CAMBRIDGE GREEK AND LATIN CLASSICS

HELLENISTIC
EPIGRAMS
A SELECTION

EDITED BY
ALEXANDER SENS
Georgetown University

CAMBRIDGE
UNIVERSITY PRESS

Shaftesbury Road, Cambridge CB2 8EA, United Kingdom

One Liberty Plaza, 20th Floor, New York, NY 10006, USA

477 Williamstown Road, Port Melbourne, VIC 3207, Australia

314–321, 3rd Floor, Plot 3, Splendor Forum, Jasola District Centre, New Delhi – 110025, India

103 Penang Road, #05–06/07, Visioncrest Commercial, Singapore 238467

Cambridge University Press is part of Cambridge University Press & Assessment, a department of the University of Cambridge.

We share the University's mission to contribute to society through the pursuit of education, learning and research at the highest international levels of excellence.

www.cambridge.org
Information on this title: www.cambridge.org/9780521614818

DOI: 10.1017/9781139024839

© Cambridge University Press & Assessment 2020

First published 2020

A catalogue record for this publication is available from the British Library

Library of Congress Cataloging-in-Publication data
NAMES: Sens, Alexander, author.
TITLE: Hellenistic epigrams : a selection / Alexander Sens.
OTHER TITLES: Cambridge Greek and Latin classics.
DESCRIPTION: New York : Cambridge University Press, 2020. | Series:
Cambridge Greek and Latin classics | Includes
bibliographical references and index.
IDENTIFIERS: LCCN 2020021824 (print) | LCCN 2020021825 (ebook) |
ISBN 9780521849555 (hardback) |
ISBN 9781139024839 (ebook)
SUBJECTS: LCSH: Epigrams, Greek. | Epigrams, Greek – History and criticism.
Classification: LCC PA3123 .S46 2020 (print) |
LCC PA3123 (ebook) | DDC888/.010208–dc23
LC record available at https://lccn.loc.gov/2020021824
LC ebook record available at https://lccn.loc.gov/2020021825

ISBN   978-0-521-84955-5   Hardback
ISBN   978-0-521-61481-8   Paperback

For Serena

CONTENTS

PREFACE

Greek "literary" epigrams constitute one of the most versatile and dynamic poetic forms in the Hellenistic period. Originally modeled on the anonymous epitaphs and dedications inscribed on monuments throughout antiquity, these short poems came to include a variety of subtypes and served as a vehicle for Hellenistic poets to experiment with themes and motifs from other genres. Epigram thrived into the Imperial and Byzantine periods and exerted a great influence on Latin poetry; its afterlife in other literatures continues to the present day.

The modern study of Hellenistic epigram is built on the philological foundations of A. S. F. Gow and D. L. Page's edition of epigrams which seem to have been collected in antiquity in the anthologies of Meleager (*HE*) and Philip (*GPh*). Since the publication of those works, new scholarly attitudes and approaches have helped transform our understanding of the form and its literary and cultural context, as have papyrological discoveries; epigrams are better appreciated as works of literature, as are the ancient collections in which they were assembled. Readers approaching the form for the first time in Greek, however, still have relatively few resources for accessing a range of poems by multiple early writers.

This volume is not intended as a comprehensive survey of the long history of literary epigram; instead, it focuses on the remarkably diverse work of early Hellenistic epigrammatists, covering epigrams included in *HE* along with a handful of others discovered on papyrus since that work's publication. My goal is to provide readers, including students approaching the genre for the first time, with a sense of some of the ways in which early Hellenistic epigrams might be read, and to place the poems within the various epigraphic and literary traditions with which they engage. I also hope that the volume might serve as a partial introduction to Hellenistic poetry more broadly.

Even within the limited chronological range covered here, space has compelled difficult choices. Because I was interested in illustrating the practices of individual poets, I have omitted poems transmitted without ascription, as well as those whose ascriptions to famous poets of an earlier period are almost certainly spurious. The series editors cautioned against epigrams with complicated textual problems. In keeping with the goals of the series, I have, in general, treated those editorial matters that do arise only briefly in the commentary, and I have left the critical apparatus spare. In the end, even with these limitations, I had to cut poems I would have liked to include.

Many people have provided invaluable assistance. The series editors, Richard Hunter, Pat Easterling, and Neil Hopkinson, were patient throughout the process, read drafts acutely and quickly, and saved me from numerous errors. Charles McNelis responded to ideas about individual poems and about Greek literature more generally; another Georgetown colleague, Marden Nichols, provided advice on the introduction. Hayden Pelliccia generously shared his work on Callimachus' epigrams, especially 28 Pfeiffer, and commented on early drafts. Benjamin Millis checked references to ancient texts and offered excellent advice. The other friends and colleagues who have suggested improvements to the readings offered in this book are too many to list, but I hope they know I am deeply thankful. I am also grateful to several students: Annalisa Quinn, Allison Muth, and Caelin Ivanov, who working under the auspices of the Georgetown University Research Opportunities program helped improve early drafts of parts of the volume; Claire Healy's research assistance in 2017–18 allowed me to assemble the volume in near-final form, and her reactions to early drafts and willingness to talk about avenues of interpretation fundamentally improved the readings offered in the commentary. The project was supported by the Loeb Classical Library Foundation and by funds attached to the Markos and Eleni Tsakopoulos Kounalakis Chair in Hellenic Studies at Georgetown University. Needless to say, I claim sole responsibility for the infelicities that remain.

ABBREVIATIONS

Abbreviations of authors and works often appear in fuller form than in LSJ. Most epigrams are cited by their enumeration in the Greek Anthology (*AP*, *Pl*), except that poems preserved exclusively in other sources are cited from the editions of A. S. F. Gow and D. L. Page (GP), *HE* and *GPh*, and epigrams by Asclepiades, Posidippus, and Callimachus are enumerated as in A. Sens, *Asclepiades of Samos* (Oxford 2011), C. Austin and G. Bastianini, *Posidippi Pellaei quae supersunt omnia* (Milan 2002) (AB), and R. Pfeiffer, ed., *Callimachus* (Oxford 1949–52), respectively. Except where noted, other fragments of Callimachus are cited from Pfeiffer's edition. Euphorion is cited from B. A. van Groningen's edition (Amsterdam 1977), fragments of Attic drama from *PCG* and *TrGF*, lyric and elegy from *PMG* and *IEG*. Some inscribed epigrams originally written in the Attic alphabet are given using the more familiar Ionic alphabet.

Roman numerals are used in the commentary to refer to entire poems included in this volume; italicized Arabic numerals to refer to specific lines in the continuous enumeration, which is indicated in lemmata with square brackets.

Bernabé	A. Bernabé, ed., *Poetae epici Graeci* I, Leipzig 1987.
Buck	C. D. Buck, *The Greek dialects*, Chicago 1955.
CA	J. U. Powell, *Collectanea Alexandrina*, Oxford 1925.
CEG	P. A. Hansen, ed., *Carmina epigraphica Graeca*, 2 vols., Berlin and New York 1983–9.
Denniston	J. D. Denniston, *The Greek particles*, 2nd edn., Oxford 1954.
Ep. Gr.	G. Kaibel, ed., *Epigrammata Graeca ex lapidibus conlecta*, Berlin 1878.
FD	*Fouilles de Delphes*, Paris 1848–1925.
FGE	D. L. Page, ed., *Further Greek epigrams: epigrams before A.D. 50 from the Greek Anthology and other sources*, Cambridge 1981.
FGrH	F. Jacoby, *Die Fragmente der griechischen Historiker*, Berlin 1923–30, Leiden 1940–58.
FHG	C. Müller, *Fragmenta historicorum Graecorum*, Paris 1841–70.
GPh	A. S. F. Gow and D. L. Page, eds., *The Greek Anthology: The Garland of Philip*, Cambridge 1968.
GVI	W. Peek, ed., *Griechische Vers-Inschriften* I: *Grab-Epigramme*, Berlin 1957.
HE	A. S. F. Gow and D. L. Page, eds., *The Greek Anthology: Hellenistic epigrams*, Cambridge 1965.
IEG	M. West, *Iambi et elegi Graeci*, 2nd edn., Oxford 1992.
IG	*Inscriptiones Graecae*, Berlin 1873–.

IMEGR	É. Bernand, ed., *Inscriptions métriques de l'Égypt gréco-romaine*, Paris 1969.
K–B	R. Kühner, *Ausführliche Grammatik der griechischen Sprache* I, 3rd edn., rev. F. Blass, Hanover 1890–2.
K–G	R. Kühner, *Ausführliche Grammatik der griechischen Sprache, Zweiter Teil: Satzlehre*, rev. B. Gerth, Hanover 1898–1904.
LfgrE	Snell, B. *et al.*, eds., *Lexicon des frühgriechischen Epos*, Göttingen 1955–2010.
LGPN	P. M. Fraser, E. Matthews *et al.*, eds., *Lexicon of Greek personal names*, Oxford 1987–.
LIMC	*Lexicon iconographicum mythologiae classicae*, Zurich 1981–2009.
LSJ	H. G. Liddell, R. Scott, H. Stuart Jones, and R. Mackenzie, *A Greek–English lexicon*, 9th edn., Oxford 1968.
OGIS	W. Dittenberger, ed., *Orientis Graecae inscriptiones selectae*, Leipzig 1903–5.
PCG	R. Kassel and C. Austin, eds., *Poetae comici Graeci*, Berlin and New York 1983–.
PMG	D. L. Page, ed., *Poetae melici Graeci*, Oxford 1962.
Powell	J. U. Powell, ed., *Collectanea Alexandrina*, Oxford 1925.
RE	A. Pauly, G. Wissowa, and W. Kroll, *Realencyclopädie der classischen Altertumswissenschaft*, Stuttgart 1893–1978.
RECAM II	S. Mitchell, ed., *Regional epigraphic catalogues of Asia Minor* II: *The Ankara District: the inscriptions of North Galatia*, Oxford 1982.
SEG	*Supplementum epigraphicum Graecum.*
ΣEMA	V. N. Bardani and G. K. Papadopoulos, eds., Συμπλήρωμα τῶν ἐπιτυμβίων μνημείων τῆς Ἀττικῆς, Athens 2006.
SGO	R. Merkelbach and J. Stauber, eds., *Steinepigramme aus dem griechischen Osten*, Stuttgart and Leipzig 1998–2004.
SH	H. Lloyd-Jones and P. Parsons, eds., *Supplementum Hellenisticum*, Berlin and New York 1983.
Smyth	H. W. Smyth, *A Greek grammar*, Cambridge, Mass. 1920.
TrGF	B. Snell, R. Kannicht, and S. Radt, eds., *Tragicorum Graecorum fragmenta*, Göttingen 1971–2004.

INTRODUCTION

1 THE ORIGINS OF LITERARY EPIGRAM

In its original sense, "epigram," ἐπίγραμμα (cf. Hdt. 5.59, Thuc. 6.59.2),[1] refers to short poems that, from the archaic period on, were inscribed on stone and other durable materials for a variety of purposes. These were the first Greek poems designed to be experienced in writing rather than in performance. Some of them marked publicly funded monuments honoring individuals or commemorating war dead; others contained private claims of ownership of an object. The great majority, however, marked graves or recorded dedications to the gods. Some of these were probably written by persons who had a direct interest in commemorating an event or death, others perhaps by professional epigrammatists working on commission; in any case, the writers of these early epigrams generally made no effort to ensure that their names would be attached to their compositions in the way that the authors of other archaic genres did (e.g. Hes. *Th.* 22–4, Sappho, fr. 1.20; Thgn. 19–23).[2]

By the end of the fifth century, at least one famous poet was explicitly connected with epigrams: Simonides allegedly wrote an epigram for a seer killed at Thermopylae (Hdt. 7.228) and, according to a tradition probably rooted in the fifth century and in any case established by Aristotle's day,[3] composed other famous epitaphs for casualties of the Persian Wars. Whether or not the ascription of any of these epigrams to him is correct, the association of such an illustrious poet with the genre seems at least to reflect, and perhaps to have contributed to, an elevation in the status of epigrammatists as authors and of epigram as a form of literature. In the fourth century, poets sometimes included their own names in epigrams that they composed for others (cf. *CEG* 819, 888.18–19, 889.8): these "seals" (σφραγῖδες) suggest a more elevated conception of the role of the epigrammatist, and indeed the terms in which they describe their activity are reminiscent of more traditionally elevated forms of praise poetry.[4] In the fourth century, if not earlier,[5] epigrams appear to have been collected

---

[1] Cf. Puelma 1996; Gutzwiller 1998a: 15–20.
[2] On authorial self-references in Greek poetry, see Peirano 2013.
[3] Arist. *Rhet.* 1367b20 attributes to him an epigram cited as anonymous by Thuc. 6.59.2; for the role of Peripatetic biography in the formation of the "Simonidean" corpus, cf. Gutzwiller 1998a: 49–50.
[4] Cf. *CEG* 819.5 κρηπῖδ' ἐστεφάνωσ[ε; *CEG* 888.19 and 889.8 use the language of gift-exchange, for which cf. Kurke 1991.
[5] Professional poets may have drawn material from "handbooks" containing exemplary epigrams; the existence of such collections would explain the presence of shared language in epigrams from diverse places and times.

and circulated in books in which they were presented as literary objects
divorced from an original material context.[6] These collections provided
a model for a different type of epigram: "fictive" experiments playing on
the conventions of a popular, inscribed form but intended for the papyrus
roll rather than the stone.

Such fictive epigrams are already presupposed by "embedded" commemorations such as that at *Il.* 7.89–90, where, as ancient critics recog-
nized, Hector invents a hypothetical epitaph for Ajax (cf. Σ^{bT} on *Il.* 7.86).
Though, in the absence of most fourth-century literature, the history of
the development of freestanding, fictive epigrams must remain obscure,
by the late classical or early Hellenistic period, poems playing on the formal and thematic features of anonymous, inscribed verse had become a
popular vehicle for competition and display by literary elites from around
the Greek-speaking world,[7] including women. Such epigrams were collected in books early in their history, and are copiously preserved in the
Byzantine-era collections cumulatively known as the Greek Anthology and
in a handful of ancient papyri (see below section 5a).

2 "GENRES" OF HELLENISTIC EPIGRAM

Early Hellenistic epigrams were diverse and innovative. A large group
retained the traditional themes and content of dedications and epitaphs but handled them in novel ways, for example by employing atyp-
ical meters, imagining events that could not have – or at least would not
ordinarily have – been recorded with an inscription (e.g. the deaths of
sea creatures, insects, and other animals, or implausible dedications), or
playing creatively with voice and perspective. Many epigrams, however,
did not present themselves as dedications or epitaphs but instead drew
their themes and subject matter from elegy, lyric, comedy, mime, and

---

[6] Examples include the historian Philochorus' now lost collection of Attic epigrams (*Suda* φ 441 = *FGrH* 328 T 1; a germinal form of the "sylloge Simonidea,"
a lost collection that ultimately came to include a number of Hellenistic compositions spuriously attributed to Simonides, might be as old as the fifth century (cf.
Sider 2007). For the possible classical origins of the "Aristotelian" *Peplos* containing a collection epitaphs for heroes, cf. Gutzwiller 2010.

[7] A number of epigrams are ascribed to famous poets and philosophers of the
archaic and classical periods, including Sappho, Anacreon, and Plato, but these
are unlikely to be authentic: whether they are deliberately forged or simply mis-
attributed, they probably reflect the desire of subsequent writers to find or invent
predecessors for the sort of poetry they were producing; cf. *FGE* 119–30. For the
"erotic" epigrams attributed to Plato, see Ludwig 1963. On the Hellenistic quest
for authoritative literary ancestors in general, see Fantuzzi in Fantuzzi and Hunter
2004: 1–41.

other genres. These novel poetic types reflect a broader set of Hellenistic concerns. The interest in the power of eros and in the emotional experiences of "ordinary" individuals that one finds in amatory epigrams has counterparts in a variety of Hellenistic poems; "ecphrastic" epigrams form part of a broader Hellenistic discourse on the power of art to imitate life. Even the most generically innovative of these new epigrammatic types often advert to or resonate against their inscribed ancestors. Thus "sympotic" and "erotic" epigrams not only exploit the formal resemblance between epigrams and other poetic genres, including the short elegies collected in the corpus of Theognis, but also play on the linkage between love and death and the frequently looming presence of death in erotic and sympotic literature. "Ecphrastic" poems containing descriptions or appreciations of art play with elements drawn not only from statue bases (cf. xxx introductory n.) but from epic, drama, and elsewhere. These categories are inherently flexible and unstable: although early papyrological evidence suggests that some ancient readers divided epigrams into subgenres (below pp. 14, 170–1), the ingenuity of many epigrams lies in the ways they blur the boundaries among different epigrammatic forms or combine elements from multiple types.

3 "FICTIVE" AND "INSCRIBED" EPIGRAMS

Of the Hellenistic epigrams preserved in the Greek Anthology and on papyri (as opposed to the anonymous Hellenistic-era compositions preserved on stone), a substantial majority were probably not intended for inscription.[8] Often, however, the distinction between "fictive" and "inscribed" epigrams is difficult to draw.[9] Our corpus includes epigrams by elite Hellenistic poets in honor of important people and events, including members of the royal families and building projects such as the Pharos lighthouse and the Temple of Arsinoe-Aphrodite at Zephyrium; these played an important role in the creation and promulgation of the image of the Hellenistic royal houses, and some may have been intended for public inscription. Some other epigrams may commemorate the deaths or dedications of real, ordinary individuals. Satisfactory criteria for determining the original function of any given poem are hard to identify, however. The presence of traditional features such as deictic pronouns does not prove that a poem was designed for inscription, since Hellenistic

---

[8] Some inscribed epigrams did find their way into the Anthology (cf. e.g. *CEG* 467 = *AP* 7.245).
[9] For the permeability of the boundary between "inscribed" and "literary" epigrams, see Bing 1998.

poets were well attuned to and capable of imitating the features of real epitaphs and dedications; that they composed at least some clearly fictive epigrams allows for skepticism even about those poems that most closely resemble real inscriptions. Conversely, neither artifice nor ingenuity necessarily shows that a poem was only "literary," and even the presence of information that would be superfluous in a material context – such as the identity of a dedicated object – can at best be suggestive.

In a broader sense, scholarly debates about the original intended context of individual Hellenistic epitaphs and dedications are surrogates for the larger debate about the nature of the audience for the compositions of the elite poets working in places such as the Ptolemaic Museum.[10] Though we have far more information about the literary culture of Alexandria than about other contexts in which epigrams were produced, we still know too little about the professional realities of scholar-poets like Callimachus to be certain whether an elegant and poignant epitaph such as LVII, honoring a dead child, was originally designed as a real epitaph or as a literary exercise; nor, in the latter case, is it clear who its original intended audience would have been. Similarly, Posidippus' three epigrams (39, 116, 119) on the temple of Arsinoe-Aphrodite at Zephyrium share verbal and thematic points of connection, and although they could easily have been inscribed together or separately in the temple precinct, neither their form nor their content proves that they were: one or more of them could have been designed as a variation of the others for a purely "literary" context. At least some other poems in honor of Hellenistic royalty, at any rate, are unlikely to have been inscribed (e.g. XII, Asclep. *44 Sens).

It is clear, in any case, that many Hellenistic epigrams are the product of a competitive literary environment in which poets knew and engaged closely with one another's work and displayed their ingenuity by varying themes and language they found in other epigrams. The speakers of some epigrams represent themselves as participants in symposia, and it has been suggested that at Hellenistic drinking parties the production of epigrams served as a vehicle for elite competition and display, much as the composition or performance of lyric and elegy had in earlier periods.[11] Epigrams such as Hedylus LXX, in which convivial drinking is represented as a source of poetic inspiration, may reflect actual practice in some form

---

[10] These poets were once viewed as cloistered residents of an "ivory tower," but both the dissemination of the poems and the outward-facing perspective of many of them make this difficult to sustain; see Cameron 1995, Selden 1998, Stephens 2003.

[11] Reitzenstein 1893, Cameron 1995: 71–103, Gutzwiller 1998a: 21–2.

(cf. Ath. 3.125c–d), but the picture they present is at best elliptical and stylized; even poems composed for or at drinking parties must have been polished and revised before they were collected in the books from which our versions derive. Like erotic epigrams in which the speaker claims to be in love (cf. below p. 71), these epigrams are inspired at least as much by literature as by life, and, whatever their first performance context, they are ultimately literary pieces designed for the written scroll.

The poems preserved in the Greek Anthology and on papyrus survived precisely because they were included in books either at the time of their composition or not long after. Some of these collections were almost certainly produced by their authors themselves (see below section 5a). Papyri such as *P.Mil.Vogl.* VIII 209 reveal the artistry with which these collections could be arranged, and indeed some individual epigrams in the Anthology seem designed to be read in conjunction with one another, presumably in the context of a collection (cf. LIX introductory n.). Whatever their genesis, then, Hellenistic epigrams in the form we have them are fundamentally literary artifacts.

The popularity of the form as a medium for literary expression seems to have been widely dispersed. Known Hellenistic epigrammatists hailed from around the Greek-speaking world, including the Peloponnese and Magna Graecia (Anyte, Nossis, Leonidas, Theocritus), Central Greece and Macedonia (Alexander, Perses, Posidippus), the islands of the Eastern Aegean (Philitas, Simias, Asclepiades, Hedylus), North Africa (Callimachus), and the Near East (Antipater of Sidon, Meleager). Some, but apparently not all, spent part of their lives in Ptolemaic Alexandria. Reitzenstein (1893) posited that early Hellenistic epigrammatists could be divided into "schools" with distinct thematic and generic interests: a "Peloponnesian" school of Doric-speaking poets from the Peloponnese and Magna Graecia such as Anyte, Nossis, and Leonidas, who mostly played with the features of the traditional epigram forms; and an "Alexandrian" school comprising poets associated with the Ptolemaic court, including Asclepiades, Posidippus, Callimachus, and Hedylus, who introduced subject matter from other genres. Although the distinction does not acknowledge the overlap between these groups, it remains useful: local networks may well have played a role in the early development of Hellenistic epigram. At the same time, poets from both groups knew and engaged with one another's work, and papyrological evidence suggests that epigrams circulated throughout the Mediterranean world and that their audience was not restricted to literary elites.[12]

---

[12] For epigrams in paraliterary compilations, including school texts, cf. Petrovic 2019.

4 FORMAL AND LITERARY ASPECTS OF HELLENISTIC EPIGRAMS

(a) Length

The length of inscribed epitaphs and dedications was generally restricted by the space available on their monuments. Like their inscribed antecedents, the majority of early Hellenistic epigrams were relatively short, typically no more than about four or five couplets in length, and often shorter. Even if, as papyrus evidence suggests, a random sample of Hellenistic epigrams might have a slightly greater average, brevity was clearly a defining feature of the genre and probably contributed to its popularity in the Hellenistic period.[13] Indeed, one of the ways in which epigrammatists played with genre was to condense elements treated at greater length in other genres within the narrow confines of a few verses;[14] conversely, the slightly greater length of an epigram may sometimes reflect its affiliation with other poetic forms (cf. XXIII, c introductory nn.).

At a basic level, the restricted space posed an attractive challenge to poets seeking to demonstrate wit and skill. At the same time, however, the challenge of composing within a small compass helps explain the programmatic value of brevity for Hellenistic poets, who sometimes drew on an interrelated set of oppositions – between brevity and length, lightness and weight, novelty and familiarity, clarity and murkiness, purity and squalor, exclusivity and vulgarity, truthfulness and falsehood – to define their aesthetic values and position in the tradition. For at least some of these poets, brevity is one of a set of qualities that define refined and elegant (λεπτός, λεπταλέος) poetry in which every element is chosen with exquisite precision and care. Callimachus, most notoriously, defends himself against the charge that he has not composed work of sufficient length by asserting his preference for poetry that is small, light, fine, and clear like the chirruping of a cicada or the trickling of a small, pure spring rather than long, heavy, and raucous like the braying of an ass or a raging, filthy river (Call. fr. 1.29–36, h. 2.108–12). Callimachus' framing of these oppositions was not shared by all poets, however. Hedylus, in one epigram, links the production of novel, refined poetry not with spring water but with copious amounts of wine,[15] and, in another, describes the clear sound produced by wine in Callimachean terms but simultaneously

---

[13] For brevity as a marker of the genre, cf. Philip *AP* 4.2.1–6; Magnelli 2006, Kimmel-Clauzet 2017.

[14] Harder 2019.

[15] Callimachus' *Aetia* probably included a poetic initiation from the waters of Mt. Helicon; cf. fr. 2 with Harder's note; Asclep. *45 with Sens's note.

assimilates it with the "song" of the torrential Nile. Similarly, whereas Callimachus in the *Aetia*-prologue (fr. 1) allusively links his poetic refinement to the subtlety of Euripides as he is depicted in Aristophanes' *Frogs*, Dioscorides lauds the grandness of Aeschylus in terms that evoke his competition with Euripides in that comedy.

A number of other Hellenistic epigrammatists by implication reflect on the small scale of their own compositions. Epitaphs contrasting the small size of a grave with the greatness of its occupant (e.g. CXXIII) may be read as self-referential comments on the paradox of great content within a small form. A number of epigrams in the Milan Posidippus papyrus describe diminutive but finely wrought and realistic artifacts in ways that seem to comment on the poet's project, sometimes contrasting the small scale of their subject matter with the greatness of the effect they produce.[16]

(b) Variatio

Among the most striking features of many Hellenistic epigrams is their reworking of the linguistic or thematic features of other epigrams. In some cases, an individual epigrammatist treated a single subject or theme in multiple ways or from multiple perspectives (e.g. CXXVII–CXXXI); more often, poets played with the language, themes, or subject matter they found in other poets' work. Both sorts of variation have models in the epigraphic tradition. For all their diversity, inscribed epitaphs and dedications relied on a relatively stable and limited set of formal structures and motifs, and Hellenistic readers may have found in them a tension between repetition and variation, especially when they were copied together in books. Some monuments, indeed, contained several epigrams which treated a single death or dedication from different perspectives (e.g. *CEG* 543).

(c) Voice and Perspective

Inscribed epigrams made use of a variety of speaking voices and internal addressees. Epitaphs could be addressed to or spoken by an anonymous reader (sometimes identified as a passing traveler), by the deceased, or by the monument; dedications were sometimes spoken by a third-person narrator and sometimes by the dedicated objects. In some cases, the voice shifts without clear marking, as in poems where the passerby and the deceased converse.

---

[16] Cf. Porter 2011.

In their original contexts, these inscribed poems formed part of a semantic system in which text and monument each contributed to meaning.[17] Deciphering and making sense of them could be very challenging, and in fact literary epigrammatists sometimes call attention to the process of interpretation involved in reading inscriptions (cf. LXXI, CI, CXXVI). In a purely literary context, the absence of a monument allowed poets to imagine new situations and contexts, and to play with ambiguities of voice and perspective that would be clarified in an inscriptional context. All these features posed challenges for readers; indeed, perhaps more than almost any other genre, literary epigrams invite their audience to participate in the process of interpretation by filling in gaps and drawing inferences from a limited set of information.[18]

(d) Tone

Hellenistic epigrams are capable of an enormous tonal range. Many are seriously pathetic, poignant, or solemn; others jocularly bathetic, obscene, even parodic. In some poems, the humorous point is revealed by a "punch line" in the final word or words, but this phenomenon is less common than it becomes in epigrams of the Imperial period and in the poems of Martial that they influenced. The wit of many poems resides in the subtle, ironic characterization of the speaker, in the contrast between grandiose language and humble content, or in sexual innuendo.

(e) Materiality

The essential materiality of epigram in its original inscriptional context made it well suited to Hellenistic "book culture" and an excellent canvas on which Hellenistic poets, who knew the literary tradition primarily through books and who regularly represented themselves as writers rather than singers (e.g. Call. fr. 1.21–8, Asclepiades *45.8 Sens) or treated their inspiration as deriving from books (e.g. Call. fr. 75.54–77), could project their literary values. Some epigrams, for example, treat other forms of poetry, such as tragedy, as though it were inscribed (543–4n.); in others, the written poetry-book plays the role occupied in the epigraphic tradition by the engraved stone (e.g. Asclep. 28 Sens).

---

[17] This is particularly clear in epitaphs which omit the name of the deceased because it was included elsewhere on the grave (e.g. *CEG* 524), and in inscribed dedicatory epigrams which refer to the dedication only by means of a pronoun, since they had no need to identify further the object on which they were inscribed.

[18] See e.g. Bing 1995, Hunter 1992.

(f) Language and Style

Hellenistic epigrams are stylistically variable; some individual epigrams juxtapose words from different registers. Many use relatively straightforward language, morphology, and syntax with few traces of the obscure vocabulary, unusual morphology, or difficult word order found in some other Hellenistic genres. Notably, erudite poets like Callimachus and Euphorion who regularly used rare, disputed, or otherwise difficult language in their other compositions mostly eschew lexical or syntactic obscurity in their epigrams. The difficulty of these and many other epigrams lies less in their language than in their elliptical nature and in the interpretive demands they thus impose on readers.[19]

Epigrammatists sometimes drew on a far more elevated stylistic register. Many play with form and content by applying high-style language, including extravagant, "dithyrambic" compound adjectives (many of them novel), to humble subject matter. The phenomenon is particularly prominent in the epigrams of Leonidas of Tarentum and his imitators Antipater of Sidon and Phanias, but it is not restricted to them. The tone of the contrast between style and subject matter is not always easy to determine; in some cases, it is clearly playful, even approaching parodic (cf. *619–20*n.).

Any assessment of the style of a given author must acknowledge the role played by the stylistic preferences of the editors of the ancient anthologies which lie behind our extant corpus. A number of the epigrams preserved on the Milan Posidippus papyrus (below pp. 14, 170–1), for instance, have a more elaborate, "baroque" style than do the epigrams of the same poet preserved in the Anthology. Some of this difference may be a function of genre, since the poems in the Anthology are principally of types which do not appear in the extant sections of the papyrus.

(g) Dialect

Greek poetic language was inherently artificial and included elements drawn from multiple traditions. Although inscribed epigrams were often based on the local, spoken dialect, many included phonological and morphological features foreign to local speech and drawn from the inherited, artificial language of epic and elegy (e.g. genitive singular in -οιο, dative plurals in -οισι/-αισι in Attic inscriptions). The authors of literary epigrams also exploited multiple poetic dialect traditions. These

[19] Cf. Magnelli 2007: 165–9.

traditions are not "pure" in the sense that they reflect actual local speech, but draw on a generalized poetic language and morphology with an overlay of specific dialectal features.

The dialectal substratum of the vast majority of Hellenistic literary epigrams is either the Ionic poetic *koine* or its Doric counterpart; markedly local forms appear rarely. Many epigrammatists, including Asclepiades, Callimachus, Posidippus, and Leonidas, composed in both Ionic and Doric. The assessment of dialect is often complicated by uncertainties about the text. Many features are not guaranteed by the meter, and dialect was easily altered in transmission; in many cases, the manuscripts disagree on the dialect of a given word. Even when they agree, there is ground for skepticism: in one case, the Milan papyrus preserves Doric forms that have been completely lost in the manuscripts of the Anthology (LXXXIII). Inconsistent dialect features sometimes coexist in a given poem: the extent to which they should be regularized (especially when they are isolated in an otherwise regular dialectal context) is debated: in general, the artificial nature of poetic language and the explicit Hellenistic recognition of the practice of dialect mixing (e.g. Call. *Iamb* 13.18 = fr. 203.18 Pfeiffer) suggest that we should be cautious about eliminating inconsistency, and at least in some cases, there appear to be good literary reasons for incongruous forms.

Dialect contributed to meaning in several ways. The traditional association of specific dialects with particular genres (e.g. Doric with choral lyric, Ionic with iambus) meant that they could serve as a signifier of literary heritage and generic affiliation. Moreover, in a few epigrams, the dialect seems to imitate the native language of the imagined speaker (e.g. XXVIII, LXXV, LXXXIII, LXXXVIII). In epigrams on Macedonian royalty, Doric may have played an important ideological role by evoking the Argead claim to Argive ancestry (cf. XII, Hunter in Fantuzzi and Hunter 2004: 371–7, Sens 2004: 74–5).

The following features of Doric appear in the poems of the present collection (for a fuller treatment of Hellenistic literary Doric, see Hunter 1999: 24–6):

Phonology and orthography

(a) ᾱ rather than η is the reflex of inherited *ā*. It occasionally appears in "hyper-Doricisms" as the reflex of inherited *ē*, for which Doric properly has η (cf. Pos. *405*n.). Doric α is regularly overlaid on epic forms.

(b) σδ is sometimes used for medial ζ.

(c) The secondary lengthening of inherited *e* and *o* by contraction or compensatory lengthening is handled in different ways by specific local versions of Doric: the so-called "milder" Doric dialects have ει and ου, as in Ionic dialects, while "more severe" dialects have η and ω. Both forms appear in Doric-colored epigrams; in at least one case, "more severe" Doricisms suit the Cretan ethnicity of the honorand (cf. LXXV introductory n.).

(d) Contractions

    i. The contraction of ε + ο is usually ευ.

    ii. Endings beginning in ε and η contract with preceding α to produce η in alpha-contract verbs. Thus, ὁρῆι (3rd pers. pres. indic. act. of ὁράω), ποθορῆν (pres. infin. act. of ποθοράω = Attic/Ionic προσορᾶν).

    iii. On one occasion, ο + ο produces ευ in a poem with mostly Doric forms (*121*n.); the form is more characteristic of Ionic.

Nouns

(a) 1st declension

    i. gen. sing. of masculine nouns ends in -ᾱ.

    ii. gen. pl. in -ᾶν.

(b) 2nd declension

    i. gen. sing. in -ω or -ου (see above).

    ii. acc. pl. in -ως or -ους (see above).

Pronouns

(a) 1st pers.: nom. pl. ἁμές; acc. pl. ἁμέ.

(b) 2nd pers.: nom. sing. τύ; dat. sing. τίν, τοι; dat. pl. ὑμίν.

(c) 3rd pers.: neither νιν nor μιν occurs in Doric-flavored poems in the selection, though both occur in other Hellenistic poetry in Doric. τῆνος and apparently κῆνος (cf. *188*n.) are used in addition to ἐκεῖνος (e.g. *471*; cf. Gow on Theocr. 7.104).

Verbs

(a) 1st pers. pl. ending in -μες.

(b) 3rd pers. pl. ending in -ντι.

(c) One case of a future in -σέω with contraction is possible at Asclep. *49* (αὐδασοῦντι, dat. sing. fut. participle).

(d) Fem. pres. participle in -οισα as well as -ουσα. The former is a feature of archaic Doric lyric and appears in Hellenistic literary Doric, as well as in the spoken language of some local Aeolic (Lesbos) and Doric (Cyrene) dialects.

(e) Forms of εἰμί include ἐντί (3rd pl. pres. indic.), ἔμμεν (pres. infin.), and ἦς (3rd sing. imp. indic.).

(f) ἐνθ- for ἐλθ- as the aorist stem of ἔρχομαι.

(h) Meter

Although some early inscribed epigrams were composed in dactylic hexameters or iambic trimeters, the principal meter of epigram was the elegiac couplet, an epodic form in which a dactylic hexameter is followed by an elegiac pentameter:

$$- \smile\smile \: - \smile\smile \: - \smile\smile \: - \smile\smile \: - \smile\smile \: - \times$$
$$- \smile\smile \: - \smile\smile \: - \:|\: - \smile\smile \: - \smile\smile \: \times$$

The majority of extant Hellenistic epigrams, including all the poems on the Milan Posidippus papyrus, are in this meter. Although it is possible that editorial selection bias (cf. below section 5a) may have distorted the picture to some extent (the collection of "Theocritean" epigrams, which seems not to have survived via Meleager's anthology, includes a number of non-elegiac poems),[20] it seems clear that Hellenistic poets considered it the default rhythm of the genre.

Several features of the Hellenistic elegiac couplet are worth noting.

(i) The Hexameter

Most Hellenistic poets favored dactyls ($-\smile\smile$) over spondees ($--$) in the hexameter and consequently tended to use fewer of the possible arrangements of dactyls and spondees within the verse. Whereas earlier hexameters sometimes had their principal caesura in the fourth foot ("hephthemimeral"), Hellenistic hexameters restricted it to the third; the preference for dactyls is naturally correlated with the predominance of the "feminine" caesura (between the bicipitia of the third foot) over the "masculine" caesura (following the third longum).

In Greek hexameters of all periods words tended to end in certain places in the verse more often than others. Most notably, throughout the history of the form, it was very rare for a word to end after the first short of a fourth-foot dactyl (Hermann's Bridge). Hellenistic poets regularized the hexameter by further limiting some combinations of word-breaks and restricting the places in which words of certain shapes could end, with the result that they used fewer of the total number of theoretically available rhythmical possibilities than their predecessors.[21] Callimachus was particularly restrictive, and the extent to which individual poets shared his

---

[20] Dale 2010 argues that there is little evidence that non-elegiac poems in the Anthology derived from Meleager's *Garland*.

[21] To some extent, their practice may reflect a broader trend that is also reflected in inscriptions; cf. Fantuzzi and Sens 2006.

practices was an important marker of their "modernity." These metrical practices have been described via a set of "laws":

(1) Words do not end after the first short of a second-foot dactyl ("Meyer's First Law") or at the end of a dactylic second foot ("Giseke's Law") if they begin in the first foot, and they never end after a spondaic second foot ("Hilberg's Law").
(2) Words of iambic shape (⌣ –) do not end before the masculine caesura ("Meyer's Second Law").
(3) Lines with word-end following the third foot also have a regular caesura in the third foot and word-end after a dactylic fourth foot (bucolic diaeresis), along with sense-pause at either the main caesura or the bucolic diaeresis ("Bulloch's Law").
(4) Word-end does not follow a fourth-foot spondee ("Naeke's Law").
(5) A line with word-end after the first syllable of the fourth foot does not have word-end after the first syllable of the fifth ("Tiedke's Law").
(6) Verses ending in a monosyllable normally have word-end after a dactylic fourth foot (bucolic diaeresis) and have a dactylic fifth foot, but see 569n.

(ii) The Pentameter

Antipater of Sidon is the first poet to avoid accented syllables at the end of the pentameter; the avoidance of accented final syllables became common in the Imperial period. Early Hellenistic epigrammatists avoid monosyllables at line end. There is a clear break between the two halves of the verse; this caesura may be preceded by elision, and the preceding syllable may be lengthened by position. Rhyme at caesura and line end is common. It is often the product of an adjective and a noun in grammatical agreement; this phenomenon occurs at different rates in different poets, but it is probably not a significant marker of stylistic affiliation.[22]

(iii) Non-Elegiac Meters

Most of the extant non-elegiac epigrams in the Anthology derive from the early Hellenistic period,[23] and it may be that metrical experimentation was especially robust at a relatively early phase in the development of the

---

[22] Slings 1993, Hutchinson 2016.
[23] Non-elegiac meters are somewhat more common in epigrams from Philip's *Garland*; cf. *GPh* i.xxxvii–xxxvii; Magnelli 2007: 179.

literary epigram:[24] most non-elegiac poems have dedicatory or funerary themes, and this relatively traditional content provided the generic foundation for experimentation with form. In some cases, meter marks generic affiliation, as in Leonidas' use of iambic trimeter in an epitaph with comic overtones or Theocritus' use of choliambs to honor Hipponax, with whom the meter was closely associated. As in other Hellenistic poems, a meter traditionally found in combination with other meters is sometimes used by itself. A number of poems combine longer and shorter lines into couplets (e.g. x); a smaller group reverses the order of shorter and longer lines (xc, Call. *AP* 13.24) or combines three or more lines into stanzas of several verses (xlv).

5 TRANSMISSION

(a) Epigram Collections

Hellenistic literary epigrams may sometimes have circulated individually or in small clusters, but most extant poems survived because they came to be organized into and published as larger collections. Some contained the work of a single author. These include both "libelli" produced by the poet and "syllogae" in which an editor gathered together a poet's works.[25] The most extensive ancient single-authored collection is *P.Mil.Vogl.* viii 309, apparently containing an extensive and artfully arranged collection of epigrams by Posidippus of Pella copied no more than a few decades after the last of them was composed. The care with which the collection is arranged allows for the possibility that it was produced by the author himself, though it does not prove this.[26] The basic organizational principle is thematic: the poems are divided into labeled groups, including some groups otherwise poorly attested in the literary tradition.[27] Within and between individual sections there are signs of artful structural marking.

---

[24] A few poems included in the "Vienna incipit list" (below p. 15) appear to be in non-elegiac meters; cf. Parsons *et al.* 2015: 14.

[25] See Argentieri 1998.

[26] See especially the papers in Gutzwiller 2005. Parsons *et al.* (2015: 12–13) question as anachronistic the assumption that all the poems must be by Posidippus because the individual poems lack indications of authorship and the only two previously known poems are by him; doubts based on style are less compelling. Other early collections perhaps containing the work of a single author include *P.Köln* v 204 and possibly *P.Petrie* ii 49b.

[27] The extant papyrus contains no erotic epigrams of the sort attributed to Posidippus in the Anthology; whether these appeared in a part now lost is unknowable.

Other early collections included the works of multiple authors (e.g. *P.Lond.Lit.* 60, *P.Oxy.* IV 662). The so-called "Vienna incipit list" provides the first lines of 226 epigrams, organized into four books; one opening is identical to that of Asclepiades XIX. The purpose of this list, the nature of the collection it presupposes, and the authorship of the poems to which it refers are uncertain, but it is possible that it consisted of a multi-author anthology. For the mysterious collection known as the Σωρός, see p. 68.

In his *Garland*, published around 100 BCE, Meleager of Gadara juxtaposed his own compositions with the work of earlier epigrammatists; the collection was the source of the vast majority of extant Hellenistic epigrams and included works by all the poets in this volume except Theocritus. Changes to the original structure of Meleager's *Garland* were made in the tenth-century collection by Cephalas which forms the basis of the Greek Anthology (see below),[28] but many original sequences do survive, and it is possible to identify some organizing principles of the *Garland* and of its individual components. The anthology seems originally to have been arranged in four books, consisting of erotic, dedicatory, funerary, and epideictic poems. Individual sequences were grouped artistically by theme. Often, Meleager showcases his engagement with the tradition by juxtaposing his own compositions with a series of earlier epigrams on the same themes. The collection also included thematically grouped sequences by individual poets, including cycles of Meleager's own work.

Epigram continued to be a vibrant form throughout antiquity and beyond, and poems from a number of subsequent collections, including Philip's *Garland* (*ca.* 40 CE) and the *Cycle* of Agathias (6th cent. CE), and others, were ultimately included in the Greek Anthology.

(b) Sources of the Text

The majority of Hellenistic epigrams are preserved in either or both of the two principal collections that constitute the Greek Anthology. These derive from a now-lost collection of Greek epigrams assembled by Constantine Cephalas in the tenth century. Cephalas' work included poems from a number of epigram anthologies, including the *Garland* of Meleager, the *Garland* of Philip (*ca.* 40 CE), and several other later collections (see Cameron 1993, Lauxtermann 2003: 88).

The Palatine Anthology (P), dating from the tenth century CE, survives in a single manuscript, now divided into two unequal parts housed in Heidelberg and Paris. It comprises fourteen books of epigrams, mostly but

[28] See Cameron 1993, Gutzwiller 1995.

not entirely organized by theme, and a fifteenth containing miscellaneous epigrams and other poetic material; after it was assembled by a group of scholars working from several copies of Cephalas' *Anthology*, it was partly revised by a "Corrector" who used a different exemplar of Cephalas' work. Transcriptions ("apographa") of P circulated in Europe even before the manuscript was discovered in 1606; the apographa were heavily emended by a number of scholars, including Saumaise and Scaliger.

The Planudean Anthology (Pl), now in Venice, is Maximus Planudes' autograph of a collection that he assembled in 1301. Its epigrams fall into groups, the first organized in seven sections, the second containing additional poems roughly corresponding to the first four of those sections and copied from a different exemplar. The epigrams unique to Pl are sometimes erroneously referred to as "Book 16" of the Anthology. Several smaller collections ("syllogae") derive from Cephalas' collection by routes independent of P and Pl and thus offer valuable evidence for the text of some epigrams.

A smaller number of epigrams survive exclusively in ancient and Byzantine authors and lexica, including Plutarch, Pollux, Athenaeus, Stobaeus, and Tzetzes. The tenth-century lexicon called the *Suda* preserves lines and phrases from many poems, apparently relying on a copy of Cephalas' anthology different from those used by P and Pl. A number of epigrams not found in the Greek Anthology appear on papyri, most notably *P.Mil.Vogl.* VIII 309 (above p. 14) and *P.Louvre* 7172 (cf. LXXVIII introductory n.). The present edition omits some papyrological details for poems preserved in these collections.

6 ORGANIZING PRINCIPLES OF THIS ANTHOLOGY

No scheme for arranging epigrams within an anthology is wholly unproblematic. Because the absolute and relative dates of individual poets and their work are not secure, and because the careers of many of them overlapped, no clear chronological arrangement is possible. Organizing epigrams by theme or "type," despite the ancient antecedent of the Milan Posidippus, risks effacing some of the generic complexity of the poems. The organizing principles of this collection are as follows:

(a) Individual poems are grouped by author.
(b) Within individual author-sections poems are broadly arranged by genre: epitaphs and dedications appear first, followed by epigrams most closely playing on these forms, and then by other types (ecphrastic, sympotic, erotic).

(c) Authors are arranged alphabetically within four imperfectly defined chronological groups:
  i. epigrammatists active in the late fourth/early third centuries (e.g. Anyte, Asclepiades, Nossis, Perses);
  ii. slightly later poets, whose activity may have covered some of the same period as that of the first group (Callimachus, Theocritus, Posidippus, Hedylus);
  iii. poets flourishing in the second half of the third century (Dioscorides, Rhianus, Euphorion, Theodoridas);
  iv. subsequent poets down to the end of the second century (Alcaeus, Antipater of Sidon, Phanias, Meleager).

SIGLA

P	Palatinus gr. 23 + Parisinus suppl. gr. 384
C	codicis P partim corrector, partim lemmatista
Pl	Ven. Marc. 481
	Pl^A Planudis fons primus, foll. 2^r–76^v capita VII Anthologiae complectentia
	Pl^B Planudis fons alter, foll. 81^v–100^v supplementa ad capita I–IV complectentia
Σ^π	Sylloge Σ^π (Palatinus graecus 23)
Syll.ς	Sylloge Σ (Parisinus gr. 1773, Laurentianus plut. 57.29)
Syll.s	Sylloge S (Parisinus suppl. 352, Parisinus gr. 1630)
apogr.	apographon uel apographa codicis P
corp. buc.	corpus poetarum bucolicorum extra Anthologiam Graecam traditum
D	Parisinus gr. 2726, uariis manibus emendatus
K	Ambrosianus 886 (C 222 inf.)
Cal.	editio Romana Zachariae Calliergis anno 1516 impressa
Iunt.	editio Florentina Philippi Iuntae anno 1516 impressa
P.Mil.	*P.Mil.Vogl.* VIII 309
P.Louvre	*P.Louvre* 7172 (*P.Firmin-Didot*)
P.Oxy.	*The Oxyrhynchus Papyri*
ed. pr.	editio princeps *P.Mil.Vogl.* VIII 309
Ep.Gr.	Kaibel, *Epigrammata Graeca* (supra, p. xi)
marg.	uocabulum in margine scriptum
v.l.	uaria lectio
γρ	uaria lectio signo γρ(άφεται) notata

ΕΠΙΓΡΑΜΜΑΤΑ

ΕΠΙΓΡΑΜΜΑΤΑ

I. ANYTE *AP* 7.724 (4 GP)

ἤβαν μὲν σύ, Πρόαρχ᾽, ὄλεσας, καὶ δώματα πατρός
Φειδία ἐν δνοφερῶι πένθει ἔθου φθίμενος·
ἀλλὰ καλόν τοι ὕπερθεν ἔπος τόδε πέτρος ἀείδει,
ὡς ἔθανες πρὸ φίλας μαρνάμενος πατρίδος.

II. ANYTE *AP* 7.649 (8 GP)

5   ἀντί τοι εὐλεχέος θαλάμου σεμνῶν θ᾽ ὑμεναίων
μάτηρ στᾶσε τάφωι τῶιδ᾽ ἐπὶ μαρμαρίνωι
παρθενικὰν μέτρον τε τεὸν καὶ κάλλος ἔχοισαν,
Θερσί· ποτιφθεγκτὰ δ᾽ ἔπλεο καὶ φθιμένα.

III. ANYTE *AP* 7.646 (7 GP)

    λοίσθια δὴ τάδε πατρὶ φίλωι περὶ χεῖρε βαλοῦσα
10   εἶπ᾽ Ἐρατὼ χλωροῖς δάκρυσι λειβομένα,
"ὦ πάτερ, οὔ τοι ἔτ᾽ εἰμί, μέλας δ᾽ ἐμὸν ὄμμα καλύπτει
ἤδη ἀποφθιμένας κυάνεος θάνατος."

IV. ANYTE *AP* 7.490 (6 GP)

    παρθένον Ἀντιβίαν κατοδύρομαι, ἇς ἐπὶ πολλοὶ
νυμφίοι ἱέμενοι πατρὸς ἵκοντο δόμον,
15   κάλλευς καὶ πινυτᾶτος ἀνὰ κλέος· ἀλλ᾽ ἐπιπάντων
ἐλπίδας οὐλομένα Μοῖρ᾽ ἐκύλισε πρόσω.

V. ANYTE 10 GP (APUD POLLUCEM 5.48)

ὤλεο δή ποτε καὶ σὺ πολύρριζον παρὰ θάμνον,
Λόκρι, φιλοφθόγγων ὠκυτάτη σκυλάκων·

I.   1 ἤβαν μὲν σύ, Πρόαρχ᾽, ὄλεσας καὶ δώματα πατρός Ypsilanti: ἤβα μέν σε πρόαρχε ἔσαν παίδων ἅτε ματρός P: alii alia

II.   2 στᾶσε Gow: στῆσε PPl   2 μαρμαρίναν Pl

III.   1 δὴ om. Pl   4 ἀποφθιμένας Stadtmüller: ἀποφθιμένης PPl

IV.   Pl Ionice passim Ἀντιβίην ... ἧς [1], πινυτῆτος [3], οὐλομένη [4]   3 ἀγακλέος Pl

V.   1 καὶ σύ Pollux: Μαῖρα Schneider, Ypsilanti

21

τοῖον ἐλαφρίζοντι τεῶι ἐγκάτθετο κώλωι
20   ἰὸν ἀμείλικτον ποικιλόδειρος ἔχις.

VI. ANYTE AP 6.123 (1 GP)
ἔσταθι τᾶιδε, κράνεια βροτοκτόνε, μηδ᾽ ἔτι λυγρὸν
χάλκεον ἀμφ᾽ ὄνυχα στάζε φόνον δαΐων,
ἀλλ᾽ ἀνὰ μαρμάρεον δόμον ἥμενα αἰπὺν Ἀθάνας,
ἄγγελλ᾽ ἀνορέαν Κρητὸς Ἐχεκρατίδα.

VII. ANYTE AP 9.745 (14 GP)
25   θάεο τὸν Βρομίου κεραὸν τράγον, ὡς ἀγερώχως
ὄμμα κατὰ λασιᾶν γαῦρον ἔχει γενύων
κυδιόων ὅτι οἱ θάμ᾽ ἐν οὔρεσιν ἀμφὶ παρῆιδα
βόστρυχον εἰς ῥοδέαν Ναῒς ἔδεκτο χέρα.

VIII. ANYTE AP 9.313 (16 GP)
ἵζευ ἅπας ὑπὸ καλὰ δάφνας εὐθαλέα φύλλα
30   ὡραίου τ᾽ ἄρυσαι νάματος ἁδὺ πόμα,
ὄφρα τοι ἀσθμαίνοντα πόνοις θέρεος φίλα γυῖα
ἀμπαύσηις πνοιᾶι τυπτόμενα Ζεφύρου.

IX. ANYTE APL 291 (3 GP)
φριξοκόμαι τόδε Πανὶ καὶ αὐλιάσιν θέτο Νύμφαις
δῶρον ὑπὸ σκοπιᾶς Θεύδοτος οἰονόμος,
35   οὕνεχ᾽ ὑπ᾽ ἀζαλέοιο θέρευς μέγα κεκμηῶτα
παῦσαν ὀρέξασαι χερσὶ μελιχρὸν ὕδωρ.

X. ASCLEPIADES AP 13.23 (33 GP = SENS)
ἰὼ παρέρπων, μικρόν, εἴ τι κἀγκονεῖς, ἄκουσον
τὰ Βότρυος περισσὰ δῆτα κήδη,

VI.   1 τᾶιδε Meineke: τῆιδε P Suda   κράνεια C: -αι P   2 δαΐων Küster: δηΐων P:
δαίδων Suda   3 ἥμένα Salmasius: εἱ- P   4 ἠνορέην Suda

VII.   3 οἱ Brunck: οὐ P

VIII.   1 τῆσδε δάφνης P   2 ἡδὺ Pl   4 πνοιᾶι Stadtmüller: πνοιῆι PPl

IX.   3 αἵ μιν ὑπὸ ζαθέοιο θέρευς Pl^A: οὕνεχ᾽ ὑπ᾽ ἀζαλέου θέρεος Pl^B

X.   1 τι κἀγκονεῖς Meineke: τι κακὸν εἰς P   2 Βότρυος Jacobs: -ύου P

ὃς πρέσβυς ὀγδώκοντ᾿ ἐτῶν τὸν ἐκ νέων ἔθαψεν
40   ἤδη τι τέχναι καὶ σοφὸν λέγοντα.
       φεῦ τὸν τεκόντα, φεῦ δὲ καὶ Βότρυος φίλος παῖ,   5
       ὀσσᾶν ἄμοιρος ἀδονᾶν ἀπώλευ.

XI. ASCLEPIADES *AP* 6.308 (27 GP = SENS)

νικήσας τοὺς παῖδας ἐπεὶ καλὰ γράμματ᾿ ἔγραψεν
       Κόνναρος ὀγδώκοντ᾿ ἀστραγάλους ἔλαβεν,
45   κἀμὲ χάριν Μούσαις τὸν κωμικὸν ὧδε Χάρητα
       πρεσβύτην θορύβωι θῆκ᾿ ἐνὶ παιδαρίων.

XII. ASCLEPIADES OR ARCHELAUS *APL*ᴬ
120 (43 GP = SENS)

τόλμαν Ἀλεξάνδρου καὶ ὅλαν ἀπεμάξατο μορφὰν
       Λύσιππος· τίν᾿ ὁδὶ χαλκὸς ἔχει δύναμιν.
       αὐδασοῦντι δ᾿ ἔοικεν ὁ χάλκεος ἐς Δία λεύσσων·
50   "γᾶν ὑπ᾿ ἐμοὶ τίθεμαι, Ζεῦ, σὺ δ᾿ Ὄλυμπον ἔχε."

XIII. ASCLEPIADES *AP* 5.185 (26 GP =SENS)

εἰς ἀγορὰν βαδίσας, Δημήτριε, τρεῖς παρ᾿ Ἀμύντου
       γλαυκίσκους αἴτει καὶ δέκα φυκίδια,
       καὶ κυφὰς καρῖδας – ἀριθμήσει δέ σοι αὐτός –
       εἴκοσι καὶ τέτορας. δεῦρο λαβὼν ἄπιθι
55   καὶ παρὰ Θαυβαρίου ῥοδίνους ἓξ πρόσλαβε ‹ – ×›   5
       καὶ Τρυφέραν ταχέως ἐν παρόδωι κάλεσον.

XIV. ASCLEPIADES *AP* 5.169 (1 GP = SENS)

ἡδὺ θέρους διψῶντι χιὼν ποτόν, ἡδὺ δὲ ναύταις
       ἐκ χειμῶνος ἰδεῖν εἰαρινὸν Στέφανον·
       ἥδιον δ᾿ ὁπόταν κρύψηι μία τοὺς φιλέοντας
60   χλαῖνα, καὶ αἰνῆται Κύπρις ὑπ᾿ ἀμφοτέρων.

6   ὀσσᾶν Page dubitanter: ὀσσαν P: ὀσᾶν Sternbach: ὅσων apogr. ἀδονᾶν Sternbach:
ἡδονὰν P: ἡδονῶν apogr

XI.   2 Κώναρος Pl   3 Μούσης Pl   4 θῆκ᾿ἐνὶ Hecker: θῆκέ με PPl

XII.   2 τίνα δή Hermann   3 αὐδασοῦντι, αὐδας ουν τι , αὐδαν ουν τι, αὐδάσοντι,
αὐδήσοντι Plut. codices varii, αὐδασεῦντι possis: αὐδάσοντι PlΣᵖ   4 ἐμὲ Tzetzes

XIII. 5 Θαυβαρίου Gow: Θαυβορίου P

XIV.   2 στέφανον CPl: στέφος P   3 ἡδεῖον (-ιον Jacobs) δ᾿ ὁπόταν P: ἥδιστον Cʸᵖ: ἡδὺ δὲ
καὶ ὁπότε (δὲ καὶ manu recent.) Pl: ἡδὺ ὁπότε spatio relicto post ἡδὺ Q   4 αἰνεῖται P

XV. ASCLEPIADES *AP* 5.85 (2 GP = SENS)

φείδηι παρθενίης. καὶ τί πλέον; οὐ γὰρ ἐς Ἅιδην
ἐλθοῦσ᾽ εὑρήσεις τὸν φιλέοντα, κόρη.
ἐν ζωοῖσι τὰ τερπνὰ τὰ Κύπριδος· ἐν δ᾽ Ἀχέροντι
ὀστέα καὶ σποδιή, παρθένε, κεισόμεθα.

XVI. ASCLEPIADES *AP* 5.210 (5 GP = SENS)

65 τὠφθαλμῶι Διδύμη με συνήρπασεν, ὤμοι, ἐγὼ δὲ
τήκομαι ὡς κηρὸς πὰρ πυρὶ κάλλος ὁρῶν.
εἰ δὲ μέλαινα, τί τοῦτο; καὶ ἄνθρακες· ἀλλ᾽ ὅτε κείνους
θάλψωμεν λάμπουσ᾽ ὡς ῥόδεαι κάλυκες.

XVII. ASCLEPIADES *AP* 5.64 (11 GP = SENS)

νεῖφε, χαλαζοβόλει, ποίει σκότος, αἶθε, κεραύνου,
70 πάντα τὰ πορφύροντ᾽ ἐν χθονὶ σεῖε νέφη·
ἢν γάρ με κτείνηις, τότε παύσομαι, ἢν δέ μ᾽ ἀφῆις ζῆν
καὶ διαθῆις τούτων χείρονα, κωμάσομαι·
ἕλκει γάρ μ᾽ ὁ κρατῶν καὶ σοῦ θεός, ὧι ποτε πεισθείς,   5
Ζεῦ, διὰ χαλκείων χρυσὸς ἔδυς θαλάμων.

XVIII. ASCLEPIADES *AP* 5.145 (12 GP = SENS)

75 αὐτοῦ μοι, στέφανοι, παρὰ δικλίσι ταῖσδε κρεμαστοὶ
μίμνετε, μὴ προπετῶς φύλλα τινασσόμενοι
οὓς δακρύοις κατέβρεξα — κάτομβρα γὰρ ὄμματ᾽ ἐρώντων —
ἀλλ᾽ ὅταν οἰγομένης αὐτὸν ἴδητε θύρης,
στάξαθ᾽ ὑπὲρ κεφαλῆς ἐμὸν ὑετόν, ὡς ἂν ἐκείνου   5
80 ἡ ξανθή γε κόμη τἀμὰ πίηι δάκρυα.

XIX. ASCLEPIADES *AP* 12.46 (15 GP = SENS)

οὔκ εἰμ᾽ οὐδ᾽ ἐτέων δύο κεἴκοσι καὶ κοπιῶ ζῶν.
ὤρωτες, τί κακὸν τοῦτο; τί με φλέγετε;
ἢν γὰρ ἐγώ τι πάθω, τί ποιήσετε; δῆλον, Ἔρωτες,
ὡς τὸ πάρος παίξεσθ᾽ ἄφρονες ἀστραγάλοις.

XVI. 1 τὠφθαλμῶι Wilamowitz (ὀφθαλμῶι Jacobs): τῷ θαλλῶι PPl: τῷ θάλπει
Wilamowitz: alii alia   3 ἀλλ᾽ ὅτε κείνους Jacobs: ἀλλὰ τὸ κείνου P: ἀλλὰ τὰ κείνης C

XVII. 3 ἀφῆις ζῆν P *Suda*: ἀφείης Pl   4 διαθῆις Pl (-ης) *Suda*: διαθεὶς P

XVIII. 3 ἐρώντων CPl *P.Oxy.*: ἐρώτων P   4 ὅταν οἰγομένης Jacobs: ὅτ᾽ ἂν οἰγ- C: ὅτ᾽
ἀνοιγ- PPl   αὐτὸν PPl: αὐτὴν C   5 ἐκείνου *P.Oxy.*: ἄμεινον PPl   6 πίηι δάκρυα P *P.Oxy.*:
δάκρυα πίηι Pl

XX. ASCLEPIADES AP 12.135 (18 GP = SENS)

85 οἶνος ἔρωτος ἔλεγχος· ἐρᾶν ἀρνεύμενον ἡμῖν
ἤτασαν αἱ πολλαὶ Νικαγόρην προπόσεις·
καὶ γὰρ ἐδάκρυσεν καὶ ἐνύστασε καί τι κατηφὲς
ἔβλεπε, χὠ σφιγχθεὶς οὐκ ἔμενε στέφανος.

XXI. ERINNA AP 6.352 (3 GP)

ἐξ ἀταλᾶν χειρῶν τάδε γράμματα· λῷστε Προμαθεῦ,
90 ἔντι καὶ ἄνθρωποι τὶν ὁμαλοὶ σοφίαν.
ταύταν γοῦν ἐτύμως τὰν παρθένον ὅστις ἔγραψεν,
αἰ καὐδὰν ποτέθηκ’, ἦς κ’ Ἀγαθαρχὶς ὅλα.

XXII. LEONIDAS AP 7.655 (17 GP)

ἀρκεῖ μοι γαίης μικρὴ κόνις· ἡ δὲ περισσὴ
ἄλλον ἐπιθλίβοι πλούσια κεκλιμένον
95 στήλη, τὸ σκληρὸν νεκρῶν βάρος. εἴ με θανόντα
γνώσοντ’, Ἀλκάνδρωι τοῦτο τί Καλλιτέλευς;

XXIII. LEONIDAS AP 6.657 (19 GP)

ποιμένες, οἳ ταύτην ὄρεος ῥάχιν οἰοπολεῖτε
αἶγας κεὐείρους ἐμβοτέοντες ὄις,
Κλειταγόρηι, πρὸς Γῆς, ὀλίγην χάριν, ἀλλὰ προσηνῆ
100 τίνοιτε χθονίης εἵνεκα Φερσεφόνης.
βληχήσαιντ’ ὄιές μοι, ἐπ’ ἀξέστοιο δὲ ποιμὴν   5
πέτρης συρίζοι πρηέα βοσκομέναις·
εἴαρι δὲ πρώτωι λειμώνιον ἄνθος ἀμέρσας
χωρίτης στεφέτω τύμβον ἐμὸν στεφάνωι,
105 καί τις ἀπ’ εὐάρνοιο καταχραίνοιτο γάλακτι
οἰός, ἀμολγαῖον μαστὸν ἀνασχόμενος,   10
κρηπῖδ’ ὑγραίνων ἐπιτύμβιον. εἰσὶ θανόντων,
εἰσὶν ἀμοιβαῖαι κἀν φθιμένοις χάριτες.

XX. 2 ἤτησαν ἐν πολλαῖς νικασόρην προποσις P, corr. apogr.   3 ἐνύστασε καί τι apogr.: ἐνύσταξε κητι P   4 σφιγχθεὶς Brunck: σφιχθεὶς P

XXI. 1 ἐξ PPl: δέξ’ C   ἀταλᾶν P: ἀπαλᾶν Pl   Προμαθεῦ P: -μηθ- Pl   2 τὶν P: τὴν Pl   4 αἰ καὐδὰν Weiske: αἴκ’ αὐγὰν PPl   ποτέθηκ’ P (-θήκ’) apogr.: ποτε θῆκ’ PlC (ποτὲ) κ’ om. Pl

XXII. 3 εἴ Hermann: οἱ P: οἱ Pl

XXIII. 2 κεὐείρους Salmasius: κεὐήρους P: κεὐμάλους Pl   ἐμβοτέοντες Scaliger: -βατ- PPl   7 ἀμέρξας Scaliger

XXIV. LEONIDAS *AP* 7.295 (20 GP)

Θῆριν τὸν τριγέροντα, τὸν εὐάγρων ἀπὸ κύρτων

110   ζῶντα, τὸν αἰθυίης πλείονα νηξάμενον,

    ἰχθυσιληιστῆρα, σαγηνέα, χηραμοδύτην,

    οὐχὶ πολυσκάλμου πλώτορα ναυτιλίης,

    ἔμπης οὔτ' Ἀρκτοῦρος ἀπώλεσεν, οὔτε καταιγὶς   5

    ἤλασε τὰς πολλὰς τῶν ἐτέων δεκάδας·

115   ἀλλ' ἔθαν' ἐν καλύβηι σχοινίτιδι λύχνος ὁποῖα

    τῶι μακρῶι σβεσθεὶς ἐν χρόνωι αὐτόματος.

    σῆμα δὲ τοῦτ' οὐ παῖδες ἐφήρμοσαν οὐδ' ὁμόλεκτρος,

    ἀλλὰ συνεργατίνης ἰχθυβόλων θίασος.   10

XXV. LEONIDAS *AP* 7.740 (75 GP)

αὗτα ἐπὶ Κρήθωνος ἐγὼ λίθος, οὔνομα κείνου

120   δηλοῦσα· Κρήθων δ' ἐγχθόνιος σποδιά,

    ὁ πρὶν καὶ Γύγηι παρισεύμενος ὄλβον, ὁ τὸ πρὶν

    βουπάμων, ὁ πρὶν πλούσιος αἰπολίοις,

    ὁ πρίν — τί πλείω μυθεῦμ' ἔτι; — πᾶσι μακαρτός,   5

    φεῦ, γαίης ὄσσης ὄσσον ἔχει μόριον.

XXVI. LEONIDAS *AP* 7.283 (63 GP)

125   τετρηχυῖα θάλασσα, τί μ' οὐκ οἰζυρὰ παθόντα

    τηλόσ' ἀπὸ ψιλῆς ἔπτυσας ἠιόνος,

    ὡς σεῦ μηδ' Ἀίδαο κακὴν ἐπιειμένος ἀχλὺν

    Φιλλεὺς Ἀμφιμένευς ἄσσον ἐγειτόνεον;

XXVII. LEONIDAS *AP* 7.455 (68 GP)

Μαρωνὶς ἡ φίλοινος, ἡ πίθων σποδός,

130   ἐνταῦθα κεῖται γρηῦς, ἧς ὑπὲρ τάφου

    γνωστὸν πρόκειται πᾶσιν Ἀττικὴ κύλιξ.

    στένει δὲ καὶ γᾶς νέρθεν, οὐχ ὑπὲρ τέκνων

    οὐδ' ἀνδρός, οὓς ἔλειπεν ἐνδεεῖς βίου,

    ἓν δ' ἀντὶ πάντων, οὔνεχ' ἡ κύλιξ κενή.   5

XXV.   2 ἐγχθόνιος Kaibel: ἐν χθονὶ οἷς P: ἐν χθονίοις Pl

XXVI.   1 τετρηχυῖα CPl: -αν P   3 ὡς CPl: ὃς P

XXVII.   epigramma iteravit (= P[b]) C in margine iuxta Antip. *AP* 7.353 (de Maronide)   3 γνωστὴ Pl   4 γῆς Pl   5 οὐδ' P: οὐκ P[b]Pl   λέλοιπεν Pl

XXVIII. LEONIDAS *AP* 7.408 (58 GP)

135 ἀτρέμα τὸν τύμβον παραμείβετε, μὴ τὸν ἐν ὕπνωι
πικρὸν ἐγείρητε σφῆκ' ἀναπαυόμενον.
ἄρτι γὰρ Ἱππώνακτος ὁ καὶ τοκεῶνε βαΰξας
ἄρτι κεκοίμηται θυμὸς ἐν ἡσυχίηι.
ἀλλὰ προμηθήσασθε· τὰ γὰρ πεπυρωμένα κείνου   5
140 ῥήματα πημαίνειν οἶδε καὶ εἰν Ἀίδηι.

XXIX. LEONIDAS *AP* 7.13 (98 GP)

παρθενικὰν νεαοιδὸν ἐν ὑμνοπόλοισι μέλισσαν
"Ηρινναν Μουσέων ἄνθεα δρεπτομέναν
"Αιδας εἰς ὑμέναιον ἀνάρπασεν. ἦ ῥα τόδ' ἔμφρων
εἶπ' ἐτύμως ἁ παῖς· "βάσκανός ἐσσ', Ἀίδα."

XXX. LEONIDAS *AP* 9.719 (88 GP)

145 οὐκ ἔπλασέν με Μύρων, ἐψεύσατο· βοσκομέναν δὲ
ἐξ ἀγέλας ἐλάσας δῆσε βάσει λιθίνωι.

XXXI. LEONIDAS *AP* 6.263 (49 GP)

πυρσῶ τοῦτο λέοντος ἀπεφλοιώσατο δέρμα
Σῶσος ὁ βουπάμων δουρὶ φονευσάμενος
ἄρτι καταβρύκοντα τὸν εὐθηλήμονα μόσχον·
150 οὐδ' ἵκετ' ἐκ μάνδρας αὖτις ἐπὶ ξύλοχον,
μοσχείω δ' ἀπέτισεν ὁ θὴρ ἀνθ' αἵματος αἷμα   5
βληθείς· ἀχθεινὰν δ' εἶδε βοοκτασίαν.

XXXII. LEONIDAS *APL* 230 (86 GP)

μὴ σύ γ' ἐπ' οἰονόμοιο περίπλεον ἰλύος ὧδε
τοῦτο χαραδραίης θερμόν, ὁδῖτα, πίηις·
155 ἀλλὰ μολὼν μάλα τυτθὸν ὑπὲρ δαμαλήβοτον ἄκρην
κεῖσέ γε πὰρ κείναι ποιμενίαι πίτυϊ

XXVIII. 3 τοκεῶνε βαΰξας Headlam: τοκέων εἶα P: τοκέων ἔο βαύξας Pl

XXIX. 1 παρθενικὰν Brunck: -ὴν PPl   2 "Ηρινναν P: "Ηρ- Pl Syll.Σ   Μουσέων Syll.Σ:
Μουσῶν PPl   δρεπτομέναν P: -ην Pl Syll.Σ   3 ἀνάρπασεν P: ἀνήρπ- Pl Syll.Σ   4 ἀίδα
P: -δη Pl Syll.Σ

XXXI. 1 πυρσῶ Meineke: -ῶι P: -οῦ Pl   2 βουπάμων Valckenaer: -παλίων PPl   5
μοσχείω Meineke: -είωι P: -είου Pl: -ίω *Suda*

XXXII. 1 γε ποιονόμοιο Geffcken

εὑρήσεις κελαρύζον ἐυκρήνου διὰ πέτρης   5
νᾶμα Βορειαίης ψυχρότερον νιφάδος.

XXXIII. LEONIDAS *AP* 9.99 (32 GP)

ἴξαλος εὐπώγων αἰγὸς πόσις ἔν ποτ' ἀλωῆι
160 οἴνης τοὺς ἁπαλοὺς πάντας ἔδαψε κλάδους.
τῶι δ' ἔπος ἐκ γαίης τόσον ἄπυε· "κεῖρε, κάκιστε,
γναθμοῖς ἡμέτερον κλῆμα τὸ καρποφόρον·
ῥίζα γὰρ ἔμπεδος οὖσα πάλιν γλυκὺ νέκταρ ἀνήσει   5
ὅσσον ἐπισπεῖσαι σοί, τράγε, θυομένωι."

XXXIV. MOERO *AP* 6.119 (1 GP)

165 κεῖσαι δὴ χρυσέαν ὑπὸ παστάδα τὰν Ἀφροδίτας,
βότρυ, Διωνύσου πληθόμενος σταγόνι,
οὐδ' ἔτι τοι μάτηρ ἐρατὸν περὶ κλῆμα βαλοῦσα
φύσει ὑπὲρ κρατὸς νεκτάρεον πέταλον.

XXXV. NOSSIS *AP* 6.275 (5 GP)

χαίροισάν τοι ἔοικε κομᾶν ἄπο τὰν Ἀφροδίταν
170 ἄνθεμα κεκρύφαλον τόνδε λαβεῖν Σαμύθας·
δαιδάλεός τε γάρ ἐστι καὶ ἁδύ τι νέκταρος ὄσδει·
τούτωι καὶ τήνα καλὸν Ἄδωνα χρίει.

XXXVI. NOSSIS *AP* 6.353 (8 GP)

Αὐτομέλιννα τέτυκται· ἴδ', ὡς ἀγανὸν τὸ πρόσωπον.
ἁμὲ ποτοπτάζειν μειλιχίως δοκέει·
175 ὡς ἐτύμως θυγάτηρ τᾶι ματέρι πάντα ποτώικει.
ἦ καλόν, ὅκκα πέληι τέκνα γονεῦσιν ἴσα.

XXXVII. NOSSIS *AP* 6.354 (9 GP)

γνωτὰ καὶ τηλῶθε Σαβαιθίδος εἴδεται ἔμμεν
ἅδ' εἰκὼν μορφᾶι καὶ μεγαλεοσύναι.
θάεο· τὰν πινυτὰν τό τε μείλιχον αὐτόθι τήνας
180 ἔλπομ' ὁρῆν. χαίροις πολλά, μάκαιρα γύναι.

XXXIV.   2 σταγόνι apogr.: -ῶνι P

XXXV.   3 ὄσδει apogr.: ὄζει P (δ supra ζ scr.) *Suda*

XXXVI.   3 ποτώικει Bentley: προσ- P   4 πέληι Schaefer: πέλοι P

XXXVII.   1 τηλῶθε Meineke: τηνῶθε P   εἴδεται ἔμμεν Meineke: εἴδετε μὲν P   3
μεγαλειοσύναι Reiske: μεγαλωσύναι C: μεγαλωσύνα P   4 ὁρῆν Brunck: ὁρᾶν P

XXXVIII. NOSSIS *AP* 9.604 (7 GP)

Θαυμαρέτας μορφὰν ὁ πίναξ ἔχει· εὖ γε τὸ γαῦρον
τεῦξε τό θ' ὡραῖον τᾶς ἀγανοβλεφάρου.
σαίνοι κέν σ' ἐσιδοῖσα καὶ οἰκοφύλαξ σκυλάκαινα
δέσποιναν μελάθρων οἰομένα ποθορῆν.

XXXIX. NOSSIS *AP* 5.170 (1 GP)

185 ἅδιον οὐδὲν ἔρωτος· ἃ δ' ὄλβια, δεύτερα πάντα
ἐστίν· ἀπὸ στόματος δ' ἔπτυσα καὶ τὸ μέλι.
τοῦτο λέγει Νοσσίς· τίνα δ' ἁ Κύπρις οὐκ ἐφίλησεν,
οὐκ οἶδεν κήνα γ', ἄνθεα ποῖα ῥόδα.

XL. PERSES *AP* 7.539 (9 GP)

οὐ προϊδών, Θεότιμε, κακὴν δύσιν ὑετίοιο
190 Ἀρκτούρου κρυερῆς ἥψαο ναυτιλίης,
ἤ σε δι' Αἰγαίοιο πολυκλήϊδι θέοντα
νηὶ σὺν οἷς ἑτάροις ἤγαγεν εἰς Ἀίδην.
αἰαῖ, Ἀριστοδίκη δὲ καὶ Εὔπολις, οἵ σ' ἐτέκοντο,   5
μύρονται κενεὸν σῆμα περισχόμενοι.

XLI. PERSES *AP* 7.501 (4 GP)

195 Εὔρου χειμέριαί σε καταιγίδες ἐξεκύλισαν,
Φίλλι, πολυκλαύτωι γυμνὸν ἐπ' ἠιόνι,
οἰνηρῆς Λέσβοιο παρὰ σφυρόν· αἰγίλιπος δὲ
πέτρου ἁλιβρέκτωι κεῖσαι ὑπὸ πρόποδι.

XLII. PERSES *AP* 7.730 (7 GP)

δειλαία Μνάσυλλα, τί τοι καὶ ἐπ' ἠρίωι οὗτος
200 μυρομέναι κούραν γραπτὸς ἔπεστι τύπος
Νευτίμας, ἃς δή ποκ' ἀπὸ ψυχὰν ἐρύσαντο
ὠδῖνες; κεῖται δ' οἷα κατὰ βλεφάρων
ἀχλύι πλημύρουσα φίλας ὑπὸ μητρὸς ἀγοστῶι,   5
αἰαῖ, Ἀριστοτέλης δ' οὐκ ἀπάνευθε πατὴρ

XXXVIII. 2 θ' Brunck: δ' PPl   τῆς PL   3 ἐσιδοῦσα Pl   4 οἰομένη Pl

XXXIX. 1 ἃ δ' apogr.: τἀδ' P   4 κήνα γ' Reitzenstein: κῆνα τ' P

XLI. 1 ἐξεκύλισαν Pl: ἐξεκύλισσαν P

XLII. 2 κούραν Hecker: κούρα P   3 ἃς C: τε P (ut videtur)   ἐρύσαντο C: ἐρεα P (ut videtur)   4 βλεφάρων C: φαεφάρων P   5 ὑπὸ C: ἀπὸ P

205   δεξιτερᾶι κεφαλὰν ἐπεμάσσατο. ὦ μέγα δειλοί,
       οὐδὲ θανόντες ἑῶν ἐξελάθεσθ' ἀχέων.

XLIII. PERSES *AP* 6.112 (1 GP)

    τρεῖς ἄφατοι κεράεσσιν ὑπ' αἰθούσαις τοι, Ἄπολλον,
    ἄγκεινται κεφαλαὶ Μαιναλίων ἐλάφων,
    ἃς ἕλον ἐξ ἵππων †γυγερῶι χέρε† Δαΐλοχός τε
210   καὶ Προμένης, ἀγαθοῦ τέκνα Λεοντιάδου.

XLIV. PERSES *AP* 6.272 (2 GP)

    ζῶμά τοι, ὦ Λατωί, καὶ ἀνθεμόεντα κύπασσιν
    καὶ μίτραν μαστοῖς σφιγκτὰ περιπλομέναν
    θήκατο Τιμάεσσα, δυσωδίνοιο γενέθλας
    ἀργαλέον δεκάτωι μηνὶ φυγοῦσα βάρος.

XLV. PHALAECUS *AP* 13.27 (4 GP)

215   Φῶκος ἐπὶ ξείνηι μὲν ἀπέφθιτο· κῦμα γὰρ μέλαινα
    νεῦς οὐχ ὑπεξήνεικεν οὐδ' ἐδέξατο
    ἀλλὰ κατ' Αἰγαίοιο πολὺν βυθὸν ὤιχετο πόντου
    βίηι Νότου πρήσαντος ἐσχάτην ἅλα.
    τύμβου δ' ἐν πατέρων κενεοῦ λάχεν, ὃν πέρι Προμηθὶς   5
220   μήτηρ, λυγρῆι ὄρνιθι πότμον εἰκέλη,
    αἰαῖ κωκύει τὸν ἑὸν γόνον ἤματα πάντα,
    λέγουσα τὸν πρόωρον ὡς ἀπέφθιτο.

XLVI. PHILITAS 13 SBARDELLA (3 GP [VV. 1–2], 23 SPANOUDAKIS)

    — ἐκ θυμοῦ κλαῦσαί με τὰ μέτρια καί τι προσηνὲς
    εἰπεῖν, μεμνῆσθαί τ' οὐκέτ' ἐόντος ὁμῶς.

---

7 ὦ Wilamowitz: κοὺ Stadtmüller: κ' ὦ P

XLIII.   2 ἄγκεινται *Suda:* ἔγκεινται P *Suda*   3 Μαιναδίων *Suda*

XLIV.   1 Λατωί Graefe: Λατοῖ P   2 μαστοῖς apogr.: μαστοῖο P   3 Τιμήεσσα C   δυσωδίνοιο C: διωδίνοιο P

XLV.   2 ὑπεξήνικεν P, corr. Brunck   3 πολὺν βυθὸν Meineke: πολὺ βαθὺν P   4 ἐσχατάτην P, corr. Brunck   5 Προμηθὶς Brunck: -θεὶς P   6 εἰκέλη Brunck: ἱκ- P   8 πρόορον P, corr. Salmasius

XLVI.   1–2 et 3–4 coniunxit Schneidewin   1 με τὰ Jacobs: μέγα Stob.

225   — οὐ κλαίω ξείνων σε φιλαίτατε· πολλὰ γὰρ ἔγνως
       καλά, κακῶν δ' αὖ σοι μοῖραν ἔνειμε θεός.

XLVII. SIMIAS, "SIMONIDES," OR SAMIUS
AP 7.647 (SIMIAS 7 GP)

ὕστατα δὴ τάδ' ἔειπε φίλαν ποτὶ ματέρα Γοργώ
δακρυόεσσα δέρας χερσὶν ἐφαπτομένα·
"αὖθι μένοις παρὰ πατρί, τέκοις δ' ἐπὶ λώιονι μοίραι
230   ἄλλαν σῶι πολιῶι γήραϊ καδεμόνα."

XLVIII. SIMIAS AP 7.22 (5 GP)

ἠρέμ' ὑπὲρ τύμβοιο Σοφοκλέος, ἠρέμα, κισσέ,
ἑρπύζοις χλοερούς ἐκπροχέων πλοκάμους,
καὶ πέταλον πάντηι θάλλοι ρόδου ἥ τε φιλορρὼξ
ἄμπελος ὑγρὰ πέριξ κλήματα χευαμένη,
235   εἵνεκεν εὐμαθίης πινυτόφρονος, ἣν ὁ μελιχρὸς   5
       ἤσκησεν Μουσῶν ἄμμιγα καὶ Χαρίτων.

XLIX. SIMIAS AP 7.203 (1 GP)

οὐκέτ' ἀν' ὑλῆεν δρίος εὔσκιον, ἀγρότα πέρδιξ,
ἠχήεσσαν ἱεῖς γῆρυν ἀπὸ στομάτων,
θηρεύων βαλιοὺς συνομήλικας ἐν νομῶι ὕλης·
240   ὤιχεο γὰρ πυμάταν εἰς Ἀχέροντος ὁδόν.

L. CALLIMACHUS AP 7.517 (20 PF., 32 GP)

ἠῶιοι Μελάνιππον ἐθάπτομεν, ἠελίου δὲ
δυομένου Βασιλὼ κάτθανε παρθενικὴ
αὐτοχερί· ζώειν γὰρ ἀδελφεὸν ἐν πυρὶ θεῖσα
οὐκ ἔτλη. δίδυμον δ' οἶκος ἐσεῖδε κακὸν
245   πατρὸς Ἀριστίπποιο, κατήφησεν δὲ Κυρήνη   5
       πᾶσα τὸν εὔτεκνον χῆρον ἰδοῦσα δόμον.

---

4 ἔνειμε Gesner: νέμει Stob.

XLVII.   1 δὴ om. P   φίλην, μητέρα P   2 δέρας Stadtmüller: δέρης PPl   4 καδεμόνα
apogr.: καδομέναν PPl (in κηδομένην corr. P)

XLVIII.   1 τύμβου Σοφοκλέους P   4 κλίματα P   5 μελιχροῦς P

XLIX.   1 δρίος C Suda: δρυὸς Pl: δρύσὲς P   2 στομάτων P: στόματος CPl Suda   3
βαλιοὺς συνομήλικας Pl   4 ὤιχεο CPl Suda: ὤιχετο P

L.   6 εὔτεκνον C: εὐτέκνων P: εὔτακτον Pl

LI. CALLIMACHUS *AP* 7.80 (2 PF., 34 GP)
εἶπέ τις, Ἡράκλειτε, τεὸν μόρον, ἐς δέ με δάκρυ
ἤγαγεν· ἐμνήσθην δ' ὁσσάκις ἀμφότεροι
ἥλιον λέσχῃ κατεδύσαμεν. ἀλλὰ σὺ μέν που,
250   ξεῖν' Ἁλικαρνησεῦ, τετράπαλαι σποδιή,
αἱ δὲ τεαὶ ζώουσιν ἀηδόνες, ἧισιν ὁ πάντων   5
ἁρπακτὴς Ἀΐδης οὐκ ἐπὶ χεῖρα βαλεῖ.

LII. CALLIMACHUS *AP* 7.447 (11 PF., 35 GP)
σύντομος ἦν ὁ ξεῖνος, ὃ καὶ στίχος οὐ μακρὰ λέξων
"Θῆρις Ἀρισταίου Κρής" ἐπ' ἐμοὶ δολιχός.

LIII. CALLIMACHUS *AP* 7.272 (18 PF., 38 GP)
255   Νάξιος οὐκ ἐπὶ γῆς ἔθανεν Λύκος, ἀλλ' ἐνὶ πόντωι
ναῦν ἅμα καὶ ψυχὴν εἶδεν ἀπολλυμένην,
ἔμπορος Αἰγίνηθεν ὅτ' ἔπλεε· χὠ μὲν ἐν ὑγρῆι
νεκρός, ἐγὼ δ' ἄλλως οὔνομα τύμβος ἔχων
κηρύσσω πανάληθες ἔπος τόδε· "φεῦγε θαλάσσηι   5
260   συμμίσγειν Ἐρίφων, ναυτίλε, δυομένων."

LIV. CALLIMACHUS *AP* 7.451 (9 PF., 41 GP)
τῆιδε Σάων ὁ Δίκωνος Ἀκάνθιος ἱερὸν ὕπνον
κοιμᾶται· θνήισκειν μὴ λέγε τοὺς ἀγαθούς.

LV. CALLIMACHUS *AP* 7.521 (12 PF., 43 GP)
Κύζικον ἢν ἔλθηις, ὀλίγος πόνος Ἱππακὸν εὑρεῖν
καὶ Διδύμην· ἀφανὴς οὔτι γὰρ ἡ γενεή·
265   καί σφιν ἀνιηρὸν μὲν ἐρεῖς ἔπος, ἔμπα δὲ λέξαι
τοῦθ', ὅτι τὸν κείνων ὧδ' ἐπέχω Κριτίην.

LVI. CALLIMACHUS *AP* 7.271 (17 PF., 45 GP)
ὤφελε μηδ' ἐγένοντο θοαὶ νέες· οὐ γὰρ ἂν ἡμεῖς
παῖδα Διοκλείδου Σώπολιν ἐστένομεν·

LI.   3 ἥλιον Pl D.L.: ἥλιον P *Suda*   ἐν λέσχηι PPl, ἐν secl. Bentley
LII. 1 λέξων C: λέξω PPl
LIII. 4 ἔχων CPl: ἔχω P   6 δυομένων CPl: δυσμενέων P
LIV. 2 θνάσκειν P
LV.   3 λέξον Pl   4 ὧδ' ἐπέχω C (ὧδ' om. P): υἱὸν ἔχω Pl

νῦν δ' ὁ μὲν εἰν ἁλί που φέρεται νέκυς, ἀντὶ δ' ἐκείνου
270 οὔνομα καὶ κενεὸν σῆμα παρερχόμεθα.

LVII. CALLIMACHUS AP 7.453 (19 PF., 46 GP)

δωδεκέτη τὸν παῖδα πατὴρ ἀπέθηκε Φίλιππος
ἐνθάδε, τὴν πολλὴν ἐλπίδα, Νικοτέλην.

LVIII. CALLIMACHUS AP 7.317 (4 PF., 51 GP)

Τίμων (οὐ γὰρ ἔτ' ἐσσί), τί τοι, σκότος ἢ φάος, ἐχθρόν;
— τὸ σκότος· ὑμέων γὰρ πλείονες εἰν Ἀΐδηι.

LIX. CALLIMACHUS AP 7.525 (21 PF., 29 GP)

275 ὅστις ἐμὸν παρὰ σῆμα φέρεις πόδα, Καλλιμάχου με
ἴσθι Κυρηναίου παῖδά τε καὶ γενέτην.
εἰδείης δ' ἄμφω κεν· ὁ μέν κοτε πατρίδος ὅπλων
ἦρξεν, ὁ δ' ἤεισεν κρέσσονα βασκανίης.
οὐ νέμεσις· Μοῦσαι γὰρ ὅσους ἴδον ὄμματι παῖδας   5
280 μὴ λοξῶι, πολιοὺς οὐκ ἀπέθεντο φίλους.

LX. CALLIMACHUS APUD ATH. 7.318B
(5 PF., 14 GP)

κόγχος ἐγώ, Ζεφυρῖτι, παλαίτερον· ἀλλὰ σὺ νῦν με,
Κύπρι, Σεληναίης ἄνθεμα πρῶτον ἔχεις,
ναυτίλος ὃς πελάγεσσιν ἐπέπλεον, εἰ μὲν ἄηται,
τείνας οἰκείων λαῖφος ἀπὸ προτόνων,
285 εἰ δὲ Γαληναίη, λιπαρὴ θεός, οὖλος ἐρέσσων   5
ποσσίν (ἴδ' ὡς τὦργωι τοὔνομα συμφέρεται)
ἔστ' ἔπεσον παρὰ θῖνας Ἰουλίδας, ὄφρα γένωμαι
σοὶ τὸ περίσκεπτον παίγνιον, Ἀρσινόη,
μηδέ μοι ἐν θαλάμηισιν ἔθ' ὡς πάρος (εἰμὶ γὰρ ἄπνους)
290 τίκτηται νοτερῆς ὤεον ἀλκυόνος.   10

LVIII. 1 φάος ἢ σκότος Pl   2 ὑμείων P

LIX. 5–6 secl. Pfeiffer   6 μὴ λοξῶι schol. Hes.; cf. Call. Aet. fr. 1.38: ἄχρι βίου PPl

LX. 1 παλαίτερον Bentley: -ρος Ath.: πάλαι τέρας Schneider (cf. Plin. NH 9.88)
3 ναυτίλος Kaibel: -λον Ath.   6 ἴδ'ὡς τὦργωι Schneider: ἱν' ὡσπεργωι Ath.   10
ἀλκυόνος Bentley: ἀλκυόνης Ath.

Κλεινίου ἀλλὰ θυγατρὶ δίδου χάριν· οἶδε γὰρ ἐσθλὰ
ῥέζειν καὶ Σμύρνης ἐστὶν ἀπ' Αἰολίδος.

LXI. CALLIMACHUS AP 6.351 (34 PF., 22 GP)

τίν με, λεοντάγχ' ὦνα συοκτόνε, φήγινον ὄζον
θῆκε — τίς; — Ἀρχῖνος. — ποῖος; — ὁ Κρής. — δέχομαι.

LXII. CALLIMACHUS AP 6.149 (56 PF., 25 GP)

295 φησὶν ὅ με στήσας Εὐαίνετος (οὐ γὰρ ἔγωγε
      γινώσκω) νίκης ἀντί με τῆς ἰδίης
      ἀγκεῖσθαι χάλκειον ἀλέκτορα Τυνδαρίδηισι·
      πιστεύω Φαίδρου παιδὶ Φιλοξενίδεω.

LXIII. CALLIMACHUS AP 12.102 131 PF., 1 GP)

      ὠγρευτής, Ἐπίκυδες, ἐν οὔρεσι πάντα λαγωὸν
300   διφᾶι καὶ πάσης ἴχνια δορκαλίδος
      στίβηι καὶ νιφετῶι κεχρημένος· ἢν δέ τις εἴπηι
      "τῆ, τόδε βέβληται θηρίον," οὐκ ἔλαβεν.
      χοὐμὸς Ἔρως τοιόσδε· τὰ μὲν φεύγοντα διώκειν   5
      οἶδε, τὰ δ' ἐν μέσσωι κείμενα παρπέταται.

LXIV. CALLIMACHUS AP 12.43 (28 PF., 2 GP)

305 ἐχθαίρω τὸ ποίημα τὸ κυκλικόν, οὐδὲ κελεύθωι
      χαίρω, τίς πολλοὺς ὧδε καὶ ὧδε φέρει·
      μισέω καὶ περίφοιτον ἐρώμενον, οὐδ' ἀπὸ κρήνης
      πίνω· σικχαίνω πάντα τὰ δημόσια.
      Λυσανίη, σὺ δὲ ναίχι καλός — "καλός" — ἀλλὰ πρὶν εἰπεῖν   5
310   τοῦτο σαφῶς Ἠχώ, φησί τις ἄλλος ἔχειν.

LXV. CALLIMACHUS AP 12.118 (42 PF., 8 GP)

εἰ μὲν ἑκών, Ἀρχῖν', ἐπεκώμασα, μυρία μέμφου·
εἰ δ' ἄκων ἥκω, τὴν προπέτειαν ἔα.
ἄκρητος καὶ ἔρως μ' ἠνάγκασαν· ὧν ὁ μὲν αὐτῶν

LXIII.   4 τῇ Brunck: τῆι P

LXIV.   3 οὐδ' Brunck: οὔτ' P   4 σικχαίνω Brunck: -άνω P   6 ἔχειν Petersen: ἔχει P

LXV.   1 Ἀρχῖν' Bentley: ἄρχειν P

εἶλκεν, ὁ δ᾽ οὐκ εἴα τὴν προπέτειαν ἐᾶν.
315 ἐλθὼν δ᾽ οὐκ ἐβόησα, τίς ἢ τίνος, ἀλλ᾽ ἐφίλησα   5
τὴν φλιήν· εἰ τοῦτ᾽ ἔστ᾽ ἀδίκημ᾽, ἀδικέω.

LXVI. CALLIMACHUS AP 12.134 (43 PF., 13 GP)

ἕλκος ἔχων ὁ ξεῖνος ἐλάνθανεν· ὡς ἀνιηρὸν
πνεῦμα διὰ στηθέων (εἶδες;) ἀνηγάγετο,
τὸ τρίτον ἡνίκ᾽ ἔπινε, τὰ δὲ ῥόδα φυλλοβολεῦντα
320 τὠνδρὸς ἀπὸ στεφάνων πάντ᾽ ἐγένοντο χαμαί·
ὤπτηται μέγα δή τι, μὰ δαίμονας· οὐκ ἀπὸ ῥυσμοῦ   5
εἰκάζω, φωρὸς δ᾽ ἴχνια φὼρ ἔμαθον.

LXVII. CALLIMACHUS AP 9.507 (27 PF., 56 GP)

Ἡσιόδου τό τ᾽ ἄεισμα καὶ ὁ τρόπος· οὐ τὸν ἀοιδὸν
ἔσχατον, ἀλλ᾽ ὀκνέω μὴ τὸ μελιχρότατον
325 τῶν ἐπέων ὁ Σολεὺς ἀπεμάξατο· χαίρετε λεπταὶ
ῥήσιες, Ἀρήτου σύμβολον ἀγρυπνίης.

LXVIII. HEDYLUS APUD ATH. 11.497D (4 GP)

ζωροπόται, καὶ τοῦτο φιλοζεφύρου κατὰ νηὸν
τὸ ῥυτὸν εὐδίης δεῦτ᾽ ἴδετ᾽ Ἀρσινόης,
ὀρχηστὴν Βησᾶν Αἰγύπτιον· ὃς λιγὺν ἦχον
330 σαλπίζει κρουνοῦ πρὸς ῥύσιν οἰγομένου,
οὐ πολέμου σύνθημα, διὰ χρυσέου δὲ γέγωνεν   5
κώδωνος κώμου σύνθεμα καὶ θαλίης,
Νεῖλος ὁκοῖον ἄναξ μύσταις φίλον ἱεραγωγοῖς
εὗρε μέλος θείων πάτριον ἐξ ὑδάτων.
335 ἀλλὰ Κτησιβίου σοφὸν εὕρεμα τίετε τοῦτο,
δεῦτε, νέοι, νηῶι τῶιδε παρ᾽ Ἀρσινόης.   10

---

4 τὴν προπέτειαν ἐᾶν Dressel ex]ετηανεαν Ep. Gr. 1111: τὴν βίαν ὅσσην ὅρα Syll.s:
σώφρονα θυμὸν ἔχειν P 6 ἀδικέω Meineke: ἀδικῶ P Syll.s Ep. Gr.

LXVII. 1 ἀοιδόν P, Achilles ap. Vit. Arat. 5: -ῶν P.Oxy. 4648 4 σύμβολον Ruhnken:
σύντονος P: σύγγονος Achilles: σύντομος Stewart ἀγρυπνίης Achilles: -ίη P

LXVIII. 2 εὐδίης Kaibel: εἰδείης Ath.: αἰδοίης Jacobs 4 οἰγομένου Salmasius:
ἠγομένου Ath. 5 οὐ Jacobs: καὶ Ath. 6 σύνθεμα Musurus: σύνθημα Ath. 7 ὁκοῖον
Schweighäuser: ὁκοῖος Ath. 9 ἀλλ᾽ εἰ Meineke

LXIX. HEDYLUS AP 5.199 (2 GP)

οἶνος καὶ προπόσεις κατεκοίμισαν Ἀγλαονίκην
αἱ δόλιαι καὶ ἔρως ἡδὺς ὁ Νικαγόρεω,
ἧς πάρα Κύπριδι ταῦτα μύροις ἔτι πάντα μυδῶντα
340   κεῖνται παρθενίων ὑγρὰ λάφυρα πόθων,
σάνδαλα καὶ μαλακαί, μαστῶν ἐκδύματα, μίτραι,   5
ὕπνου καὶ σκυλμῶν τῶν τότε μαρτύρια.

LXX. HEDYLUS APUD ATH. 11.472F–3A (5 GP)

πίνωμεν· καὶ γάρ τι νέον, καὶ γάρ τι παρ' οἶνον
εὕροιμ' ἂν λεπτὸν καί τι μελιχρὸν ἔπος.
345   ἀλλὰ κάδοις Χίου με κατάβρεχε καὶ λέγε "παῖζε,
Ἡδύλε." μισῶ ζῆν ἐς κενὸν οὐ μεθύων.

LXXI. HERACLITUS AP 7.465 (1 GP)

ἁ κόνις ἀρτίσκαπτος, ἐπὶ στάλας δὲ μετώπων
σείονται φύλλων ἡμιθαλεῖς στέφανοι·
γράμμα διακρίναντες, ὁδοιπόρε, πέτρον ἴδωμεν,
350   λευρὰ περιστέλλειν ὀστέα φατὶ τίνος.
– ξεῖν', Ἀρετημιὰς εἰμι· πάτρα Κνίδος· Εὔφρονος ἦλθον   5
εἰς λέχος· ὠδίνων οὐκ ἄμορος γενόμαν·
δισσὰ δ' ὁμοῦ τίκτουσα τὸ μὲν λίπον ἀνδρὶ ποδηγὸν
γήρως, ἐν δ' ἀπάγω μναμόσυνον πόσιος.

LXXII. NICIAS AP 6.127 (2 GP)

355   μέλλον ἄρα στυγερὰν κἀγώ ποτε δῆριν Ἄρηος
ἐκπρολιποῦσα χορῶν παρθενίων ἀίειν
Ἀρτέμιδος περὶ ναόν, Ἐπίξενος ἔνθα μ' ἔθηκεν,
λευκὸν ἐπεὶ κείνου γῆρας ἔτειρε μέλη.

LXX.   2 εὕροιμ' ἂν Jacobs: εὕροιμεν Ath.   4 μισῶ ζῆν Jacobs: με σωζην Ath.

LXXI.   1 ἀρτίσκαπτος CPl: -τρος P (ut videtur)   μετώπωι Pl   2 σεύονται . . .
ἡμιθανεῖς Pl   4 λευρὰ C et in marg. γρ. λευρὰ ἢ ἄλλως πως et subter λευκὰ: λύρα P:
λυγρὰ Pl   5 Ἀρετιμιάς P   6 ἐς Pl   8 ἐν Jacobs: ὃν PPl   μνημ- Pl

LXXII.   1 Ἄρηος apogr.: -ηι P Suda

LXXIII. NICIAS AP 6.270 (3 GP)

Ἀμφαρέτας κρήδεμνα καὶ ὑδατόεσσα καλύπτρα,
360   Εἰλείθυια, τεᾶς κεῖται ὑπὲρ κεφαλᾶς,
ὡς σὲ μετ' εὐχωλᾶς ἐκαλέσσατο λευγαλέας οἱ
κῆρας ἀπ' ὠδίνων τῆλε βαλεῖν λοχίων.

LXXIV. POSIDIPPUS *131 AB (AP 7.170 = 21 GP)

τὸν τριετῆ παίζοντα περὶ φρέαρ Ἀρχιάνακτα
εἴδωλον μορφᾶς κωφὸν ἐπεσπάσατο,
365   ἐκ δ' ὕδατος τὸν παῖδα διάβροχον ἥρπασε μάτηρ
σκεπτομένα ζωᾶς εἴ τινα μοῖραν ἔχει.
Νύμφας δ' οὐκ ἐμίηνεν ὁ νήπιος, ἀλλ' ἐπὶ γούνοις   5
ματρὸς κοιμασθεὶς τὸν βαθὺν ὕπνον ἔχει.

LXXV. POSIDIPPUS 102 AB

τί πρὸς ἔμ' ὧδ' ἔστητε; τί μ' οὐκ ἠάσατ' ἰαύειν,
370   εἰρόμενοι τίς ἐγὼ καὶ πόθεν ἢ ποδαπός;
στείχετέ μου παρὰ σῆμα· Μενοίτιός εἰμι Φιλάρχω
Κρής, ὀλιγορρήμων ὡς ἂν ἐπὶ ξενίης.

LXXVI. POSIDIPPUS 100 AB

ἡνίκ' ἔδει Ζήνωνα τὸν ἥσυχον ὕπνον ἰαύειν,
πέμπτον ἐπ' εἰκοστῶι τυφλὸν ἐόντα θέρει,
375   ὀγδωκονταέτης ὑγιὴς γένετ', ἠέλιον δὲ
δὶς μοῦ[νον βλέψας τὸ]ν βαρὺν εἶδ' Ἀίδην.

LXXIII.   1 Ἀμφαρέτας Meineke: -τις P: -τρις C   2 Εἰλείθυια C: Εἰλήθυια P   3 εὐχωλᾶς apogr.: -αῖς P Suda   οἱ apogr.: τοι Suda

LXXIV.   post 7.481 idem carmen habet P Callimacho adscriptum (= Pᵇ)   1 περὶ CᵃPᵇPl: παρὰ Pᵃ   Ἀρχεάνακτα Pᵇ   2 μορφῆς Pᵇ   3 ἄρπ- Pᵃ   4 σκεπτομένη ζωῆς Pᵇ   5 ἐμίηνεν Cᵃᵇ: μίηνεν Pᵃ (ut videtur): ἐμίκηνεν Pᵇ   γούνων PᵇPlᵖᶜ   6 κοιμανθεὶς τὸν μακρὸν Pᵃ

LXXV.   3 στείχετε ed. pr.: στειχεμου P.Mil.

LXXVI.   4 μοῦ[νον βλέψαϲ τὸ]ν ed. pr.: alii alia

LXXVII. POSIDIPPUS 33 AB

μεῖζον Ἀριστόξεινος ἐνύπνιον ἢ καθ' ἑωυτὸν
Ὡρκὰς ἰδὼν μεγάλων νήπιος ὠρέγετο·
ὤιετ' Ἀθήνης γαμβρὸς Ὀλυμπίου ἐν Διὸς οἴκωι
380   εὕδειν χρυσείωι πάννυχος ἐν θαλάμωι·
ἦρι δ' ἀνεγρόμενος δήιων προσέμισγε φάλαγγι,   5
ὡς τὸν Ἀθηναίης ἐν φρενὶ θυμὸν ἔχων·
τὸν δὲ θεοῖς ἐρίσαντα μέλας κατεκοίμισεν Ἄρης,
ὤιχετο δὲ ψευδὴς νυμφίος εἰς Ἀΐδεω.

LXXVIII. POSIDIPPUS 116 AB
(12 GP = P.LOUVRE 7172 [P.FIRMIN-DIDOT])

385   μέσσον ἐγὼ Φαρίης ἀκτῆς στόματός τε Κανώπου
ἐν περιφαινομένωι κύματι χῶρον ἔχω,
τήνδε πολυρρήνου Λιβύης ἀνεμώδεα χηλὴν
τὴν ἀνατεινομένην εἰς Ἰταλὸν ζέφυρον,
ἔνθα με Καλλικράτης ἱδρύσατο καὶ βασιλίσσης   5
390   ἱερὸν Ἀρσινόης Κύπριδος ὠνόμασεν.
ἀλλ' ἐπὶ τὴν Ζεφυρῖτιν ἀκουσομένην Ἀφροδίτην,
Ἑλλήνων ἁγναί, βαίνετε, θυγατέρες
οἵ θ' ἁλὸς ἐργάται ἄνδρες· ὁ γὰρ ναύαρχος ἔτευξεν
τοῦθ' ἱερὸν παντὸς κύματος εὐλίμενον.

LXXIX. POSIDIPPUS 36 AB

395   Ἀρσινόη, σοὶ τοῦτο διὰ στολίδων ἀνεμοῦσθαι
βύσσινον ἄγκειται βρέγμ' ἀπὸ Ναυκράτιος,
ὧι σύ, φίλη, κατ' ὄνειρον ὁμόρξασθαι γλυκὺν ἱδρῶ
ἤθελες, ὀτρηρῶν παυσαμένη καμάτων·
ὡς ἐφάνη⟨ς⟩, Φιλάδελφε, καὶ ἐν χερὶ δούρατος αἰχμήν,   5
400   πότνα, καὶ ἐν πήχει κοῖλον ἔχουσα σάκος·
ἡ δὲ σοὶ αἰτηθεῖσα τὸ λευ⟨χ⟩έανον κανόνισμα
παρθένος Ἡγησὼ θῆκε γένος Μακέ[τη.

LXXVII. 1 ἑωυτὸν ed. pr.: εωτον *P.Mil.*   2 Ὡρκὰς ed. pr.: οαρκας *P.Mil.*   3 Ἀθήνης
ed. pr.: αθηναιης   6 ἐν φρενὶ ed. pr.: εμφρενι *P.Mil.*

LXXVIII. multos errores orthographicos ab editoribus pr. correctos non
notaui   3 τήνδε Reitzenstein: τῆσδε *P.Louvre*

LXXX. POSIDIPPUS 87 AB

π[ῶλοι] ἔθ᾽ ἁμὲς ἐοῦσαι Ὀλυμ[πια]κὸν Βερενίκας,
Π[ι]σᾶ[τ]αι, Μακέτας ἀγάγομ[ε]ς στέφανον,
405 ὃς τὸ [πο]λυθρύλητον ἔχει κλέος, ὧι τὸ Κυνίσκας
ἐν Σπάρται χρόνιον κῦδος ἀφειλόμεθα.

LXXXI. POSIDIPPUS 88 AB

πρῶτο[ι] τρεῖς βασιλῆες Ὀλύμπια καὶ μόνοι ἁμὲς
ἅρμασι νικῶμες καὶ γονέες καὶ ἐγώ·
εἷς μὲν ἐγὼ [Π]τολεμαίου ὁμώνυμος, ἐκ Βερενίκας
410 υἱ[ός], Ἐορδαία γέννα, δύω δὲ γονεῖς·
πρὸς μέγα πατρὸς ἐμὸν τίθεμαι κλέος, ἀλλ᾽ ὅτι μάτηρ   5
εἷλε γυνὰ νίκαν ἅρματι, τοῦτο μέγα.

LXXXII. POSIDIPPUS 63 AB

τόνδε Φιλίται χ[αλ]κὸν [ἴ]σον κατὰ πάνθ᾽ Ἐκ[α]ταῖος
ἀ]κριβὴς ἄκρους [ἔπλ]ασεν εἰς ὄνυχας,
415 καὶ με]γέθει κα[ὶ σα]ρκὶ τὸν ἀνθρωπιστὶ διώξας
γνώμο]ν᾽, ἀφ᾽ ἡρώων δ᾽ οὐδὲν ἔμειξ᾽ ἰδέης,
ἀλλὰ τὸν ἀκρομέριμνον ὅλ[ηι κ]ατεμάξατο τέχνηι   5
πρ]έσβυν, ἀληθείης ὀρθὸν [ἔχων] κανόνα·
αὐδήσ]οντι δ᾽ ἔοικεν ὅσωι ποικίλλεται ἤθει,
420 ἔμψυχ]ος, καίπερ χάλκεος ἐὼν ὁ γέρων·
ἐκ Πτολε]μαίου δ᾽ ὧδε θεοῦ θ᾽ ἅμα καὶ βασιλῆος
ἄγκειτ]αι Μουσέων εἵνεκα Κῶιος ἀνήρ.   10

LXXX. 1 π[ῶλοι] Haslam, de Stefani: ἵπ[ποι] ed. pr.   3 πο]υθρύλητον Janko, Sens: -ατον *P.Mil.* (α ex η corr.)

LXXXI. 3 ἐκ Βερενίκας ed. pr.: εγβερενικας *P.Mil.*   5 πρὸς ed. pr.: πρου *P.Mil.*   ἐμὸν ed. pr.: εμου *P.Mil.*: κού Gronewald   6 αρματοτουτο *P.Mil.*

LXXXII. 1 πανταε.[.] ταιος *P.Mil.*   3 καὶ με]γέθει ed. pr.: ἐν με]γέθει Ferrari   4 γνώμο]ν᾽ ed. pr.: alii alia   εμειξειδεησ *P.Mil.*   5 ὅλ[ηι ed. pr.: ὅλ[ως vel ὅλ[ον Lapini   6 [ἔχων] ed. pr.: [ἄγων] De Stefani   7 αὐδής]οντι ed. pr.: cυννοέ]οντι Gärtner: ζητής]οντι Livrea: alii alia   ποικίλλεται ed. pr.: ἰνδάλλεται Livrea   8 ἔμψυχ]οc ed. pr..: alii alia   9 ἐκ Πτολε]μαίου Gascou, ed. pr.: ἐν Πτ- Bernardini–Bravi   βασιλειοc *P.Mil.*, corr. ed. pr.   10 ἄγκειτ]αι ed. pr.: ἄγκειμ]αι Scodel

LXXXIII. POSIDIPPUS 65 AB (*APL* 119 = 18 GP)
Λύσιππε, πλάστα Σικυώνιε, θαρσαλέα χείρ,
δάϊε τεχνίτα, πῦρ τοι ὁ χαλκὸς ὁρῆι
425 ὃν κατ' Ἀλεξάνδρου μορφᾶς ἔθευ· οὔ τί γε μεμπτοὶ
Πέρσαι· συγγνώμα βουσὶ λέοντα φυγεῖν.

LXXXIV. POSIDIPPUS 15 AB (20 GP)
οὐ ποταμὸς κελάδων ἐπὶ χείλεσιν ἀλλὰ δράκοντος
εἶχέ ποτ' εὐπώγων τόνδε λίθον κεφαλὴ
πυκνὰ φαληριόωντα· τὸ δὲ γλυφὲν ἄρμα κατ' αὐτοῦ
430 τοῦθ' ὑπὸ Λυγκείου βλέμματος ἐγλύφετο
ψεύδεϊ χειρὸς ὅμοιον· ἀποπλασθὲν γὰρ ὁρᾶται   5
ἄρμα, κατὰ πλάτεος δ' οὐκ ἂν ἴδοις προβόλους·
ἧι καὶ θαῦμα πέλει μόχθου μέγα πῶς ὁ λιθουργὸς
τὰς ἀτενιζούσας οὐκ ἐμόγησε κόρας.

LXXXV. POSIDIPPUS 139 AB (*AP* 12.131 = 8 GP)
435 ἃ Κύπρον ἅ τε Κύθηρα καὶ ἃ Μίλητον ἐποιχνεῖς
καὶ καλὸν Συρίης ἱπποκρότου δάπεδον,
ἔλθοις ἵλαος Καλλιστίωι ἢ τὸν ἐραστὴν
οὐδέποτ' οἰκείων ὦσεν ἀπὸ προθύρων.

LXXXVI. POSIDIPPUS 135 AB (*AP* 12.45 = 5 GP)
ναὶ ναὶ βάλλετ', Ἔρωτες· ἐγὼ σκοπὸς εἷς ἅμα πολλοῖς
440 κεῖμαι. μὴ φείσησθ' ἄφρονες· ἢν γὰρ ἐμὲ
νικήσητ', ὀνομαστοὶ ἐν ἀθανάτοισιν ἔσεσθε
τοξόται ὡς μεγάλης δεσπόται ἰοδόκης.

LXXXVII. POSIDIPPUS 138 AB
(*AP* 12.120 = 7 GP)
εὐοπλῶ καὶ πρός σὲ μαχήσομαι, οὐδ' ἀπεροῦμαι
θνητὸς ἐών· σὺ δ', Ἔρως, μηκέτι μοι πρόσαγε.

LXXXIII. 1]αλεα *P.Mil.*: θαρσαλέη Pl: δαιδαλέη Himerius   3 εθευουτιγε *P.Mil.*: χέες·
οὐκέτι Pl   4]μα *P.Mil.*: συγγνώμη Pl

LXXXIV. 3 πυκνα *P.Mil.*: λευκὰ Tzetzes   4 βλέμματος Tzetzes: γλυμματος *P.Mil.*   5
χειρὸς Tzetzes: χρειος *P.Mil.*   6 αρμα *P.Mil.*: γλύμμα Tzetzes   προβολους *P.Mil.*:
προβόλου Tzetzes   7 ηι *P.Mil.*: εἰ Tzetzes

LXXXVI. 1 πολλοῖς apogr.: βαλλοις P

445   ἤν με λάβῃς μεθύοντ', ἄπαγ' ἔκδοτον, ἄχρι δὲ νήφω
      τὸν παραταξάμενον πρὸς σὲ λογισμὸν ἔχω.

LXXXVIII. THEOCRITUS 19 GOW
(AP 13.3 = 13 GP)

ὁ μουσοποιὸς ἐνθάδ' Ἱππῶναξ κεῖται.
εἰ μὲν πονηρός, μὴ προσέρχευ τῷ τύμβωι·
εἰ δ' ἐσσὶ κρήγυός τε καὶ παρὰ χρηστῶν,
450   θαρσέων καθίζευ, κἢν θέλῃς, ἀπόβριξον.

LXXXIX. THEOCRITUS 15 GOW
(AP 7.658 = 7 GP)

γνώσομαι εἴ τι νέμεις ἀγαθοῖς πλέον ἢ καὶ ὁ δειλὸς
ἐκ σέθεν ὡσαύτως ἶσον, ὁδοιπόρ', ἔχει.
"χαιρέτω οὗτος ὁ τύμβος," ἐρεῖς, "ἐπεὶ Εὐρυμέδοντος
κεῖται τῆς ἱερῆς κοῦφος ὑπὲρ κεφαλῆς."

XC. THEOCRITUS 20 GOW (AP 7.663 = 11 GP)

455   ὁ μικκὸς τόδ' ἔτευξε τᾷ Θραΐσσαι
      Μήδειος τὸ μνᾶμ' ἐπὶ τᾷ ὁδῷι κἠπέγραψε Κλείτας.
      ἕξει τὰν χάριν ἁ γυνὰ ἀντὶ τήνων
      ὦν τὸν κῶρον ἔθρεψε· τί μάν; ἔτι χρησίμα καλεῖται.

XCI. [THEOCRITUS] 25 GOW (AUTOMEDON AP 7.534 = AUTOMEDON 12 GP = ALEXANDER AETOLUS FR. DUB. 25 MAGNELLI)

      ἄνθρωπε, ζωῆς περιφείδεο μηδὲ παρ' ὥρην
460   ναυτίλος ἴσθι· καὶ ὡς οὐ πολὺς ἀνδρὶ βίος.
      δείλαιε Κλεόνικε, σὺ δ' εἰς λιπαρὴν Θάσον ἐλθεῖν
      ἠπείγευ Κοίλης ἔμπορος ἐκ Συρίης,ν
      ἔμπορος, ὦ Κλεόνικε· δύσιν δ' ὑπὸ Πλειάδος αὐτὴν   5
      ποντοπορῶν αὐτῇ Πλειάδι συγκατέδυς.

LXXXVIII.   2 μὴ προσέρχευ Ahrens (-χου corp. buc.): μήποτ' ἔρχευ PPl

LXXXIX.   1 νέμοις PKD¹   2 ἔχεις corp. buc.

XC.   2 Μνήδειος . . . κἠνέγραψε corp. buc.   3 τὴν χάριν ἡ γυνὴ corp. buc.   ἀντεκείνων P   4 κοῦρον corp. buc.   μην; ἔτι χρησίμη corp. buc.   τελευτᾷ P

XCI.   3–6 om. Pl   5 Πληάδων P, corr. Graevius   6 ποντοπόρωι ναύτηι P, corr. Pierson

XCII. THEOCRITUS 6 GOW (*AP* 9.432 = 22 GP)

465 ἇ δείλαιε τὺ Θύρσι, τί τὸ πλέον εἰ κατατάξεις
δάκρυσι διγλήνους ὦπας ὀδυρόμενος;
οἴχεται ἁ χίμαρος, τὸ καλὸν τέκος, οἴχετ᾽ ἐς Ἅιδαν·
τραχὺς γὰρ χαλαῖς ἀμφεπίαξε λύκος.
αἱ δὲ κύνες κλαγγεῦντι· τί τὸ πλέον, ἀνίκα τήνας   5
470 ὀστίον οὐδὲ τέφρα λείπεται οἰχομένας;

XCIII. THEOCRITUS 1 GOW (*AP* 6.336 = 5 GP)

τὰ ῥόδα τὰ δροσόεντα καὶ ἁ κατάπυκνος ἐκείνα
ἕρπυλλος κεῖται ταῖς Ἑλικωνιάσιν·
ταὶ δὲ μελάμφυλλοι δάφναι τίν, Πύθιε Παιάν,
Δελφὶς ἐπεὶ πέτρα τοῦτό τοι ἀγλάισε·
475 βωμὸν δ᾽ αἱμάξει κεραὸς τράγος οὗτος ὁ μαλὸς   5
τερμίνθου τρώγων ἔσχατον ἀκρεμόνα.

XCIV. THEOCRITUS 8 (*AP* 6.337 = 1 GP)

ἦλθε καὶ ἐς Μίλητον ὁ τοῦ Παιήονος υἱός,
ἰητῆρι νόσων ἀνδρὶ συνοισόμενος
Νικίαι, ὅς μιν ἐπ᾽ ἦμαρ ἀεὶ θυέεσσιν ἱκνεῖται
480 καὶ τόδ᾽ ἀπ᾽ εὐώδους γλύψατ᾽ ἄγαλμα κέδρου,
Ἠετίωνι χάριν γλαφυρᾶς χερὸς ἄκρον ὑποστὸς   5
μισθόν· ὁ δ᾽ εἰς ἔργον πᾶσαν ἀφῆκε τέχνην.

XCV. THEOCRITUS 22 GOW (*AP* 9.598 = 16 GP)

τὸν τοῦ Ζανὸς ὅδ᾽ ὑμὶν υἱὸν ὠνὴρ
τὸν λεοντομάχαν, τὸν ὀξύχειρα,
485 πρᾶτος τῶν ἐπάνωθε μουσοποιῶν
Πείσανδρος συνέγραψεν οὐκ Καμίρου,
χὤσσους ἐξεπόνασεν εἶπ᾽ ἀέθλους.   5

XCII. 1 ὦ δειλὲ D (δειλὲ post spatium K)   τί τοι P   2 διγλήνως P   4 χαλᾶς corp.
buc.   ἀμφὶ πίαξε P   5 καλεῦντι P   6 λείπετ᾽ ἀποιχ- P

XCIII. 1 ἡ corp. buc.   4 ἐπεὶ Iunt. Cal.: ἐπὶ cet.   5 ὁ μάνος KD   6 τερμίνθου C
corp. buc.: περ- P

XCIV. 1 Μίλατον P   τῶι P   2 νόσων C corp. buc.: νοῦσον P   3 ὅς corp. buc.: ὅσα
P   ἆμαρ P   6 τέχναν P

XCV. 1 τῶι Ζηνὸς P   ἡμῖν … ἀνήρ corp. buc.   3 τᾶν ἔτ᾽ ἄνωθεν P   4 οὐκ Ahrens:
ὤ(κ) corp. buc.   5 χὤσσους Ahrens: χὤσους corp. buc.: χὄσσ- P

τοῦτον δ' αὐτὸν ὁ δᾶμος, ὡς σάφ' εἰδῆις,
ἔστασ' ἐνθάδε χάλκεον ποήσας
490   πολλοῖς μησὶν ὄπισθε κἠνιαυτοῖς.

XCVI. THEOCRITUS 17 GOW (AP 9.599 = 15 GP)

θᾶσαι τὸν ἀνδριάντα τοῦτον, ὦ ξένε,
σπουδᾶι, καὶ λέγ' ἐπὴν ἐς οἶκον ἔνθηις·
'Ἀνακρέοντος εἰκόν' εἶδον ἐν Τέωι
τῶν πρόσθ' εἴ τι περισσὸν ὡιδοποιῶν."
495   προσθεὶς δὲ χὤτι τοῖς νέοισιν ἅδετο   5
ἐρεῖς ἀτρεκέως ὅλον τὸν ἄνδρα.

XCVII. DIOSCORIDES AP 7.708 (24 GP)

τῶι κωμωιδογράφωι, κούφη κόνι, τὸν φιλάγωνα
κισσὸν ὑπὲρ τύμβου ζῶντα Μάχωνι φέροις·
οὐ γὰρ ἔχεις κύφωνα παλίμπλυτον, ἀλλά τι τέχνης
500   ἄξιον ἀρχαίης λείψανον ἠμφίεσας.
τοῦτο δ' ὁ πρέσβυς ἐρεῖ· "Κέκροπος πόλι, καὶ παρὰ Νείλωι   5
ἔστιν ὅτ' ἐν Μούσαις δριμὺ πέφυκε θύμον."

XCVIII. DIOSCORIDES AP 7.76 (33 GP)

ἐμπορίης λήξαντα Φιλόκριτον, ἄρτι δ' ἀρότρου
γευόμενον ξείνωι Μέμφις ἔκρυψε τάφωι·
505   ἔνθα δραμὼν Νείλοιο πολὺς ῥόος ὕδατι λάβρωι
τἀνδρὸς τὴν ὀλίγην βῶλον ἀπημφίασε.
καὶ ζωὸς μὲν ἔφευγε πικρὴν ἅλα, νῦν δὲ καλυφθεὶς   5
κύμασι ναυηγὸν σχέτλιος ἔσχε τάφον.

XCIX. DIOSCORIDES AP 7.229 (30 GP)

τὰν Πιτάναν Θρασύβουλος ἐπ' ἀσπίδος ἤλυθεν ἄπνους,
510   ἑπτὰ πρὸς Ἀργείων τραύματα δεξάμενος,

7 ἔστασεν P   ποιήσας corp. buc.   8 μασὶν vel μισὶν corp. buc.

XCVI. 2 σπουδαῖε corp. buc.   ἐπὴν D²: ἐπὰν cett.   4 προσθέντι . . . ὡδοποιοῦ
P   περισσῶν KD¹   5 ἤδετο P

XCVII. 3 ἔχεις κύφωνα Gow: ἔχεις κηφῆνα Ath.: ἔχει σφῆναγε P

XCVIII. 2 ξείνωι PPlᴬ: ξείνη Plᴮ   3 Νείλοιο PPlᴮ: Νείλου ὁ Plᴬ   λάβρωι PPlᴮ: λάυρωι
Plᴬ   4 ὀλίγαν Plᴬ

XCIX. post 7.721 iteravit P (=Pᵇ)   1 τὰν Πιτάναν Plut.: τᾶι Πιτάναι PPl
3 πρόσθια πάντα PPl: ἀντία πάντα C Plut.: ἀντί' ἅπαντα Pᵇ   4 πυρκαϊῆς Pl: πυρκαϊὴν P

δεικνὺς πρόσθια πάντα· τὸν αἱματόεντα δ' ὁ πρέσβυς
παῖδ' ἐπὶ πυρκαϊῆς Τύννιχος εἶπε τιθείς·
"δειλοὶ κλαιέσθωσαν· ἐγὼ δὲ σέ, τέκνον, ἄδακρυς 5
θάψω, τὸν καὶ ἐμὸν καὶ Λακεδαιμόνιον."

C. DIOSCORIDES AP 6.220 (16 GP)

515 Σάρδις Πεσσινόεντος ἀπὸ Φρυγὸς ἦθελ' ἱκέσθαι,
ἔκφρων μαινομένην δοὺς ἀνέμοισι τρίχα,
ἁγνὸς Ἄτυς, Κυβέλης θαλαμηπόλος· ἄγρια δ' αὐτοῦ
ἐψύχθη χαλεπῆς πνεύματα θευφορίης
ἑσπέριον στείχοντος ἀνὰ κνέφας· εἰς δὲ κάταντες 5
520 ἄντρον ἔδυ νεύσας βαιὸν ἄπωθεν ὁδοῦ.
τοῦ δὲ λέων ὤρουσε κατὰ στίβον, ἀνδράσι δεῖμα
θαρσαλέοις, γάλλωι δ' οὐδ' ὀνομαστὸν ἄχος,
ὃς τότ' ἄναυδος ἔμεινε δέους ὕπο καί τινος αὔρηι
δαίμονος ἐς τὸν ἑὸν τύμπανον ἧκε χέρας· 10
525 οὗ βαρὺ μυκήσαντος ὁ θαρσαλεώτερος ἄλλων
τετραπόδων ἐλάφων ἔδραμεν ὀξύτερον,
τὸν βαρὺν οὐ μείνας ἀκοαῖς ψόφον· ἐκ δ' ἐβόησεν·
"μῆτερ, Σαγγαρίου χείλεσι πὰρ ποταμοῦ,
ἱρὴν σοὶ θαλάμην, ζωάγρια καὶ λαλάγημα 15
530 τοῦτο τὸ θηρὶ φυγῆς αἴτιον ἀντίθεμαι."

CI. DIOSCORIDES AP 7.430 (31 GP)

τίς τὰ νεοσκύλευτα ποτὶ δρυῒ τᾶιδε καθᾶψεν
ἔντεα; τῶ πέλτα Δωρὶς ἀναγράφεται;
πλάθει γὰρ Θυρεᾶτις ὑφ' αἵματος ἅδε λοχιτᾶν,
χἇμὲς ἀπ' Ἀργείων τοὶ δύο λειπόμεθα.
535 – πάντα νέκυν μάστευε δεδουπότα, μή τις ἔτ' ἔμπνους 5
λειπόμενος Σπάρται κῦδος ἔλαμψε νόθον.
– ἴσχε βάσιν. νίκα γὰρ ἐπ' ἀσπίδος ὧδε Λακώνων
φωνεῖται θρόμβοις αἵματος Ὀθρυάδα,
χὠ τόδε μοχθήσας σπαίρει πέλας. ἇ πρόπατορ Ζεῦ,
540 στύξον ἀνικάτω σύμβολα φυλόπιδος." 10

C. 1 Πεσσινόεντος apogr.: Πισσ- P   3 Ἄτυς Cᵐᵃʳᵍ·: Ἄτις P   5 στείχοντος C: στείχοντας
P   13 ἀκοαῖς Jacobs, Gow: ἀκοῆς P: ἀκοῆι Salmasius: alii alia

CII. DIOSCORIDES *AP* 7.411 (21 GP)

Θέσπιδος εὕρεμα τοῦτο· τὰ δ᾽ ἀγροιῶτιν ἀν᾽ ὕλαν
παίγνια καὶ κώμους τούσδε τελειοτέρους
Αἰσχύλος ἐξύψωσεν, ὁ μὴ σμιλευτὰ χαράξας
γράμματα, χειμάρρωι δ᾽ οἷα καταρδόμενα,
545   καὶ τὰ κατὰ σκηνὴν μετεκαίνισεν. ὦ στόμα πάντων   5
δεξιόν, ἀρχαίων ἦσθά τις ἡμιθέων.

CIII. DIOSCORIDES *AP* 5.55 (5 GP)

Δωρίδα τὴν ῥοδόπυγον ὑπὲρ λεχέων διατείνας
ἄνθεσιν ἐν χλοεροῖς ἀθάνατος γέγονα.
ἡ γὰρ ὑπερφυέεσσι μέσον διαβᾶσά με ποσσὶν
550   ἤνυσεν ἀκλινέως τὸν Κύπριδος δόλιχον,
ὄμμασι νωθρὰ βλέπουσα· τὰ δ᾽, ἠΰτε πνεύματι φύλλα,   5
ἀμφισαλευομένης ἔτρεμε πορφύρεα,
μέχρις ἀπεσπείσθη λευκὸν μένος ἀμφοτέροισιν,
καὶ Δωρὶς παρέτοις ἐξεχύθη μέλεσι.

CIV. DIOSCORIDES *AP* 5.138 (2 GP)

555   Ἵππον Ἀθήνιον ᾖσεν ἐμοὶ κακόν· ἐν πυρὶ πᾶσα
Ἴλιος ἦν, κἀγὼ κείνηι ἅμ᾽ ἐφλεγόμαν,
οὐ δείσας Δαναῶν δεκέτη πόνον· ἐν δ᾽ ἑνὶ φέγγει
τῶι τότε καὶ Τρῶες κἀγὼ ἀπωλόμεθα.

CV. DIOSCORIDES *AP* 5.54 (7 GP)

μήποτε γαστροβαρῆ πρὸς σὸν λέχος ἀντιπρόσωπον
560   παιδογόνωι κλίνηις Κύπριδι τερπόμενος.
μεσσόθι γὰρ μέγα κῦμα καὶ οὐκ ὀλίγος πόνος ἔσται
τῆς μὲν ἐρεσσομένης, σοῦ δὲ σαλευομένου.
ἀλλὰ πάλιν στρέψας ῥοδοειδέι τέρπεο πυγῆι,   5
τὴν ἄλοχον νομίσας ἀρσενόπαιδα Κύπριν.

CII.   2 τοὺς δὲ τελειοτέρους P (corr. Meineke): τοὺς ἀτελειοτέρους Salmasius: τούσδε
γελοιοτέρους Heinsius   3 ὁ μὴ σμιλευτὰ Salmasius: ομὴ σμιαευτα P

CIII.   4 ἤνυσεν P: ἤνυεν C   7 ἀπεσπείσθη apogr.: ἀπεσπείθη P

CIV.   3 οὐδείσας: varia proposuerunt edd.

CV.   5 πάλιν apogr.: πρὶν P

CVI. EUPHORION *AP* 7.651 (2 GP)

565 οὐχ ὁ τρηχὺς ἔλαιος ἐπ' ὀστέα κεῖνα καλύπτει
οὐδ' ἡ κυάνεον γράμμα λαχοῦσα πέτρη·
ἀλλὰ τὰ μὲν Δολίχης τε καὶ αἰπεινῆς Δρακάνοιο
Ἰκάριον ῥήσσει κῦμα περὶ κροκάλαις·
ἀντὶ δ' ἐγὼ ξενίης Πολυμήδεος ἡ κεινὴ χθὼν   5
570 ὠγκώθην Δρυόπων διψάσιν ἐν βοτάναις.

CVII. MNASALCES *AP* 7.171 (8 GP)

ἀμπαύσει καὶ τᾶιδε θοὸν πτερὸν ἱερὸς ὄρνις
τᾶσδ' ὑπὲρ ἀδείας ἑζόμενος πλατάνου.
ὤλετο γὰρ Ποίμανδρος ὁ Μάλιος οὐδ' ἔτι νεῖται
ἰξὸν ἐπ' ἀγρευταῖς χευάμενος καλάμοις.

CVIII. MNASALCES *AP* 7.242 (7 GP)

575 οἵδε πάτραν πολύδακρυν ἐπ' αὐχένι δεσμὸν ἔχουσαν
ῥυόμενοι δνοφερὰν ἀμφεβάλοντο κόνιν,
ἄρνυνται δ' ἀρετᾶς αἶνον μέγαν. ἀλλά τις ἀστῶν
τούσδ' ἐσιδὼν θνάισκειν τλάτω ὑπὲρ πατρίδος.

CIX. MNASALCES *AP* 9.324 (16 GP)

ἁ σῦριγξ, τί τοι ὧδε παρ' Ἀφρογένειαν ὄρουσας;
580 τίπτ' ἀπὸ ποιμενίου χείλεος ὧδε πάρει;
οὔ τοι πρῶνες ἔθ' ὧδ' οὔτ' ἄγκεα, πάντα δ' Ἔρωτες
καὶ Πόθος· ἁ δ' ἀγρία Μοῦσ' ἐν ὄρει μενέτω.

CX. RHIANUS *AP* 6.173 (7 GP)

Ἀχρυλίς, ἡ Φρυγίη θαλαμηπόλος, ἡ περὶ πεύκας
πολλάκι τοὺς ἱεροὺς χευαμένη πλοκάμους,
585 γαλλαίωι Κυβέλης ὀλολύγματι πολλάκι δοῦσα
τὸν βαρὺν εἰς ἀκοὰς ἦχον ἀπὸ στομάτων,
τάσδε θεῆι χαίτας περὶ δικλίδι θῆκεν ὀρείηι,   5
θερμὸν ἐπεὶ λύσσης ὧδ' ἀνέπαυσε πόδα.

CVI. 1 ἔλαιος Meineke: σελι θαῖος P   2 λαχοῦσα Hecker: λαβοῦσα P
CVII. 1 τᾶιδε Jacobs: τῆιδε PPl   4 ἀγρευτῆι . . . καλάμωι Pl
CVIII. 3 ἀστῶν CPl: αὐτῶν P
CIX. 2 πάρει Pl: πάρη P   3 οὐδ' Pl   4 μενέτω Brunck: μένεται P: νέμεται Pl
CX. 1 Ἀχρυλίς P *Suda*: Ἀρχ- apogr.   5 περικλεῖδι *Suda*   ὀρείηι Powell: -αι P *Suda*

CXI. RHIANUS *AP* 12.93 (3 GP)

οἱ παῖδες λαβύρινθος ἀνέξοδος· ἦι γὰρ ἂν ὄμμα
590 ῥίψηις, ὡς ἰξῶι τοῦτο προσαμπέχεται.
τῆι μὲν γὰρ Θεόδωρος ἄγει ποτὶ πίονα σαρκὸς
ἀκμήν, καὶ γυίων ἄνθος ἀκηράσιον·
τῆι δὲ Φιλοκλῆος χρύσεον ῥέθος, ὅς τε καθ᾽ ὕψος 5
οὐ μέγας, οὐρανίη δ᾽ ἀμφιτέθηλε χάρις.
595 ἢν δ᾽ ἐπὶ Λεπτίνεω στρέψηις δέμας, οὐκέτι γυῖα
κινήσεις, ἀλύτωι δ᾽ ὡς ἀδάμαντι μενεῖς,
ἴχνια κολληθείς· τοῖον σέλας ὄμμασιν αἴθει
κοῦρος, κὰς νεάτους ἐκ κορυφῆς ὄνυχας. 10
χαίρετε καλοὶ παῖδες, ἐς ἀκμαίην δὲ μόλοιτε
600 ἥβην, καὶ λευκὴν ἀμφιέσαισθε κόμην.

CXII. RHIANUS *AP* 12.121 (4 GP)

ἦ ῥά νύ τοι, Κλεόνικε, δι᾽ ἀτραπιτοῖο κιόντι
στεινῆς ἤντησαν ταὶ λιπαραὶ Χάριτες·
καί σε ποτὶ ῥοδόεσσιν ἐπηχύναντο χέρεσσιν,
κοῦρε· πεποίησαι δ᾽ ἡλίκος ἐσσὶ Χάρις·
605 τηλόθι μοι μάλα χαῖρε· πυρὸς δ᾽ οὐκ ἀσφαλὲς ἆσσον 5
ἕρπειν αὐηρήν, ἆ φίλος, ἀνθερίκην.

CXIII. RHIANUS *AP* 12.142 (10 GP)

ἰξῶι Δεξιόνικος ὑπὸ χλωρῆι πλατανίστωι
κόσσυφον ἀγρεύσας εἷλε κατὰ πτερύγων·
χὠ μὲν ἀναστενάχων ἀπεκώκυεν ἱερὸς ὄρνις.
610 ἀλλ᾽ ἐγώ, ὦ φίλ᾽ Ἔρως, καὶ θαλεραὶ Χάριτες,
εἴην καὶ κίχλη καὶ κόσσυφος, ὡς ἂν ἐκείνου 5
ἐν χερὶ καὶ φθογγὴν καὶ γλυκὺ δάκρυ βάλω.

CXI. 2 ῥίψηις ὡς Reiske: ῥιψως P 5 χρύσεον Brunck: -ειον P τε Brunck: τὸ P
6 οὐρανίη Brunck: -ίης P 7 Λεπτίνεω Brunck: -ήνεω P 10 κὰς Brunck: καὶ P
11 ἐς Brunck: εἰς P μόλοιτε Elmsley: μολεῖτε P 12 ἀμφιέσαισθε Elmsley: -σεσθε P

CXII. 6 ἀνθερίκην Gow: -αν Brunck: ἀθερίκαν P

CXIII. 4 ὦ Brunck: ὁ P

CXIV. RHIANUS *AP* 12.38 (1 GP)

᾿Ωραί σοι Χάριτές τε κατὰ γλυκὺ χεῦαν ἔλαιον,
  ὦ πυγά· κνώσσειν δ' οὐδὲ γέροντας ἐᾷς.
615 λέξον μοι, τίνος ἐσσὶ μάκαιρα τύ, καὶ τίνα παίδων
  κοσμεῖς; ἁ πυγὰ δ' εἶπε· "Μενεκράτεος."

CXV. THEODORIDAS *AP* 6.155 (1 GP)

ἅλικες αἵ τε κόμαι καὶ ὁ Κρωβύλος, ἃς ἀπὸ Φοίβωι
  πέξατο μολπαστᾶι κῶρος ὁ τετραετής·
αἰχμητὰν δ' ἐπέθυσεν ἀλέκτορα καὶ πλακόεντα
620 παῖς Ἡγησιδίκου πίονα τυροφόρον.
῎Ωπολλον, θείης τὸν Κρωβύλον εἰς τέλος ἄνδρα   5
  οἴκου καὶ κτεάνων χεῖρας ὕπερθεν ἔχειν.

CXVI. THEODORIDAS *AP* 6.222 (4 GP)

μυριόπουν σκολόπενδραν ὑπ' ᾿Ωρίωνι κυκηθεὶς
  πόντος Ἰαπύγων ἔβρασ' ἐπὶ σκοπέλους,
625 καὶ τοδ' ἀπὸ βλοσυροῦ σελάχευς μέγα πλευρὸν ἀνῆψαν
  δαίμοσι βουφόρτων κοίρανοι εἰκοσόρων.

CXVII. THEODORIDAS *AP* 7.406 (14 GP)

Εὐφορίων, ὁ περισσὸν ἐπιστάμενός τι ποῆσαι,
  Πειραϊκοῖς κεῖται τοῖσδε παρὰ σκέλεσιν.
ἀλλὰ σὺ τῶι μύστηι ῥοιὴν ἢ μῆλον ἄπαρξαι
630 ἢ μύρτον· καὶ γὰρ ζωὸς ἐὼν ἐφίλει.

CXVIII. ALCAEUS *AP* 9.518 (1 GP)

μακύνου τείχη, Ζεῦ ᾿Ολύμπιε· πάντα Φιλίππωι
  ἀμβατά· χαλκείας κλεῖε πύλας μακάρων.
χθὼν μὲν δὴ καὶ πόντος ὑπὸ σκήπτροισι Φιλίππου
  δέδμηται, λοιπὰ δ' ἁ πρὸς ῎Ολυμπον ὁδός.

CXV. 2 παίξατο P: πλέξ- P^marg. *Suda* (v.l.)   μολπαστᾶι CPl *Suda* (v.l.): μολπαστὰ P
Suda (v.l.) κῶρος Scaliger: κῶμος PPl *Suda*

CXVI. 3 σελάχευς apogr.: σελάγευς P   πλευρὸν C *Suda*: -ραν P

CXVII. 3 σὺ Reiske: σοὶ P

CXVIII. 1 πάντα Φιλίππωι P: ῥέξε Φίλιππος Pl

CXIX. ALCAEUS *AP* 7.247 (4 GP)

635 ἄκλαυστοι καὶ ἄθαπτοι, ὁδοιπόρε, τῶιδ᾽ ἐπὶ νώτωι
    Θεσσαλίας τρισσαὶ κείμεθα μυριάδες,
    Αἰτωλῶν δμηθέντες ὑπ᾽ Ἄρεος ἠδὲ Λατίνων,
    οὓς Τίτος εὐρείης ἤγαγ᾽ ἀπ᾽ Ἰταλίης,
    Ἠμαθίηι μέγα πῆμα. τὸ δὲ θρασὺ κεῖνο Φιλίππου   5
640   πνεῦμα θοᾶν ἐλάφων ὦιχετ᾽ ἐλαφρότερον.

CXX. ALCAEUS *AP* 7.55 (12 GP)

    Λοκρίδος ἐν νέμεϊ σκιερῶι νέκυν Ἡσιόδοιο
    Νύμφαι κρηνίδων λοῦσαν ἀπὸ σφετέρων
    καὶ τάφον ὑψώσαντο· γάλακτι δὲ ποιμένες αἰγῶν
    ἔρραναν ξανθῶι μιξάμενοι μέλιτι·
645 τοίην γὰρ καὶ γῆρυν ἀπέπνεεν, ἐννέα Μουσέων   5
    ὁ πρέσβυς καθαρῶν γευσάμενος λιβάδων.

CXXI. ALCAEUS *AP* 7.1 (11 GP)

    ἡρώων τὸν ἀοιδὸν Ἴωι ἔνι παῖδες Ὅμηρον
    ἤκαχον ἐκ Μουσέων γρῖφον ὑφηνάμενοι·
    νέκταρι δ᾽ εἰνάλιαι Νηρηίδες ἐχρίσαντο
650   καὶ νέκυν ἀκταίηι θῆκαν ὑπὸ σπιλάδι,
    ὅττι Θέτιν κύδηνε καὶ υἱέα καὶ μόθον ἄλλων   5
    ἡρώων Ἰθακοῦ τ᾽ ἔργματα Λαρτιάδεω.
    ὀλβίστη νήσων πόντωι Ἴος, ὅττι κέκευθε
    βαιὴ Μουσάων ἀστέρα καὶ Χαρίτων.

CXXII. ALCAEUS *AP* 12.30 (8 GP)

655 ἡ κνήμη, Νίκανδρε, δασύνεται· ἀλλὰ φύλαξαι
    μή σε καὶ ἡ πυγὴ ταὐτὸ παθοῦσα λάθηι
    καὶ γνώσηι φιλέοντος ὅση σπάνις. ἀλλ᾽ ἔτι καὶ νῦν
    τῆς ἀμετακλήτου φρόντισον ἡλικίης.

CXIX. 1 ἄκλαυτοι Pl   ἐπὶ νώτωι Plut.: ἐπὶ τύμβωι PPl   2 Θεσσαλίας P: Ἠμαθίας
Pl   3-4 om. PPl

CXX. 2 κρηνίδων Wakefield: κρηνιάδων PPl   4 μιξάμενοι CPl: μιξάμεναι P   5
Μουσῶν Pl

CXXI. 5 ἄλλων CPl: ἄλλον P   6 Ἰθακοῦ J: Ἰακοῦ PPl   Λαρτιάδεω CPl: Λαρτίδεω P   7
νῆσος Pl

CXXII. 4 ἀμετακλήτου Buherius: -βλήτου P

CXXIII. ANTIPATER OF SIDON *AP* 7.2 (8 GP)

τὰν μερόπων Πειθώ, τὸ μέγα στόμα, τὰν ἴσα Μούσαις
660   φθεγξαμέναν κεφαλάν, ὦ ξένε, Μαιονίδεω
        ᾅδ' ἔλαχον νασῖτις Ἴου σπιλάς· οὐ γὰρ ἐν ἄλλαι
        ἱερὸν ἀλλ' ἐν ἐμοὶ πνεῦμα θανὼν ἔλιπεν,
        ὧι νεῦμα Κρονίδαο τὸ παγκρατές, ὧι καὶ Ὄλυμπον   5
        καὶ τὰν Αἴαντος ναύμαχον εἶπε βίαν
665   καὶ τὸν Ἀχιλλείοις Φαρσαλίσιν Ἕκτορα πώλοις
        ὀστέα Δαρδανικῶι δρυπτόμενον πεδίωι.
        εἰ δ' ὀλίγα κρύπτω τὸν ταλίκον, ἴσθ' ὅτι κεύθει
        καὶ Θέτιδος γαμέταν ἁ βραχύβωλος Ἴκος.   10

CXXIV. ANTIPATER OF SIDON *AP* 7.34 (18 GP)

Πιερικὰν σάλπιγγα, τὸν εὐαγέων βαρὺν ὕμνων
670   χαλκευτάν, κατέχει Πίνδαρον ἅδε κόνις,
        οὗ μέλος εἰσαΐων φθέγξαιό κεν ὡς ἀπὸ Μουσῶν
        ἐν Κάδμου θαλάμοις σμῆνος ἀπεπλάσατο.

CXXV. ANTIPATER OF SIDON *AP* 7.218 (23 GP)

τὴν καὶ ἅμα χρυσῶι καὶ ἀλουργίδι καὶ σὺν Ἔρωτι
        θρυπτομένην ἁπαλῆς Κύπριδος ἁβροτέρην,
675   Λαΐδ' ἔχω, πολιῆτιν ἁλιζώνοιο Κορίνθου,
        Πειρήνης λευκῶν φαιδροτέρην λιβάδων,
        τὴν θνητὴν Κυθέρειαν, ἐφ' ἧς μνηστῆρες ἀγαυοὶ   5
        πλείονες ἢ νύμφης εἵνεκα Τυνδαρίδος
        δρεπτόμενοι χάριτάς τε καὶ ὠνητὴν Ἀφροδίτην,
680   ἧς καὶ ὑπ' εὐώδει τύμβος ὄδωδε κρόκωι,
        ἧς ἔτι κηώεντι μύρωι τὸ διάβροχον ὀστεῦν
        καὶ λιπαραὶ θυόεν ἄσθμα πνέουσι κόμαι,   10
        ἧς ἔπι καλὸν ἄμυξε κάτα ῥέθος Ἀφρογένεια
        καὶ γοερὸν λύζων ἐστονάχησεν Ἔρως.

CXXIII.   2 φθεγξαμέναν Pl: -ην P   3 νασίτης P   8 δρυπτόμενον CPl *Suda*: -να P

CXXIV.   1 βαρὺ ὕμνων C (βαρυύμνων Pl): β. ὕπν- P

CXXV.   2 ἁβροτέρην *Suda*: -αν PPl   3–4 habet P inter disticha praecedentis epi-
grammatis (= Pᵃ) et iterum suo loco   ἐυζώνοιο *Suda*   λευκοτέρην λιβάδος Pᵃ   5 ἧς
Suda: ἧι P   ἀγαυοὶ PPl *Suda*: ἀγανοὶ *Suda* (v.l.)   8 ὑπ' CPl *Suda*: ἐπ' P   9 ἔτι PPl: αἰεὶ
Suda   11 ἧς ἔπι CPl: ἧς καὶ P

685   εἰ δ' οὐ πάγκοινον δούλην θέτο κέρδεος εὐνήν,
      Ἑλλὰς ἂν ὡς Ἑλένης τῆσδ' ὕπερ ἔσχε πόνον.

CXXVI. ANTIPATER OF SIDON AP 7.427 (32 GP)

      ἁ στάλα, φέρ' ἴδω, τίν' ἔχει νέκυν. ἀλλὰ δέδορκα
      γράμμα μὲν οὐδέν που τμαθὲν ὕπερθε λίθου,
      ἐννέα δ' ἀστραγάλους πεπτηότας· ὧν πίσυρες μὲν
690   πρᾶτοι Ἀλεξάνδρου μαρτυρέουσι βόλον,
      οἱ δὲ τὸ τᾶς νεότατος ἐφάλικος ἄνθος, ἔφηβον,   5
      εἷς δ' ὅ γε μανύει Χῖος ἀφαυρότερον.
      ἦ ῥα τόδ' ἀγγέλλοντι· "καὶ ὁ σκάπτροισι μεγαυχὴς
      χὠ θάλλων ἥβαι τέρμα τὸ μηδὲν ἔχει";
695   ἦ τὸ μὲν οὔ; δοκέω δὲ ποτὶ σκοπὸν ἰθὺν ἐλάσσειν
      ἰὸν Κρηταιεὺς ὥς τις ὀϊστοβόλος·   10
      ἧς ὁ θανὼν Χῖος μέν, Ἀλεξάνδρου δὲ λελογχὼς
      οὔνομ', ἐφηβείηι δ' ὤλετ' ἐν ἁλικίαι.
      ὡς εὖ τὸν φθίμενον νέον ἄκριτα καὶ τὸ κυβευθὲν
700   πνεῦμα δι' ἀφθέγκτων εἶπέ τις ἀστραγάλων.

CXXVII. ANTIPATER OF SIDON AP 9.720 (36 GP)

      εἰ μή μου ποτὶ τᾶιδε Μύρων πόδας ἥρμοσε πέτραι,
      ἄλλαις ἂν νεμόμαν βουσὶν ὁμοῦ δάμαλις.

CXXVIII. ANTIPATER OF SIDON AP 9.721 (37 GP)

      μόσχε, τί μοι λαγόνεσσι προσέρχεαι, ἐς δὲ τί μυκᾶι;
      ἁ τέχνα μαζοῖς οὐκ ἐνέθηκε γάλα.

CXXIX. ANTIPATER OF SIDON AP 9.722 (38 GP)

705   τὰν δάμαλιν, βουφορβέ, παρέρχεο μηδ' ἀπάνευθε
      συρίσδηις· μαστῶι πόρτιν ὑπεκδέχεται.

CXXVI.   1 ἔχει P: ἐρεῖ Herwerden   2 που C: πω P   τμαθὲν Salmasius: δμα- P   3
πεπτηότας P: -ηῶτ- C   5 νεότατος C: -ας P   8 χὠ C: θὠ P   10 ἰὸν C: ἰὼν P   ὥς τις
Reiske: ὦτος C in rasura   12 δ' Reiske: θ' P

CXXVIII.   1 ἐς δὲ τί Jacobs: τίππε PPl

CXXIX.   2 συρίσδηις PPl: συρίξηις Boissonade   ὑπεκδέχεται Pl: ἀπεκ- P

CXXX. ANTIPATER OF SIDON AP 9.723 (39 GP)
ἁ μόλιβος κατέχει με καὶ ἁ λίθος· εἵνεκα δ᾽ ἂν σεῦ,
πλάστα Μύρων, λωτὸν καὶ θρύον ἐδρεπόμαν.

CXXXI. ANTIPATER OF SIDON AP 9.724 (40 GP)
ἁ δάμαλις, δοκέω, μυκήσεται· ἦ ῥ᾽ ὁ Προμηθεὺς
710   οὐχὶ μόνος, πλάττεις ἔμπνοα καὶ σύ, Μύρων.

CXXXII. PHANIAS AP 6.307 (7 GP)
Εὐγαθὴς λαπιθανὸς ἐσοπτρίδα καὶ φιλέθειρον
σινδόνα καὶ πετάσου φάρσος ὑποξύριον
καὶ ψήκτραν δονακῖτιν ἀπέπτυσε καὶ λιποκώπους
φασγανίδας καὶ τοὺς συλόνυχας στόνυχας,
715   ἔπτυσε δὲ ψαλίδας, ξυρὰ καὶ θρόνον, εἰς δ᾽ Ἐπικούρου,   5
κουρεῖον προλιπών, ἅλατο κηπολόγος,
ἔνθα λύρας ἤκουεν ὅπως ὄνος, ὤλετο δ᾽ ἄν που
λιμώσσων εἰ μὴ στέρξε παλινδρομίαν.

CXXXIII. SAM(I)US AP 6.116 (2 GP)
σοὶ γέρας, Ἀλκείδα Μινυαμάχε, τοῦτο Φίλιππος
720   δέρμα ταναιμύκου λευρὸν ἔθηκε βοός
αὐτοῖς σὺν κεράεσσι, τὸν ὕβρεϊ κυδιόωντα
ἔσβεσεν Ὀρβηλοῦ τρηχὺν ὑπὸ πρόποδα.
ὁ φθόνος αὐαίνοιτο, τεὸν δ᾽ ἔτι κῦδος ἀέξοι   5
ῥίζα Βεροιαίου κράντορος Ἠμαθίας.

CXXXIV. MELEAGER AP 7.419 (4 GP)
725   ἀτρέμας, ὦ ξένε, βαῖνε· παρ᾽ εὐσεβέσιν γὰρ ὁ πρέσβυς
εὕδει κοιμηθεὶς ὕπνον ὀφειλόμενον

CXXX.   2 θρύον P: θρίον Pl

CXXXII.   2 φάρσος Toup: φᾶρος P   3 δονακῖτιν P: δονακῆτιν C: ἄκιτιν
Suda   λιποκώπους Toup: λιποκόπτους P: λιποκόπρους Suda: -κόπους Suda (alibi)   4
συλόνυχας C Suda: συνον- P   στόνυχας Salmasius: ὄν- P Suda   5 δὲ ψαλίδας Jacobs: δ᾽
ἰταλίας P   6 κηπολόγους C

CXXXIII.   3 τὸν ὕβρεϊ apogr.: τό νυ βρεγμῶ C: τό νυ βρεχμῶ P: τὸν βρεχμῶι
Pl   κυδιόωντα Pl: κυδιαῶντα P (-α- del. C)   5 αὐαίνυτο P   ἀέξει P

CXXXIV.   1 παρ᾽ CPl: παν P

Εὐκράτεω Μελέαγρος, ὁ τὸν γλυκύδακρυν Ἔρωτα
καὶ Μούσας ἱλαραῖς συστολίσας Χάρισιν,
ὃν θεόπαις ἤνδρωσε Τύρος Γαδάρων θ᾽ ἱερὰ χθών,   5
730   Κῶς δ᾽ ἐρατὴ Μερόπων πρέσβυν ἐγηροτρόφει.
αλλ᾽ εἰ μὲν Σύρος ἐσσί, σαλάμ᾽ εἰ δ᾽ οὖν σύ γε Φοῖνιξ,
ναίδιος᾽ εἰ δ᾽ Ἕλλην, χαῖρε᾽ τὸ δ᾽ αὐτὸ φράσον.

CXXXV. MELEAGER AP 7.196 (13 GP)

ἀχήεις τέττιξ, δροσεραῖς σταγόνεσσι μεθυσθεὶς
ἀγρονόμαν μέλπεις μοῦσαν ἐρημολάλον,
735   ἄκρα δ᾽ ἐφεζόμενος πετάλοις πριονώδεσι κώλοις
αἰθίοπι κλάζεις χρωτὶ μέλισμα λύρας᾽
ἀλλά, φίλος, φθέγγου τι νέον δενδρώδεσι Νύμφαις   5
παίγνιον, ἀντωιδὸν Πανὶ κρέκων κέλαδον,
ὄφρα φυγὼν τὸν Ἔρωτα μεσημβρινὸν ὕπνον ἀγρεύσω
740   ἐνθάδ᾽ ὑπὸ σκιερᾶι κεκλιμένος πλατάνωι.

CXXXVI. MELEAGER AP 5.176 (6 GP)

δεινὸς Ἔρως, δεινός᾽ τί δὲ τὸ πλέον ἦν πάλιν εἴπω
καὶ πάλιν οἰμώζων πολλάκι, "δεινὸς Ἔρως";
ἦ γὰρ ὁ παῖς τούτοισι γελᾶι καὶ πυκνὰ κακισθεὶς
ἥδεται, ἢν δ᾽ εἴπω λοίδορα, καὶ τρέφεται.
745   θαῦμα δέ μοι πῶς ἄρα διὰ γλαυκοῖο φανεῖσα   5
κύματος, ἐξ ὑγροῦ, Κύπρι, σὺ πῦρ τέτοκας.

CXXXVII. MELEAGER AP 5.192 (57 GP)

γυμνὴν ἢν ἐσίδηις Καλλίστιον, ὦ ξένε, φήσεις
"ἤλλακται διπλοῦν γράμμα Συρηκοσίων."

CXXXVIII. MELEAGER AP 12.52 (81 GP)

οὔριος ἐμπνεύσας ναύταις Νότος, ὦ δυσέρωτες,
750   ἥμισύ μευ ψυχᾶς ἅρπασεν Ἀνδράγαθον.

---

4 Μούσαις P   5 δ᾽ ἱερή Pl   6 δ᾽ CPl, om. P   8 τὸ CPl: τὶ P (ut videtur)

CXXXV.   1 ἀχήεις CPl: ἀχείης P (ut videtur)   2 ἀγρονόμαν P: -ον Pl *Suda*   4 λύρας
CPl *Suda*: -ης P   8 σκιερᾶι Jacobs: -ῆι PPl

CXXXVI.   5 γλυκοῖο P

τρὶς μάκαρες νᾶες, τρὶς δ' ὄλβια κύματα πόντου,
τετράκι δ' εὐδαίμων παιδοφορῶν ἄνεμος·
εἴθ' εἴην δελφίς, ἵν' ἐμοῖς βαστακτὸς ἐπ' ὤμοις   5
πορθμευθεὶς ἐσίδηι τὰν γλυκύπαιδα Ῥόδον.

CXXXIX. MELEAGER AP 12.137 (118 GP)

755   ὀρθροβόας, δυσέρωτι κακάγγελε, νῦν, τρισάλαστε,
ἐννύχιος κράζεις πλευροτυπῆ κέλαδον
γαῦρος ὑπὲρ κοίτας ὅτε μοι βραχὺ τοῦτ' ἔτι νυκτὸς
παιδοφιλεῖν, ἐπ' ἐμαῖς δ' ἁδὺ γελᾶις ὀδύναις.
ἅδε φίλα θρεπτῆρι χάρις; ναὶ τὸν βαθὺν ὄρθρον,   5
760   ἔσχατα γηρύσηι ταῦτα τὰ πικρὰ μέλη.

CXL. MELEAGER AP 5.151 (33 GP)

ὀξυβόαι κώνωπες, ἀναιδέες, αἵματος ἀνδρῶν
σίφωνες, νυκτὸς κνώδαλα διπτέρυγα,
βαιὸν Ζηνοφίλαν, λίτομαι, πάρεθ' ἥσυχον ὕπνωι
εὕδειν, τἀμὰ δ', ἰδού, σαρκοφαγεῖτε μέλη.
765   καίτοι πρὸς τί μάτην αὐδῶ; καὶ θῆρες ἄτεγκτοι   5
τέρπονται τρυφερῶι χρωτὶ χλιαινόμενοι.
ἀλλ' ἔτι νῦν προλέγω, κακὰ θρέμματα λήγετε τόλμης,
ἢ γνώσεσθε χερῶν ζηλοτύπων δύναμιν.

CXXXVIII.   3 τρὶς δ' Brunck: τρεῖς δ' P   6 γλυκύπαιδα Brunck: γλυκό- P

CXXXIX.   3 ὅτε Hermann: ὅτι P   4 παιδοφιλεῖν Huschke: καὶ τὸ φιλεῖν P   5
θρεπτῆρι Huschke: θρέπτειρα P

CXL. Meleager AP 5.151 (33 GP)
2 νυκτὸς P: ἀνδρῶν Pl   3 παράθ' P   ὕπνον Pl   4 σαρκοφαγεῖτε Pl: -ται P   5 πρὸς τί
μάτην Scaliger: προσῆ κα τὴν P: προ ση κατην Pl   ἄτεκνοι P   7 τόλμης CPl: τέλ- P

COMMENTARY

ANYTE

Twenty-four epigrams attributed to Anyte survive. She was from Arcadian Tegea (Pollux 5.48; cf. Steph. Byz. τ65.19); the ethnic Μιτυληναία in the lemma to *AP* 7.492 (cf. the lemma to Nossis *AP* 9.332 Νοσσίδος Λεσβίας) is probably an error deriving from the supposedly Sapphic character of her poetry; the same may be true for the references to her as μελοποιός or λυρική in the ascriptions of the Anthology. Paus. 10.38.13 reports that she composed hexameters, but no fragment of these remains. Anyte's work is (contra Bernsdorff 2001) probably earlier than that of Nicias and Mnasalces (cf. Sens 2006); VII may play on Nossis' ecphrastic epigrams.

Anyte draws heavily on Homeric language, often applying it to ordinary, domestic contexts. In a number of cases she alludes to specific passages of the *Iliad* and *Odyssey*. At the same time, she frequently varies Homeric phrases by including in them diction deriving from Greek tragedy, especially Euripides. Her dialect is principally Doric, often overlaid on forms derived from epic.

Anyte played a role in the development of a number of epigrammatic types, including fictive epitaphs for dead pets and wild animals (v introductory n.), and of poems in which the speaker invites exhausted travelers to relax in an idealized rural landscape (cf. VIII). These, too, play on the conventions of sepulchral epigrams (cf. 29n.)

I. Anyte AP 7.724 (4 GP)

On a dead soldier. Although the text is problematic, the most likely reconstruction places the epigram in the tradition of epitaphs on young men who have died in battle. Its novelty lies in the second couplet, in which the stone itself is explicitly characterized as a poet, and the conventional language of the final verse thus amounts to an epigram within the epigram, which thus calls attention to its status as a literary artifact.

1–2[1–2] "You lost your youth, Proarchus, and in dying put the house of your father Pheidias into dark mourning." The paradosis is intolerably awkward; Ypsilanti's emendation (a variation of Graefe's ἥβαν μὲν σύ, Πρόαρχ᾽, ὄλεσας, παῖ, δῶμά τε πατρός) produces a text that draws closely on the traditions of inscribed epitaph, but cannot be considered certain.   **ἥβαν:** that young men who have died in battle have lost their ἥβη or the equivalent is a common theme of epitaphs, e.g. *CEG* 4.3 οἵ ποτε καλλιχόρου περὶ πατρίδος ὠλέσατ{ε} ἥβην, 716.2 ὤλεσα[ς ἡ]λικία[ν]. **Πρόαρχ':** perhaps an otherwise unattested proper name rather than a military title ("captain"), in which sense the word appears first in the twelfth century CE; at *SEG* XXXII 474.4–5 (3rd cent. CE) it is a religious title, in place of the more common προάρχων. The word acquires special resonance in the final verse: the young man has died fighting at the forefront of his men (cf. Homeric πρόμαχος). **ὄλεσας:** unaugmented aorist indicative, in the verse position regularly occupied by the aorist participle ὀλέσας in Homer (e.g. *Il.* 8.498). **δώματα πατρός:** a Homeric line end (e.g. *Il.* 18.141). **Φειδία:** Doric genitive singular. **δνοφερῶι πένθει:** perhaps alluding to Aesch. *Pers.* 535–6 ἄστυ τὸ Σούσων ἠδ᾽ Ἀγβατάνων | πένθει δνοφερῶι κατέκρυψας, where Zeus's destruction of an entire army causes the grief; here a single warrior's death produces the same effect.

3–4[3–4] The representation of the tomb as a poet is a variation of the conventional depiction of the tombstone as a speaker or messenger (e.g. *CEG* 173, 429.1 αὐδὴ τεχνήεσσα λίθου, 591.4); cf. Call. 259–60n. The direct quotation of a sung "good word" recalls Thgn. 15–17, where the Muses and Graces are the source of an aphorism (καλὸν ἀείσατ᾽ ἔπος, | "ὅττι καλόν, φίλον ἐστί· τὸ δ᾽ οὐ καλὸν οὐ φίλον ἐστί"); here, the gravestone replaces the goddesses of poetry. That it is good to die fighting for one's country was a commonplace included, for example, among the Delphic maxims (132 ap. Stob. 3.1.173 θνῆισκε ὑπὲρ πατρίδος); cf. Tyrt. fr. 10.1–2 τεθνάμεναι γὰρ καλὸν ἐνὶ προμάχοισι πεσόντα | ἄνδρ᾽ ἀγαθὸν περὶ ἧι πατρίδι μαρνάμενον. **τοι ὕπερθεν** "above you." **πέτρος ἀείδει:** the distinction between writing and song is sometimes blurred in Hellenistic poetry (e.g. Call. fr. 103 ἐπεὶ τόδε κύρβις ἀείδει; Pos. 122.6 AB ᾠδῆς . . . φθεγγόμεναι σελίδες). **φίλας . . . πατρίδος:** a common Homeric phrase (e.g. *Il.* 9.428).

II. Anyte AP 7.649 (8 GP)

On Thersis, who died before marriage. The epigram draws its basic form from inscribed epitaphs naming the person who buried the deceased (e.g. *CEG* 35, 741). Here, Thersis' mother has erected a full-size likeness of her dead daughter over the tomb. Such images would usually have taken the form of a relief rather than a freestanding statue; what type of representation is meant here is not entirely clear. The theme of the epigram is the commonplace idea "death before (or 'instead of') marriage," regularly found in inscribed epigrams (cf. *CEG* 24, 584.4, 587, 591.11–12) and exploited as a source of pathos (cf. Rehm 1994).

1[5] A periphrasis for the commonplace "instead of marriage" (e.g. *CEG* 591.12 τάφον ἀντὶ γάμου), couched in language reminiscent of epic and tragedy.   τοι "for you [i.e. Thersis]." Enclitic personal pronouns tend to occupy second position in their clause ("Wackernagel's Law"), even when this causes them to intercede between prepositions and their objects.   εὐλεχέος θαλάμου reworks *Od.* 23.178 εὐσταθέος θαλάμου. The adjective is attested elsewhere only at Leon. *APl* 182.2, but has an analogue in the Sophoclean εὔλεκτρος (*Trach.* 515, *Ant.* 796).

3[7] μέτρον . . . κάλλος "size and beauty"; cf. *177–8*n.   **ἔχοισαν:** feminine participles in -οισα are a standard feature of Hellenistic literary Doric (cf. Bulloch on Call. *h.* 5.7, Introduction section 4g).

4[8] The vocative probably enacts the ritual called the προσφθεγκτήρια (cf. Pollux 2.118 προσφθεγκτήρια πρὸ γάμων ἑορτή; cf. 3.36), in which the bride was formally addressed. For the language, cf. Hermes. fr. 7.20 γνωστὴ δ' ἐστὶ καὶ εἰν Ἀΐδηι.   **Θερσί:** Θερσίς is not otherwise securely attested as a woman's name, though it is plausibly restored in a third-century Thessalian inscription (cf. *LGPN* III.B).   **ποτιφθεγκτὰ δ' ἔπλεο καὶ φθιμένα** "you were (ἔπλεο) ritually addressed though dead." ποτιφθεγκτά is Doric nominative singular. The continued honor received by the dead (e.g. *CEG* 178.4 καὶ ἐν Ἀΐδεώ περ ἐοῦσαι) is a *topos* in funerary epigrams: cf. *CEG* 571, 600, 603, Tsagalis 2008: 39.

III. Anyte AP 7.646 (7 GP)

The dying words of Erato. Grave monuments commonly depicted the deceased bidding farewell to family members, and the epigram would suit a relief in which Erato and her father appeared together. This may be the earliest surviving epigram in which the final words of the deceased are reported, and although the motif reappears several times in early Hellenistic epigram (e.g. XLVII introductory n., Leon. *AP* 7.648, Pos. 60 AB, Damag. *AP* 7.735, "Simon." *AP* 7.513), it is extant in inscriptions only later (*SGO* 14/11/02). In any case, the epigram has a literary background. That Erato addresses her final words to her father suggests that she does not have a husband, and her name, with its connection to Eros, suggests the pathos of her premature death. The representation of the dying words of a young woman is reminiscent of Attic tragedy, where young women on the verge of death sometimes bid farewell to family members (e.g. Eur. *Alc.* 372–92, *Hec.* 402–43); much of the language is distinctly tragic in coloring. The poem also recalls the poignant encounter between Odysseus and his dead mother in *Odyssey* 11. The first word, λοίσθια, which paradoxically means "last," signals the content of the entire poem and forms a frame with θάνατος, which brings to a close both the epigram and the life of its honorand.

1[9] λοίσθια: this form of the adjective (as opposed to λοῖσθος) is first attested in the fifth century, and is common in tragedy (e.g. Aesch. Ag. 120, Eur. Alc. 417).   δή suggests that the speaker is accurately reporting Erato's last words.   πατρὶ φίλωι: a Homeric collocation in a Homeric verse position (Il. 13.644, Od. 10.8).   περὶ χεῖρε βαλοῦσα "embracing." Tmesis occurs several times in Anyte but is relatively rare in Hellenistic epigram. The phrase alludes to Od. 11.211, where Odysseus laments that he and his mother cannot embrace (περὶ χεῖρε βαλόντε). Anyte reverses the relationship: an unmarried girl embraces her father at the moment of her death. The allusion has a pathetic effect: this will be Erato's last opportunity to hug her father.

2[10] Ἐρατώ: the name is well attested (cf. LGPN), but is especially poignant in an epigram recording the last words of a dying virgin.   χλωροῖς δάκρυσι: a tragic collocation (Eur. Med. 906, 922, Hel. 1189; cf. Soph. Trach. 847–8). The semantic range of χλωρός, which may mean "green," "pale," and "fresh," probably derives from a basic sense "moist"; cf. Irwin 1974: 31–78.   λειβομένα: probably passive ("poured out with tears"), as apparently at Eur. Andr. 532 λείβομαι δάκρυσιν κόρας (where κόρας seems to be accusative of respect), rather than middle ("pouring forth (with tears)"). The active with δάκρυ(α) as direct object is more common: cf. Il. 13.88.

3[11] οὔ τοι ἔτ᾽ εἰμί: probably "I am yours (τοι) no longer" rather than "know that (τοι) I am dead." This emotional expression is best paralleled in Euripides (e.g. Alc. 390, Hipp. 357 χαίρετ᾽, οὐκέτ᾽ εἴμ᾽ ἐγώ), and the deployment of similar phrases in comic parodies of tragedy (Olson on Ar. Ach. 1184–5) suggests that it should be taken as a tragic feature.

3–4[11–12] μέλας . . . κυάνεος: death is black because it brings the end of sight (cf. LXXVI); its darkness contrasts with the paleness of Erato's tears (χλωροῖς). κυάνεος is often almost synonymous with μέλας (Irwin 1974: 79–110), and some scholars have therefore changed one or the other to the accusative (modifying ὄμμα), but the tautology is emphatic (cf. Soph. Ajax 710). In Homer, both adjectives are used of metaphorical clouds covering the eyes of dying warriors (e.g. Il. 16.350, 20.417–18), and both are epithets of death in other contexts (cf. Gow on Theocr. 17.49).   ὄμμα καλύπτει varies the common Homeric line end σκότος ὄσσε κάλυψεν (e.g. Il. 13.575), "darkness covered his eyes."   ἀποφθιμένας: the genitive stands in agreement with the pronoun (ἐμοῦ) implied by the possessive adjective ἐμόν.

IV. Anyte AP 7.490 (6 GP)

A lament for Antibia. First-person expressions of grief for the deceased are common in inscribed epitaphs (e.g. *CEG* 16a = 470 ἀνιῶμαι, Tsagalis 2008: 255–6). Grave reliefs sometimes show female mourners, and the speaker might be imagined as depicted on Antibia's tomb, but the absence of internal pointers leaves the identification ambiguous (Tueller 2008: 77–9). As a freestanding poem, the epigram resembles a threnody enacting the lamentation of a mourner (cf. Bion's *Ep. Ad.* 1 αἰάζω τὸν Ἄδωνιν). At the same time, it plays with the epitaphic convention of highlighting a young woman's death before marriage by expanding the loss to include her suitors, whose disappointment is the focus of the poem.

1[13] παρθένον: cf. II introductory n. The initial position is emphatic.

1–2[13–14] ἐπὶ . . . ἱέμενοι: tmesis = ἐφιέμενοι, governing the genitive relative pronoun (cf. Eur. *Hel.* 1183 ἄλοχος ἧς ἐφίεμαι), though the expression is deceptive, since the epic models (e.g. *Il.* 1.162, 14.67 ἧι ἔπι πόλλ' ἔπαθον) initially suggest that ἐπί is a preposition in anastrophe. **νυμφίοι:** proleptic, to be understood closely with (ἐφ)ιέμενοι (i.e. "would-be bridegrooms"). **πατρὸς ἵκοντο δόμον:** a phrase redolent of epic (cf. *HHDem.* 171 ῥίμφα δὲ πατρὸς ἵκοντο μέγαν δόμον); it contributes to the representation of Antibia as a heroine (cf. 3n.).

3[15] κάλλευς καὶ πινυτᾶτος ἀνὰ κλέος "in response to her fame for appearance and intellect." ἀνά suggests movement toward a goal (e.g. A.R. 1.838); its use with κλέος is not precisely paralleled but appears to be a variation of such expressions as *Il.* 13.364 πολέμοιο μετὰ κλέος εἰληλούθει, Parth. *EP* 36.1 ἀφικέσθαι κατὰ κλέος γυναικὸς καλῆς. κάλλευς καὶ πινυτᾶτος evokes *Od.* 20.70 εἶδος καὶ πινυτήν "appearance and shrewdness," of the daughters of Pandion, who also died before marriage. The conventional praise of the deceased (e.g. *CEG* 67, 69, 650.3–4) is here introduced indirectly in the account of the suitors' motivation. The abstract noun πινυτής appears first here but is a common attribute of deceased spouses in later funerary epigrams. **ἀλλ' ἐπιπάντων** "but of all of them together," i.e. Antibia and the suitors, but also suggesting the universal experience of mortals. Reading the rare ἐπίπας (cf. Xenophan. fr. 3.4) yields better sense than treating ἐπί as a preposition ("Fate (coming) after all (the suitors)") or as a preverb in tmesis with ἐκύλισε; cf. adesp. *AP* 12.87.5–6 οὐ μούνοις δ' ἐπὶ τοῖσι δεδόρκαμεν ἀλλ' ἐπιπάντων | ἄρκυσι πουλυμανῆ κανθὸν ἐφελκόμεθα.

4[16] ἐλπίδας . . . πρόσω: fate has undone the aspirations described in 1–2; the contrast between ἱέμενοι and οὐλομένη in the same relative positions of the couplets is pointed. The fragility of human aspirations is a *topos* of epitaphs: e.g. *CEG* 630.2 ἀλλὰ Τύχη κρείσσων ἐλπίδος ἐξεφάνη, 732.4–5. **οὐλομένα Μοῖρ'**: cf. Tyrt. fr. 7.2 εὖτέ τιν' οὐλομένη μοῖρα κίχοι θανάτου. **Μοῖρ' . . . πρόσω** "fate rolled (them) far away." The verb has a similar metaphorical sense in expressions such as πῆμα θεὸς Δαναοῖσι κυλίνδει (*Il.* 17.688; cf. Lyc. *Alex.* 490), but Anyte reverses the direction of movement. For πρόσω, cf. *Od.* 9.542 τὴν δὲ πρόσω φέρε κῦμα.

V. Anyte 10 GP (apud Pollucem 5.48)

An epitaph for a dead hound. Anyte is among the earliest poets to write epitaphs for animals (cf. Gorla 1997, Díaz de Cerio Díez 1998). No extant epitaph for a dog predates Anyte, but a mid third-century papyrus (*P.Cair.Zen.* 59532) preserves a pair of epitaphs for the hunting dog Tauron, possibly designed for inscription (*SH* 977; cf. *SGO* 06/02/34, 18/01/28; for Latin examples, cf. Kay 1985: 215–16, Granino Cecere 1994). Theophrastus' characterization (*Char.* 21) of a man of petty ambition as the sort of person who would set up a funerary monument for his dog suggests that if some people in fact erected memorials for their pets, such monuments could be subject to derision; at a later period the speaking voice of an inscription from Rome asks passersby not to laugh at a tomb of a dog (*GVI* 1365.2).

The poem draws on epic and other high-style language (cf. 1, 3nn.), and καὶ σύ in the first verse seems to locate Locris' death in a tradition of commemorations. The contrast between the elevated diction and the identity of the honorand has been understood as humorously bathetic or ironic (Greene 2000), but the heroic language applied to Locris' death seems honorific, and the poem implicitly calls attention to the pathos of her death (cf. 2n.).

Formally, the epigram resembles inscribed epitaphs addressed to the deceased and describing the circumstances of the death (e.g. *CEG* 661). Those circumstances emerge only in the final verse, with the identity of Locris' killer made explicit in the last word.

The poem shares several points of contact with Nicander's *Theriaca*, a work probably of a later date: in addition to their shared use of the otherwise unattested collocation ἰὸν ἀμείλικτον, *Ther.* 672–5 reports the story of a hunting dog bitten in the eye by a "female viper" (ἔχιδνα) but saved from death by an herb.

1[17] **ὤλεο δή**: cf. *Il.* 24.725 (Andromache to the dead Hector) ἄνερ, ἀπ' αἰῶνος νέος ὤλεο, *GVI* 1462.1 ὤλεο δὴ στυγερῶι θανάτωι προλιποῦσα τοκῆας.   **ποτε καὶ σύ**: a Homeric phrase used in its Homeric verse-position (*Il.* 19.315, Achilles reminiscing about the dead Patroclus, *Od.* 11.441, 19.81). ποτε places the death at an unspecified moment in the past; καὶ σύ might refer to the epigram's position in an ongoing tradition of funerary epigrams or within a collection.   **πολύρριζον . . . θάμνον:** a variation of *Il.* 11.156–7 θάμνοι | πρόρριζοι. The adjective is otherwise prosaic, e.g. Thphr. *HP* 1.6.3. Its point emerges implicitly at the end of the poem: the serpent was making its lair in the dense root structure of the bush, as does the χέλυδρος of Nic. *Ther.* 418–19 (cf. 454–5).

2[18] Λόκρι is simultaneously an ethnic designation and a proper name; cf. *455*n. Locrian hounds are a hunting breed (Xen. *Cyn.* 10.1).   **φιλοφθόγγων** "who love to make noise"; attested only here.   **ὠκυτάτη:** swiftness is an attribute of many dogs (e.g. *Il.* 1.50, Pi. fr. 106.1–3, Lilja 1976: 15), but the adjective is significant: despite her speed, Locris could not get past the viper (cf. *Od.* 8.330–2) and is now immobile in death.   **σκυλάκων:** though generalized as a term for dogs of all ages by the classical period, the noun originally meant "puppy," "young dog," and its force here may be affectionate.

3[19] τοῖον ἐλαφρίζοντι "moving so quickly"; cf. 2n. τοῖον is adverbial, as at e.g. *Od.* 3.496 τοῖον γὰρ ὑπέκφερον ὠκέες ἵπποι. For intransitive ἐλαφρίζω, cf. Eur. fr. 530.8, Call. *h.* 4.115.   **τεῶι ἐγκάτθετο κώλωι** varies *Il.* 14.219 τεῶι ἐγκάτθεο κόλπωι, cf. 14.223 ἑῶι ἐγκάτθετο κόλπωι, *Od.* 11.614, 23.223.

4[20] ἰὸν ἀμείλικτον: i.e. "poison for which there is no antidote"; Nicander (*Ther.* 517–18, 545–9, 652–5) records several remedies for the bite of the ἔχις. The phrase recurs at *Ther.* 185, of the asp's venom, for which Nicander records no cure.   **ποικιλόδειρος:** a rare archaic epithet of birds (Hes. *WD* 203, Alc. fr. 345). Snakes are sometimes described as ποικίλος (cf. Thgn. 602, Pi. *Pyth.* 8.46, Nic. *Ther.* 155); the epithet suits Mediterranean vipers, which all have dark mottled markings, though it might also suggest the flashing movement of the strike (cf. Gutzwiller 1993: 80).

VI. Anyte AP 6.123 (1 GP)

On a spear dedicated to Athena. The epigram obliquely provides the information essential to a dedication – the identities of the dedicator and of the divine recipient. The dedicated object is personified and addressed in terms normally directed in inscribed contexts to passersby. Epigrams sometime ask travelers to "stop" and inspect a tomb or dedication, and sometimes request them to move on and transmit the information elsewhere (cf. 4n.). The poem conflates these two requests: the spear is to

announce Echecratidas' valor not by traveling but by remaining station-
ary (ἔσταθι; cf. Tueller 2008: 98–9). For the dedicated object making an
announcement, cf. *SGO* 01/08/01.3–4.
    The poem has points of contact with Nicias *AP* 6.122 and "Simon." *AP*
6.52. That Anyte's epigram is the model for Nicias' seems likely. Its relationship to "Simon." *AP* 6.52 is less secure: that the epigram does not
engage in the same play with inscriptional conventions may slightly favor
Anyte's priority.

1[21] ἔσταθι: intransitive perfect imperative of ἵστημι (cf. Ar. *Birds* 206).
The sense "stand" is appropriate for a spear, but the phrase initially suggests "stop" in the manner of inscribed epigram (e.g. *CEG* 27.1, 28.2);
both meanings are operative.   τᾶιδε "here."   κράνεια "cornel-wood
(spear)." The word is used like Homeric μελίη "ash (spear)"; elsewhere so
used only in the related epigram by Nicias (above). Cornel-wood was prized
for weapons and used for Macedonian cavalry spears (Arr. *Anab.* 1.15.5)
and probably the *sarissa*; cf. Markle 1977: 324.   βροτοκτόνε: earlier
only at Eur. *IT* 384 (cf. Aesch. *Eum.* 421 βροτοκτονοῦντας).   λυγρόν:
probably to be taken with φόνον as in expressions like λυγρὸν ὄλεθρον (*Il.*
6.16).

2[22] ὄνυχα: the personification is based on the spear-tip being a sharp
extension to a long, thin projection like a finger or claw (cf. Thphr. *HP*
4.2.1, 9.6.2 of an agriculture tool).   φόνον δαΐων "enemies' gore."
δαΐων is probably an anapest (⌣ ⌣ –), with the originally long alpha short-
ened by "internal" correption (cf. *Il.* 2.544, Gow on Theocr. 17.98).

3[23] ἀνὰ . . . δόμον "in the house," like the Homeric ἀνὰ δῶμα (*Il.* 1.570,
15.101).   μαρμάρεον: the word encompasses both "marble" and "shin-
ing" (e.g. *Il.* 14.273, Σᵇ *Il.* 3.126); cf. *Il.* 13.21–2 κλυτὰ δώματα . . . | χρύσεα
μαρμαίροντα τετεύχαται ἄφθιτα αἰεί, Alc. fr. 140.2.   ἡμένα: i.e. "having
been dedicated" (cf. *SGO* 01/08/01.4, *CEG* 120), though the literal sense
("sitting") creates a playful paradox with ἔσταθι.

4[24] ἄγγελλ᾽ evokes a *topos* first found in a famous epitaph for the
Spartan dead at Thermopylae ("Simon." *AP* 7.249 ὦ ξεῖν᾽, ἀγγέλλειν
Λακεδαιμονίοις ὅτι τῇδε | κείμεθα, τοῖς κείνων πειθόμενοι νομίμοις) and widely
taken up in both inscribed and fictive Hellenistic epigrams (*IMEGR* 30,
Tarán 1979: 132–49).   ἀνορέαν: praise of the ἠνορέη ("manly virtue")
of the deceased is a feature of funerary inscriptions (*CEG* 31.2, Hansen
on *CEG* 19).   Κρητός: Cretan mercenaries played an important
role in Hellenistic armies (cf. Spyridakis 1977). The basic point is that

Echecratidas is fighting far from his homeland (cf. *372*).   Ἐχεκρατίδα:
Doric genitive singular. Echecratidas, lit. "having force," suits the martial
context.

VII. Anyte AP *9.745 (14 GP)*

On a haughty goat. The poem shares points of contact with Nossis'
ecphrastic epigrams, which frequently urge inspection and appreciation
of the realism of an image of a woman. The tone argues for the priority of
Nossis' poetry: that Anyte is ironically appropriating the form of Nossis'
poems on images of women is more probable than that Nossis is evoking
a poem on a supercilious goat. The engagement with the ecphrastic tradition may suggest that the poem describes an artistic representation rather
than a real animal.

The wit depends on the subtle characterization of the goat. It is not
initially clear whether its behavior is viewed positively or negatively (cf.
1 ἀγερώχως). Subsequently allusions (cf. 3n.) associating it with the
Homeric Agamemnon and other self-important military leaders undercut
the creature's grandiosity. There is, then, a humorous contrast between
the poem's literary background and its lowly subject matter. If the goat is
treated as Dionysus' in that it is to be sacrificed to him, the animal's grandiosity is particularly ill-conceived.

1[25] Cf. Nossis *AP* 9.605.3 ὡς ἀγανῶς ἕστακεν· ἴδ' ἁ χάρις ἁλίκον ἀνθεῖ,
173.   θάεο: cf. *179, 491*. The opening command to "look" at an artifact
evokes requests that a passerby stop and pay attention to the grave (e.g.
CEG 597.1 ξένε, φράζεο σῆμα, *648*).   Βρομίου: the precise point of the
animal's affiliation with Dionysus is uncertain. Zeus concealed Dionysus
from Hera in the form of a kid (cf. [Apollod.] 3.4.3), and the god was
called by epithets referring to the animal (ἐρίφιος, μελαναιγίς, αἰγοβόλος),
but goats were also sacrificed to him.   κεραὸν τράγον: i.e. a mature
goat (e.g. Theocr. 1.4). The adjective focuses attention on the goat's
appearance, in which he takes particular pride.   ὡς ἀγερώχως: perhaps a humorous rewriting of Nossis' ὡς ἀγανῶς (above) "how gently."
The ancient debate about the etymology of Homeric ἀγέρωχος (variously
connected to ἀγείρειν or to ἄγαν) reflects differing views about its meaning
and tone, but in post-Homeric literature the word often has a pejorative
sense (e.g. Polyb. 2.8.7).

2[26] " . . . casts its proud gaze down over its shaggy chin." The line is
constructed in two symmetrical halves, in which nouns and their epithets
are of the same metrical shape and occupy the same relative position

(ὄμμα – γαῦρον, λασιᾶν – γενύων); κατά, with its second syllable lengthened before initial lambda as in epic (e.g. *Il.* 14.447), is metrically equivalent to ἔχει.   γαῦρον "haughty." The full significance of the word emerges with βόστρυχον (4n.).

3–4[27–8] ὅτι . . . χέρα "glorying in the fact that often in the mountains Nais took the lock on his cheek into her rosy hand." The lines recall descriptions of haughty generals, including Agamemnon in the Catalogue of Ships (cf. below), the unappealing leaders of Archil. fr. 114.1–2 οὐ φιλέω μέγαν στρατηγὸν οὐδὲ διαπεπλιγμένον | οὐδὲ βοστρύχοισι γαῦρον οὐδ' ὑπεξυρημένον, and Menelaus at Eur. *Or.* 1532 ἀλλ' ἴτω ξανθοῖς ἐπ' ὤμων βοστρύχοις γαυρούμενος.   **κυδιόων ὅτι:** an allusion to a disputed passage, *Il.* 2.579–80 κυδιόων ὅτι πᾶσι μετέπρεπεν ἡρώεσσιν | οὕνεκ' ἄριστος ἔην πολὺ δὲ πλείστους ἄγε λαούς, of Agamemnon. Agamemnon's supposed superiority was treated as a problem: Zenodotus read πᾶσιν δέ instead of ὅτι πᾶσιν but athetized the lines on the grounds that in the preceding verse Ajax is said to be the best after Achilles.   οἱ "his" (dative of reference). In Homer the original initial digamma regularly prevents correption before the reflexive personal pronoun; ὅτι οἱ is a common Homeric juncture (e.g. *Il.* 23.545, *Od.* 13.343).   **ἐν οὔρεσιν:** see 299n.   **ἀμφὶ παρῇδα |**
βόστρυχον "hair on its cheek." The disyllabic παρῄς for trisyllabic παρηῆς is a tragic form (e.g. Aesch. *Ch.* 24, Eur. *IA* 187, 681).   **ῥοδέαν . . .**
χέρα: cf. *603*. Nymphs conventionally have rosy arms (e.g. Hes. *Th.* 246, 251).   **ἔδεκτο:** a Homeric athematic form of δέχομαι that may have either an aoristic or, as apparently here, imperfective (cf. θάμ') sense.

VIII. *Anyte* AP 9.313 (16 GP)

An invitation for travelers to rest in a *locus amoenus*. Descriptions of idealized rural locations (already in Sappho fr. 2) conventionally feature cool water, shade provided by trees, and pleasing sounds and scents; cf. Schönbeck 1962. Anyte seems to have been among the first to incorporate these features into epigrams. Here, the relief afforded by the attractive location may be read against the conventional idea that death is a release from pains (e.g. *CEG* 572.3 ἧς γαίας τηλοῦ σῶμ' ἀνέπαυσε πόνων). The participle ἀσθμαίνοντα, a word sometimes used in Homer of dying warriors, is significant: the soothing features of the place restore breath to the fainting traveler.

Nicias *AP* 9.315 is probably an imitation; cf. Reitzenstein 1893: 125, Sens 2006: 154–62.

1[29] ἵζευ ἅπας: the opening command (cf. Nicias *AP* 9.315.1, Hermocr. *APl* 11.1) resonates against epitaphs requesting that passersby "stand" and pay attention to a tombstone; cf. *2*1n., *CEG* 27.1 στῆθι καὶ οἴκτιρον, 28.2. The speaker assumes that all who pass will fall into the category of tired worker described in the second couplet. For the singular (= πάντες), cf. Austin–Olson on Ar. *Thesm.* 372. **ὑπὸ καλά ... φύλλα:** cf. Hes. *Th.* 30 δάφνης ἐριθηλέος ὄζον. The speaker focuses on the aesthetic appeal of the tree (καλά, εὐθαλέα). εὐθαλής is principally lyric and tragic.

2[30] ὡραίου "seasonal." Not all springs flowed perennially, and those flowing in the summer heat (cf. on 3 θέρεος) were especially valuable. **ἀδὺ πόμα:** i.e. "fresh water" (cf. the more common γλυκὺ ὕδωρ), sweet for the refreshment it provides those suffering from heat (cf. 57). The adjective is commonly used of various aspects of Greek *loca amoena* (cf. 572n.).

3–4[31–2] "... so that you may rest your limbs, gasping from the toils of the summer through being struck by the gusts of the West Wind." The word order is intricate: the central verbal idea, that the traveler will rest his weary limbs, is framed by opposed participial phrases modifying γυῖα, which are first said to lack breath (ἀσθμαίνοντα) and then to be refreshed by the breeze. **ὄφρα τοι:** a Homeric verse opening (*Il.* 4.220, 6.308). **ἀσθμαίνοντα ... γυῖα:** the participle, here in a Homeric metrical position (e.g. *Il.* 16.826), is applied to a part of the body rather than to the person as a whole; cf. Pi. *Nem.* 3.47–8 σώματα ... ἀσθμαίνοντα. The point is clarified by πνοιᾶι: the "breath" of Zephyr provides relief to limbs craving a breeze. **πόνοις ... φίλα γυῖα** recalls *Il.* 13.85 τῶν ῥ' ἅμα τ' ἀργαλέωι καμάτωι φίλα γυῖα λέλυντο, of the Achaeans as they rest by the ships. As in epic, φίλος applied to parts of the body is virtually equivalent to a possessive adjective (here "your own"). πόνοις θέρεος may mean "from the labors of the harvest" (GP), in which case the imagined audience consists of harvesters, but it is just as likely to signify "from the toils of summer," including the difficulty of walking in the heat (cf. Anyte *APl* 228.4 ἄμπαυμ' ἐν θερινῶι καύματι τοῦτο φίλον). **πνοιᾶι ... Ζεφύρου:** a variation on the Homeric πνοιῆι Ζεφύροιο (*Il.* 19.415, *Od.* 4.402) and πνοιὴν ζεφύρου (*Od.* 10.25). **τυπτόμενα:** the word usually suggests an exhausting or painful experience but is here used of refreshment provided by pleasant gusts of wind (cf. Hes. *WD* 594).

IX. Anyte *APl* 291 (3 GP)

A thank-offering to Pan and the Nymphs, who provided Theudotus with water. The gift is not specified, so that the epigram resembles dedications that have no need to name the object on which they are inscribed. It seems designed to be read in close conjunction with other epigrams by Anyte in which the speaker urges the weary traveler to take refreshment in a cool and well-watered spot: it records the thanks felt by the passerby who has accepted the sort of benefactions advertised in those poems.

1[33] φριξοκόμαι: hair is often a focus of divine epithets (e.g. *HHDem.* 1 Δήμητρ' ἠΰκομον, *HH* 19.5 ἀγλαέθειρος, of Pan); the adjective primarily refers to the bristling hair of the goat-formed god, but might also suggest "who makes one's hair stand on end." Not elsewhere attested, it has analogues in [φρ]ιξοχαίτη (Soph. fr. **1od.5 Radt), φριξολόφος (Hsch. φ894) and φριξόθριξ (*Suda* φ718); cf. Eur. *Phoen.* 1121 χαίτηι πεφρικός. **αὐλιάσιν:** an otherwise unattested epithet of ambiguous sense. The nouns αὔλιον and αὖλις may refer to a variety of places for passing the night, including sheepfolds as well as human dwelling places, and the semantic range of αὔλιον includes "grotto, cave." Pan and the Nymphs are connected to sheep (cf. Call. *h.* 3.87–8) and to grottoes (cf. Ar. *Lys.* 721, Theodoridas *AP* 6.224.3, 6), and the point may be either that as patrons of sheepfolds they have aided Theudotus as he pastured his sheep (cf. below, on οἰονόμος) or that, as resident deities of a grotto, they have provided him with the blessing of its water. Cf. Leon. *AP* 6.334.1 αὔλια καὶ Νυμφέων ἱερὸς πάγος. **θέτο =** ἀνέθετο, "dedicated." **ὑπὸ σκοπιᾶς:** mountain peaks are haunts of Pan and the Nymphs (e.g. Eur. *El.* 447 Νυμφαίας σκοπιάς). Here the phrase suggests the sort of rocks that regularly feature in bucolic *loca amoena* (e.g. Anyte *APl* 228.1 ξεῖν', ὑπὸ τὰν πέτραν τετρυμένα γυῖ' ἀνάπαυσον): Theudotus has enjoyed the type of refreshment urged on travelers elsewhere.

2[34] δῶρον ... Θεύδοτος: Theodotus ("god granted") is an appropriate name for one offering thanks for divine favor. **οἰονόμος:** ambiguous, admitting the senses "solitary" (cf. Σ^T *Il.* 2.460) and "sheep pasturing" (Hdn. *Epim.* p. 138.7 Boissonade οἰονόμος, ὁ βοσκὸς τῶν προβάτων); cf. οἰοπόλος with 97n., Hunter on A.R. 4.1322.

3–4[35–6] Theodotus' gratitude is explicitly for the role played by the Nymphs: Pan has been silently dropped from consideration. For the explanatory clause introduced by οὕνεκα ("because"; cf. Sens on Asclep. 6.5), e.g. Phaedimus *AP* 6.271.3–4; Pl^Δ's αἵ μιν may be an attempt to avoid making the Nymphs' gift the sole reason for a dedication to multiple gods. **ὑπ' ἀζαλέοιο θέρευς** "from the dry summer." Pl's ζαθέοιο, "very numinous," could fit the moment of an encounter with gods but is less suitable to the context than a form of ἀζάλεος, "dry" (ἀζαλέου Pl^B). The collocation ἀζαλέοιο θέρευς is supported by Q.S. 13.242–3 στάχυν ... | ληΐου ἀζαλέοιο θέρευς εὐθαλπέος ὥρηι; both ἀζαλέοιο and θέρευς occur in the same respective positions in epic (ἀζαλέοιο: cf. *Il.* 20.491, ps.-Hes. *Shield* 153, A.R. 4.679; θέρευς: cf. Hes. *WD* 502). **μέγα κεκμηῶτα | παῦσαν** "they brought an end to his great exhaustion"; cf. Anyte *AP* 9.314.3 ἀνδράσι κεκμηῶσιν . . . ἄμπαυσιν ὁδοῖο. The spondaic line end suits the slow pace of an exhausted traveler.   ὀρέξασαι χερσί "reaching out with their hands (to give)"; e.g. Hes. *Th.* 433. The encounter with a group of female deities who appear to a lone herdsman on a mountain recalls initiation-scenes (e.g. Hes. *Th.* 22–34, Asclep. *45 Sens).   μελιχρὸν ὕδωρ: cf. *30*n.; the phrase plays on the conventional application of the epithet to wine (e.g. Anacr. *PMG* 383).

ASCLEPIADES

Asclepiades' name is associated with forty-seven epigrams in the Greek Anthology and with a few fragments from other sources. Of the epigrams in the Anthology, thirty-three are attributed to him alone. For the others, authorship is assigned to him or another poet; for six of them, Posidippus, whose other works show a great debt to Asclepiades, is the alternative. The Byzantine scholar Tzetzes (Σ Lyc. *Alex.*, p. 3 Scheer) mentions Asclepiades' hymns, but no fragment is clearly hymnic. Nor is it clear why the Aeolic meter that came to be called the "Asclepiadean" was specifically associated with him.

Asclepiades was one of the most influential early Hellenistic epigrammatists. Though his precise dates are uncertain, the external evidence suggests that he remained active at least into the 270s, perhaps into the 260s. At Theocr. 7.40, Simichidas refers to Sicelidas as an admired predecessor; the ancient scholia identify Sicelidas as Asclepiades. The significance of the nickname is not certain, but it is possible that he spent time in Sicily as a young man, perhaps during the period in which Samians were exiled from their island (365–322). Uncertainties of attribution complicate the internal evidence for his life, but if the Cleopatra honored in one epigram (*AP* 9.752) is the sister of Alexander the Great, the poem was probably composed by Asclepiades (rather than by Antipater of Thessalonica, to whom it is alternatively ascribed) some time before her death in 309.

Asclepiades' poetry frequently plays with the boundaries between epigram and other genres, including lyric, elegy, and mime. Whether or not he actually invented erotic and sympotic epigrams, he certainly played a fundamental role in their development. A number of his poems depart from the traditional content of epitaphs and dedications and focus on erotic themes while retaining traces of funerary language and *topoi* (cf. *63–4*, *81*nn.). In several, the speaker represents himself as standing outside a would-be lover's door; in others, he (or she) complains about the painful effects of love, comments on its symptoms, or attempts seduction. Several poems have the symposium as their setting, and in two the speaker gives a servant orders for preparing a dinner party. A hallmark of many is their subtle characterization of speakers, who often use language that resonates ironically against earlier literature or contrasts with the formal characteristics of the genre.

Asclepiades' poetry includes words from elevated genres (including epic and lyric) and ostensibly "unpoetic" forms attested in the literary *koine* but rare in verse. His surviving works show little interest in recherché vocabulary, though many poems play upon the ambiguity of words that seem superficially straightforward (cf. Arnott 1969). The dialect of most poems is the epic/Ionic *koine*, but several are in Doric.

Asclepiades, Posidippus, and Hedylus are linked in the prefatory poem of Meleager's *Garland*, and Reitzenstein (1893: 100–2) argued that Meleager's selection of poems by the three writers derived from a collection – which he identified with the mysterious Σωρός mentioned in connection with Posidippus in Σ *Il.* 11.101 – containing poems by all of them but not clearly attributing the authorship of individual epigrams. Cameron's suggestion (1995: 369–76) that Meleager drew from a collection organized by Hedylus in which he juxtaposed his own work with that of his predecessors Posidippus and Asclepiades is not implausible. The following commentary draws heavily on Sens 2011 (which treats the epigrams more fully).

X. *Asclepiades* AP *13.23 (33 GP = Sens)*

On Botrys, who late in life has buried his son. The poem opens with a traditional request for the passerby to pause in his travels (cf. VIII) but then focuses on the experience of the surviving father rather than his dead son; inscribed epitaphs often note the grief of surviving family members (e.g. *CEG* 686. 1–2), but it is unusual for this to be the central theme (cf., however, XLII). The son remains unnamed (5n.), and his death is only mentioned in a relative clause (3–4n.); nor is it clear whether he was still young at the time of his death. Part of the point may be that Botrys has survived too long for his own good and been deprived of his son's care late in his life (cf. 229–30n.). If so, the final lamentation for the pleasures lost to the dead son contrasts ironically with the experience of his father, for whom living too has long caused great unhappiness.

This is the only wholly extant epigram by Asclepiades in a non-elegiac meter. It is composed of alternating catalectic iambic tetrameters and catalectic trimeters without resolution (× – ᴗ – × – ᴗ – × – ᴗ – ᴗ – × | × – ᴗ – × – ᴗ – ᴗ – ×). The dialect is Doric.

1[37] The interposition of εἴ τι κἀγκονεῖς within the phrase μικρὸν . . . ἄκουσον disrupts the verse in a manner analogous to the interruption of travel that the speaker demands.   ἰώ: an emotional lamentation such as commonly appear at the beginning of epitaphs (e.g. *CEG* 49, 512, 556).   παρέρπων: ἕρπω was the regular word for "go" in Doric (cf. Buck 126); and though the usage was generalized to other dialects, the form suits the Doric dialectal context.   μικρόν: adv., "for a short while."   εἴ τι κἀγκονεῖς "even if you're in a bit of a hurry"; κἀγκονεῖς < καὶ ἐγκονεῖς (crasis).   ἄκουσον: more usually the passerby is asked to pay attention to or look at the information provided on the tomb.

2[38] περισσὰ δῆτα κήδη "quite (δῆτα) extraordinary troubles." The ambiguity of the noun, which encompasses "troubles," "concerns," and "grief," is resolved in the next couplet.

3–4[39–40] The relative clause provides the basic epitaphic information "*X* buried *Y*" (e.g. *CEG* 147, Call. *241*).   πρέσβυς ὀγδώκοντ᾽ ἐτῶν: more usually the focus is on the age of the deceased (e.g. *CEG* 480). Eighty was considered the outer boundary of normal human life; cf. Sol. fr. 20. 4, Hdt. 1. 32. 2–4.   τὸν ἐκ νέων . . . ἤδη "already when he was young" (e.g. Pl. *Gorg.* 483e). The precociousness of the deceased is a consolatory trope (Strubbe 1998), but Botrys' son is not necessarily still a boy.   τι τέχναι καὶ σοφόν: i.e. "something artful and clever." τέχναι is a dative of manner ("with artistry"), and the phrase is a zeugma involving typically Hellenistic *uariatio* of the construction (cf. *299–300*n.). The "wisdom" of the deceased is commonly mentioned in epitaphs (e.g. *CEG* 99a, 136.4, 306.2).

5–6[41–2] For the lamentation directed at the deceased man's surviving family, cf. *193–5*.   φεῦ . . . φεῦ: the repetition underscores the emotion.   τὸν τεκόντα: the accusative of exclamation after φεῦ, ὤ, and the like is rare; cf. Call. *h.* 5.89 with Bulloch's note. The sole focus on the father suggests that the mother is already dead.   φίλος: nominative for vocative (e.g. *Il.* 4.189, 9. 601), as often in emotionally freighted contexts (West 1967), especially with φίλος.   παῖ: this and other fictive funerary epigrams in which the deceased is not named may be inspired by real-life monuments in which the name appears separately from the epitaph; cf. Fantuzzi in Fantuzzi and Hunter 2004: 292–306.   ὀσσᾶν . . . ἀδονᾶν: Doric genitive plurals.   ἀπώλευ: Doric second person singular aorist middle indicative.

XI. *Asclepiades* AP *6.308 (27 GP = Sens)*

A dedication by a boy celebrating his victory in a handwriting competition. Such competitions were a feature of Hellenistic education (Cribiore

2001: 114), but much of the wit derives from the application of language appropriate to victories in public competitions to a minor, everyday triumph. The speaker is, as often in votive epigrams, the dedicated object, a comic mask which is here treated as a real person, an aged comic character called Chares. The implicit point may be that the dedicator has won by copying out a passage of comedy. The speaker's observation in the final couplet that he, as an old man, has been dedicated in a place noisy with children playfully evokes the conventional irritability of old men in comedy (cf. 3, 4nn.).

Some point also derives from the idea that the boy has won by writing καλὰ γράμματα, a phrase equally applicable to letters and to poems. Connarus' boyish victory and its reward may reflect the nugatory and lighthearted character of epigram; the speaker's ironic detachment matches that of the poet. In any case, there is perhaps humor in the implicit contrast between the victor's skill at letter formation and the accomplished composition of the poet.

The poem is imitated by Call. AP 6.310, where a tragic mask dedicated in a classroom is overtly irritated by its location.

1[43] νικήσας τοὺς παῖδας evokes the formal way of referring to winning the boys' competition in a variety of public festivals (e.g. [Dem.] 58.66 Ὀλυμπίασι νικήσας παῖδας στάδιον), here reapplied to a trivial context.   καλὰ γράμματ': in extant papyri, schoolteachers use the phrase to praise good handwriting (Cribiore 1996: nos. 136, 222), the teaching of which was an important part of ancient education.

2[44] Κόνναρος: an unusual name (cf. the Diegesis to Call. fr. 201, which alleges that the proverb ἁρπαγὰ τὰ Κοννίδα appeared in the false form ἁρπαγὰ τὰ Κοννάρου); as a common noun, the word refers to a type of tree (Hsch. κ3528).   ὀγδώκοντ' ἀστραγάλους: knucklebones, gaming pieces in popular children's games (cf. 83-4, Laser 1987: 118-22). These could sometimes be taken by the winner (e.g. A.R. 3.119-21). Eighty of them would probably have been a desirable but not excessive reward (cf. Call. frr. 276, 676). That playing with them sometimes distracted from schoolwork (cf. Herodas 3.24-5) contributes to the humor.

3[45] χάριν "as a thanksgiving present" (e.g. CEG 848.1).   Μούσαις: as patrons of education (Herodas 3.1, 71, 97), though their role as goddesses of poetry is also relevant (cf. introductory n.).   τὸν κωμικόν "(mask of) the comic character"; the adjective elsewhere refers to playwrights and actors.   Χάρητα: Chares is a common name, here perhaps chosen to evoke χάριν and ironic in context, since one possible implication ("he who rejoices") contrasts with the speaker's irritation (see below).

4[46] If Hecker's emendation is correct, the entire verse is chiastic, with θορύβωι . . . ἐνί surrounding the verb and the nouns at the beginning and the end of the line emphasizing the contrast between the old man and the boys among whom he finds himself. θῆκ' ἐνί (MSS θῆκέ με) is not, however, wholly certain, and it places epic/Ionic ἐνί, absent from drama, in the mouth of a comic character.   **θορύβωι:** the din of the classroom. θόρυβος and its cognates can imply disturbance (cf. [Theocr.] 21.4–5); the speaker seems to be unhappy about his location.   **παιδαρίων:** the diminutive is common in comedy and perhaps colloquial.

XII. Asclepiades or Archelaus APl^A 120 (43 GP = Sens)

On a statue of Alexander by Lysippus, who has captured his subject's appearance and character. The second couplet explains the meaning of the opening claim to verisimilitude: Alexander's upturned gaze explains what it means to have captured his whole form, while the words imputed to him explain the meaning of the morally ambiguous initial word τόλμαν (cf. 1n.) and the extent of the power claimed by the king (2n.).

Some of the vocabulary is equally applicable to Alexander and to his image: like Lysippus, the epigram effaces the distinction between image and reality (cf. 2, 3nn.).

By 331 BCE Alexander started calling himself "son of Zeus" (cf. Callisth., *FGrH* 124 F 36). He was sometimes depicted with a thunderbolt, suggesting power analogous to that of Zeus. The propriety of such representations was a matter of debate: Alexander himself is said to have criticized Apelles for showing him holding a thunderbolt rather than a spear. The poem may represent his arrogation of divine prerogatives as problematic (4n.).

The poem is ascribed in Pl to Asclepiades or to Archelaus; no other epigrams of Archelaus survive in the Anthology (for fragments attributed to a poet of this name, cf. *SH* 125–9). It appears to have been used as a model by Pos. LXXXII; the frequency with which Posidippus engaged with Asclepiades' work supports an attribution to Asclepiades here.

Plutarch, who cites the poem twice (*Mor.* 331a, 335b), claims that its final couplet was inscribed on a statue of Alexander by Lysippus, but even if this was so, the epigram seems unlikely to have been composed for that purpose. It is the model for Ov. *Met.* 15.858–60 *Iuppiter arces* | *temperat aetherias et mundi regna triformis,* | *terra sub Augusto est; pater est et rector uterque.*

For the dialect, see Introduction section 4g.

1[47] **τόλμαν** can connote both positive "courage" and improper "boldness."   **ὅλαν . . . μορφάν:** Plutarch reports that Lysippus' statues of

Alexander revealed the form (ἰδέα) of his body (*Alex.* 4.1). Emphasis on perfect likeness is an ecphrastic commonplace; cf. *92, 413–14.* ἀπεμάξατο "took the impression of," "copied"; cf. *323–5*n.

2[48] Λύσιππος: the Sicyonian sculptor (cf. *423*) produced numerous statues of Alexander in the latter half of the fourth century (Pliny, *NH* 34.63), but the tradition that Alexander allowed only Lysippus to produce his portrait (Hor. *Epist.* 2.1.232–44) is wrong; cf. Stewart (1993) 25–7. For Lysippus' life and work, see Ridgway (1997) 286–320.   τίν' ὁδὶ χαλκὸς ἔχει δύναμιν "what power this bronze has." The phrase is usually taken as a rhetorical question, but the use of τί as an exclamatory adverbial accusative (= "how!") in Hellenistic prose (LSJ B IV) raises the possibility that τίνα has a similar sense here.   ὁδί: this colloquial deictic, which represents the speaker as being in the presence of the statue, is more characteristic of Attic than Doric.   δύναμιν applies both to the bronze's ability to imitate life and to the real-life power of the figure it depicts.

3[49] αὐδασοῦντι δ' ἔοικεν: the speaker imagines that the statue will acquire a voice, thus effacing a conventional distinction between live humans and even the most realistic representations; cf. *709*n. The Doric contracted future αὐδασοῦντι seems to lie behind the several variants in the manuscripts of Plutarch and is here preferred to -οντι as *lectio difficilior*, though it could be a hyper-Doric correction.   ὁ χάλκεος: both literally the "bronze" statue and figuratively the "brazen" ruler it depicts (cf. LSJ 2; cf. Theocr. 22.47 σαρκὶ σιδηρείηι, σφυρήλατος οἷα κολοσσός, Alc. *AP* 9.588.1–2).   ἐς Δία λεύσσων: Alexander habitually maintained an upturned gaze (cf. Plut. *Alex.* 4.2). The phrase plays on the literal sense "Zeus" and the metonymic sense "sky."

4[50] Alexander's words recall the division of the cosmos among Zeus and his brothers by lot (cf. *Il.* 15.185–93) or by Zeus himself (Hes. *Th.* 881–5). Alexander asserts his authority over a sphere in which the gods have a strong interest (*Il.* 15.193 γαῖα δ' ἔτι ξυνὴ πάντων καὶ μακρὸς Ὄλυμπος, Pi. *Olymp.* 7.55). The division of the verse into neat halves mirrors the proposed division of the universe.   ὑπ' ἐμοὶ τίθεμαι "assume for my command."   Ὄλυμπον ἔχε "keep Olympus" (rather than "take charge of, rule" GP), a variation of the common clausula (θεοὶ) οἳ Ὄλυμπον ἔχουσιν (e.g. *Il.* 5.404, 13.68): since to "hold Olympus" is to live there, Alexander restricts Zeus's power to his home.

XIII. Asclepiades AP 5.185 (26 GP = Sens)

Instructions for shopping for a symposium. Though instructions for preparing parties are attested in archaic lyric (Alc. fr. 368, Anacr. *PMG* 396), the scene imagined here most obviously recalls the numerous food catalogues and discussions for buying and preparing food in Middle and New Comedy. The names of the fishmonger and garland-seller suggest a setting in Hellenistic Egypt: Thaubarion is markedly Egyptian, Amyntas probably Macedonian. The poem may be read as a rewriting of comedy in an Alexandrian context, but it resembles the short depictions of daily life found in the mimes of Theocritus and Herodas.

The absence of a dramatic context requires readers to reconstruct the scene. The speaker is an experienced shopper who knows the market-place well. He orders some delicacies but generally asks for simple and inexpensive commodities; the six garlands suggest that there will be six partiers, and the quantities he orders for that number are not particularly lavish, at least by comparison with the elaborate dinners depicted regularly in comedy. "Demetrius" is not a slave-name: he may be the sort of loyal friend who helps the lovers in New Comedy (cf. Arnott 1996: 156–7). If so, the speaker's final, nonchalant request for a girl called Tryphera ("Luxury") hints at his interest in her, so that the poem subtly characterizes its speaker as a shy young man who is afraid to mention the true object of his interest directly (cf. e.g. Moschion in Menander's *Samia*).

There seems to be an effort to capture "ordinary" speech. The syntax of the opening couplets is paratactic, the diction is of a low stylistic register, and line 5 contains an unrefined metrical feature.

1[51] εἰς ἀγορὰν βαδίσας "going to the market" (Ar. *Eccles.* 711, Lys. 1.8, 16). **τρεῖς:** like the twenty-four prawns, the three *glaukiskoi* are easily divisible among six diners; cf. 2n. **Ἀμύντου** is a markedly but not exclusively Macedonian name (Hatzopoulos 2000: 99–117).

2[52] The (colloquial?) diminutives may be a sign of real or feigned frugality; cf. Ephipp. fr. 15.3–9. **γλαυκίσκους:** diminutive of γλαῦκος, a large fish (perhaps a small shark), often cited as a delicacy (cf. Olson–Sens on Archestr. fr. 21.1). **αἴτει** "order" (e.g. Ar. *Wasps* 496–8). **φυκίδια:** neuter plural diminutive of φυκίς, an unidentified species of wrasse (*Labridae*), one of the πετραῖοι ("rockfish"), small fish that Archestr. fr. 46 treats as of lower quality and thus requiring elaborate preparation and saucing. Such fish were often stewed, presumably in pieces, and that fact may explain why the number requested is not divisible by six.

3[53] κυφὰς καρῖδας: αἱ κυφαὶ καρῖδες are named as a particular type of shrimp at Arist. *Hist. anim.* 525b1–2.   **ἀριθμήσει . . . αὐτός:** comic fishmongers were conventionally arrogant and untrustworthy (cf. Ath. 6.224c–8c). Amyntas may be different, and the point seems to be that he will ensure that Demetrius knows he is getting the correct number. Gow proposed ἀριθμῆσαί σε δεῖ αὐτάς "you must count them" to make the danger of being cheated explicit.

4[54] τέτορας: a markedly Doric form, perhaps suggesting the language that would be used by the Macedonian Amyntas (cf. Sens 2004).   **δεῦρο λαβὼν ἄπιθι:** cf. *Il.* 13.235 ἀλλ᾽ ἄγε τεύχεα δεῦρο λαβὼν ἴθι. The reuse of a Homeric phrase might be bathetic, though similar expressions were doubtless common in real life.

5[55] The speaker moves on to preparations for the after-dinner symposium. The last word of the line has been lost, but the basic sense is clear: Demetrius should acquire a garland of roses (cf. ῥοδίνους) for each guest. The making and selling of garlands was piecework for those of very low social status, and the vendor's Egyptian name may thus reflect the real ethnic stratification of the marketplace. A disyllabic word is missing at the end of the line; the solutions proposed have been words meaning "garlands," but none is convincing.   **ἕξ** reveals the number of participants, each of whom will wear a garland. This is the only Asclepiadean violation of "Naeke's Law" (cf. Introduction section 4h[i]).   **πρόσλαβε** "buy in addition" (e.g. Xen. *Mem.* 3.14.4).

6[56] Female performers were often hired for symposia, sometimes providing sex in addition to entertainment like music, dance, and acrobatics. Tryphera's precise role and the nature of her relationship to the host are unspecified, and though it is likely that she is a hired entertainer (cf. *Anacreont.* 32. 14–15 μύρισον, ῥόδοις δὲ κρᾶτα | πύκασον, κάλει δ᾽ ἑταίρην, Gow on Theocr. 14. 21), that does not exclude the speaker's having a personal interest in her (cf. Pos. 124.1–2 AB τέσσαρες οἱ πίνοντες· ἐρωμένη ἔρχεθ᾽ ἑκάστωι | ὀκτὼ γινομένοις Χῖον ἐν οὐχ ἱκανόν).   **Τρυφέραν:** though attested in the inscriptional record, the name suggests a sexiness (τρυφή) appropriate to a symposium entertainer.   **ταχέως ἐν παρόδωι:** the speaker, perhaps disguising his true interest (see introductory n.), represents the errand as something incidental to his main task.

XIV. Asclepiades AP *5.169 (1 GP = Sens)*

Lovemaking provides the greatest pleasure. The poem is constructed as a priamel, a rhetorical structure in which the speaker enumerates a series of items as a foil to emphasize the main focus of his attention (see Race 1982). Its background lies in a series of poems in which a list of different types of excellence culminates in the superior pleasure to be derived from what one desires, as in an epigram inscribed on the Letoön at Delos (209 Preger ap. Arist. *Eud. Eth.* 1214a5–6; cf. xxxix, Thgn. 255–6, Soph. fr. 356; Sappho, fr. 16.1–4 treats what one desires as κάλλιστον). Asclepiades differs from those predecessors in making the greatest pleasure sexual. The epigram distinguishes pleasures that are restricted to a particular season from lovemaking, which is both sweeter and independent of time, and reframes pleasure as the product of a reciprocal activity from which both lovers derive satisfaction.

The importance of cool drinking-water to travelers and of fair weather to sailors appear explicitly or implicitly as themes of early epigrams (cf. VIII, IX, XXXII). Gutzwiller 1998a: 72 reads the poem as a programmatic assertion of preference for erotic themes and suggests that it may have introduced a collection of epigrams. This may be correct, but we do not know how Asclepiades "published" his poems.

1–2[57–8] A rewriting of Aesch. *Ag.* 899–901, where Clytemnestra calls Agamemnon "land appearing to sailors unexpectedly, a most beautiful day to see after a storm/winter (εἰσιδεῖν ἐκ χείματος), a flowing spring to a thirsty traveler (ὁδοιπόρωι διψῶντι πηγαῖον ῥέος)" (cf. Di Marco 2002); Asclepiades' version includes references to particular times of year (θέρους; ἐκ χειμῶνος . . . εἰαρινόν). **ἡδύ . . . ἡδύ:** anaphora with grammatical variation, with the adjective first agreeing with ποτόν in apposition to χιών (for the idea, cf. Theocr. 11.47–8), and then as predicate to ἰδεῖν. **χιών:** i.e. snow-cooled water (LSJ II). **ἐκ χειμῶνος** "at the end of winter," when sailing becomes safer. **εἰαρινὸν Στέφανον** "the Crown, sign of spring," a reference to *Corona borealis*, allegedly Ariadne's catasterized ivy crown (Arat. 71–3, Call. fr. 110.59–60, A.R. 3.1003–4), but the phrase also suggests a garland composed of spring flowers.

3[59] ἥδιον: the comparative, less usual than the superlative in the capping sections of priamels (Bundy 1986: 111 n. 33), is to be preferred to ἥδιστον as *difficilior* (since difficult readings are more easily corrupted). **ὁπόταν:** unlike the previously mentioned activities, the sweetness of lovemaking is not dependent on the season.

3–4[59–60] μία . . . χλαῖνα: clothes served as bedding, and the sharing of a cloak is a discreet way of talking about sex; e.g. Theocr. 18. 19 ὑπὸ τὰν μίαν ἵκετο χλαῖναν. The word order, with adjective and noun surrounding τοὺς φιλέοντας, mirrors the encircling of two bodies by one cover. **τοὺς φιλέοντας:** the masculine plural includes both sexes. **αἰνῆται Κύπρις:**

i.e. both parties reach orgasm; cf. 553n.   ὑπ' ἀμφοτέρων: that ἔρως and its satisfaction will be reciprocal and mutual is desirable in erotic relationships (e.g. Theocr. 2.143 ἐς πόθον ἤνθομες ἄμφω).

XV. Asclepiades AP 5.85 (2 GP = Sens)

An attempt at seduction. The speaker advises a girl not to conserve her virginity, since there is no pleasure after death. In providing advice on sexual conduct, the poem resembles some passages of sympotic poetry, especially elegy (e.g. Thgn. 1327–30), but it also draws on the motifs and language of funerary epigram. Its wit depends on the ambiguous relationship between amatory and funerary elements and also on the engagement with and subversion of the commonplace idea that like Persephone dead virgins become brides of Hades (cf. XXIX introductory n).

1[61] φείδηι παρθενίης: the speaker treats the girl's virginity as a commodity that she is preserving too frugally; for the idea, cf. Ameipsias, fr. 21.4–5 οὐ χρὴ πόλλ' ἔχειν θνητὸν ἄνθρωπον | ἀλλ' ἐρᾶν καὶ κατεσθίειν· σὺ δὲ κάρτα φείδηι.   τί πλέον; "what benefit will you receive?" a common colloquialism that picks up the economic connotations of φείδηι.

1–2[61–2] οὐ ... φιλέοντα "Nor going to Hades will you find anyone to love you." The phrase plays on the ambiguity of "Hades" as place and god. Despite the commonplace identification of dead girls with Persephone, this one will not find a lover in Hades, nor will the god Hades be her partner (cf. Cairns 1993, 1996a).   κόρη evokes Persephone's cult title Kore.

3–4[63–4] Pleasures are inaccessible to the dead, and must therefore be enjoyed during life (cf. Thgn. 567–9, Ameling 1985). The second couplet picks up the themes and language of the first (1 οὐ γὰρ ἐς Ἅιδην ~ 3 ἐν δ' Ἀχέροντι, 2 κόρη ~ 4 παρθένε); these links lend special weight to κεισόμεθα, which responds to the evocation of the "marriage to death" theme in the previous couplet.   τὰ τερπνά: cf. Mimn. fr. 1.1 τίς δὲ βίος, τί δὲ τερπνὸν ἄτερ χρυσῆς Ἀφροδίτης;   ὀστέα καὶ σποδιή evokes the language of epitaphs (e.g. CEG 545.1 ὀστέα μὲν καὶ σάρκας ἔχει χθὼν παῖδα τὸν ἡδύν; cf. Phoenix, fr. 1. 22–4 "I went to Hades bringing neither gold nor horse nor silvery wagon; I, the mitre-bearer, lie as dark ash").   κεισόμεθα: that the verb is appropriate to both sex and death contributes to the speaker's point: he and the girl will lie together joylessly in the future even if she does not sleep with him now. Cf. Di Marco 2002: 261–4.

XVI. Asclepiades AP 5.210 (5 GP = Sens)

On Didyme, an attractive woman with a dark complexion. The poem plays with the intersection of amatory and funerary language (cf. 1n.), but its more obvious background lies in the commonplace idea that lovers can see no imperfection in their beloveds (e.g. Pl. *Rep.* 474d–475a, *Phaedr.* 233a, 240e, Theocr. 6.18–19, 10.20). It illustrates this by having the speaker express his feelings in response to imagined objections to Didyme's complexion.

The speaker's heightened emotion in 1–2 (cf. 1 ὤμοι) contrasts with his more distanced recognition, in 3–4, that not all agree with his views. The first couplet casts the speaker as the passive victim and Didyme as the aggressor; in the second, the idea that he himself will warm her and thus bring out her beauty suggests that he is at least complicit in his own burning.

Cameron 1995: 236–7 notes that Ptolemy Philadelphus is alleged to have had a mistress called Didyme (Ptol. Euerg. II *FGrH* 234 F 4) and speculates that the poem is a homage to her.

1[65] τὠφθαλμῶι "with her eye," the conventional source from which desire emanates (cf. Mel. *AP* 12.109. 1–2; Propert. 1.1.1 *Cynthia prima suis miserum me cepit ocellis*). συνήρπασεν: with Didyme as subject, the verb reverses the more common use of forms of ἁρπάζω to refer to sexual violence toward a woman (e.g. *HHDem.* 3, 19) and evokes its regular application to sudden death (e.g. *SGO* 20/03/05.5 ἀπροϊδὴς νοῦσ[ό]ς με συνήρπασε, Magini 2000: 22–4). ὤμοι: expressions of lamentation are common in funerary contexts, too.

2[66] Cf. Pi. fr. 123.10–12 ". . . but because of her [Aphrodite], I melt (τάκομαι) like wax (κηρὸς ὥς) of sacred bees, stung by the sun whenever I look (ἴδω) at the fresh-limbed youth of boys." τήκομαι: literally "am turning to liquid," and thus appropriate to melting wax, but also regularly used to denote wasting away from love sickness (e.g. Pi. fr. 123.11, A.R. 3.1019–21, Theocr. 2.28–9, Call. fr. 75.14–15; cf. Ibyc. *PMG* 287.1–2). κάλλος ὁρῶν picks up 1 τὠφθαλμῶι.

3–4[67–8] Like Didyme, charcoal is dark, but when heated it takes on the color of roses, a proverbial image of beauty; for the conflation of fire and botanical imagery, see Borthwick 1969. The passage seems related to Theocr. 10.26–8, where the singer similarly responds to the criticism of Bombyca's dark complexion by citing violets and hyacinths; cf. 28 καὶ τὸ ἴον μέλαν ἐστί, καὶ ἁ γραπτὰ ὑάκινθος. Cameron 1995: 236 argues for the priority of the Theocritean passage on the grounds that it closely reworks Plato's account of the verbal contortions in which lovers engage (*Rep.* 5.474d–475a), whereas Asclepiades' does not.   **μέλαινα:** for the idea that dark skin was a defect in women, cf. Diph. fr. 91.3. There is no way to identify Didyme's ethnicity, since the word is used of a range of complexions, and the comparison to charcoal is probably inspired by the adjective.   **τί τοῦτο; καὶ ἄνθρακες** "so what? Charcoal <is> too."   **ὅτε . . . θάλψωμεν:** for the omission of ἄν in a generalizing temporal clause, cf. Smyth §2402.   **ῥόδεαι κάλυκες:** perhaps a sexual double entendre: roses, apart from their proverbial beauty (e.g. Men. *Mon.* 403), could serve as an image for female genitalia (cf. Sandin 2000).

XVII. *Asclepiades* AP *5.64 (11 GP = Sens)*

The speaker swears that Zeus will not drive him from his beloved's door. The epigram is thus a variation of a παρακλαυσίθυρον, in which a speaker appeals to his beloved for entry into his or her house or complains about being denied access; such poems represent themselves as a product of the κῶμος, a drunken revel following a symposium (cf. Copley 1956). Though these appear already in the archaic period (cf. Alc. fr. 374), Asclepiades' engagement with their conventions probably reflects the influence of New Comedy (cf. Thomas 1979).

Rather than address his beloved, the speaker complains to Zeus, who is directly named only in the final verse. His determination to abide any weather produced by the god resembles Prometheus' unwillingness to yield as it is depicted in the *Prometheus Bound* (1043–53; cf. Aesch. *Sept.* 427–31, 441–6, Eur. *Phoen.* 1172–6, of Capaneus), though read against the backdrop of Prometheus' principled resistance, the speaker's stance is undercut by the reality that he is merely vowing to persist in his κῶμος, and his promise to withstand even more terrible assaults appears naïvely grandiose.

Naïve, too, is his attempt to draw a connection between himself and the god by adducing the story of Danae, a myth that actually emphasizes the differences between them (5–6n.). Although "the lover's hope of entering the chamber is figured in Zeus's success in entering Danae's" (Garrison 1978: 43), only Zeus has the power to get access that way.

The diction includes grand and commonplace elements. The first couplet has rare words and a high-style periphrasis, the second several colloquial elements, and the third a lofty analogy cast in epicizing terms. See Tarán 1979: 51–114, with discussion of the epigram's substantial afterlife.

1–2[69–70] νεῖφε . . . νέφη creates a jingle framing the couplet. χαλαζοβόλει: first attested here. ποίει σκότος "make darkness!"; cf. Diph. fr. 91.3. σκότος is here third declension neuter.   αἶθε, κεραύνου: sc. με. αἴθω is commonly used of the passion engendered by Eros (Call. fr. 67.2, A.R. 3.296, Theocr. 2.40), and its use here implicitly justifies the speaker's resistance: nothing Zeus can do to him matches what Eros has done already.   πορφύροντ' . . . νέφη: a variation of the epic phrase πορφυρέηι νεφέληι (*Il.* 17.551, *HHMerc.* 217), of clouds cloaking gods.   ἐν χθονὶ σεῖε: an elaborate way to describe the rain of a thunderstorm, with ἐν probably a preposition in a "pregnant" sense ("shake all the dark clouds <so that they are> on the ground"; cf. A.R. 3.1308 τὸν δ' ἐν χθονὶ κάββαλεν); alternatively, ἐν . . . σεῖε could be taken as a unit in tmesis, which is, however, not elsewhere attested in Asclepiades. σεῖε refers to the rumble accompanying a thunderstorm; cf. Ar. *Birds* 1751, Soph. *Trach.* 1087–8 ἔνσεισον, ὦναξ, ἐγκατάσκηψον βέλος, | πάτερ, κεραυνοῦ.

3–4[71–2] For the lover's determination to continue even at the risk of death, cf. Thgn. 1327–8 ὦ παῖ, ἕως ἂν ἔχηις λείαν γένυν, οὔποτέ σ' αἰνῶν | παύσομαι, οὐδ' εἴ μοι μόρσιμόν ἐστι θανεῖν, Soph. *Ant.* 883–4, *OC* 1040–1. ἢν γάρ με κτείνηις: cf. *Il.* 20.186 αἴ κεν ἐμὲ κτείνηις.   τότε: i.e. "in that case."   ἀφῆις: ἀφίημι, "allow," with acc. and infin. is a prosaic usage (LSJ IV) and perhaps colloquial: the speaker addresses Zeus in informal, familiar terms (cf. next n.).   διαθῆις . . . χείρονα: διατίθημι κακόν (-ά) with the accusative of the person harmed is common in the Hellenistic *koine* (e.g. Jos. *Ant. Jud.* 2.242, Philo, *Jos.* 156) and is likely to be felt as colloquial.

5–6[73–4] That even Zeus and the other gods are susceptible to the power of Eros (cf. Lasserre 1946: 130–49) is often used to justify mortal sexual behavior (e.g. [Thgn.] 1345–50, Eur. *Tr.* 948–50, Ar. *Clouds* 1080–2, Isocr. 10.59, [Theocr.] 20.34–41). The specific reference is to the story of Danae, locked by her father in a bronze chamber, which Zeus entered as a shower of gold. As an exemplum (cf. Men. *Sam.* 592–5) the story is ironic, since it shows the weakness of the drenched, excluded lover in relation to the god, who easily slipped into Danae's chamber; that the god does so in the form of rain adds to the irony.   ἕλκει . . . πεισθείς: the opposition between the emotional compulsion (for ἕλκω, cf. *314*) and persuasion at the beginning and end of the verse highlights the difference between the speaker's and the god's experiences. Persuasion is commonly associated with Eros and Aphrodite (e.g. Hes. *WD* 73, Sappho, fr. 1.18–19, Ibyc. *PMG* 288, Pi. *Pyth.* 4.218–19).   ὁ κρατῶν: a rejection of Zeus's supreme κράτος (e.g. *Od.* 5.4, Hes. *Th.* 385–8, Theocr.

22.213). διὰ ... ἔδυς θαλάμων "slipped through (the walls of) the chamber," with the preposition used with the genitive of motion through a penetrable substance (LSJ 1.1, *hypoth.* ad [Eur.] *Danae* fr. 1132.4–8, p. 1030 Kannicht).   χαλκείων χρυσός: the juxtaposition evokes Glaucus' folly in exchanging his golden armor with Diomedes for bronze (*Il.* 6.235–6 τεύχε' ἄμειβεν | χρύσεα χαλκείων), and suggests both the lengths to which Zeus will go and the vast difference between divine and mortal lovers.   θαλάμων may denote any inner room, but its regular use in the sense "bridal chamber" (LSJ 1.2.a) makes it especially appropriate (cf. Pherecydes *FGrH* 3 F 10, Soph. *Ant.* 947, Paus. 2.23.7).

XVIII. Asclepiades AP 5.145 (12 GP = Sens)

A παρακλαυσίθυρον (cf. XVII introductory n.). The speaker (almost certainly a man, though the *Fragmentum Grenfellianum*, lyr. adesp. pp. 177–9 Powell, contains a woman's παρακλαυσίθυρον) addresses garlands he has left on his beloved's door after a κῶμος, urging them to stay fresh until the boy emerges. Excluded lovers regularly pledge not to abandon their station (e.g. 71–2); this speaker is leaving, and the garlands are to stay and represent him.

The poem falls into two groups of three lines – the first focused on instructions for the present and the second on the future; they are linked by the representation of tears as figurative rain (3, 6). The soaking of the garlands with tears inverts the conventional soaking of rained-on excluded lovers. Eventually, the boy will emerge for a reason other than granting the speaker access; what would under different conditions have been a source of triumph will result only in tears.

1[75] αὐτοῦ "here."   μοι "I beg you" (Smyth §1486).   παρὰ δικλίσι ταῖσδε: i.e. by the outer doors of the house (for δικλίς, cf. 587n.), the position currently occupied by the speaker.   κρεμαστοί: excluded lovers frequently leave the garlands they wore at the symposium by their beloveds' doors (cf. Theocr. 2. 153, Headlam on Herodas 2.34–7).

2[76] προπετῶς "hastily, prematurely," though the etymological connection to πίπτω "fall" is also active.   φύλλα τινασσόμενοι "causing your petals to scatter."

3[77] οὕς: i.e. the garlands.   κάτομβρα ... ἐρώντων "for the eyes of lovers drip with rain." Excluded lovers are often rain-soaked, but here the "rain" is a metaphor for tears, with which the speaker has thoroughly drenched (κατέβρεξα) the garlands. For the idea cf. the allegorization of rain as the tears of Zeus or the heavens ([Orph.] 407F Bernabé, Heraclitus, *All.* 42.5), an idea that apparently lies behind *Il.* 16.459–60; the metaphor does not seem to be attested of human tears before this passage. The jingly alliteration of κατέβρεξα – κάτομβρα . . . ὄμματ᾽ seems playful and at odds with the speaker's claim to be distraught. κάτομβρος is a prosaic adjective.

4[78] οἰγομένης . . . θύρης "when the door is opened."

5–6[79–80] The boy will experience metaphorically what many excluded lovers experience from literal rain in other poems.   **στάξαθ᾽:** στάζω is commonly used of shedding tears (e.g. Eur. *Ion* 876).   **ὑετόν:** apparently the first attestation of the noun in the metaphorical sense "tears" (cf. Lat. *imber*).   **πίηι** extends the association of tears and rain, since πίνω may be used of the earth absorbing rainwater (LSJ iii). The speaker, who previously had been at a symposium, imagines his beloved drinking at a later time.

XIX. *Asclepiades AP 12.46 (15 GP = Sens)*

A complaint to the Erotes. The intersection of amatory and funerary themes creates a pointed irony: the opening words resemble numerous epitaphs for young people (1n.), and the poem exploits the distance between the speaker's overwrought understanding of his condition and the pathos of premature death as it is depicted in epigrams; readers familiar with the conventions of funerary epigram understand, as the speaker does not, the difference between his pain and the permanence of death. Against this backdrop, the Erotes' cruel obliviousness about the consequences of their games contrasts with the way epitaphs treat the emotional burden left to surviving family members. The young man has little experience: the funerary elements of the poem show how naïve his desperation is.

The imagery of the second couplet derives from Anacr. *PMG* 398 ἀστράγαλαι δ᾽ Ἔρωτός εἰσιν | μανίαι τε καὶ κύδοιμοι, where ἀστράγαλαι is metaphorical. Eros and the Erotes are often depicted playing games such as knucklebones in literature and art (e.g. Anacr. *PMG* 358.1–4, A.R. 3.117–24, Pos. 135 AB, *LIMC* Eros nos. 755–78).

The fundamental idea is that the Erotes are unaffected by the sufferings they cause, and will continue to be unaffected by the speaker's misery and death (cf. Defreyne 1993: 207); the final line is thus an indictment of their irresponsible cruelty (cf. A.R. 3.129, 4.445–9) rather than "a calm realization of love's neutrality" (Garrison 1978: 58). But the apparent gravity is undercut by the cool playfulness created by the speaker's language (cf. 3–4n.).

1[81] Specifications of age are common in funerary poems (especially in epitaphs for those who have died young; cf. LVII), and the claim that the speaker is not even twenty-two would fit an epitaph spoken by the deceased. But unlike the speakers of such poems, who regularly express their regret for pleasures and opportunities lost, the speaker is already tired of living and is willing to die.   κοπιῶ ζῶν "I'm tired of living." κοπιάω, common in comedy and prose but absent from higher poetic genres, is probably colloquial.

2[82] ὥρωτες: crasis (ὦ Ἔρωτες). Though the plural of Ἔρως is common from the fifth century on, it here underscores the weakness of the speaker in the face of assault from multiple deities.

2–3[82–3] τί . . . τί . . . τί: the rapid anaphora reflects the speaker's disturbed state.   τί κακὸν τοῦτο; "Why this trouble?"   ἤν . . . τι πάθω: a common euphemism for "if I die" (cf. Eng. "if something happens to me").

3–4[83–4] δῆλον . . . | ὡς τὸ πάρος παίξεσθ' answers the speaker's rhetorical question τί ποιήσετε; since ὡς τὸ πάρος is always treated as a unit (e.g. Od. 24.486, Nic. Alex. 86), δῆλον here must be equivalent to δῆλον ὅτι (cf. Pearson on Soph. fr. 63, Theocr. 10.13). Line 4 is alliterative and assonant. Its words increase in length from one to four syllables; this progressive "racking up" of syllables ("rhopalic" structure) may suggest the scoring of the game of knucklebones (McKay 1968: 173); cf. Olson–Sens on Archestr. fr. 16. 6–9.   ἄφρονες "heedless(ly)," an otherwise unattested sense (cf. Theocr. 10.20 ὠφρόντιστος Ἔρως; contrast Pos. 135.2 AB, where the adj. has its usual sense "foolish"). Their insouciance makes them all the more dangerous.   ἀστραγάλοις: see 44n.

XX. Asclepiades AP 12.135 (18 GP = Sens)

Nicagoras' drunken behavior shows that he is in love. The opening comment on wine's capacity to expose emotions resembles passages of Theognis in which the speaker reflects on the effects of drinking. These archaic models express such observations as generalized truths (e.g. Thgn. 211–12, 497–8, 873–6) or as comments made during a drinking-party (Thgn. 487–8, 503–8); here, by contrast, the speaker reflects on a past event to illustrate his point. His location and audience are unspecified: he might be addressing the fellow symposiasts implied by 1 ἡμῖν or speaking to another group after the event.

The poem plays on the commonplace that drinking leads to the truth (cf. 1n.) by compelling people to speak openly about things that they would otherwise keep to themselves (e.g. Alc. fr. 366 οἶνος, ὦ φίλε παῖ, καὶ ἀλάθεα, Philoch. *FGrH* 328 F 170, Ephipp. fr. 25, Theocr. 29.1). The present situation is different: Nicagoras continues to deny the truth, but his drunken state has undermined his self-control so much that he behaves in revealing ways. Although the point of 2 πολλαὶ . . . προπόσεις seems initially to be that the nature and number of Nicagoras' toasts expose his feelings (cf. Giangrande 1968: 121), the behaviors described in 3–4 are all non-verbal. The implied situation resembles scenes from comedy (cf. Antiph. fr. 232 "Someone could hide all but two things: when he's drinking wine or when he's fallen in love. The result is that those who make toasts are particularly obvious," Men. *Mis.* 761–6, *Dis Ex.* 104–5 τί κατηφὴς καὶ σκυθρωπός, εἰπέ μοι; | καὶ βλέμμα τοῦθ᾽ ὑπόδακρυ;), and the overall effect is perhaps humorous (Garrison 1978: 59).

LXVI is a variation on the epigram; cf. LXIX introductory n.

1–2[85–6] The hexameter and the first part of the pentameter consist entirely of words beginning with vowels, followed by the alliterative πολλαὶ . . . προπόσεις.   **οἶνος ἔρωτος ἔλεγχος** "wine is the test (that exposes) love." For the language, cf. Eur. *HF* 162 ἀνδρὸς δ᾽ ἔλεγχος οὐχὶ τόξ᾽ εὐψυχίας. That wine reveals a person's true state is a traditional idea (e.g. Thgn. 500, Aesch. fr. 393, Theopomp. Com. fr. 33. 3).   **ἐρᾶν ἀρνεύμενον** . . . **προπόσεις:** the narrative illustrates and explains the opening generalization; ἐρᾶν corresponds to ἔρωτος, πολλαὶ . . . προπόσεις to οἶνος, ἀρνεύμενον . . . | ἤτασαν to ἔλεγχος. The absence of a connective between this and the previous sentence isolates the initial aphorism and presents it as a topical heading.   **Νικαγόρην:** a common name, perhaps ironic here, since it implies a persuasiveness at odds with his failure to deceive.   **ἤτασαν** "proved false." The compound ἐξετάζω is more common.   **αἱ πολλαὶ . . . προπόσεις:** cf. adesp. lyr. fr. 3.4–5, p. 181 Powell ὑπὸ γὰρ τῶν πολλῶν προπόσεων | [βακχεύων ἄ]λλομαι. The article suits either "our many toasts (as a regular part of the symposium)" or "his many toasts (to his beloved)."

3–4[87–8] The enumeration of the physical symptoms of love belongs to a tradition going back to Sappho (fr. 31). Here, the behaviors adduced as evidence of love sickness are not exclusive to it, though they are characteristic of the young lovers of comedy (above, introductory n.).   **καὶ γάρ** "for in fact" (cf. Denniston 108–9).   **ἐνύστασε** "he nodded his head" (cf. Pl. *Ion* 533a), an act which may be caused by drinking alone (e.g. Thgn. 503–4 οἰνοβαρέω κεφαλήν, Ὀνομάκριτε, καί με βιᾶται | οἶνος, Pl. *Symp.* 223d) and offers little proof of Nicagoras' emotional state.   **τι κατηφὲς | ἔβλεπε** "he had a quite downcast look" (cf. Eur. *Med.* 1012, *Heracl.* 633, Men. *Dis Ex.* 104–5). βλέπω with an adverbial internal accusative is characteristic of comedy and probably colloquial in tone (Olson on Ar. *Ach.*

95; *Frogs* 562 ἔβλεψεν . . . δριμύ). τι functions as an intensifying adverb; cf. Bulloch on Call. *h.* 5.58, Hopkinson on Call. *h.* 6.57.   χὠ σφιγχθεὶς . . . στέφανος "the garland bound (to his head)," a reference to the "pathetic fallacy" that the disintegration of garlands was an indication that a person was in love (cf. Ath. 15.669f–70e, citing Clearchus fr. 24; *319*n., Theocr. 7.63–4, Hangard 1971); but here the garlands may simply have slipped from Nicagoras' head because he nodded off.

ERINNA

Erinna's biography was controversial: ancient sources identified her birthplace as Teos, Tenos, Telos, Rhodes, or Lesbos (*Suda* η521; Steph. Byz. τ116) and placed her *floruit* variously in the time of Sappho (*Suda* loc. cit.) or (more plausibly) in the late fifth or early fourth century (Tatian 33.2) or in the mid fourth century (Eus. *Chron.* Ol. 107.1); cf. Neri 2003: 42–7. Her *Distaff*, a poem of some 300 hexameter verses in mixed Aeolic and Doric dialect, was admired by Hellenistic poets. In the poem, fragments of which are preserved on papyrus (*SH* 401), Erinna laments her friend Baucis' premature death; the funerary epigrams of Asclepiades and Leonidas map Baucis' fate on Erinna's own (cf. XXIX introductory n.). In addition, three epigrams attributed to her appear in the Greek Anthology via the *Garland* of Meleager, who includes her in his prefatory poem (*AP* 4.1.12; cf. *Suda* η521).

The authenticity of the epigrams is questionable. Two are epitaphs for Baucis, and it is easy to suppose that they derive from the same context in which Asclepiades and Leonidas composed tributes to Erinna and that they were assigned to her on the basis of their content: one (*AP* 7.710) assigns Tenos as a birthplace to Baucis and may readily be understood as engaging in a Hellenistic debate about Erinna's homeland; the other (*AP* 7.712) appears to quote the *Distaff*, as does Leonidas' epitaph for Erinna. The third (below), an ecphrasis of a painting, resembles the epigrams of Nossis, and was assigned to that poet by West 1977, who improbably argued that Erinna herself was a fiction and that the *Distaff* was the work of a male poet. The case against Erinna's authorship of the epigrams depends on the resemblance of the poem to later works and on assumptions about the development of ecphrastic epigram. It is inherently circular but has some weight (cf. *FGE* p. 155, Neri 2003: 85–8). *AP* 6.352 is thus included here either as a precursor to a form later developed by third-century poets or, more probably, as an elegant Hellenistic example spuriously assigned to Erinna; cf. Peirano Garrison 2017.

XXI. Erinna AP 6.352 (3 GP)

On a painting of Agatharchis. The basic theme – that the artist has created such an accurate representation of the subject that it seems to be
alive except for the absence of voice – is first attested at Aesch. fr. 78a.6–7
εἴδωλον εἶναι τοῦτ᾽ ἐμῆι μορφῆι πλέον, | τὸ Δαιδάλου μίμημα· φωνῆς δεῖ μόνον,
which similarly positions the work against a legendary artistic predecessor
(cf. 1n.). If the epigram is by Erinna, the development of the motif in
Hellenistic poetry (49–50, Herodas 4.32–4) may be due to its influence
(Gutzwiller 2002a, Skinner 2001). The language of the opening line creates slippage between two types of γράμματα, those of the painting and
of the poem in which it is described (cf. Männlein-Robert 2007: 255–6,
Tueller 2008: 142–5), and thus suggests the shared delicacy of both. The
subtle assimilation of artist and subject (cf. 1n.), artwork and poem, is
anticipated by the dictum attributed to Simonides (Plut. Mor. 346f) that
"a painting is a silent poem, a poem a chattering painting"; Erinna's poem
enacts the creation of voice that it describes.

1[89] ἀταλᾶν "delicate." Like ἀπαλός (with which it is sometimes confused
in manuscripts, as here; cf. Aesch. Pers. 537), ἀταλός is often applied to
young people (e.g. Od. 11.39), or to their state of mind (e.g. Il. 18.567,
Hes. Th. 989). Here it may imply artistic subtlety, but since it would apply
well to the virgin Agatharchis, it also assimilates the artist to the artist's subject (cf. LXXXII, LXXXIII introductory nn.).   **χειρῶν:** see 423n.   **τάδε
γράμματα** "these marks," including both the painting (cf. Theocr. 15.81–
3) and the poem itself.   **λῶιστε:** an affectionate and lighthearted
address ("my good man"), more common in prose than verse (e.g. Pl.
Gorg. 467b, Laws 1.638a; in poetry, Call. fr. 191.33).   **Προμαθεῦ:**
Prometheus is invoked as the paradigmatically wise (Thphr. fr. 50) figure
responsible for creating humans from mud and thus analogous to an artist; cf. Aesop 240 Perry; Philemon fr. 93.1; Men. fr. 508.5; in Hellenistic
art, he is often depicted in the process of forming individual people or
parts of the body (LIMC 80–112).

2[90] ἔντι: Doric third person plural of εἰμί.   **τίν:** see 293n.   **σοφίαν:**
the word may be used of both poetic (e.g. Pi. Isthm. 7.18, Call. fr. 1.18)
and artistic skill (e.g. Arist. Nic. Eth. 1141a9–12).

3–4[91–2] "To be sure, if the person who painted this maiden had added
a voice, truly she would be Agatharchis in her entirety." Contrafactual
conditions of this sort are an ecphrastic topos: e.g. Asclep. 21 "if wings
were added to you and there were a bow and arrow in your hand, not

Eros but you would have been inscribed as son of Cypris," Herodas
4.32–3.   **γοῦν** introduces evidence that confirms the preceding
assertion (Denniston 451); compare, in a parallel context, Herodas
4.32.   **ἐτύμως:** cf. *175*n. For "truthfulness" as a desideratum in art and
literature, cf. *418*n.   **ὅστις ἔγραψεν:** the speaker claims ignorance as
to the identity of the artist (cf. Herodas 4.21–2); the masculine relative
pronoun could refer to an artist of either sex.   **ποτέθηκ':** προστίθημι
and its intransitive complement πρόσκειμαι are standard words for adding
elements to a work of art; cf. *Il.* 18.379, Headlam on Herodas 4.60.   **ἦς:**
Doric = ἦν.   **ὅλα:** cf. Theocr. *496.*

LEONIDAS OF TARENTUM

Leonidas of Tarentum probably flourished in the first third of the third
century. Points of contact between his epigrams and one by Asclepiades,
for example, seem more likely to reflect borrowing from than by Leonidas
(cf. Sens on Asclep. 30). More than ninety poems are assigned to him in
the Anthology (with or without ethnic specification), and several more
name him as a possible author. Most of his extant compositions play on
the formal features of epitaphs or dedications, and in this sense his corpus resembles that of Peloponnesian epigrammatists such as Anyte (cf.
pp. 5, 55). A number of the epigrams focus on humble working people,
including herdsmen, hunters, and fishermen, as well as entertainers,
weavers, and the like, and on the broader theme of poverty. Several
poems reflect on the uselessness of wealth and prestige after death;
these moralizing poems have sometimes been associated with a Cynic
world-view (cf. Gutzwiller 1998a: 104–8, Solitario 2015), but the links to
Cynicism seem more conceptual than specific. Many epigrams exploit a
tension between humble subject matter and elevated language, including
numerous high-style compound adjectives, glosses, and other unusual
words, as well as alliteration and other forms of phonetic play. Leonidas'
work shares this tension with Theocritean bucolic, whose conventions he
sometimes seems to evoke (XXXII introductory n.). His metrical practice, too, resembles that of Theocritean bucolic in that his hexameters
are relatively more spondaic that most third-century hexameter, which
tends to be more dactylic than early epic and to avoid multiple spondees;
Theocritus' bucolic poems, though not his "epic" ones, are likewise more
spondaic than the contemporary norm (cf. Hunter 1996: 18–19).

XXII. Leonidas AP *7.655 (17 GP)*

A simple grave is sufficient. The epigram resembles epitaphs in which the
deceased provides biographical information, but the speaker proclaims

that he does not need or wish to be commemorated with an identifying monument; the commonplace wish (cf. 1–3n.) that the earth lie lightly on the dead person is converted into a reason to reject the burden of an elaborate memorial. The epigram is one of several poems on the vanity of material prosperity in life (cf. xxv introductory n.): in the final couplet, the speaker denies the traditional idea that posthumous commemoration is a compensation for death (3–4n.), and the implication is that things valued by the living are insignificant to the dead.

1[93] γαίης μικρή κόνις "a small dusting of soil," without a conspicuous burial mound. κόνις is used of the dirt covering a grave occasionally in pre-Hellenistic epitaphs (e.g. *CEG* 576.2, 657.8, 709.2) and commonly in Hellenistic literary epigrams.

1–3[93–5] ἡ περισσή . . . στήλη "a superfluous grave marker." The article is generalizing: Smyth §§1122–3. The semantic range of περισσός includes "unnecessary, superfluous" and "extraordinary," and the postponement of στήλη makes the phrase initially deceptive, since ἡ περισσή seems to stand in contrast to μικρή κόνις and to mean "an extravagant burial," though the noun suggests that the speaker is rejecting even a tombstone marking his name.   **ἐπιθλίβοι** "press upon," a deliberate reversal of prayers for the earth to rest lightly on a dead person (e.g. Eur. *Alc.* 462–3, *Hel.* 852–3); cf. 3 βάρος.   **πλούσια κεκλιμένον** "richly laid to rest" (cf. Eur. *Alc.* 56 πλουσίως ταφήσεται). For the language, cf. Zenod. *AP* 7.315.4 ἥσυχα κεκλιμένος, LSJ κλίνω II.3.   **σκληρὸν . . . βάρος** "a difficult burden for corpses"; cf. Luc. *DMort.* 29.2 τὸ βάρος τοῦ τάφου, Call. fr. 1.35–6.

3–4[95–6] The speaker provides his biographical information even as he rejects the importance of preserving one's identity after death (cf. *Od.* 24.93–4).   **γνώσοντ'** "will recognize"; cf. *CEG* 19.2 σῆμα τὸ σὸν προσιδὼν γνώ[σετ]αι ἢν[ορέαν].   **Ἀλκάνδρωι . . . Καλλιτέλευς:** these are not unusual names, but Calliteles, suggesting "Beautiful End," is ironic in a poem asserting the meaningless of a marked burial.   **τοῦτο τί** "what difference does it make?"; e.g. Asclep. 5.3 with Sens's note.

XXIII. Leonidas AP 6.657 (19 GP)

A request for passing shepherds to make an offering. The ποιμένες play the part of the ξεῖνοι or παριόντες who are typically urged to stop at a tomb. A Hellenistic epigram from Egypt (*IMEGR* 34) contrasts wandering herdsmen with the learned passerby who is asked to wish the dead woman well. For Leonidas' treatment of bucolic themes, see above p. 86 and XXXII introductory n. The relative length of the poem perhaps marks its affiliation with bucolic poetry.

1[97] ὄρεος ῥάχιν "mountain ridge" (cf. Hdt. 3.54.2, 7.216).   **οἰοπολεῖτε:** the verb (elsewhere at Eur. *Cycl.* 74) can mean both "walk alone" and "pasture sheep," since the Homeric adjective οἰοπόλος on which it is based is explained as meaning either "isolated" (οἶος) or "sheep-pasturing" (for οἶς as a by-form of ὄις, cf. Σ *Il.* 13.473, A.R. 4.1322); cf. *34*n., Rengakos 1994: 119, *LfgrE.* The word is picked up phonetically by ὄις at the end of line 2.

2[98] κευείρους (< καὶ εὐ-) "woolly." For the Ionic form of the adjective (Attic εὔερος, Soph. *Ajax* 297, Ar. *Birds* 121), e.g. Soph. *Trach.* 675, [Hp.] *Mul.* II 8.368.8–9 Littré. In an equivalent sense, Homer has ὄις λάσιος (*Il.* 24.125).   **ἐμβοτέοντες** "pasturing." The verb (βόσκω), restored here by Scaliger, is not elsewhere attested; it may have been created from the rare βοτέω (Nic. *Ther.* 394; cf. Hsch. β853).   **ὄις:** accusative plural.

3[99] πρὸς Γῆς: Earth is invoked in anticipation of the chthonic rites requested in 9–11.

3–4[99–100] χάριν . . . τίνοιτε: the phrase more commonly means "repay a favor" (e.g. [Aesch.] *Prom.* 985), but here seems to have the sense "do a favor."   **προσηνῆ** "kind."   **εἵνεκα** "in honor of," as e.g. *422* ἄγκειτ]αι Μουσέων εἵνεκα.

5–6[101–2] The bleating of sheep and the music of the shepherd replace the greeting and mourning usually requested in epitaphs; the ordinary activities of literary herdsmen (cf. Theocr. 6.8–9 κάθησαι | ἁδέα συρίσδων) are thus reframed as gifts to the deceased. The "pathetic fallacy" (*87–8*n.) is a fundamental feature of bucolic poetry; cf. Theocr. 1.71–5 with Hunter's note.   **ἀξέστοιο** "unpolished," in contrast to a wrought tombstone; e.g. Pi. *Nem.* 10.67 ξεστὸν πέτρον, of a grave stele.   **πρηέα** "softly" (neuter plural as adverb), qualifying συρίζοι.   **βοσκομέναις:** that shepherds play for their animals rather than for their own entertainment (subsequently a prominent feature of Longus' *Daphnis and Chloe*) is implicit in Theocr. 6.45, where heifers dance in response to herdsmen's song.

7[103] λειμώνιον ἄνθος: collective singular. The collocation appears at Aesch. fr. 374 (ἄνθεα λειμώνια).   **ἀμέρσας:** aorist participle of ἀμέργω "gather"; the more common form is ἀμέρξας.

8[104] χωρίτης "local resident," e.g. Aesch. *Eum.* 1035, Soph. fr. 226. Leonidas is fond of adjectives in -ίτης and -ῖτις, many of which are unique to him (e.g. *115* σχοινίτιδι, *118* συνεργατίνης).   **στεφέτω . . . στεφάνωι:** a *figura etymologica*; at Greek funerals, στέφανοι were regularly placed on the head of the deceased (Garland 1985: 26).

9[105] εὐάρνοιο "which has produced beautiful lambs." First here; in two later passages (Crates of Mallos, fr. 4 Broggiato, Myrinus *AP* 6.108.3) the adjective means "rich in sheep." καταχραίνοιτο "might be sprinkled," without the common implication of defilement (cf. uncompounded χραίνω at e.g. Bacchyl. 10.111). γάλακτι: milk could be offered to the dead (cf. Alc. *643–4*n.) and is regularly used in libations in bucolic poetry (Theocr. 1.143–4, 5.53–4).

10[106] ἀμολγαῖον "ready to be milked." Leonidas' usage makes clear the etymological connection to milking (< ἀμέλγω), but in its one other literary attestation (Hes. *WD* 590 μᾶζα . . . ἀμολγαίη) the word was variously interpreted by ancient critics to mean "dense," "best," "made of cheese," "having to do with shepherds," and "leavened with milk." μαστόν: ordinarily "breast," but here "udder," a rare usage (Eur. *Cycl.* 55, 207; cf. Call. *h.* 1.48–9, Arat. 163) that personifies the sheep.

11[107] κρηπῖδ᾽ . . . ἐπιτύμβιον "the base of the tomb that lies above the grave." Cf. Eur. *Hel.* 547 τύμβου 'πὶ κρηπῖδ᾽, Lyc. *Alex.* 882–3 τυμβείαν θ᾽ ὕπερ | κρηπῖδ᾽, *CEG* 819.6 κρηπῖδ᾽ ἐστεφάνωσ[ε]. The adjective is very rare in extant earlier literature (Aesch. *Ag.* 1547), but not morphologically unusual.

11–12[107–8] εἰσὶ θανόντων, | . . . κἂν φθιμένοις: even the dead feel gratitude; cf. *CEG* 640 "his wife and children erected the tomb over Echenicus, in case even one lying dead in Hades feels gratitude" (εἴ τις κἢν Ἄιδαι κειμένωι ἐστὶ χάρις). The repetition of εἰσί marks the speaker's insistence on a controversial point. ἀμοιβαῖαι . . . χάριτες: both "thanks felt in response," and "goodwill that brings a response" (cf. A.R. 3.82 ἀμοιβαίη χάρις). Leonidas and Apollonius reverse the formal relationship of adjective and noun in *Od.* 3.58 χαρίεσσαν ἀμοιβήν.

XXIV. Leonidas *AP* 7.295 (20 GP)

On a fisherman who after years of dangerous work died of old age in his hut, without family to bury him. The poem reflects a broader interest in fishermen in Hellenistic poetry (e.g. Theocr. 1.39–42, [21] *passim*, Leon. *AP* 6.4). It depends on the existence of numerous Hellenistic epitaphs for the graves of drowned sailors: the first two couplets set up an initial, false expectation that Theris, like many other sailors in epigram, has perished at sea. Instead, the remainder of the poem makes clear that he has reached the end of his life in the company of others like him, without a family to see to his burial. The ornate language, including several novel coinages, contrasts with the simplicity of Theris' life and the banality of his death. See further Bruss 2005: 97–101.

1[109] Θῆριν: cf. 254; here a speaking name suggesting hunting (for θηρεύω of catching fish, cf. Arist. *Hist. anim.* 603a7, Apollonides *AP* 7.702.1 ἰχθυοθηρητῆρα). **τριγέροντα** "tremendously old"; cf. Aesch. *Ch.* 314. τρι- is a general intensifier, probably colloquial in tone, despite the claim of *Suda* τ960 that the word refers specifically to three generations (i.e. ninety years). **κύρτων** "weels," funnel-shaped fish-traps woven from reeds; cf. Gow on Theocr. 21.11.

2[110] ζῶντα "making his living" (e.g. Thgn. 1156). **πλείονα:** the primary sense is "more often" rather than "better," since the point is that Theris regularly engaged in activities that put him in danger of drowning (cf. Call. fr. 178.33–4 ναυτιλίης εἰ νῆιν ἔχεις βίον· ἀλλ' ἐμὸς αἰὼν | κύμασιν αἰθυίης μᾶλλον ἐσωικίσατο), but the latter may remain operative. **αἰθυίης:** the comparison of a swimmer to the αἴθυια, probably the shearwater, has its roots in *Od.* 5.337; in Hellenistic poetry, the bird comes to be a "symbol of the restless and endangered sailor" (Kidd 1997: 293; cf. Arat. 296, Call. *Epigr.* 58.4 αἰθυίηι δ' ἴσα θαλασσοπορεῖ) and associated with death at sea (cf. Pos. 21 AB, *Suda* αι1155) and also with successful fishing (cf. Pos. 23 AB).

3[111] The asyndetic series of unusual substantives illustrating the variety of ways in which Theris catches sea creatures has an elevated stylistic register contrasting with his humble status. **ἰχθυσιληιστῆρα** "fish snatcher," only here, with the first element formed from ἰχθυσι-, by false analogy with the numerous adjectives in which the first element ends in -εσι- (K–B §340.12); cf. Philip *AP* 6.90.5 ὑδασιστεγῆ. **σαγηνέα:** accusative < σαγηνεύς "wielder of the seine net" (cf. Hegesippus *AP* 7.276.1). σαγῆναι were large nets capable of catching great numbers of fish. **χηραμοδύτην:** the noun χηραμός (lit. "hollow spot," cf. *Il.* 21.495) is used of the hiding places of a variety of creatures (cf. Hsch. χ410), and the novel adjective suggests that Theris did the dangerous work of diving to catch them one by one in their underwater lairs.

4[112] πολυσκάλμου . . . ναυτιλίης: a σκαλμός was the tholepin to which the oar was attached, and the point of the otherwise unattested epithet (varying the Homeric πολυκληίς "with many tholepins") is that Theris' sea voyages did not involve large, relatively safe, ships with many oars. **πλώτορα:** a novel variation of the more usual πλωτήρ, on the analogy of doublets like δωτήρ/δώτωρ.

5[113] ἔμπης: i.e. despite his risky profession. Ἀρκτοῦρος: here the star is a metonym for the bad storms which were closely associated with it: cf. Perses *189–90*n.; Plautus, *Rud.* 1–82. καταιγίς: see *195*n.

6[114] ἤλασε "smote." πολλάς ... δεκάδας: probably a metonym equivalent to τὸν τριγέροντα, to which it refers back, rather than (*pace* Bruss 2005: 98) an accusative of extent of time ("over the course of many decades"). For the language, cf. *CEG* 592.4 ἀριθμ[ή]σασ᾽ ἐννέ᾽ ἐτῶν δεκά<δ>ας, Call. fr. 1.6 τῶν δ᾽ ἐτέων ἡ δεκὰς οὐκ ὀλίγη.

7–8[115–16] The terrestrial death of a sailor, a well-developed theme in later epigram (e.g. Antip. Thess. *AP* 7.289, Flaccus *AP* 7.290, Secundus *AP* 9.36.3–5), is bathetic. καλύβηι σχοινίτιδι: a cabin with wattled walls, a typical fisherman's dwelling; cf. [Theocr.] 21.7 ὑπὸ πλεκταῖς καλύβαισι with Gow's note. σχοινῖτις (for σχοίνινος) occurs only here. λύχνος ὁποῖα | . . . σβεσθείς: the treatment of death as an extinguishing of light has its origin in the ubiquitous association of death with darkness (σκότος) and life with light (cf. Call. 273). Theris died of natural causes (αὐτόματος; cf. Dem. 18.205), just as an unattended lamp will eventually die out. For the metaphorical use of the passive of uncompounded σβέννυμι in the sense "die," cf. *IMEGR* 11.2; more commonly the compound ἀποσβέννυμι is used in related contexts (e.g. Eur. *Med.* 1218 χρόνωι . . . ἀπέσβη; cf. Antip. *AP* 7.303.4 κῦμα δ᾽ ἀπὸ ψυχὴν ἔσβεσε).

9–10[117–18] Having a tomb erected by one's surviving family is a consolation for the dead (e.g. *CEG* 640.1 σᾶμα γυνὰ καὶ παῖδες ἐπέστησαν, 703), and the implication is either that Theris never had a wife or children or that he has outlived them all. σῆμα . . . ἐφήρμοσαν: ἐφαρμόζω ordinarily is to fit one thing (accusative) on another (dative), but it is used absolutely here as a variation of verbs such as ἐπιτίθημι (cf. *CEG* 638, 647) and ἐφίστημι (e.g. *CEG* 640, 706). ὁμόλεκτρος, | . . . συνεργατίνης: the synonymous prefixes call attention to the contrast between the fellowship of a wife and that offered by colleagues. In antiquity, professional colleagues commonly contributed to the expense of burial or the erection of a funeral monument; cf. van Nijf 1997: 36–68. ὁμόλεκτρος is an adjective at Eur. *Or.* 476, 508, first here as a substantive meaning "wife." συνεργατίνης is also a novel word, formed on the model of the apparently Hellenistic ἐργατίνης (Theocr. 10.1, [21].3, A.R. 2.376). ἰχθυβόλων: the first attestation of ἰχθυβόλος as a noun (an adjective at Aesch. *Sept.* 131) equivalent to ἰχθυβολεύς (ps.-Hes. fr. 372.2, Call *h.* 4.15, Nic. *Ther.* 793). θίασος "professional association"; cf. Arnaoutoglou 2003: 60–70.

XXV. *Leonidas* AP *7.740 (75 GP)*

An epitaph for Crethon, a man rich in herds. The poem draws on the theme of wealth's uselessness after death (Thgn. 725–6, Theocr. 16.42, Phoenix fr. 1.22–4 Powell ἐγὼ δ' ἐς Ἅιδην οὔτε χρυσὸν οὔθ' ἵππον | οὔτ' ἀργυρῆν ἅμαξαν ὠιχόμην ἕλκων | σποδὸς δὲ πελλὴ χὼ μιτρηφόρος κεῖμαι). Unlike numerous other epitaphs in which the voices of the tomb and of the deceased are conflated (e.g. *CEG* 24), here the speaking stone carefully distinguishes itself from the honorand in the opening couplet, and this distinction sets up a reflection on the reality that death leaves even a once wealthy man only a small plot of earth. The humor of the poem, however, resides in Crethon's assessment of his wealth: though he equated it to Gyges', he was wealthy in animals and, even if objectively prosperous in that regard, rather different from the Lydian dynast. The final, pathetic explanation is thus a reflection on the vanity of wealth.

1–2[119–20] "I here (αὗτα) am a stone over Crethon, revealing his name, but Crethon is dust under the earth." The distinction between the dead man himself and the stone is emphasized by the repetition of the man's name in parallel positions of the hexameter and pentameter; cf., e.g., *CEG* 153 ἀντὶ γυναικὸς ἐγὼ Παρίου λίθου ἐνθάδε κεῖμαι | μνημόσυνον Βίττης.   Crethon is the name of a young son of a wealthy man killed along with his twin at *Il.* 5.541–53.   **λίθος:** as often, feminine when referring to a wrought stone; cf. Headlam on Herodas 4.21.   **ἐγχθόνιος σποδιά:** cf. Call. *149–50*, *SGO* 03/06/04.4 ὀστέα καὶ σποδιὴ κειμένη ἐνχθόνιος.

3–5[121–3] ὁ πρὶν . . . πρὶν | . . . πρὶν . . . πρίν: for the contrast between the dead man's former wealth and his current state, e.g. Phoenix fr. 1.16–24, a mock epitaph for the Assyrian king Ninus.   **Γύγηι παρισεύμενος** "equating his own wealth with (that of) Gyges." The Lydian king Gyges is a paradigm for extreme wealth already at Archil. fr. 19 and commonly thereafter, but Crethon's perspective on his own wealth is hyperbolic (though cf. Augeas at [Theocr.] 25.7–32). The contraction of ο + ο > ευ in the present participle (= παρισούμενος) appears to be a feature of Ionic (e.g. Hdt. 4.166.1); in the generally Doric context of the epigram it may be based by analogy on the fact that in both Ionic and Doric ε + ο > ευ (cf. μυθεῦμ'). **βουπάμων** "endowed with cattle" (< πάομαι, "acquire"), only here and in *148*; cf. *Il.* 4.433–4 ὥς τ' ὄϊες πολυπάμονος ἀνδρὸς ἐν αὐλῆι | μυρίαι ἑστήκασιν. **αἰπολίοις** "in flocks of goats." **τί πλείω μυθεῦμ';** cf. *Od.* 7.213 καὶ δ' ἔτι κεν καὶ πλείον' ἐγὼ κακὰ μυθησαίμην; 12.450 τί τοι τάδε μυθολογεύω; The statement reflects a common rhetorical strategy by which the speaker "breaks off" enumerating his honorand's accomplishments in order to avoid the audience's hostility (cf. Bundy 1972), but here the aposiopesis may have a specific, witty point: the speaker has enumerated Crethon's material wealth in diminishing order of agricultural value, moving from cattle to goats (cf. Berman 2005), and his silence allows him to avoid engaging in further diminuendo. πᾶσι "in all respects," parallel to αἰπολίοις (cf. βουπάμων). μακαρτός: a rare variant of μακαριστός, as if from unattested μακαίρω.

6[124] Similar expressions of lamentation are common in the final verses of epitaphs; cf. *41.* γαίης ὅσσης ὅσσον ἔχει μόριον "how little a portion of earth he possesses." A carefully constructed, chiastic expression concludes the poem with a rhetorical flourish.

XXVI. Leonidas AP *7.283 (63 GP)*

A complaint to the sea for having cast the speaker upon the shore. Though the opening reference to the sea's turbulence and the speaker's implicit but obvious hostility to it suggest that he has died in a shipwreck caused by a stormy sea, the circumstances of his death are unspecified. The theme of the poem is related to that of Asclep. 30 Sens and Pos. 132 AB, in which the speakers complain that the sea is too near the grave, but here the speaker has not been buried at all (cf. XLI). The language is notably epicizing (cf. 1, 3–4nn.), and the emphasis on the corpse's maltreatment in the water implicitly links its sufferings to those of Odysseus, whose experiences make him the most οἰζυρός of all men (*Od.* 5.105).

1–2[125–6] "Rough sea, why did you not spit me out, after I suffered grievously, far from the bare beach?" τετρηχυῖα θάλασσα: τετρηχυῖα is properly the intransitive perfect participle of ταράσσω, but it seems to have been connected by Hellenistic poets with τρηχύς, e.g. A.R. 1.1167, 3.1393, Nic. *Ther.* 267; the related expression τρηχεῖα θάλασσα appears at line end in the nominative at Leon. *AP* 7.665.7 and in the vocative at Asclep. 30.1 Sens. οὐκ: with ἔπτυσας. οἰζυρὰ παθόντα: the speaker's corpse has been damaged by its time in the water. οἰζυρός is characteristic of epic, and the phrase as a whole is Homeric in flavor (e.g. *Od.* 13.131 κακὰ πολλὰ παθόντα). ψιλῆς . . . ἠιόνος, i.e. a bare beach without vegetation; cf. 3–4n. The words recur in the same positions in the verse at Pos. 19.12 AB ψιλὴν μὴ φέρ' ἐπ' ἠιόνα, 93.4 ψιλὴν ἔκθες ἐπ' ἠιόνα. ἔπτυσας: the verb is regularly used, in both simplex and compounds, of the sea casting out flotsam or foam (e.g. *Il.* 4.426 ἀποπτύει δ' ἁλὸς ἄχνην).

3–4[127–8] "... so that Philleus, son of Amphimenes, would not, cloaked in the terrible darkness of Hades, be your close neighbor." σεῦ: governed by ἆσσον ἐγειτόνεον. The genitive is explained by the adverb, but it would be equally appropriate with γειτονέω alone (cf. Mel. *AP* 7.207.8 κοίτης γειτονέοντα). μηδ᾽, though strictly negating the participial clause, logically covers the entire clause (i.e. "so that I wouldn't be your neighbor even in death"). Ἀίδαο κακὴν ἐπιειμένος ἀχλύν "cloaked in the bad mist of Hades." Shipwrecked sailors are frequently naked (γυμνός; cf. *196*, Asclep. *40.3–4 with Sens's note); here the dead man is metaphorically clothed, in contrast with the bare beach on which he lies. The expression combines the Homeric representation of mist covering the eyes of a dying man (e.g. *Il.* 5.696 κατὰ δ᾽ ὀφθαλμῶν κέχυτ᾽ ἀχλύς) with the common metaphorical use of ἕννυμι and compounds of a body covered by earth (e.g. Pi. *Nem.* 11.16). The general shape of the expression resembles phrases such as μεγάλην ἐπιειμένον ἀλκήν (*Od.* 9.214, etc.); κακὴν ... ἀχλύν recalls *Od.* 20.357 κακὴ δ᾽ ἐπιδέδρομεν ἀχλύς, portending the suitors' death. Ἀμφιμένευς: genitive of Ἀμφιμένης. ἐγειτόνεον: imperfect indicative expressing purpose after an unfulfilled main clause (Smyth §2185c).

XXVII. Leonidas *AP* 7.455 (68 GP)

On a bibulous old woman's grave, above which a drinking cup has been placed. The κύλιξ takes the place of the oil flasks (λήκυθοι) commonly associated with funerary contexts. That women were fond of drinking was a widespread notion (cf. Anacr. *PMG* 427, Ath. 10.440e), and drunken old women were popular subjects in Hellenistic art (cf. Venit 1998) as well as in Old and Middle comedy (e.g. Pherecr. fr. 152, Ar. *Clouds* 555, *Thesm.* 735–8, Antiph. frr. 161, 163; cf. Arnott 1996: 503–4). This comic background is perhaps evoked by the iambic trimeter, and by language characteristic of dramatic poetry (cf. 4, 5, 6nn.). The poem falls into two groups of three lines: the first (1–3) describes the tomb, the second (4–6) Maronis' response to death. Neuters in apposition (3 γνωστόν, 6 ἕν) appear in the last line of each, and each concludes with a reference to the κύλιξ. These references provide crucial information: the identification of the object in the first case, the broader point to the poem in the second; though Maronis has left her surviving family penniless she regrets only that she has no more access to drink, since the cup laid out with her is empty. The opposition of ἐνδεεῖς βίου and ἡ κύλιξ κενή at the ends of 5 and 6 emphasizes the distortion of Maronis' priorities. The dialect seems to be Ionic, except for 4 γᾶς.

1[129] Μαρωνίς evokes Maron, the priest of Apollo said by Odysseus to have provided the wine with which he intoxicates Polyphemus (*Od.* 9.193–215) and frequently connected with wine thereafter (cf. Alexis fr. 113.2–3 with Arnott's note).   **ἡ πίθων σποδός:** probably "the ash of (a person who consumed) barrels of wine"; but the significance of this striking and initially obscure phrase emerges only in the final verses, which imply that Maronis' heavy drinking has left her family destitute: her ashes are all that is left (cf. Aesch. *Ag.* 435–6, Phoenix fr. 1.24).

2[130] γρηΰς: epic/Ionic form of γραῦς.

3[131] γνωστὸν . . . πᾶσιν "(a thing) recognizable to everyone," with the neuter adjective in apposition to 4 κύλιξ. The expression may mean that anyone who sees the monument understands what it signifies about Maronis' drinking rather than that the cup is well known; if so, it resonates against epigrams in which the speaker must puzzle out a monument's meaning; cf. cxxvi introductory n.   **πρόκειται** picks up κεῖται in 2 and evokes the laying out of the deceased that was a part of the Greek funeral (πρόθεσις: LSJ προτίθημι II, Garland 1985: 23–31), during which objects such as oil flasks were sometimes placed with the corpse.   **Ἀττική** perhaps hints at the poem's broader connection to Attic drama. It may suggest that Maronis was from Attica, though Athenian pottery circulated internationally.

4[132] στένει: more usually, the lamentation noted in epitaphs is that of a dead person's survivors.   **γᾶς νέρθεν:** a tragic phrase, occurring with the Doric form in a lyric context at Aesch. *Ch.* 40 and with an Attic/Ionic genitive at Eur. *Hec.* 791, *HF* 516, both in the same position in the trimeter as here.

5[133] ἔλειπεν ἐνδεεῖς βίου: that Maronis' family has been left economically destitute (for the language, cf. Xen. *Cyr.* 7.5.81) is a twist on the commonplace that the deceased has left survivors bereaved (cf. *Il.* 24.725–6, Andromache to Hector, κὰδ δέ με χήρην | λείπεις) or bequeathed them pain or consolations such as glory. GP suggest that she spent the family's fortune on drink.

6[134] ἐν . . . ἀντὶ πάντων: object of 4 στένει, in apposition to οὕνεχ' ("but (for) one reason alone, because . . .").   **κενή:** the punch line. The dead were commonly provided with offerings of wine and other substances (cf. Garland 1985: 114), but Maronis will not receive any from her impoverished family.

XXVIII. Leonidas AP *7.408 (58 GP)*

The tomb of Hipponax. Unless Theocr. *AP* 13.3 is older, this is the earliest in a series of Hellenistic epigrams honoring the sixth-century Ephesian iambographer (cf. Alc. *AP* 7.536, Philip *AP* 7.405, Rosen 2007), famous for his ferocious invective in response to perceived injury (*Suda* 1588). No details of an attack on his parents are extant, but the larger point of καὶ τοκεῶνε βαύξας (3) is that not even traditional figures of authority and respect were safe from his censure. Several passages of Hellenistic iambic poetry treat Hipponax as literary ancestor: Callimachus in his *Iambi* represents Hipponax as a literary ancestor and preceptor, and in Herodas' eighth *Mimiamb* Hipponax seems to have appeared to the poet in a dream (cf. Fantuzzi in Fantuzzi and Hunter 2004: 8–17, Klooster 2011: 49–53).

The opening request for the passerby to move on without disturbing Hipponax' "sleep" is a variation of the epitaphic *topos* in which travelers are asked to pause and greet or listen to the deceased. Hipponax is identified first metaphorically as a wasp, then by name; the second couplet picks up the elements of the first (1–2 ἐν ὕπνωι | . . . ἀναπαυόμενον ~ 4 κεκοίμηται . . . ἐν ἡσυχίηι) while introducing a canine metaphor (3 βαύξας). The wasp imagery is reactivated in πεπυρωμένα (5–6n.). The final couplet implies the vitality of his poetic legacy, here embodied in Leonidas' epigram; cf. "Simon." *AP* 7.25.9–10 (of Anacreon) μολπῆς δ' οὐ λήγει μελιτερπέος ἀλλ' ἔτ' ἐκεῖνον | βάρβιτον οὐδὲ θανὼν εὔνασεν εἰν Ἀίδηι.

1–2[135–6] ἀτρέμα "calmly," i.e. without making noise or engaging in the sort of conversations often requested by epitaphs.   τὸν ἐν ὕπνωι | . . . ἀναπαυόμενον plays on the commonplace representation of death as sleep (cf. *261*–2n.); Hipponax is finally resting his anger, but can still wake up to cause pain.   σφῆκ': the association of angry people with wasps (cf. Ar. *Wasps* 1060–1121) appears already in a Homeric simile (*Il.* 16.257–65, where the scholia note that part of the comparison depends on the Myrmidons' anger).

3–4[137–8] Reworked at Mel. *AP* 7.79.3–4 λάξ γὰρ καὶ τοκεῶνας, ἰὼ ξένε, δύσφρονας ἄνδρας | ὑλακτεῖν.   ἄρτι . . . | ἄρτι pointedly locates the speaker's words close to the time of the poet's death and thus implies their antiquity. If the text is correct, the unusual anaphora within a single sentence underscores the speaker's anxiety about reawakening freshly calmed anger, but the repetition of the word at the heads of two successive verses perhaps suggests corruption.   τοκεῶνε: dual accusative, i.e. "his mother and father," restored by Headlam 1901 from the corrupt variants of the manuscripts. τοκεών is an old Ionic word (Heraclitus, fr. 74, Call. fr. 191.72) appropriately used in connection with Hipponax.   βαΰξας "barking at." For the verb, cf. Heraclitus, fr. 97, Headlam on Herodas 6.13. The image of the iambic poet as simultaneously a wasp and a dog has a parallel in Call. fr. 380 (Archilochus) εἷλκυσε δὲ δριμύν τε χόλον κυνὸς ὀξύ τε κέντρον | σφηκός, ἀπ' ἀμφοτέρων δ' ἰὸν ἔχει στόματος.   θυμὸς ἐν ἡσυχίηι: a pointed juxtaposition of Hipponax' anger (θυμός) and his current calm state.

5–6[139–40] πεπυρωμένα . . . οἶδε: the participle, here used in its common metaphorical sense "fiery," is ordinarily used of people rather than language, but οἶδε suggests that ῥήματα is a personified stand-in for Hipponax himself.

XXIX. Leonidas AP *7.13 (98 GP)*

On Erinna, snatched by Hades for marriage. The poem is one of several Hellenistic epigrams honoring her (cf. p. 84, Asclep. 28 with Sens's note, Neri 2003). The opening implicitly associates the virgin (παρθενικήν) Erinna with Persephone by closely reworking the opening of the *Homeric Hymn to Demeter*, where Persephone is abducted as she gathers flowers. The poem concludes with the quotation of a line that is here attributed to Erinna and that in an epigram ascribed to her appears as a comment on the death of Baucis. The quotation creates a parallelism between Erinna and her honorand but enacts the survival of Erinna's words beyond the grave.

The poem is attributed in the manuscript to "Leonidas or Meleager" (who at *AP* 4.1.1–4 describes his own project in terms similar to those of 1–2). The manuscripts vary between Doric and Attic/Ionic forms, though a consistent Doric coloring seems likely; the *Distaff* was composed in a mixture of Aeolic and Doric.

1–2[141–2] νεαοιδὸν . . . Μουσέων ἄνθεα: cf. Pi. *Olymp.* 9.47–9 ἔγειρ' ἐπέων σφιν οἶμον λιγύν, | αἴνει δὲ παλαιὸν μὲν οἶνον, ἄνθεα δ' ὕμνων | νεωτέρων, where the point is that newer songs are preferable (cf. *Od.* 1.351–2). The *hapax legomenon* νεαοιδόν suggests Erinna's youth ("a young singer") and also the superior quality of her poetry ("a singer of new songs"), cf. *343*, Neri 2003: 193.   ὑμνοπόλοισι "poets," without implying a particular genre; cf. Emped. fr. 146, Nic. *Alex.* 629.   μέλισσαν: poets are commonly represented as bees (e.g. Pi. *Pyth.* 6.52–4, 10.53–4, Pl. *Ion* 534b λέγουσι . . . οἱ ποιηταὶ ὅτι . . . δρεπόμενοι τὰ μέλη ἡμῖν φέρουσι ὥσπερ αἱ μέλιτται, Theocr. 7.78–85). This is connected to the idea that good poetry, like honey, is "sweet" (Σ^AbT *Il.* 2.87). Possibly Erinna used the image of her own work in the *Distaff* (cf. adesp. *AP* 7.12.1, Asclep. 28.1 Sens γλυκὺς Ἠρίννης . . . πόνος). **Ἤριννᾰν**: the name derives from Hera and seems originally to have been aspirated; the psilotic form would then reflect the tradition associating her with Aeolic Lesbos; cf. Neri 2003: 35–7. **δρεπτομέναν**: cf. Ar. *Frogs* 1300 λειμῶνα Μουσῶν ἱερὸν . . . δρέπων, Pl. *Ion* 534b.

3–4[143–4] The second couplet, framed by references to Hades, with variation on the form of the name (Ἀίδας . . . Ἀίδα; cf. Leon. *AP* 7.67. 1, 7), conflates two motives for Erinna's premature death: Hades' interest in marriage and his jealousy. **Ἀίδας . . . ἀνάρπασεν**: cf. *HHDem.* 2–3 (Persephone) ἣν Ἀιδωνεὺς | ἥρπαξεν. **ἔμφρων** entails both "with good sense" and "while still alive" (cf. Soph. *Ant.* 1237). **εἶπ' ἐτύμως**: the insistence on the truth of the embedded quotation resembles, e.g., 259 πανάληθες ἔπος; contrast Leon. *AP* 7.273.6 ψευστὴς δ' οὗτος ἔπεστι λίθος. For the programmatic value of "truthfulness," cf. *418*n. **βάσκανός ἐσσ'**: the same words are used of the death of Baucis, the honorand of the *Distaff*, in an epigram attributed to Erinna, *AP* 7.712; both instances may well derive from the *Distaff* (for discussion, cf. Neri 2003: 89). If Erinna used the phrase of Baucis' death, the present passage creates a parallelism between the death of the poet and that of her honorand. Divine *inuidia* is sometimes mentioned in epitaphs (e.g. *CEG* 635.4, *IMEGR* 64.5–6 (σε) ἄρπασε Βασκανίη, *GVI* 1941.3), but the word may also evoke the *topos* of literary envy directed at a poet (cf. 277–8n., Sens 2018: 105–8).

XXX. Leonidas *AP* 9.719 (88 GP)

On Myron's statue of a cow. Myron of Eleutherae, on the border of Attica and Boeotia, was probably active in the first half of the fifth century; cf. Stewart 1990: 1.255–6. His bronze sculpture of a cow, dedicated on the Athenian Acropolis, was seen there by Cicero (*Verr.* 4.60); later it was moved to Rome (Tzetzes, *Chil.* 8.194). Its realism became a commonplace in Hellenistic epigram: the Greek Anthology preserves thirty-six poems on the subject (*AP* 9.713–42, 793–8; cf. Fuà 1973, Speyer 1975, Lausberg 1982: 223–37, Laurens 1989: 83–5, Gutzwiller 1998a: 245–50, Squire 2010); another is preserved in the Milan Posidippus. The gusto with which Hellenistic epigrammatists praised the cow reflects their engagement with their predecessors' work more than it does the statue's impact: Cicero (*Brut.* 18.70) notes that Myron's sculptures did not achieve "full naturalness"; cf. Pliny, *NH* 34.57, Ridgway 1981: 160.

This epigram may be the earliest in the series. As on many inscribed statue bases, the cow speaks in the first person, but here she rejects the information normally provided by the inscription (whether or not one really accompanied Myron's statue is irrevelant). Her explanation of how she came into existence thus represents a "better" alternative to the epigrammatic claims that one must imagine were made by the statue base. For discussion, see Gutzwiller 1998a: 247.

The epigram is in Doric, though any inscription originally accompanying the cow would probably have been in Attic. Leonidas' poem seems to have influenced both the dialect and the length of subsequent epigrams.

1[145] οὐκ ἔπλασέν με Μύρων: inscriptions on statue bases commonly state "so-and-so made (me)," usually with the verb ἐποίησε (με)," though ἔπλασε "sculpted" appears at *IG* XII.4 972.4 (*ca.* 225–200 BCE) ἔπλασε Λύσιππός με ὁ νέ[ος]. Here the cow rejects the sort of claim made by other statues. **ἐψεύσατο:** i.e. it is false to say that the statue is an artifact. Appraisals of art in Hellenistic poetry regularly associate realism with truthfulness (cf. *417–19*n., Theocr. 15.82–3, Herodas 4.72–3 ἀληθιναὶ . . . αἱ . . . χεῖρες | ἐς πάντ' Ἀπελλέω γράμματ'), but here the claim of falsehood is based paradoxically on the cow's being too "true" to be a sculpture. **βοσκομέναν δέ:** cf. the Homeric line end βοσκομενάων (e.g. *Il.* 5.162).

2[146] ἐξ ἀγέλας ἐλάσας: a reversal of *Il.* 19.281 εἰς ἀγέλην ἔλασαν. **βάσει λιθίνωι:** reference to the statue base and the material from which it was made picks up the play with inscriptional language in 1. The dative is probably local ("bound to a statue base") rather than instrumental ("bound by means of a statue base"); cf. Soph. *Ajax* 240 κίονι δήσας. The adjective more commonly has three terminations.

XXXI. Leonidas AP 6.263 (49 GP)

On the skin of a lion killed after it has eaten a calf. The use of demonstrative τοῦτο in 1 is familiar from numerous votive epigrams, but the poem contains no explicit reference to a dedication and is instead constructed as a narrative account of the killing of the animal. Lions probably existed in some parts of mainland Greece and Macedonia in the Hellenistic period, though probably not in Leonidas' native Sicily (cf. Hunter on Theocr. 1.71–2); the event described here is in any case a literary fiction evoking Homeric lion similes, which regularly describe attacks on domestic stock and responses to them.

1[147] A carefully patterned line, with nouns and their modifiers in inter-locking order. πυρσῶ: the conventional color of lions (e.g. Aesch. fr. 110, Eur. *HF* 361–3, Arist. *Gen. an.* 785b17). Such "more severe" (see Introduction section 4g) Doric forms of the genitive singular (= ου) are common in literature (Pindar, Theocritus), though not universal in Leonidas' Doric poems (e.g. *AP* 7.463.2). ἀπεφλοιώσατο "stripped (like) bark."

2[148] Σῶσος: the name (< σώζω; Hdn. *De pros. cath.* 1.207 Lentz, "Simon." *AP* 6.216) suits a cattle-owner who has killed the predator which attacked his herd. βουπάμων: see *121–3*n.

3[149] ἄρτι: with the following participle. In sepulchral epigrams, refer-ence to activities in which the deceased was "just recently" engaged some-times suggests the suddenness of death and fragility of life; e.g. Diosc. *AP* 7.167.5–6, adesp. *AP* 7.12.1–3. καταβρύκοντα "while devouring," a verb perhaps with colloquial resonance (despite Nic. *Ther.* 675), given its initial appearance in Hipponax (fr. 26a.1) and its frequent use in com-edy. εὐθηλήμονα "well suckled," only here; a development of εὐθηλής, used of cattle at Eur. *Ba.* 737, *IA* 579.

4[150] The diction evokes epic. οὐδ' ἵκετ(ο) is a Homeric clause opening (*Il.* 11.352, *Od.* 15.246 οὐδ' ἵκετο γήραος οὐδόν). ξύλοχος frequently refers to the haunts of wild beasts, including lions, in Homeric similes (cf. *Od.* 4.335, 17.126), though in early epic animals regularly emerge "from" the woods (*Il.* 11.415, 21.573, ἐκ ξυλόχοιο, always at line end): Leonidas reverses the direction of movement. μάνδρας "pen." The noun occurs occasionally elsewhere in Hellenistic poetry (Theocr. 4.61, Call. *h.* 6.105) and is common in Hellenistic prose.

5[151] ἀπέτισεν . . . αἷμα "paid the penalty in blood."

6[152] ἀχθεινὰν δ' εἶδε βοοκτασίαν "and he came to regret his cattle kill-ing," a common use of ὁράω (e.g. *Od.* 17.448, Aesch. *Sept.* 883, Eur. *Supp.* 832–3). In similar expressions, the adjective modifying its object is more often πικρός; a different variation appears at Lyc. *Alex.* 1107 λυπρὰν . . . εἰσιδοῦσ' οἰκουρίαν. ἀχθεινός appears first in Euripides (*Hipp.* 94, *Hec.* 1240). βοοκτασία is a Hellenistic formation (A.R. 4.1724, Antip. *AP* 6.115.8), on the model of *Il.* 5.909 ἀνδροκτασιάων.

XXXII. Leonidas APl 230 (86 GP)

The speaker urges a traveler not to drink from the nearby muddy spring, but to continue to a limpid stream. The poem probably plays on epigrams that give instructions on arriving at a sacred place; cf. *SGO* 01/01/03, 01/12/08 (both Hellenistic). Here the addressee is directed to a *locus amoenus*, and the point depends on the existence of epigrams inviting a traveler to rest (e.g. Anyte VIII). The tone is playful: the speaker does not, as elsewhere (e.g. Theocr. 1.12–14, 20–2), invite his interlocutor to join him in an idealized spot, but rather urges him to visit a place from which he marks his distance (1–4 ὧδε . . . κεῖσε). In this sense, the poem may both endorse a "bucolic" poetic mode and hint at its artificiality by contrasting an idealized countryside with the less pleasant one in which the speaker is actually located; cf. Sens 2006: 149–54.

1[153] ἐπ' οἰονόμοιο "in a sheep-pasturing (place)"; cf. *34*n. περίπλεον ἰλύος "completely full of mud," unlike the pure springs which typically flow in *loca amoena*; cf. Theocr. 22.38 ὕδατι . . . ἀκηράτωι, Call. *h.* 6.28.

2[154] χαραδραίης: perhaps a unique instance of the word as a substantive (=χαράδρη), rather than adjectival (with 1 ἰλύος); cf. *285*Γαληναίη. A χαράδρη is a raging torrent, often associated with loud and roaring sounds and with the great destructive force of nature; cf. *Il.* 16.391 μεγάλα στενάχουσι ῥέουσαι, Ar. *Peace* 757 φωνὴν δ' εἶχεν χαράδρας ὄλεθρον τετοκυίας. θερμόν: sc. ὕδωρ; cf. Ar. *Clouds* 1044. ὁδῖτα: usually in such addresses the traveler is asked to pause (e.g. *37–8*); here he is encouraged to keep moving. The noun was a Homeric hapax (*Od.* 23.274) and became popular in Hellenistic poetry (e.g. Theocr. 7.11).

3[155] μάλα τυτθόν "a very short distance." δαμαλήβοτον "grazed by cows," only here.

4–6[156–8] The spring to which the speaker directs the addressee is cool and pleasantly gurgling, conventional characteristics of water in *loca amoena*; cf. Call. *h.* 6.28 with Hopkinson's note, Anyte *APl* 228.3 πίδακά τ' ἐκ παγᾶς ψυχρὸν πίε. The heavy alliteration of κ and π in 4–5 may suggest the gurgling (κελαρύζον) of the brook. ποιμενίαι πίτυϊ: the pine tree is a feature of the countryside in which literary herdsmen work (cf. Theocr. 1.1), and the epithet simultaneously suggests "used by shepherds" (cf. Theocr. 1.22–3 ὁ θῶκος | τῆνος ὁ ποιμενικός) and "featuring in bucolic poetry"; cf. Sens 2006: 151–2. κελαρύζον . . . διὰ πέτρης: cf. Sappho fr. 2.5, Theocr. 1.7–8 ἅδιον, ὦ ποιμήν, τὸ τεὸν μέλος ἢ τὸ καταχὲς | τῆν' ἀπὸ τᾶς πέτρας καταλείβεται ὑψόθεν ὕδωρ, 7.136–7 τὸ δ' ἐγγύθεν ἱερὸν ὕδωρ | Νυμφᾶν ἐξ ἄντροιο κατειβόμενον κελάρυζε. εὐκρήνου: elsewhere only at Call. fr. 75.72.

XXXIII. Leonidas AP 9.99 (32 GP)

A vine grazed by a goat promises vengeance. The same story appears in the *Aesopica* (374 Perry), and it is likely that Leonidas has reworked a popular fable in the manner of a miniature Hellenistic "epyllion" framed in elevated and epicizing language (cf. 1, 3nn.). The epigram appears to have been influential: it resembles and is probably the model of adesp. *APl* 17, where the grazing of goats leads to the bloodying of Pan's altars (cf. 1 ἄπυε, 5 πόσις αἰγῶν); the final couplet is reworked at Ov. *F.* 1.357–8 (cf. Virg. *Georg.* 2.380–1) and appears on a fresco showing a goat eating vine leaves in a house on the Via Stabiana in Pompeii; the last pentameter is taken over verbatim at Euenus *AP* 9.75.2.

1[159] ἴξαλος: the collocation of the adjective with εὐπώγων ("having a good beard") may suggest that Leonidas is endorsing the ancient interpretation "fully grown" for its unique Homeric attestation at *Il.* 4.105 (of a wild goat), where the scholia offer other possibilities, including "bounding" and "impetuous."   εὐπώγων: elsewhere of goats at Leon. *AP* 9.744.4, Herodas 8.17, Nonn. *Dion.* 19.61.   αἰγὸς πόσις: i.e. τράγος. Periphrases based on familial relationships are extremely common (cf. *167–8*n.), but the present formulation (cf. [Theocr.] 8.49 αἰγῶν ἄνερ, adesp. *APl* 17.5) is deliberately playful; cf. Lyc. *Alex.* 750 τῆς κηρύλου δάμαρτος (i.e. the halcyon).   ἕν ποτ᾽ ἀλωῆι: the word order and postponement of ποτε most closely resemble those of Call. fr. 230 (1 Hollis) Ἀκταίη τις ἔναιεν Ἐρεχθέος ἕν ποτε γουνῶι, though similar phrases appear at the opening of other Hellenistic narratives: e.g. Call. fr. 194.6 ἕν κοτε Τμώλωι, *h.* 5.57, Theocr. 18.1 ἕν ποκ᾽ ἄρα Σπάρται.

2[160] τοὺς ἁπαλούς: tender, potentially grape-bearing growth (cf. 4 καρποφόρον), not old woody stems.

3[161] ἔπος . . . τόσον: an unusual variation of the common Hellenistic speech introduction τοῖον ἔπος (e.g. A.R. 1.277, Call. *h.* 4.265), with the quantitative adjective calling attention to the paradoxical contrast between the physical destruction of the vine and sound of the voice.   ἐκ γαίης: only the vine-stock remains.   ἄπυε: *sc.* ἡ οἴνη. Just as the grammatical subject is invisible, so too the vine speaks but is nowhere to be seen.

3–4[161–2] The striking alliteration of κ and γ heightens the intensity and may sound harsh and menacing.   κλῆμα τὸ καρποφόρον: i.e. a shoot with the capacity to bear fruit; the adjective's full point emerges only in the final line.

5[163] γλυκύ νέκταρ: taken from *Il.* 1.598 οἰνοχόει γλυκύ νέκταρ, where Hephaestus serves nectar to the gods as if it were wine; the Hellenistic treatment of wine as νέκταρ (e.g. Call. fr. 399.2, Nic. *Alex.* 44) is an easy extension. **νέκταρ ἀνήσει:** the grapevine speaks as if it were the direct producer of wine, though it will actually produce grapes. For the verb in an agricultural sense, cf. *HHDem.* 332 καρπὸν ἀνήσειν.

6[164] ὅσσον ἐπισπεῖσαι σοί "enough (wine) for me to pour a libation over you": cf. LSJ ὅσος IV.1.

MOERO

Two poems are attributed to Moero, whose name is sometimes given as Myro, though the short first syllable of the latter does not fit the meter of *AP* 4.1.5, where Meleager associates her with Anyte and Sappho. According to the *Suda* (which calls her Myro), she was from Byzantium, author of "hexameters, elegy, lyric" (μ1464), and mother of the tragedian Homerus (0253; σ 860; μ1464 makes her his daughter), a member of the tragic Pleiad, and flourished around 284–281 BCE. If this information is reliable, Moero would belong to the first generation of Hellenistic epigrammatists, though if, as seems to be the case, XXXIV is related to Anyte III, Moero is more likely the borrower.

XXXIV. Moero AP 6.119 (1 GP)

On a cluster of grapes lying in Aphrodite's temple. The epigram plays on the intersection between the conventions of funerary and dedicatory epigram (cf. 1n.), and evokes the funerary *topos* emphasizing the permanent separation of a dead youth from his or her parents (*pace* Cairns 2016: 341–4, who reads it as an extended metaphor for the separation of a newly married girl from her mother). The simple subject matter contrasts with the high-style language in 2 and 4; the second couplet resonates bathetically against Odysseus' failed attempts to embrace his mother in the *Odyssey*, and more generally against the death of children in epigram.

1[165] κεῖσαι: a play on the senses "you are dedicated" (= ἀνάκεισαι) and "lie dead" (cf. e.g. *130*); cf. Tueller 2008: 95–6. The first use is implied by the location, the inner recess of Aphrodite's temple, but the second is picked up in the next couplet, where the grape-cluster is treated as if a dead youth. There is a general resemblance to Achilles' speech over the body of Iphition at *Il.* 20.389–92 (Pelliccia 1995: 169 n. 106). χρυσέαν ὑπὸ παστάδα: a παστάς is an open portico or porch, and the point is apparently that the grapes have been left in the πρόναος of Aphrodite's temple (cf. Hegesippus *AP* 6.178.2 = *HE* 1902 with Gow ad loc.). The adjective is commonly used of Aphrodite herself; its transference to her temple is facilitated by the fact that the houses of the gods on Olympus are conventionally described as golden (e.g. *Il.* 13.22, Asclep. *34.2 Sens = Pos. *126.2 AB Κύπριδος ἐκ χρυσέων . . . θαλάμων).

2[166] Διωνύσου . . . σταγόνι: a "dithyrambic" periphrasis for wine; for σταγών, cf. Ephipp. 29 πολλὴ δὲ Λεσβία σταγὼν ἐκπίνεται. The phrase is ironic in context, since the cluster will never yield wine; it thus anticipates the pathos of loss and unrealized possibility developed in 3–4.

3–4[167–8] That the deceased man's family will no longer receive him home (e.g. *Il.* 11.452–3, Pelliccia 1995: 162–3) is a commonplace, but the passage has more specific roots in the encounter between Odysseus and his mother at *Od.* 11.211, with κλῆμα taking the place of the phonetically similar χεῖρα; for the embrace no longer available to the parent, cf. 9n. **μάτηρ:** the poetic image of grapes as children of the vine (cf. Archestr. fr. 37.2 with Olson–Sens ad loc.) is deployed to cast the plant as a grieving parent. **ἐρατόν** entails both "lovely" and "beloved." **φύσει ὑπὲρ κρατός:** cf. "Simon." *AP* 7.24.7–8, where the speaker hopes that grapes will grow above the head of the dead Anacreon, κἠν χθονὶ πεπτηὼς κεφαλῆς ἐφύπερθε φέροιτο | ἀγλαὸν ὡραίων βότρυν ἀπ᾽ ἀκρεμόνων. **νεκτάρεον πέταλον:** the adjective may be applied to sweet-smelling flowers (cf. *Cypria* fr. 4.4–5 ῥόδου τ᾽ ἐνὶ ἄνθεϊ καλῶι | ἡδέι νεκταρέωι, Pi. fr. 75.15), but is here loosely used of the grape leaf on the basis of the common association of wine and nectar (e.g. *Od.* 9.359, Eub. fr. 121.2, Call. fr. 399.2).

NOSSIS

The Anthology ascribes eleven epigrams to Nossis; the lemma ὡς Νόσσιδος of another (*AP* 6.273) seems a stylistic observation rather than an attribution. Nossis was from Epizephyrian Locri in Southern Italy and must have been active before the second quarter of the third century, since she was mentioned by Herodas (6.20–36, 7.57–8). One epigram (*AP* 7.414) purports to be for the tomb of Rhinthon, an author of "phlyax plays" (Southern Italian burlesque dramas; cf. Taplin 1993) who flourished under Ptolemy I (*Suda* ρ171). Several of her epigrams record fictive dedications by women or describe artistic representations of them. The use of the metronymic ἁ Κλεόχας at *AP* 6.265.4 may reflect a female linguistic practice; for the imitation of female speech, see e.g. Asclep. 19.1 with Sens's note. It has been argued (cf. esp. Skinner 1991) that Nossis' epigrams were designed for a private circle of female readers, but this does not account for the way in which they participate in the broader literary strategies of the Hellenistic period (cf. Bowman 1998). The representation of Thaumarete at *181–2*, at any rate, could reflect the perspective of a sexually interested man. *AP* 7.718 seems to construct Sappho as Nossis' literary ancestor, and in XXXIX Sapphic influence is perhaps implicit in the representation of Aphrodite as the inspirer of her poetic project.

Nossis' diction juxtaposes elements drawn from epic (e.g. *177–8*n.) with more colloquial features (cf. *183, 187–8*nn.).

XXXV. Nossis AP 6.275 (5 GP)

On a headband dedicated to Aphrodite. Some dedicatory epigrams pray for the divine recipient to rejoice at the offering (e.g. *CEG* 822.3); this poem, by contrast, reflects retrospectively on the gift, which the speaker imagines to have been received with pleasure. The first couplet records Aphrodite's reaction to the offering; the second justifies the speaker's guess. The opening and closing verses focus on the actions of Aphrodite in both the more and less distant past, while the central verses treat the band itself.

1–2[169–70] "I imagine that Aphrodite received with pleasure this headband offered from the hair of Samytha." The verses end respectively with the name of the divine recipient and the dedicator.   ἄνθεμα = ἀνάθεμα: predicate, "as an offering"; e.g. Antip. *AP* 6.47.2, Mnas. *AP* 6.128.2.   κεκρύφαλον: a band of cloth worn by women to keep their hair tidy (cf. Austin–Olson on Ar. *Thesm.* 137–8). The word is a Homeric hapax at *Il.* 22.469, where it has the same prosody; elsewhere the υ is sometimes long.   Σαμύθας: the name, emphatically placed at the end of the couplet, is very rare.

3[171] For the phrasing, cf. Callinus fr.1.6 τιμῆέν τε γάρ ἐστι καὶ ἀγλαὸν ἀνδρὶ μάχεσθαι.   δαιδάλεος "embroidered"; so of a veil at Hes. *Th.* 574–5 καλύπτρην | δαιδαλέην.   ἁδύ τι "very sweet"; for intensifying τι, cf. *39–40*n.

3–4[171–2] νέκταρος . . . χρίει: νέκταρ is often a metaphor for pleasantly fragrant substances (cf. Olson–Sens on Archestr. fr. 16.3–4), and in early epic the adjective νεκτάρεος is used of sweet-smelling garments (*Il.* 3.385, 18.25; cf. *Cypria* fr. 4.5). Here, what appears initially to be a metaphorical usage is made concrete in the pentameter: the nectar is that which Aphrodite actually uses. The ι of χρίω is elsewhere long.   Ἄδωνα χρίει: probably a reference to the anointing of Adonis' corpse by Aphrodite; cf. Theocr. 15.114 with Reed 2000: 332, Il. 19.38–9, where Thetis helps preserve Patroclus' body. The more common Greek form Ἄδωνις is probably derived from Semitic Adon "lord"; the present form reflects the god's Near Eastern origins; Theocr. 15.149 has the vocative Ἄδων in a hymnic context, and Alcm. PMG 109 seems to use it as a Phrygian slave name.

XXXVI. Nossis AP 6.353 (8 GP)

On an image of Melinna or her daughter. The poem conflates artistic verisimilitude and filiation. Though the absence of any reference to a specific artistic medium and the use of the passive voice leave open the precise identity of the subject, the first line gives the impression that it is an image of Melinna, and that, as in other ecphrastic epigrams, the point will be the realism with which her demeanor is captured. As evidence of verisimilitude, the speaker refers to an identifiable feature, the gentleness with which the girl gazes at the viewers. The second verse, however, takes the argument in a surprising direction by focusing on the resemblance of mother and daughter. The image may be metaphorical, in which case the "daughter" of 3 is the painting, depicted as the offspring of the woman it represents (see Parker 2004). Nothing precludes understanding 3–4 as commenting on a real mother–daughter pair (see Tueller 2008: 169–72), however, in which case the first word may retrospectively be understood to refer to Melinna's real-life daughter, praised for her resemblance to her mother. So understood, the epigram applies the conventional, elevated language of ecphrasis to an everyday observation on the similarity between a mother and her daughter (cf. 4n.). In any case, the poem plays on the traditional representation of viewing in ecphrastic epigram by making the subject both the viewer (cf. ποτοπτάζει) and the viewed (ποτώικει).

1[173] Αὐτομέλιννα "Melinna her very self." Ar. Thesm. 514, where a nurse deceives the presumptive father by calling a supposititious child αὐτέκμαγμα σόν "your very image," suggests the possibility of a wider use of such phrases to assure parents of the legitimacy of their children.   ἀγανόν "gentle"; cf. Nossis AP 9.605.3, 182n.

1–2[173–4] πρόσωπον | . . . ποτοπτάζειν: the compounded verb is not otherwise attested either in this Doric form or as προσοπτάζω, but here picks up and explains πρόσωπον "face," a noun entailing both the active

sense "that which looks" and the passive sense "that which is viewed."
ποτοπτάζειν suggests the former, while ποτώικει in 3 corresponds to the
latter. Ecphrastic epigrams commonly refer to the viewer's inspection of
the artwork (cf. *184* ποθορῆν); here Nossis treats the object as staring at
the viewer.   ἀμέ: Doric = ἡμᾶς (cf. Buck §118.5, Introduction section
4g).   μειλιχίως: the adverb explains ἀγανόν; cf. *179* τό . . . μείλιχον.

3[175] ἐτύμως: ἔτυμος and its cognates regularly express the verisimilitude
with which a work captures its subject (e.g. Theocr. 15.82).   πάντα "in
all respects"; cf. *413*, Nossis *AP* 9.605.2 πάντ' ἀνέθηκεν ἴσαν.   ποτώικει =
προσεώικει (pluperfect in imperfect sense). The past tense refers to the
moment of creation, like ἐποίει in artists' signatures.

4[176] ἠ . . . ἴσα: the claim that it is good for children to resemble their
parents derives from Hesiod's account of the benefits befalling the just
city, *WD* 235 τίκτουσιν δὲ γυναῖκες ἐοικότα τέκνα γονεῦσι; epic πέλη suits the
Hesiodic background. The idea is here put to new use, since whereas the
resemblance of children to their father is a proof of their legitimacy and
thus of the fidelity of the mother, the resemblance of a mother and her
daughter reveals nothing about the identity of the father or the stability
of the family line. See Parker 2004, who argues that this is evidence for
understanding the "daughter" to be the painting itself.

XXXVII. Nossis AP 6.354 (9 GP)

On a statue of Sabaethis. The poem's basic structure is defined by the
spatial adverbs in the hexameters. In the first couplet, Sabaethis' physical attributes are said to be recognizable even from a distance (τηλῶθε).
In the next, the speaker urges the addressee to look more closely and
then recounts the experience of doing so: in addition to her appearance,
Sabaethis' intelligence and kindness appear to be present "on the spot"
(αὐτόθι), i.e. to be immanent in the figural representation. By the final
line, the distinction between the image and Sabaethis is gone, and the
speaker addresses her directly as a woman: in representing the totality of
her attributes, both physical and non-physical, the epigram effaces the
distinction between representation and reality (see Tueller 2008: 168–9).
The rhetoric enacts the growing appreciation of Sabaethis in her entirety:
first, a general recognition of her appearance from a distance; then, on
closer consideration (cf. 3 θάεο), fuller comprehension of her intellectual and social qualities. The speaker's involvement in the interpretation
becomes more explicit as the poem proceeds, as the third-person assertion εἴδεται ἔμμεν (1) is picked up by the first-person ἔλπομ' ὁρῆν (4). The

two central verses contribute to the ring composition: each focuses on two pairs of attributes, having to do first with Sabaethis' appearance (2) and then with her intelligence and character (3).

1–2[177–8] "Even from afar, this image seems to be recognizable (as that) of Sabaethis for her form and stature." Inscriptions on statue bases sometimes observe that the representation is identical in stature and form to its subject; e.g. *CEG* 814.5. The passage rewrites *Od.* 11.336–7 Φαίηκες, πῶς ὔμμιν ἀνὴρ ὅδε φαίνεται εἶναι | εἶδός τε μέγεθός τε ἰδὲ φρένας ἔνδον ἐΐσας;, which similarly focuses first on matters of appearance and then on intelligence (cf. 3n.).   **γνωτά** "known, recognizable" (cf. *Il.* 7.401, *Od.* 24.182).   **τηλῶθε:** this rare adverb is mentioned as a poetic form by Hdn. *De pros. cath.* 1.501 Lentz; it suits the spacial dynamics of the poem (cf. introductory n.). Transmitted τηνῶθε "from there" (e.g. Ar. *Ach.* 754, Theocr. 3.10) would imply that the speaker and addressee are in different locations.   **Σαβαιθίδος:** the name is otherwise attested only in a few inscriptions from Caria. It could be non-Greek; cf. *170* Σαμύθας.   **ἔμμεν:** present infinitive of εἰμί.   **ἄδ᾽ εἰκών:** though εἰκών can be used of paintings, the assimilation of the image and the real Sabaethis here (see introductory n.) suggests that it is a statue. In the latter sense, the word generally designates a representation of a human being rather than of a god (properly ἄγαλμα), though Hellenistic poets sometimes play on the boundaries between them; cf. Asclep. *39.1 Sens = Pos. *141.1 AB Κύπριδος ἄδ᾽ εἰκών with Sens's note.   **μορφᾶι καὶ μεγαλειοσύναι** "appearance and grandeur," a reworking of the conventional conjunction of form (εἶδος) and size (μέγεθος) in Homer (cf. *Od.* 11.337). μεγαλειοσύνη is not otherwise attested, though it has a morphological analogue in μεγαλειότης (e.g. LXX 1 Esdras 4.40), which refers to metaphorical greatness.

3[179] θάεο: cf. *25*.   **τὰν πινυτάν:** cf. *15*n.   **τό . . . μείλιχον** "kindness." For the neuter abstract, cf. *181*.   **αὐτόθι** "right here"; Sabaethis' intelligence and kindness are present in the statue.

4[180] ἔλπομ᾽ "think," a common Homeric usage (LSJ II.3).   **ὁρῆν:** -ῆν is the standard Doric treatment of the infinitive of verbs in -άω (e.g. Ar. *Lys.* 1077).   **χαίροις . . . μάκαιρα:** μάκαρ/μάκαιρα may refer to fortunate, living humans as well as gods and the dead; the point is apparently that the attributes enumerated in the poem make Sabaethis blessed (cf. Nossis *AP* 9.605.4 χαιρέτω, οὔ τινα γὰρ μέμψιν ἔχει βιοτᾶς). Epigrams attached to statues of humans sometimes address them directly (e.g. *CEG* 877.7 ὦ μάκαρ εὐκλείας Ἄρχων), but the phrase may also evoke the *envoi* of rhapsodic hymns, which often end with a request for the god to "rejoice" (χαῖρε). The poem "approximates a divine epiphany" (Skinner 1991: 29); it blurs the distinction between divine and human to suggest that Sabaethis occupies an ambiguous position between them.

XXXVIII. Nossis AP 9.604 (7 GP)

A painting of Thaumarete. Initially, the speaker/viewer's perspective is sexualized, as the focus on attractiveness (2 ὡραῖον) and the evocation of Ibycus in 2 ἀγανοβλεφάρου make clear; but the poem concludes by locating Thaumarete in the domestic sphere, and replaces the conventional hypothetical reaction of a human viewer with that of her dog. The wit depends on this play with ecphrastic convention, and on the juxtaposition of high-style with colloquial language. As often in inscribed epigrams, the distinction between the object and the person it represents is fragile, and like other poems by Nossis, this epigram enacts the blurring of boundaries between image and reality: after the third-person exegesis of the opening couplet, the second-person address (3 σ') seems initially to be directed at Thaumarete herself, until the speaker's claim about the reaction of her dog reveals that it must refer to the painting (see Tueller 2008: 168).

1[181] Θαυμαρέτας: the name "Wondrous virtue" is significant in the context of the sexualized description that follows.   **μορφάν . . . ἔχει:** inscriptions attached to reliefs and statues sometimes identify the person they represent in similar terms; e.g. CEG 481.3 τούτου τῶν τ' ἄλλων ὧν τύπος εἰκόν' ἔχει, 877.5.   **ὁ πίναξ** "the painting"; cf. Anyte AP 9.605.1.   **τὸ γαῦρον** "sauciness," wantonness"; cf. 26n., Eur. Supp. 217 τὸ γαῦρον δ' ἐν φρεσὶν κεκτημένοι.

2[182] τεῦξε: the grammatical subject ὁ πίναξ is here treated as if it were the artist.   **τὸ . . . ὡραῖον** "nubility." The adjective is regularly used of both boys and young women at the prime of physical attractiveness.   **ἀγανοβλεφάρου:** the adjective is borrowed from Ibyc. PMG 288.3–4 ἅ τ' ἀγανοβλέφαρος Πειθὼ ῥοδέοισιν ἐν ἄνθεσι θρέψαν, where Peitho is a divine embodiment of sexual desire. The second element here refers to Thaumarete's eyes rather than her eyelids (cf. LSJ βλέφαρος II); the eyes were treated as the source of sexual desire, imagined as a physical property emerging from them.

3–4[183–4] Dogs are uniquely equipped to recognize their owners (cf. Od. 17.301–2): the representation is so good that even Thaumarete's dog is deceived. Greek ecphrases commonly comment on a viewer's hypothetical reaction to a work of art (cf. Goldhill 1994), sometimes imagining what the viewer would *say* about it (cf. *49*). The fawning of Thaumarete's dog takes the place of a human viewer's reaction; the humor is enhanced by the contrast between the colloquialism of σκυλάκαινα and the grandness of δέσποιναν μελάθρων. The sigmatism and assonance of -οι- are striking.   ἐσιδοῖσα: forms of ὁράω are standard in ecphrases, e.g. *58*, A.R. 1.765. For -οῖσα, cf. 7n.   οἰκοφύλαξ: attested earlier only at Aesch. *Supp.* 26, of Zeus. The word is probably elevated in tone, despite its appearance in later prose.   σκυλάκαινα: see *18*n. The feminine form is not elsewhere attested and is perhaps colloquial, though it has analogues in the names of female animals (e.g. δράκαινα, ὕαινα); by the end of the fifth century, dogs were commonly represented as female (cf. Lilja 1976: 5). In Old Comedy, neologisms ending in -αινα are used for absurd or derisive effect (Fraenkel 1955: 44–5), sometimes in the mouths of women (Ar. *Lys.* 146, *Eccles.* 713).   μελάθρων: an epic word, typically used for grand houses (i.e. "palace") and thus standing in pointed contrast to the stylistic level of σκυλάκαινα.

XXXIX. *Nossis AP 5.170 (1 GP)*

Love is the sweetest of all things. The theme is that of xiv, but instead of adopting the form of a priamel, the epigram opens in the aphoristic manner of poems in the elegiac corpus (cf. 1–2n., xx introductory n.), and especially the reflections on ἔρως in the Theognidea (e.g. Thgn. 1353–4). The second couplet, however, is a σφραγίς identifying the speaker of 1–2 as Nossis herself and attributing to her special knowledge. The poem is a self-reflexive assertion of Nossis' place in the poetic tradition. As a whole, it is an extended reworking of Hes. *Th.* 96–7 (ὃ δ᾽ ὄλβιος ὅντινα Μοῦσαι | φίλωνται· γλυκερή οἱ ἀπὸ στόματος ῥέει αὐδή) that also incorporates imagery drawn from Sappho. The point is that Aphrodite's favor provides Nossis with special knowledge, and by implication even greater poetic sweetness than poetry on other themes. In this sense, the epigram locates its speaker in a tradition of amatory poetry originating with Sappho (cf. esp. fr. 16), who treats Aphrodite as an ally (fr. 1).

AP 5.170 is sometimes assumed to be the opening poem in a book of Nossis' epigrams. It is, however, different in its focus from other extant poems, and it is impossible to know precisely what position it occupied; Nossis may well have produced multiple epigram collections. Cillacter *AP* 5.29 is an obscene parody.

1–2[185–6] "Nothing is sweeter than eros. The things that are a source of happiness are all secondary. I reject from my mouth even honey." Line

1 is a chiastic verse in which initial ἄδιον οὐδέν is answered by δεύτερα πάντα at line end, and Eros and other unspecified alternatives (ἃ δ᾽ ὄλβια) are juxtaposed on opposite sides of the caesura.   **ἄδιον οὐδέν:** the negative comparison resembles the openings of some individual *Theognidea*, e.g. 117 κιβδήλου δ᾽ ἀνδρὸς γνῶναι χαλεπώτερον οὐδέν, 131–2, 411–12.   **ἃ δ᾽ ὄλβια:** the relative clause provides the subject. ὄλβια is commonly used in the *Odyssey* of the pleasurable gifts of the gods (e.g. *Od.* 7.148 θεοὶ ὄλβια δοῖεν, 8.413). The language mirrors that of Hes. *Th.* 96 (cf. introductory n.), but ἃ is relative rather than demonstrative, as ὅ is there.   **δεύτερα πάντα:** a prosaic idiom (e.g. Arist. fr. 565, p. 348.8–9 Rose ἅπαντα δεύτερα τοῦ ζητεῖν τὸν φόνον ἐποιοῦντο).   **ἀπὸ στόματος** is used in epic in contexts where song emanates from the mouths of poets (Hes. *Th.* 97, *HH.* 25.5); here it stands as a marker of the speaker's preference for erotic over non-erotic subject matter.   **δ᾽:** cf. Introduction section 4h(ii).   **ἔπτυσα:** although the compound ἀποπτύω is often used metaphorically to express loathing, the simplex is rarely so employed (cf. Griffith on Soph. *Ant.* 653); the usage is facilitated by ἀπὸ στόματος. The aorist may be used (especially in dramatic contexts) to express the speaker's strong approval or disapproval of an action without reference to past time; cf. Smyth §1937.   **τὸ μέλι:** honey is the sweetest substance available to the ancient imagination (cf. Diogen. VI 51), and commonly a metaphor or comparandum for poetic "sweetness" (e.g. Pi. *Olymp.* 10.98, *Nem.* 3.77, *Ismth.* 5.54, [Theocr.] 20.26–7 ἐκ στομάτων δὲ | ἔρρεέ μοι φωνὰ γλυκερωτέρα ἢ μέλι κηρῶ; cf. *141*n.). The rejection of it here implies the superiority of Nossis' poetry to others'.

3–4[187–8] τοῦτο λέγει Νοσσίς: a self-referential σφραγίς (cf. Thgn. 19–23) in which τοῦτο looks back to the preceding couplet, converting the opening aphorism into a quotation.   **τίνα . . . ῥόδα** "she whom Aphrodite does not love does not know what sort of flowers roses are." The lines continue the allusion to Hes. *Th.* 96–7 (cf. 1–2n.), but couch the point in negative terms. They appear to evoke Sappho fr. 55 οὐ γὰρ πεδέχηις βρόδων | τῶν ἐκ Πιερίας (cf. *471–2*n., Mel. *AP* 4.1.6): like Sappho, Nossis has special (poetic) knowledge and ability that other women do not. Cf. Call. fr. 1.37–8 Μοῦσαι γὰρ ὅσους ἴδον ὄθματι παῖδας | μὴ λοξῶι, πολιοὺς οὐκ ἀπέθεντο φίλους.   **τίνα:** a generalizing relative pronoun (= ἥντινα), as occasionally in Hellenistic poetry and later Greek (cf. Pfeiffer on Call. frr. 75.60 and 191.67), apparently on the analogy of the use of τίς for ὅστις in indirect questions; it is perhaps a feature of ordinary discourse (cf. LSJ B.ii.d).   **οὐκ ἐφίλησεν:** gnomic aorist, lending the claim the authority of timeless truth. ἐφίλησεν (not -ασεν) is the expected form in Doric.   **κήνα γ᾽:** the demonstrative serves the same function as ὅ in

Hes. *Th.* 96. κῆνος is a feature of some Doric dialects (cf. Buck §125) and of Aeolic; it would generally suit the Sapphic flavor.   ἄνθεα ποῖα ῥόδα: the rose is proverbially the most beautiful flower (e.g. Men. *Mon.* 403, Rhianus *AP* 12.58.3–4); the literal point is that someone who has not experienced the favor of Aphrodite cannot appreciate its superiority to other good things, but there is also an evocation of the Sapphic association of roses with poetry (cf. above).

PERSES

The Anthology preserves nine epigrams attributed to Perses. Of these, one identifies him as Theban (*AP* 7.445), another calls him Macedonian (*AP* 7.487), and the rest offer no ethnic. The name Perses is relatively rare, and most of its occurrences are clustered in Thessaly and Macedonia. The geographical designations in the lemmata of the Anthology are not consistently reliable (cf. p. 55, on Anyte), and in the absence of any stylistic grounds for distinguishing between two homonymous poets, the surviving epigrams need not be assigned to different men.

One epigram, at least, reveals a possible connection to Thebes. A Delphic inscription datable to the first half of the 320s (*FD* III.1 356) records the granting of proxeny to a Theban named Promenes, son of Leontiades, and to his family, including a son named Leontiades, and descendants. A Leontiades and a Promenes appear as father and son in XLIII, and though there is reason to be cautious about assuming they are to be connected to the Theban father and son (cf. Habicht 1994), Perses may have had real individuals in mind; even if the pairs are connected, it is impossible to know whether the Promenes named in the epigram is the man granted Delphic proxeny, since it was common to call children after their grandparents and thus for names to alternate through the generations.

Perses' style suggests an early date in the development of Greek epigram. In particular, the extant poems more closely resemble inscribed epigrams than those of many later authors; it has sometimes been thought that at least some were designed for real-life monuments, though in most cases even those poems that seem most traditional contain subtle clues that they are in fact intended as literary fictions rather than for inscription (cf. Tueller 2008: 58–61). At the level of diction, Perses' epigrams, like those of Anyte, frequently use language drawn from Homer, but reapply it to "ordinary," fictive individuals instead of heroes.

XL. Perses AP 7.539 (9 GP)

For Theotimus, drowned in a shipwreck. Some archaic and classical epitaphs for people who died at sea survive (*CEG* 132, 143, 166, 466, 544,

664, Bruss 2005: 88–96), but the form became disproportionately popular as a vehicle for experimentation by Hellenistic epigrammatists. The speaker begins by addressing the deceased, whose body is not present to hear the words. Such second-person addresses are rare in cenotaphs for victims of shipwreck (cf. "Anacr." *AP* 7.263); occasionally, cenotaphic epigrams are spoken by the deceased, who is thus simultaneously present and absent (cf. *CEG* 166, Asclep. 31).

The opening couplet casts an unflattering light on the victim, who has brought about his own death through inattention to a basic nautical rule, well established in the literary tradition from Hesiod on, by embarking during the winter (cf. 259–60), and his negligence causes the death of numerous, anonymous crewmates and leads to the suffering of his parents. The Homeric language of the second couplet represents Theotimus' fatal adventure as an epic voyage, and an allusion to Odysseus' katabasis in *Odyssey* 11 contributes to representing him as a modern-day Odysseus with marked differences: whereas Odysseus' crew died through their own recklessness, Theotimus seems to have caused the death of his ἑταῖροι; nor will he return from the Underworld to his family.

1–2[189–90] Theotimus sailed in late October at the time of Arcturus' evening setting (i.e. the moment in the calendar year when Arcturus seems to set just after dusk). Arcturus appears as a weather-sign first in Aratus (745–7). Kidd on Arat. 745 argues that that passage was the source of Arcturus' association with storms at sea in poetry (cf. A.R. 2.1098–9, Leon. *AP* 7.295.5, 7.503.4, Alc. *AP* 7.495.1), including here, but the relative chronology is uncertain.　　**κρυερῆς ἥψαο ναυτιλίης** "you set your hand to chilly sailing." κρυερῆς . . . ναυτιλίης glosses Hes. *WD* 618 ναυτιλίης δυσπεμφέλου. κρυερός can be used both metaphorically ("grievous") and literally of the coldness of death (e.g. "Simon." *AP* 7.496.5 ἐν πόντωι κρυερὸς νέκυς), and it thus doubly suits a fatal sailing expedition in the early winter.

3–4[191–2] Theotimus' voyage is described in conspicuously Homeric terms: cf. introductory n.　　**ἥ:** i.e. ναυτιλίη.　　**πολυκλήιδι ... | νηί:** a variation of the Homeric νηὶ πολυκλήιδι, with the noun and epithet reversed and divided between two verses. The epithet has special point: Theotimus' ship had a large crew, all of whom died at sea.　　**οἷς ἑτάροις** "with your companions." The phrase οἷς ἑτάροισι occurs in this verse-position in epic (*Il.* 5.165, 23.5, *Od.* 1.237, 14.413), but οἷς is here a second-person rather than third-person possessive adjective (= σοῖς), as often in Hellenistic poetry (cf. Call. *h.* 3.103, A.R. 2.634, 3.140, Theocr. 17.50, Apollon. Dysc. *Pron.* p. 109.20–6).　　**ἤγαγεν εἰς Ἀίδην:** cf. *Od.* 11.164 μῆτερ ἐμή, χρειώ με κατήγαγεν εἰς Ἀΐδαο. To express the idea "to Hades," Hellenistic poets preferred the accusative with εἰς, whereas earlier poets preferred the genitive; cf. Magnelli 1999: 188.

5[193] αἰαῖ . . . Εὔπολις: for the exclamation expressing the speaker's sympathy for the mourning of the parents, e.g. *204, CEG* 686.1–2.

6[194] κενεὸν σῆμα περισχόμενοι "embracing your empty tomb," since the parents will never again be able to embrace their son (cf. Moero *167–8*n.). The phrase acquires point from the phonetic similarity of σῆμα and σῶμα (cf. Pl. *Gorg.* 493a): the tomb replaces the missing body. The phrase bears a phonetic resemblance to Call. *Epigr.* 17.4 κενεὸν σῆμα παρερχόμεθα, where going past a tomb is a more traditional idea.

XLI. Perses AP 7.501 (4 GP)

On Phillis, drowned at sea and washed ashore in a deserted location. The poem is a second-person address to the deceased. Its first line sets up expectations that are quickly disappointed. It begins as if it were describing the moment at which storm winds rolled Phillis from his ship (1 ἐξεκύλισαν) and drowned him, and thus seems initially to be an account of the loss of his body at sea. By the end of the first couplet, however, the ferocious winds are revealed to have cast his body ashore (1, 2nn.). The poem thus plays on real and fictive cenotaphs in which the body of the deceased has been lost and is now represented only by his tomb. Whereas in cenotaphs the grave is a stand-in for a dead person whose actual location is unknown, here the narrator knows the precise location of Phillis' body, and addresses it as if it were actually buried. The remote beach takes the place traditionally occupied by the tomb (cf. 2, 3–4nn.), and the inaccessible promontory that of the grave stele.

1[195] Cf. Leon. *AP* 7.273.1–3 Εὔρου με τρηχεῖα καὶ αἰπήεσσα καταιγὶς | καὶ νὺξ καὶ δνοφερῆς κύματα πανδυσίης | ἔβλαψ᾽ Ὠρίωνος. **Εὔρου χειμέριαι . . . καταιγίδες:** Hes. *WD* 618–22 warns that winter storm winds are particularly dangerous. A καταιγίς is a violent blast falling suddenly from above ([Arist.] *Mund.* 395a5–6), and the entire expression thus initially seems to explain the cause of Phillis' death at sea; as it turns out, the winds, whatever their role in his drowning, are here the cause of his beaching. **ἐξεκύλισαν:** the Homeric use of the verb of riders thrown from chariots (*Il.* 6.42 = 23.394 ἐκ δίφροιο . . . ἐξεκυλίσθη) creates the mistaken expectation that it refers to Phillis' ejection from his ship rather than to the rolling of his corpse in the surf.

2[196] πολυκλαύτωι . . . ἐπ᾽ ἠιόνι poignantly evokes πολυκλαύτωι ἐπὶ τύμβωι (cited as πολυκλαύτου ἐπὶ τύμβου by Pl. *Phaedr.* 264d) in a well-known archaic epigram ("Homer" or Cleobulus *AP* 7.153.3) spoken by a statue on Midas' tomb: here, the shore of Lesbos must serve as the final resting place, and while a tomb in a well-visited spot may be "much lamented" (cf. "Erinna" *AP* 7.712.1–2), lines 3–4 reveal that the corpse is inaccessible. For γυμνόν, cf. *127–8*n. ἐπιειμένος ἀχλύν.

3–4[197–8] Cf. Hermesianax fr. 7.54–5 οἰνηρῆι δειρῆι κεκλιμένην πατρίδα | Λέσβον ἐς εὔοινον, where the shape of the island is similarly depicted via an anatomical metaphor ("neck"). οἰνηρῆς "wine-producing," as at Call. fr. 399.1. The adjective more commonly means "containing wine" (e.g. Pi. *Nem.* 10. 43, Hdt. 3.6.1) or "(consisting) of wine" (e.g. Eur. *IT* 163). The reference to Lesbos' excellent wine (cf. Archestr. fr. 59.4 with Olson–Sens's note) is pathetic: Phillis can no longer enjoy such things. παρὰ σφυρόν "along the shore, coast" (cf. Gow on Theocr. 16.77); the phrase is used by Homer (*Il.* 4.518, 17.290) in an anatomical sense ("near the ankle"). αἰγίλιπος . . . ὑπὸ πρόποδι "you lie under the jutting base, wet from the sea, of a lofty cliff." Ancient scholarship took αἰγίλιψ to mean "steep," and explained its literal force as either "so high that even a goat would not leave it" (cf. Σ (D) *Il.* 9.15) or "so high that even a goat would not ascend it" (Apoll. Soph. p. 14.31–2). αἰγίλιπος δὲ | πέτρου varies the Homeric αἰγίλιπος πέτρης. πέτρη is the more expected word for a cliff; although Hellenistic epigrammatists use both it and πέτρος of tombstones, the latter is more commonly applied to graves. The change of form thus contributes to the larger point: the cliff-face takes the place of a tomb-stone. ἁλιβρέκτωι "wetted by the sea" (for the idea, cf. Soph. *Ajax* 1219 πρόβλη᾽ ἁλίκλυστον), rather than by the tears of mourners; the adjective appears first here. ὑπὸ πρόποδι: a πρόπους is a spur of land jutting from the base of a mountain (Hsch. π3637). The word is rare in poetry, and may have been chosen here because its derivation from πούς suits the metaphorical use of σφυρόν: the body lies by the "ankle" of Lesbos, under the "forefoot" of a cliff. Cf. Samius 772.

XLII. Perses AP 7.730 (7 GP)

On the tomb of Mnasylla. The poem is cast as a question posed by a viewer, who asks why the painting on the tomb depicts the deceased mourning the death of her daughter. Questions posed to the tomb or its occupant occur occasionally in the classical period (cf. *CEG* 429) and are more fully developed in dialogue-epigrams of the Hellenistic period.

The nature of the image emerges slowly and elliptically. The opening couplet, in which Mnasylla is simultaneously treated as a mourner grieving her daughter (μυρομέναι κούραν) and as the deceased, is explained in the last verse: she is so depicted because she still mourns in death. A painted grave stele (Arbanitopoulos 1928: 147–9 with Plate II) from Demetrias-Pagasae in Thessaly depicts a scene like that imagined in the epigram. As the inscribed poem (GVI 1606) accompanying it reveals, it represents a young woman who has died in childbirth lying on a bed, mourned by her husband and, at a distance in the background, accompanied by an older woman holding the dead infant (cf. Pollitt 1986: 4, 194). Here too the body of the deceased is accompanied by a pair of mourners, Mnasylla and her husband, one in physical proximity, the other a short distance away.

The handful of extant painted stelae do not allow us to know how common such scenes were, but the Thessalian example casts light on the poem's innovative approach. Although it describes the image on Mnasylla's tomb, its focus is on her daughter's death, which is treated as if in an epitaph (4–5; cf. e.g. 9, 227); although the attention paid to the grief of the deceased mother has a parallel in CEG 526, the extent to which it is developed here is marked; see x introductory n. The shift from present to aorist in 7–8 obscures the difference between the actual mourning of Neutima's parents in the past and its representation on Mnasylla's tomb.

Unusually, there is consistent enjambment between the pentameters and the succeeding hexameter, with syntactically necessary enjambment at both 4–5 and 6–7. The dialect is predominantly Doric, but cf. 4–5n.

1–3[199–201] "Wretched Mnasylla, why for you (τοι), mourning your child, is there a depiction of Neutima painted even on (your) tomb?" γραπτός . . . τύπος "painted representation"; cf. introductory n. For τύπος of the depiction of the deceased on a tomb, cf. CEG 481.3. ποκ' = ποτ(ε). That Neutima's death is set at an unspecified past time (cf. CEG 576.3 ἅ ποτε . . . κατέφθιτο) emphasizes the continuity of Mnasylla's grief. ἀπὸ ψυχὰν ἐρύσαντο "tore away her soul" (tmesis), a variation of Homeric expressions such as ἀπὸ θυμὸν ὄλεσσεν (e.g. Il. 8.90, cf. Philitas fr. 20.1; cf. Emped. 31 B 138 χαλκῶι ἀπὸ ψυχὴν ἀρύσας); Perses substitutes the Homeric rarity ἀπερύω, which occurs (also in tmesis) only at Od. 14.134 (of the destruction of a corpse) ῥινὸν ἀπ' ὀστεόφιν ἐρύσαι.

4–5[202–3] οἷα κατὰ βλεφάρων | ἀχλύι πλημύρουσα "as though overflowing with the dark mist (that had been poured) down over her eyes." The simile is based on metaphorical Homeric expressions in which a dark mist pours over the eyes of a dying person (e.g. Il. 5.696, 16.344 κατὰ δ' ὀφθαλμῶν κέχυτ' ἀχλύς): πλημύρουσα ("overflowing") develops the image of the mist as a pourable liquid (cf. κέχυτ'); κατὰ βλεφάρων (*Il.* 17.438) suggests movement, as in the Homeric model. **μητρός:** the Ionic form (P) might be explained as suiting the epic flavor of ἀγοστῶι. **ἀγοστῶι** "forearm," one of the competing senses assigned to this Homeric word by ancient scholars (cf. Σ *Il.* 14.452, Rengakos 1994: 31–2) and taken up by Hellenistic poets (cf. Theocr. 17.129, Livrea on A.R. 4.1734). Mnasylla places her arm on her dead daughter as she sits by her side.

6[204] αἰαῖ, Ἀριστοτέλης δ': see *193*n.

7[205] δεξιτερᾶι κεφαλὰν ἐπεμάσσατο: Aristoteles held his head with his right hand in an expression of mourning. ἐπεμάσσατο (aorist of ἐπιμαίομαι) is here "clutched" (e.g. A.R. 4.18) rather than "stroked." The change in tense blurs the boundary between the real event in the past (here represented by the aorist, cf. 8 ἐξελάθεσθ') and its present representation on the tomb (cf. 2 ἔπεστι). **ὦ μέγα δειλοί:** cf. 1 δειλαία, *Or. Sib.* 2.161, Nonn. *Dion.* 6.259. The text is uncertain: κ(αί) in P's κ' ὦ is unwelcome and may reflect a desire to avoid the hiatus before ὦ, but Perses may be following Homeric practice, which occasionally allows hiatus before the bucolic diaeresis (K–B 1.192). Stadtmüller's κοὐ is also possible.

8[206] An allusion to *Od.* 11.553–5 "Ajax, blameless son of Telemon, not even in death, then, were you bound to forget your anger (οὐδὲ θανὼν λήσεσθαι) at me over the terrible armor." **ἐῶν:** second person plural = ὑμετέρων; cf. *192*n.

XLIII. *Perses* AP *6.112 (1 GP)*

A dedication by brothers of three deer-heads and antlers to Apollo. The names Leontiades and Promenes coincide with those of a Theban father and son in an inscription from the end of the fourth century (see above p. 112); the poem may have been composed to accompany a real dedication, but it is uncertain that it was, or that it celebrates a real hunting expedition. Epigrams allegedly recording the dedication of antlers to Apollo at Delphi are attributed to Alexander the Great (Ael. *NA* 10.40) and to Nicocreon, king of Cypriote Salamis in the late fourth century (Ael. *NA* 11.40); literary epigrams recording similar dedications include Leon. *AP* 6.110, Antip. *AP* 6.111; cf. cxxxiii. Mt. Maenalus is a conventional haunt of wild beasts in Hellenistic poetry (e.g. Call. *h.* 3.88–9, A.R. 1.168); that the deer were killed there could be a literary fiction as easily as a reflection of reality.

The diction is heavily indebted to epic and implicitly assimilates Leontiades' sons to Homeric heroes.

1–2[207–8] τρεῖς . . . κεφαλαί: dedicated objects named in the nominative are relatively rare in the inscriptional record (*CEG* 390, 822, 830.8). **ἄφατοι** "amazing" (*Suda* α4564; cf. Pi. *Nem.* 1.47), an extension of the literal meaning "unmentioned, unspoken" (Hes. *Op.* 3), and thus "unspeakable." Before the Hellenistic period, the adjective is mostly restricted to lyric, and it is probably elevated in tone (cf. Bulloch on Call. *h.* 5.77). The epigrams attached to dedications by Alexander and Nicocreon (above, introductory n.) both emphasize the extraordinary character of the horns (Ael. *NA* 10.40 χρῆμά τι δαιμόνιον, 11.40 τετράκερων). **κεράεσσιν** "with respect to their antlers"; cf. *HHMerc.* 192 (cows) πάσας κεράεσσιν ἑλικτάς. **ὑπ' αἰθούσαις:** i.e. in the portico of Apollo's temple. The phrase is a variation of the Homeric ὑπ' αἰθούσηι, used in this verse-position at *Od.* 3.399, 7.345, 20.176. **ἄγκεινται** "have been dedicated" (< ἀνάκεινται), e.g. *CEG* 822.1, Theocr. 10.33 with Gow's note.

3[209] ἕλον "killed" (e.g. *Il.* 16.697); cf. the epigram ap. Ael. *NA* 11.40 σῆς ἕνεκεν, Λητοῦς τοξαλκέτα κοῦρ', ἐπινοίας | τήνδ' ἕλε Νικοκρέων τετράκερων ἔλαφον. **ἐξ ἵππων** "on horseback," as e.g. App. *BC* 2.10.70 οἱ μὲν ἐξ ἵππων, οἱ δὲ πεζοί; ἀπό is more commonly used in this context. Perses varies the meaning of the expression in Homer, where it always refers to dismounting or falling from a chariot; e.g. *Il.* 7.16 ἐξ ἵππων χαμάδις πέσε, 11.94 ἐξ ἵππων κατεπάλμενος. **†γυγερῶι χέρε†:** incurably corrupt, but perhaps masking the name of a third son of Leontiades. The line end Δαΐλοχός τε resembles Homeric expressions such as *Il.* 17.378 Θρασυμήδης Ἀντίλοχός τε, *Od.* 11.23, 12.195, 15.248, in all of which two proper names are conjoined. The existence of a third brother would explain why three heads have been dedicated. Attempts to preserve a form of χείρ are less satisfactory (σθεναρῆι χερί Salmasius, γυμνῆι χερί Hiller von Gaertringen).

XLIV. Perses AP 6.272 (2 GP)

A dedication of clothing to Artemis by a woman who survived a difficult labor. Greek women often dedicated textiles to Artemis to celebrate childbirth (Σ Call. *h.* 1.77) and other important transitional moments (Cole 1998); sanctuary inventories, especially at Brauron, list numerous items of clothing, including belts (cf. *IG* II² 1514.15 ζῶμα) and a variety of finely wrought linen. Some such dedications may have been marked by epigrams (perhaps embroidered; cf. *IG* II² 1514.8–9), but this poem is probably a fiction.

The poem has a form common in inscribed dedicatory epigram: σοι/τοι + address of divine recipient (vocative) + dedicator (nominative) + τίθημι + dedicated item(s) in the accusative. Lines 1–2 name the divine recipient and list the dedicated items in a tricolon of ascending length (a common Homeric structure), of which the last element is a high-style description of an intimate garment; two of the items appear together as part of a warrior's armor in Homer (1–2n.), and the lines gain point from the application of Homeric language to a feminized context (cf. 1 ἀνθεμόεντα, 2 περιπλομέναν). Lines 3–4 name the dedicator and explain the gift. The poem appears to be the model for Leon. *AP* 6.202.

1–2[211–12] Cf. *Il.* 4.216, where ζῶμα and μίτρη are the loin-cloth and bronze waist-guard worn by Menelaus.   **ζῶμα . . . κύπασσιν:** ζῶμα, here equivalent to ζώνη, refers to a girdle or belt worn around a woman's waist. A κύπασσις is a chiton used by both sexes (cf. Hecat. *FGrH* 1 F 284; Hippon. fr. 32.4; Aesch. fr. dub. ****473), though ancient lexicographers disagreed about whether it was a male or female garment (Harpocr. κ96). It is associated with the East and with Asiatic luxury (Hecat. loc. cit., Diotimus *AP* 6.358.1–2). ζώματα and κυπάσσιδες are juxtaposed at Alc. fr. 140.13.   **ὦ Λατωί:** vocative of Λατωΐς "daughter of Leto," i.e. Artemis, here invoked as goddess of childbirth (cf. Eur. *Hipp.* 166, [Theocr.] 27.29–30, Cole 1998). The adjective appears first in Hellenistic poetry in place of traditional epithets such as Λητογένεια, Λητογενής, Λητώια.   **ἀνθεμόεντα:** either "brightly colored" (cf. LSJ) or "decorated with (images of) flowers" (cf. Asclep. 4.2 ζώνιον ἐξ ἀνθέων ποικίλον with Sens's note). The adjective sometimes has the literal sense "flowery" in Homer, but ancient scholars debated whether its meaning in passages describing metallic objects was "intended for dedication" (as if from ἀνατίθημι), "bright, shining," or "variegated."   **μίτραν** "breast-band," a sense first attested in Hellenistic poetry (e.g. Call. *Epigr.* 38.3–4 μίτρην | ἣ μαστοὺς ἐφίλησε, A.R. 3.867); more commonly synonymous with ζῶμα.   **μαστοῖς σφιγκτὰ περιπλομέναν** "tightly (σφιγκτὰ) encircling her breasts," i.e. wrapped around her torso to support her breasts. The phrase explains the function of the item, not its current state. περιπλόμενος is an epic word. σφιγκτὰ is adverbial neuter plural.

3[213] **θήκατο:** an epic (e.g. *Il.* 10.31) equivalent to ἔθετο.

3–4[213–14] **δυσωδίνοιο γενέθλας | ἀργαλέον . . . βάρος** "grievous misery of an ill-labored birth." βάρος, "misery, burden," suggests the weight of pregnancy. δυσώδινος, a hapax, implies not merely a painful labor, but one that could have ended disastrously.   **δεκάτωι μηνί:** i.e. at the conclusion of a normal pregnancy.   **φυγοῦσα:** surviving childbirth; cf. Leon. *AP* 6.200.1 πικρὰν ὠδῖνα φυγοῦσα.

PHALAECUS

Five epigrams are attributed to Phalaecus. His use of non-elegiac meters suggests a *floruit* early in the Hellenistic period. Why his name was given to the so-called "Phalaecian" hendecasyllable, an archaic meter used by other early third-century epigrammatists as well, is unclear: possibly he was the first to use it in epigrams or in stichic form (cf. xcv). A *terminus post quem* is suggested by the probability that the honorand of *AP* 13.6 was Lycon of Scarphe, who was a comic actor twice victorious at the Lenaea in the mid-fourth century (*IG* II² 2325.195); he accompanied Alexander on his expeditions (Plut. *Mor.* 334e), and performed at the mass marriage at Susa (Chares *FGrH* 125 F4).

XLV. Phalaecus AP 13.27 (4 GP)

On Phocus, lost at sea. The poem comprises two four-line stanzas in which an Archilochian is followed by an iambic trimeter and then a hexameter is followed by another iambic trimeter. This metrical form is a variation of the more common epodic alternation of hexameters and trimeters. The Archilochian consists of four dactylic feet followed by a trochaic tetrapody ($- \smile\smile\, -\smile\smile\, -\smile\smile\, -\smile - \smile - \times$). It is rhythmically close to the the hexameter in that both have the same first four feet, and the adonic with which the hexameter ends can be converted to a trochaic tripody by adding a single heavy syllable ($-\smile-\smile-\times$ as opposed to $-\smile\smile-\times$); the first and third verses are thus related. The two stanzas focus respectively on Phocus' death abroad (1–4) and on his burial and his mother's grief at home (5–8); the contrast is highlighted by the identical relative positions of ἐπὶ ξείνηι and ἐν πατέρων in their verses. The structure of the poem, which opens with the narrator telling how Phocus died and ends with his mother recounting the same event, creates a parallelism between the omniscient narrator and the grieving parent, whose name, Promethis ("Foreknowing"), perhaps suggests her own special knowledge; the parallelism is reinforced by the recurrence of ἀπέφθιτο in 1 and 8 and by the ambiguous focalization of 7 αἰαῖ.

1[215] Φῶκος ("seal") is well attested as a name, but ironic of a drowned man.   **ἐπὶ ξείνηι**: the noun to be supplied is ordinarily γῆι (as in e.g. 372), but the subsequent account of the death reveals the meaning to be only that Phocus was not in his homeland rather than that he was "in" a foreign land when he perished.

1–2[215–16] μέλαινα | νεῦς: varying, by verse-position and morphology, the Homeric formulas μέλαιναι νῆες, νηὶ μελαίνηι, etc.; νεῦς is an Ionic form of the nominative singular (Ionic νηῦς, Attic ναῦς) elsewhere attested only in the lexicographical tradition.   οὐδ' ὑπεξήνεικεν "did not escape," probably evoking a disputed meaning of ὑπεκφέρω at *Il.* 22.202, where Aristarchus favored κῆρας ὑπεξέφερεν rather than vulgate κῆρας ὑπεξέφυγεν (cf. Hdt. 4.125.1).   ἐδέξατο "tolerated," "endured," with the wave represented as an attacking force (cf. Thuc. 4.126.6 τοῖς . . . τὴν πρώτην ἔφοδον δεξαμένοις).

4[218] βίηι Νότου: the expression resembles [Theocr.] 25.90–1, of clouds, ἐλαυνόμενα προτέρωσε | ἠὲ Νότοιο βίηι ἠὲ Θρηικὸς Βορέαο; cf. *Il.* 16.213, 23.713 βίας ἀνέμων.   **πρήσαντος ἐσχάτην ἅλα** "raised the sea from its depths (ἐσχάτην)." πίμπρημι typically means "blow out," of sails and the like, but the cognate πρηστήρ is used of typhoons and violent thunderstorms at sea (cf. West on Hes. *Th.* 846); cf. πρήσσω at A.R. 4.1537–8 πρήσσοντος ἀήτεω | ἂμ πέλαγος νοτίοιο.

5[219] τύμβου . . . λάχεν: cf. *566*n.   **ἐν πατέρων** "in <the land> of his ancestors."

6[220] λυγρῆι ὄρνιθι: probably a gloss on the halcyon (cf. *SGO* 05/01/44.7–8 μήτηρ δ' ἡ δύστηνος ὀδύρεται οἵα τις ἀκταῖς | ἀλκυονὶς γοεροῖς δάκρυσι μυρομένα, A.R. 4.362–3 λυγρῆισιν . . . ἀλκυόνεσσι), whose association with grief derives from the mourning of Alcyone, transformed into a halcyon after her husband Ceyx drowned at sea. The hiatus is unusual but has antecedents in epic hexameters; cf. *Il.* 10.277 χαῖρε δὲ τῶι ὄρνιθ' Ὀδυσεύς, 23.857 τύχηι ὄρνιθος.   **πότμον εἰκέλη:** i.e. they shared the loss of a loved one at sea.

7[221] αἰαῖ may be understood as a parenthetic expression of grief by the speaker, as often in epigram (*193*n., *CEG* 556.1, 686.1), or as an internal accusative with κωκύει ("she cries αἰαῖ for her child"); the grammatical ambiguity blurs the distinction between the speaker's voice and that of the grieving mother.   **κωκύει:** the *uox propria* for high-pitched female lamentation.   **ἑὸν γόνον** "her son"; the expression occurs once in Homer (*Od.* 1.216), in a different sense ("his paternity").   **ἤματα πάντα:** a Homeric tag (e.g. *Il.* 8.539, 12.133).

8[222] ". . . saying how her prematurely deceased son died." Like the narrator of the poem, the mother, perhaps implausibly, knows the details of her son's death.

PHILITAS

Philitas (or Philetas) of Cos was a scholar and poet of the generation that included Asclepiades (cf. Theocr. 7.40), Aratus, Alexander Aetolus,

and Menander; he is said to have tutored Ptolemy II Philadelphus and
Zenodotus. The influence he exerted on subsequent Hellenistic writers is
reflected in his treatment as a model poet in the prologue to Callimachus'
Aetia (fr. 1.9–12 with schol. Flor. *ad loc.*) and in Theocritus' seventh idyll
(37–41); cf. LXXXII. The exiguous fragments of his poetry include part
of a hexameter narrative (*Hermes*) and an elegy (*Demeter*). These rework
earlier poetry, especially the Homeric epics, in creative ways, and show an
interest in lexical rarities that finds a parallel in Philitas' scholarly writings,
including the Ἄτακτοι Γλῶσσαι (a collection and discussion of unusual
words) and, apparently, a work called the *Hermeneia* (see Dettori 2000).
The existence of epigrams by him is attested by the *Suda* (φ332) and by
Stobaeus (4.17.5, 56.11), but none appears in the Anthology (though two
poems attributed to "Philitas of Samos" do); Meleager does not mention
him in his preface and may not have known a collection of his work (cf.
Sbardella 2000: 49–52, Spanoudakis 2002: 327–8).

XLVI. *Philitas 13 Sbardella (3 GP [vv. 1–2])*

A dialogue between a dead man and a friend who refuses to mourn a
life well lived. The two couplets are cited separately but in succession by
Stobaeus, who attributes the first to Philitas' *Paegnia* (of which he also
quotes another fragment, 12 Sbardella), the second to his *Epigrams*. In the
first, the dead man requests a traditional response to news of his death;
in the second, the passerby responds by refusing to lament him. That
the couplets belong to the same work is suggested by close verbal and
thematic correspondences (1 ἐκ θυμοῦ ~ 3 φιλαίτατε, 1 με ~ 3 σε, 1 κλαῦσαί
~ 3 οὐ κλαίω), by the identical metrical shape of the hexameters, and by
Euphorion's apparent reworking of the epigram (fr. 22). Apart from
one relatively rare form (cf. 3–4n.), the poem lacks recherché diction.
Instead, its point depends on the play with epigrammatic conventions and
on the characterization of the speakers, especially the passerby, a scrupu-
lous man who offers thoughtful consolation instead of lamentation.

1[223] ἐκ θυμοῦ "from your heart, sincerely," suggesting strong affection
(e.g. *Il.* 9.343 ἐκ θυμοῦ φίλεον).

1–2[223–4] κλαῦσαι . . . | εἰπεῖν, μεμνῆσθαι: infinitives used as impera-
tives have a solemn tone (cf. Smyth §2013). The emotional, practical,
and intellectual responses requested by the dead man are conventional
in epigrams and elsewhere (e.g. Sol. fr. 21), and constitute a sequence
moving from immediate lamentation to lasting remembrance.   τὰ
μέτρια "in moderation," an adverbial usage common in prose but not

verse. Solon allegedly limited excessive displays of grief (Plut. *Sol.* 12.5), and moderate mourning was treated as an ideal, even if it was not always maintained in reality; cf. Eur. fr. 46, Antiph. 54.1.   τι προσηνές "a kind word."   οὐκέτ' ἐόντος ὁμῶς "(remember) me, dead, in the same way (ὁμῶς) (as if I were alive)"; cf. A.R. 1.896 μνώεο μήν, ἀπεών περ ὁμῶς καὶ νόστιμος. The expression has a Homeric antecedent at *Il.* 22.384 Ἕκτορος οὐκέτ' ἐόντος.

3–4[225–6] The speaker rejects the request for lamentation, but implicitly fulfills the dead man's wish that he respond in a consolatory and commemorative way. That life contains a mixture of good and bad is commonplace (e.g. *Il.* 24.527–33, Call. fr. 298 = *Hecale* fr. 115 with Hollis' note); the point is that the deceased, having lived a life with many blessings, does not merit grief. More commonly, the speaker of an epitaph urges the reader not to lament at all (cf. Lattimore 1942: 217–20).   ξείνων . . . φιλαίτατε: addressed to the dead man, the apostrophe reverses the usual address of the imagined passerby as ξεῖνος (cf. *CEG* 597.1, *IMEGR* 5.11–12); cf. Call. LI introductory n. The speaker's refusal to mourn is not due to a lack of fondness. φιλαίτατε is a rare superlative of φίλος, first attested in fourth-century Attic prose (Xen. *HG* 7.3.8), and subsequently in Hellenistic poetry at Theocr. 7.98, Pos. 61.5 AB.   ἔγνως "you experienced"; e.g. *GVI* 861.2, *IGUR* III 1243.4.   καλά, κακῶν: an emphatic juxtaposition encompassing the range of human experiences.   μοῖραν "(just) portion"; contrast, e.g., Asclep. 42 ἄμοιρος ἀδονᾶν.

SIM(M)IAS

Sim(m)ias of Rhodes lived early in the Hellenistic period, though his precise dates are uncertain. According to Hephaestion (p. 31.4 Consbruch), he used the choriambic hexameter before Philicus, who was active no later than the early 270s (cf. Ath. 5.198c). On the other hand, the numerous points of contact between Simias' and Anyte's epigrams seem most plausibly explained as the product of his reworking of Anyte, and if this is so, he will have been active not much earlier than the first or second decade of the third century.

The *Suda* (σ431), in an entry contaminated with information pertaining to Semonides of Amorgos, reports that Simias was a grammarian who produced three books on rare words and four books of poems of various sorts. Three pattern-poems in which the physical layout of the verses iconically represents the subject matter are attributed to him (*Axe*, *Wings*, and *Egg*); on these see, e.g., Strodel 2002, Luz 2010, Kwapisz 2013, Pappas 2013. Also extant are scanty fragments of poems entitled *Apollo*,

Months, and *Gorgo(n)*. Of the seven surviving epigrams to which his name is attached in the *Anthology*, two (*AP* 7.21, XLVIII) are ascribed to Simmias of Thebes, and may be by a different poet; another (XLVII) is assigned to him, to Simonides, or to Samius.

    Simias' diction includes elements drawn from a range of genres and stylistic levels. His poems engage in a learned manner with Homeric diction but also use un-Homeric words, especially compound epithets characteristic of lyric and dramatic poetry; when he uses a Homeric phrase, he often varies it, sometimes by substituting for one or more of its elements language drawn from other literary traditions. His use of Homeric rarities matches his scholarly interest in glosses.

XLVII. Simias, "Simonides," or Samius AP 7.647 (Simias 7 GP)

The last words of the dying Gorgo. The poem shares a number of points of contact with Anyte III. Anyte's περὶ χεῖρε βαλοῦσα, alluding to Odysseus' last encounter with his mother in the Underworld, seems less likely to have been generated by δέρας χερσὶν ἐφαπταμένα here than the other way around, and Reitzenstein (1893: 129) is probably correct to think that the epigram is a response to Anyte's. The poet has made the internal addressee the girl's mother rather than her father and has changed the focus of her final words.

    The authorship of the epigram is variously given in the Anthology and remains uncertain. The Corrector attributes it to Simonides or to Simias, while Pl assigns it to Samius. Athenaeus 11.491c reports that Simias was the author of a work entitled *Gorgo* (called *Gorgon* at Σ Eur. *Andr.* 14), whose existence could have led a reader falsely to ascribe the epigram to him.

    The manuscripts diverge on the dialect coloring, with P favoring Ionic forms in η and Pl generally preserving α, but the coloring throughout was most likely Doric, perhaps on the model of Anyte's poem.

1–2[227–8] The lines seem to rework 9. **δακρυόεσσα . . . ἐφαπτομένα** varies Anyte's περὶ χεῖρε βαλοῦσα; the feminine participle at pentameter end picks up δάκρυσι λειβομένα in the equivalent position in Anyte's poem, while the content of that phrase is expressed via the adjective δακρυόεσσα at the opening of the verse.   **τάδ᾽ ἔειπε:** τόδ᾽ ἔειπε appears in this verse-position in Homer (*Od.* 16.356, 23.273); cf. Sens on Theocr. 22.153.   **ποτί:** Doric = πρός.   **δέρας:** genitive of δέρα (epic δειρή), "neck."

3–4[229–30] Whereas Anyte's dying Erato focuses on her own condition, Gorgo expresses concern for the fate of her parents. **αὖθι μένοις:** the phrase is an adaptation of the epic line opening αὖθι μένων (etc.); e.g. *Il.* 1.492, 10.410. αὖθι "here" implies "among the living" (e.g. Ar. *Frogs* 89 ἐνταῦθα). **ἐπὶ λώιονι μοίραι** "with better fortune." The same expression occurs in a third-century funerary epigram from Egypt (*IMEGR* 28.7–8) ἀλλ' ἐπὶ λώιονι μὲν μοίρηι νύμφην τις ἄγοιτο | τοιαύτηνδε. **τέκοις . . . καδεμόνα:** Gorgo is apparently an only child; cf. A.R. 1.97–8 οὐ μὲν ἔτ' ἄλλους | γήραος υἷας ἔχεν βιότοιό τε κηδεμονῆας. The elderly depended on their grown children for care, and the loss of this support is regularly cited as an additional source of pain to parents who have lost children (e.g. Eur. *Alc.* 662–5, *Med.* 1032–5, *Hec.* 430). **πολιῶι γήραϊ:** a conventional collocation in elegy, lyric, and tragedy (e.g. Thgn. 174, Pi. *Isthm.* 6.15, Bacchyl. 3.88–9, Eur. *Supp.* 170, *Ion* 700). **καδεμόνα** "carer" (LSJ 2). The noun is commonly used of those who care for the bodies of the dead (cf. *Il.* 23.163, 674), and its use highlights the reversal of the natural order, a common theme in epitaphs for young people: Gorgo's parents will have to play the role of κηδεμών for her rather than the other way around.

XLVIII. Simias AP 7.22 (5 GP)

The speaker hopes that ivy, roses, and grapevines will grace the tomb of Sophocles. Fictive epitaphs for famous poets of the Archaic and Classical periods became popular in the Hellenistic period (cf. Gabathuler 1937, Rossi 2001: 81–102; for an inscribed analogue, cf. *CEG* 578). These often attribute to their honorands qualities that their authors sought in their own work (cf. Sens 2003): here Simias emphasizes the sweetness and learning of Sophocles' poetry (cf. 5–6n.). The poem opens with a direct address to ivy that plays on the sepulchral convention in which the speaker of the inscription appeals to passersby not to neglect or mistreat the tomb; the language of the opening couplet suggests that the plant should play the part of mourner.

  Both this epigram and *AP* 7.21 are ascribed, probably falsely, to Simias of Thebes, a follower of Socrates. *AP* 7.21 too associates Sophocles with ivy, although there the connection between the plant and the crown awarded to victorious tragedians is made explicit. Other epigrams on Sophocles include Diosc. *AP* 7.37, Eryc. *AP* 7.36 and adesp. *AP* 7.20.

1–2[231–2] The wish for ivy and other plants to flourish on the tombs of poets was conventional in epigram, perhaps via the connection between garlands and victories in poetic competitions (cf. *CEG* 578.9–10, Luck 1956: 279–82, Rossi 2001: 100–1), including the Athenian dramatic festivals (cf. Pickard-Cambridge 1968: 98); the presence of ivy on the tomb would be a mark of Dionysus' favor and of Sophocles' status as a tragic poet.   ἠρέμ᾽ . . . ἠρέμα "gently," so as not to disturb the occupant of the tomb; cf. *135* ἀτρέμα. The repetition suggests the speaker's urgency.   ἑρπύζοις "creep slowly." ἑρπύζω is a Homeric verb closely associated with contexts involving grief (cf. *Il.* 23.234–5, *Od.* 13.220) and thus especially appropriate here.   χλοερούς ἐκπροχέων πλοκάμους is multivalent. Most obviously "pouring forth green hair" is "growing an abundance of leaves"; cf. Nic. *Ther.* 658 τροχεὴν δ᾽ ἀπεχεύατο χαίτην. πλόκαμος is less commonly used of foliage than κόμη and χαίτη; cf. *Anacreont.* 41.6. At the same time, in a literal sense to pour out one's hair is to leave it unbound (cf. *584*, Call. *h.* 6.5 κατεχεύατο χαίτην), an act often signifying mourning (cf. Richardson on *HHDem.* 41). The participle may also evoke the commonplace use of χέω of tears (cf. *Il.* 1.357, etc. δάκρυ χέων, A.R. 3.1118–19 προχέουσα . . . | δάκρυα), for which χλοερός/χλωρός is sometimes an epithet (cf. Anyte *1*on., Diosc. *AP* 7.31.4 χλωρόν . . . δάκρυ χέας).

3[233] πέταλον "flower(s)" (singular for plural); cf. Eur. *Ion* 889, Mosch. 2.67. πάντηι "everywhere."   φιλορρώξ "grape-loving," i.e. "producing many grapes"; cf. LSJ ῥώξ B, Zonas *AP* 6.22.3 πυκνόρρωγα. The adjective, a hapax, occupies the standard verse-position of the (etymologically unrelated) Homeric ἀπόρρωξ, "broken off, sheer."

4[234] ἄμπελος . . . χευαμένη: like ivy, the vine was intimately linked with Dionysus (e.g. *HHDion.* 39–41). The carefully balanced, chiastic structure of this line, in which an adverb meaning "all around" is itself framed by two noun–adjective pairs (noun A–adjective B–adverb–noun B–participle A) mirrors the twining of a vine.   ὑγρά "pliant."   κλήματα "vines."   χευαμένη "pouring forth," with the implication of great abundance. The middle voice of the uncompounded verb varies the similar use of the compound ἐκπροχέων in the active (2).

5[235] εὐμαθίης: usually "ability to learn, docility" but here approximating to "learnedness" (cf., in a programmatic context, Mel. *AP* 12.257.8). The wisdom of the deceased is commonplace in epitaphs, but here also reflects the values of the scholar-poet Simias.   πινυτόφρονος "wise-minded," first attested here.   μελιχρός: Hellenistic poets frequently use the adjective of poetry and poets they admire (cf. Call *323*–5n.); and sweetness was specifically attributed to Sophocles and his work (cf. T 108–14 Radt).

5–6[235–6] ἦν . . . | ἤσκησεν "which he practiced"; cf. LSJ ἀσκέω II.2. The verb occurs frequently in funerary contexts, e.g. *CEG* 553.3, 585.1 σωφροσύνην ἦσκον ἀρετήν τε. **Μουσῶν . . . καὶ Χαρίτων:** the Muses and the Graces were sometimes associated as goddesses of poetry, cf. Eur. *HF* 673–5 οὐ παύσομαι τὰς Χάριτας | ταῖς Μούσαισιν συγκαταμεί|γνυς, ἡδίσταν συζυγίαν. **ἄμμιγα** "together with," here unusually governing a genitive rather than a dative. For the poet's collaboration with the goddesses, cf. Asclep. 32.4 Sens τὸ ξυνὸν Μουσῶν γράμμα καὶ Ἀντιμάχου, adesp. *AP* 7.12.6, Crinag. *AP* 9.513.

XLIX. Simias AP 7.203 (1 GP)

An epitaph for a dead partridge. The epigram resembles Anyte's for dead animals (cf. 1n.), but here the twist is that the bird had, in life, been used as a decoy to attract others of its kind (cf. Arist. *Hist. anim.* 614a10, 560b15, Ael. *NA* 4.16, Xen. *Mem.* 2.1.4). Some of the point derives from the initial ambiguity of ἀγρότα, which could refer either to a hunting decoy or to a bird living in the countryside, as partridges do. The allusion to the deceptive song of the Sirens (2) provides some hint of the bird's function, made explicit first in 3, where it is assimilated to a human fowler. Several other phrases evoke Homeric scenes of hunting (cf. 1, 3nn.).

1[237] οὐκέτι: cf. Anyte *AP* 7.202 (for a rooster), 215 (a beached dolphin), which similarly open with the adverb; that the dead person will no longer be able to do what he or she once did is an epitaphic commonplace (e.g. *CEG* 680.5 [ο]ὐκέτι τὰν ἁβρόπαιδα πάτραν σὰν Ἑσπερ[ίδ'] ὄψηι). **ἀν' ὑλῆεν δρίος:** a variation of the Homeric χῶρον ἀν' ὑλήενθ', used in the context of a hunting simile at *Il.* 10.360–2. For the common χῶρον, Simias substitutes a Homeric hapax, the neuter noun δρίος "thicket" (cf. *Od.* 14.353). The noun is semantically obscure and is thus glossed with multiple adjectives; cf. Sistakou 2007: 395. **εὔσκιον:** an un-Homeric word (cf. Homeric σκιοείς), first in Pindar (*Pyth.* 11.21) and Euripides (fr. 495.36). **ἀγρότα:** the sole Homeric occurrence of the word is in a simile comparing the weeping of Telemachus and Odysseus to geese or vultures whose young have been taken by ἀγρόται (*Od.* 16.216–18). It may mean either "woodsman" or "hunter" (cf. Fraenkel 1910–20: 1.57), and ancient critics debated its Homeric sense (cf. Sistakou 2007: 395); only with θηρεύων in the third verse does it become clear that the latter meaning is operative.

2[238] ἱεῖς: alternative thematic form of the second person singular present indicative active of ἵημι (Smyth §746b). **γῆρυν ἀπὸ στομάτων:** a rewriting of the Sirens' attempt to waylay Odysseus by claiming that no sailor has yet passed by without hearing their song (*Od.* 12.187 πρίν γ' ἡμέων μελίγηρυν ἀπὸ στομάτων ὄπ' ἀκοῦσαι). Like theirs, the partridge's song is deceptive and destructive. The plural στομάτων is appropriate for the Sirens, but here a poetic equivalent to the singular.

3[239] θηρεύων: cf. 1n. For the representation of the decoy as an active hunter, cf. Arist. *Hist. anim.* 614a10.   **βαλιοὺς συνομήλικας:** the common rock partridge (*Alectoris graeca*) is a slate grey bird with a black outline around its white throat and with black and white bars on its wings, but its chicks are spotted. συνομῆλιξ is attested first here; the expression ξὺν ὁμήλικι occupies the same verse-position at Thgn. 1063. The intensifying prefix συν- suggests a solidarity violated by the decoy's perfidy.   **ἐν νομῶι ὕλης** varies *Od.* 10.159 ἐκ νομοῦ ὕλης, of the woods from which a deer ultimately killed by Odysseus emerges.

4[240] Animals are sometimes represented as appearing in the Underworld (e.g. *Od.* 11.572–5), but the language here is typical of inscribed epitaphs and represents the partridge's death in markedly human terms. A similar effect occurs in Anyte *AP* 7.190.3–4; cf. Catull. 3.11–14.   **ὤιχεο γάρ:** similar explanatory expressions are common in inscribed epigrams, e.g. *CEG* 575.3–4 σὺ γάρ ... | ὤιχου.   **πυμάταν ... ὁδόν** "on the final road," a common metaphor for death in Hellenistic inscriptions and in the Anthology.   **εἰς Ἀχέροντος** "to (the house of) Acheron." The genitive is used by analogy with the more common εἰς Ἀίδου, and is not dependent on ὁδόν. Acheron, originally a body of water in the Underworld, stands by metonymy for the Underworld itself already in the fifth century (e.g. Soph. *Ant.* 812; *CEG* 119.2), but here the construction (εἰς + genitive of person) points to the personified god Hades.

CALLIMACHUS

Callimachus was the most prolific and influential Hellenistic poet. His style and manner are often viewed as coterminous with an "Alexandrian" or more broadly "Hellenistic" approach to poetic composition; such views oversimplify the diversity of Hellenistic poetry, but they reflect his importance in the canon. Internal evidence shows that he was born in Cyrene but was associated with Ptolemaic Alexandria from at least the late 270s through the mid 240s. In addition to being one of the more creative poets of antiquity, he was a prodigious scholar, whose prose treatises included work on contests, birds, winds, rivers, unusual words, the foundations of islands and cities, barbarian customs, and wonders of the world; his

Pinakes were an organized account of books held in the Library, including a quotation of the first line of each (cf. Blum 1991, Krevans 2004). This scholarship was reflected in his verse, which included a collection of six hymns, a hexameter epic called the *Hecale*, a collection of *Iambi*, elegies, and lyric poems on various topics. These sophisticated and witty works experimented in innovative ways with voice and with the traditional features of inherited forms. They included numerous rare glosses, frequently referred to obscure places, rites, and customs, and used language in ways that reflected contemporary scholarly debates, especially about the text and interpretation of the Homeric epics. His metrical technique was highly refined: cf. Introduction section 4h.

More than sixty epigrams survive. In one (*Epigr.* 35), Callimachus seems to distinguish his serious poetry (ἀοιδή) from his lighthearted, sympotic compositions, a group that probably includes epigram. In fact, Callimachus' epigrams differ somewhat from many other of his poems in the deceptive simplicity of their language. They contain relatively few obscure and unusual words and glosses; their word order is generally straightforward; they rarely refer to obscure myths and rituals, matters of scholarly controversy, or specific passages of Homeric epic. Their relatively simple diction and syntax, however, belie the interpretative questions they pose. Indeed, several epigrams that call attention to the act of interpretation may be read as reflecting on the hermeneutical challenges facing the reader: in these, the speaker moves from self-proclaimed ignorance or intellectual uncertainty to understanding or confidence (cf. LXII, LXVI introductory nn.).

L. *Callimachus* AP *7.517 (20 Pf., 32 GP)*

The tragedy befalling the house of Aristippus. The poem consists of a vivid narrative in which the death of Melanippus leads to the suicide of his unmarried sister and to the grief of the household and the wider Cyrenaean community. The sequence is underscored by the repetition of forms of (ἐσ)οράω in the identical position in the second and third pentameters: first the house witnesses the father's losses, and then Cyrene witnesses the house's bereavement.

The name Melanippus appears on coinage from Cyrene from *ca.* 325 BCE, as does that of Aristippus some time later. The poem is, however, a literary exercise that plays on the generic conventions of epitaphs. Its content evokes tragic messenger speeches reporting the desolation of a household by a succession of disasters, all occurring within a single day. The linking of individual couplets by enjambment reinforces the impression of cascading misfortunes culminating in the grief of the entire city.

Basilo's suicidal anguish at the loss of her brother may reflect the ideological importance of sisterly affection during and after the reign of Ptolemy II Philadelphus and his sister-wife Arsinoe, especially given the royal associations of the dead girl's name. On this poem, see Ambühl 2002.

1–2[241–2] ἠῶιοι . . . ἠελίου δὲ | δυομένου: the delimitation of the disaster by the rise and setting of the sun evokes the *topos* that a single day is sufficient to convert a person's fortune from good to ill (e.g. Soph. *El.* 1148–50). **ἠῶιοι Μελάνιππον:** the juxtaposition of the dead man's name and the adjective is pointed, since the horses of Dawn were conventionally white, those of Night black (cf. Aesch. fr. 69.6–7). **ἐθάπτομεν:** the imperfect tense creates vividness, as at Call. *AP* 7.519.3 τᾶι ἑτέραι κλαύσαντες ἐθάπτομεν, Pos. 46.6, 61.5 AB. **Βασιλώ:** a rare name whose implication of royalty may suggest that the family's status was elevated. **παρθενική:** cf. II, IV introductory nn. Basilo's death before marriage and child-bearing augments the misfortune.

3[243] αὐτοχερί "by her own hand." **ἀδελφεόν:** the special grief engendered by the loss of a brother finds models at e.g. Soph. *Ant.* 904–15, Hdt. 3.119.3–6. **ἐν πυρὶ θεῖσα:** < *Il.* 5.215 ἐν πυρὶ θείην.

5–6[245–6] Κυρήνη | πᾶσα . . . δόμον: for the grief of the community, e.g. *CEG* 10.10 ἄνδρας μὲν πόλις ἥδε ποθεῖ καὶ δῆ[μος Ἐρεχθέος], 643.4 πένθος ἔχει πᾶσα πόλις, *IMEGR* 67.7 π[ᾶ]σα . . . σὸν στενάχησε πόλις βαρυκαδέα πότμον, Pos. 50 AB. **κατήφησεν,** "hung its head," is here unusually applied to the city-state itself. **χῆρον ἰδοῦσα δόμον** "seeing the house bereft of children"; cf. 4 οἶκος ἐσεῖδε κακόν. The phrase resembles Antim. fr. 134 χηρήιον οἶκον, where Hesychius (χ415) glosses the otherwise unattested by-form of the adjective as "childless"; cf. Eur. *Alc.* 862 χήρων μελάθρων, of a house bereft of its mistress. The extension of the word from widows to other members of the community is analogous to the development of ὀρφανός, which is applied to parents and others as well as to orphaned children.

LI. Callimachus AP 7.80 (2 Pf., 34 GP)

A remembrance of the speaker's friend, the poet Heraclitus (cf. p. 166). The epigram plays on the commemorative function of epitaphs as a source of lasting information. Rather than being transmitted on a "memorial" (i.e. a μνῆμα), here the news of Heraclitus' death is conveyed not by a grave marker, but by an anonymous informant (1 τις) who prompts the speaker's recollection; the address to Heraclitus as the speaker's Halicarnassian guest-friend (4 ξεῖν' Ἁλικαρνησεῦ) plays on the conventional sepulchral address directed to the passing stranger and suggests the physical separation of the dead man, whose location is ambiguous (3 που; cf. Hunter 1992: 120), from the mourning speaker, who is both recipient and conveyor of information. The poem thus represents a "sequel" to epigrams in which the stone asks passersby to convey information about the dead person to his distant family: it reports the reaction of one to whom such information has been given. "Memory" in Callimachus serves as a metaphor for poets' engagement with the literary tradition (McNelis and Sens 2016: 57), and the process of transmission, reminiscence, and survival recorded here perhaps reflects the poet's dual role as recipient and transmitter of the tradition.

The epigram is divided into unequal halves, structured around the vocatives Ἡράκλειτε (1) and ξεῖν' Ἁλικαρνησεῦ (3). Both halves move from loss to recollection and preservation: they open with Heraclitus' death (1 τεὸν μόρον, 3–4 σὺ . . . σποδιή) and culminate by referring, first obliquely and then explicitly, to his poetry and its survival in the speaker's memory or in writing; the evocation of 1 τεὸν μόρον in 5 τεαὶ . . . ἀηδόνες emphasizes the contrast between Heraclitus' mortality and the destiny of his poetry. Indeed, the poem is constructed around a set of fundamental oppositions – between past and present, presence and absence, light and darkness, loss and preservation. Both parts end with night, first in the claim that the speaker and his friend often "made the sun set," and second in the designation of Heraclitus' work as "nightingales," birds which sing through the night; the metaphor forms part of an argument about their capacity to survive the danger of obliteration posed by Ἁίδης, whose name was interpreted to mean "he who makes invisible" (cf. Call. *Epigr.* 41.1–2).

The poem contains a number of marked epicisms (1 τεόν/5 -αί, 3 ἠέλιον, 5 ζώουσιν, 6 ἐπὶ . . . βαλεῖ) which distinguish the speaker's address to his dead friend from ordinary conversation and locate it in a tradition that preserves the glory of dead heroes.

1–3[247–9] εἶπέ … κατεδύσαμεν "someone mentioned your death, Heraclitus, and brought me to tears, and I remembered how often both of us brought the sun down in conversation." The opening lines narrate the speaker's reaction to news of his friend's death through a series of paratactic clauses connected by δέ: word of Heraclitus' fate leads the speaker to mourn and then to remember. Cf. Virg. *Ecl.* 9.51–2 *saepe ego longos | cantando memini puerum me condere soles*, where the literary character of "memory" is overt. **εἶπε … τεὸν μόρον:** an unusual expression, more probably meaning "someone told me of your death" than "someone mentioned your death" (as suggested by Thomson 1941), but ultimately ambiguous.   τις: the anonymity of the informant suits the uncertainty about the grave's location.   ἐς δέ με δάκρυ | ἤγαγεν "and led me to a tear." For the position of the personal pronoun, cf. 5n.   ὁσσάκις: a rare form. ὁσσάκι occurs three times in Homer (*Il.* 21.265, 22.194, *Od.* 11.585; cf. Call. *h.* 4.254), always introducing temporal relative clauses ("however often") rather than, as here, an indirect question.   ἠέλιον . . . κατεδύσαμεν "brought the sun down," a reworking of Homeric expressions in which the sun is subject (e.g. *Il.* 1.475 ἠέλιος κατέδυ) and the verb intransitive ("go down," "sink"); here it is transitive (e.g. Pherecr. fr. 12.2 "causing to sink"). The expression plays on the idea of the sun sinking as people continue with an activity, as in the Homeric phrase καί νύ κ' ὀδυρομένοισιν ἔδυ φάος ἠελίοιο, used in passages evoking "memory, friendship and loss" (Hunter 1992: 122–3; cf. *Il.* 23.154, *Od.* 16.220, 21.226). Night's arrival also evokes death, and the phrase achieves point by contrast: in the past, conversations extended into the darkness, but now only Heraclitus' poetry survives the darkness of his death. Cf. 5–6n.   λέσχηι "in conversation." Callimachus elsewhere uses the noun, which occurs once in Homer in the sense "place for conversation" (*Od.* 18.329; cf. Hes. *WD* 493, 501), of the sort of discussions that lead to the composition of poetry, including the encounter between the poet and the Muses at the opening of the *Aetia* (fr. 2a.44, Pf. addenda) and the sympotic conversation of fr. 178.16.   που: cf. 269n.

4[250] τετράπαλαι "extremely long ago," only here; a pointed exaggeration of the more usual colloquialism τρίπαλαι; cf. *109n.* τριγέροντα.

5–6[251–2] The contrast between Heraclitus' "nightingales" and Hades as a "snatcher" (ἁρπακτής) evokes the Hesiodic parable (*WD* 202–12) of the nightingale, represented as a "singer" (ἀοιδόν), and the hawk that has snatched it in its talons (204 μεμαρπώς). Heraclitus' "nightingales," the speaker claims, will remain untouched.   ἀηδόνες: probably a metonymy for "poems" (cf. the earlier use of the noun to mean poets; e.g. Bacchyl. 3.98), but possibly the title of Heraclitus' work. Nightingales were thought not to need sleep (Hes. fr. 312, *Suda* α651), and the word thus has a special significance for poems that live on after their writer's death.   ὁ πάντων | ἁρπακτής: a violent image, with parallels in expressions for other all-powerful gods or personified cosmic forces (e.g. Pi. *Olymp.* 2.17 Χρόνος ὁ πάντων πατήρ, *Isthm.* 5.53 Ζεὺς ὁ πάντων κύριος, fr. 169a.1, Bacchyl. 17.66), but πάντων is paradoxical in context: though Hades snatches all else (cf. Lyc. *Alex.* 655), he cannot touch Heraclitus' poetry. ἁρπακτής is a rare variation, first attested here, of the Homeric hapax ἁρπακτήρ. ἁρπάζω and its cognates and compounds are often used of sudden death, an idea underlying the abduction of Persephone by Hades (e.g. *HHDem.* 2–3, Hes. *Th.* 913–14, Leon. *143*).   ἐπὶ χεῖρα βαλεῖ: tmesis = χεῖρα ἐπιβαλεῖ.

LII. Callimachus AP 7.447 (11 Pf., 35 GP)

An epitaph for Theris, on whose tomb a brief phrase will be inscribed. The wit depends on the distinction between the voice of the poem itself and that of the inscription embedded in it: the speaker of line 2 is Theris, but the line he quotes has not yet been inscribed, since it is imagined as speaking in the future (1). The conclusion plays on the fact that inscriptions must fit a defined space, so that a line that was "long" would be problematic: here, however, the real problem is that the deceased spoke concisely, so that even a brief and (from the standpoint of a poem composed in elegiac couplets) metrically incomplete inscription (but cf. 2n.) is excessively verbose for his tomb.

The epigram is similar in theme to LXXV. Apart from their common focus on Cretans, both epigrams engage with the idea that it is appropriate for foreigners to mind their words (e.g. Aesch. *Supp.* 194–6, Eur. *Phoen.* 390–1). They may both also be read as evoking the esthetic significance of concision for Hellenistic poets; Cairns's view (1996b: 79–80) that they were commissioned for inscription seems less probable than that they are literary fictions playing on the brevity of the genre.

1[253] The line is framed by the contrasting terms σύντομος and μακρὰ λέξων. **σύντομος** "concise," "getting right to the point," without unnecessary verbiage. Brevity is treated as a stylistic virtue elsewhere in Callimachus (e.g. fr. 1), as it was in the Peripatetic tradition (e.g. Arist. *Nic. Eth.*1176a33). **ὁ ξεῖνος:** here not the passerby but the occupant of the tomb (cf. Philitas 225–6n.), who has died and been buried away from his homeland; his ethnic is thus required. **ὅ** "in respect to which," i.e. "for which reason" (LSJ A.b.IV.2). **καί** "even." **στίχος:** i.e. inscribed line, whether metrical or not. **οὐ μακρὰ λέξων** "which will not go on at length."

2[254] Θῆρις Ἀρισταίου Κρής: the imagined inscription; the dead man's name and ethnic and the name of his father, i.e. the most basic information necessary to identify him, fill the first half of the hexameter up to the end of the third foot (Celentano 1995: 69). **ἐπ' ἐμοί:** both "over me" (e.g. Nossis *AP* 7.414.2), with the speaker imagined to be the deceased, and "on me," with the speaker taken as the tomb.

LIII. Callimachus AP 7.272 (18 Pf., 38 GP)

A cenotaph for Lycus, who has died at sea. The poem reworks Asclep. 31, in which the narrator asks the passerby to carry news of his death at sea to his family. Here, the tomb provides details of the death directly and represents itself as a herald offering a generic warning of the dangers of winter seafaring. The message it conveys plays on the name of the deceased, Lycus: in a reversal of the natural order, here the constellation known as "the Kids" poses a mortal threat to the "Wolf."

The poem contains a number of epic phrases, and its opening lines in particular evoke the proem of the *Odyssey* (cf. 1–2n.). The reformulated epic language presents Lycus as a sort of Homeric hero, whose disappearance at sea represents the type of unmarked death that heroes dread. Structurally the poem is unified by references to the sea after the bucolic diaeresis of each hexameter (1 ἀλλ' ἐνὶ πόντωι, 3 χὦ μὲν ἐν ὑγρῆι, 5 φεῦγε θαλάσσηι).

1–2[255–6] rewrite the proem of the *Odyssey* (1.4–5), in which the opposition between land and sea is implicit in the claim that the hero both "saw" (ἴδεν) the cities of many men and suffered much on the sea (ἐν πόντωι) trying to preserve his life (ἤν τε ψυχήν) and the return of his companions. Unlike Odysseus (but like his crew), Lycus is witness (εἶδεν) only to the loss of both his vessel and his own soul. The expression involves a syllepsis in which ναῦν is the more natural object of εἶδεν than ψυχήν. **ἐπὶ γῆς ... ἐνὶ πόντωι**: the two possibilities are couched in language evocative of Homer: cf. *Od.* 4.354, 821 ἐνὶ πόντωι, 12.27 ἢ ἁλὸς ἢ ἐπὶ γῆς ἀλγήσετε.

3[257] ἔμπορος: see 462–3n. The emphatic position contrasts the commercially motivated Lycus with the heroes with whom the poem implicitly compares him (see below). **Αἰγίνηθεν ὅτ' ἔπλεε**: cf. *Il.* 14.250–1 ἤματι τῶι ὅτε κεῖνος ὑπέρθυμος Διὸς υἱός | ἔπλεεν Ἰλιόθεν Τρώων πόλιν ἐξαλαπάξας, of Heracles, who is separated from his companions as he sails away from a heroic exploit; Lycus, by contrast, dies engaging in commerce, traveling not from Troy but from Aegina, a major commercial center. **ἐν ὑγρῆι**: a variation of the Homeric ἐφ' ὑγρήν (*Od.* 1.97, etc.) that pathetically places Lycus "in" rather than "on" the sea.

4[258] ἄλλως οὔνομα ... ἔχων "having merely a name," i.e. an inscription but no body; cf. Asclep. 31.4 Sens αὐτὸ λέλειπτ' ὄνομα. For ἄλλως in the sense "only, merely," cf. e.g. Soph. *Phil.* 946–7 καπνοῦ σκιὰν | εἴδωλον ἄλλως.

5–6[259–60] The tomb appropriates the voice of Hesiodic didactic to offer general sailing advice (cf. Hes. *WD* 641–2) but varies the astronomical details (see below). For the embedding of a direct quotation by a "messenger," cf. *CEG* 632.5–6 ("Θηβαῖοι κρείσσονες ἐν πολέμωι" | καρύσσει Λεύκτροις νικαφόρα δουρὶ τρόπαια). **κηρύσσω . . . ἔπος:** cf. *3–4*n. ἔπος suits the tomb's didactic posture. Greek poets sometimes represent themselves as heralds (cf. Pi. fr. 70b23–5 ἐμὲ δ᾽ ἐξαίρετο[ν] | κάρυκα σοφῶν ἐπέων | Μοῖσ᾽ ἀνέστασ᾽), who, like poets, often insist on the accuracy of their reports (cf. Aesch. *Ag.* 680). **φεῦγε** "avoid." **συμμίσγειν** "have dealings with," a common meaning (LSJ ii), though the literal sense "mix together" also resonates in a phrase referring to a body of water (cf. e.g. Hdt. 4.202.4). **Ἐρίφων . . . δυομένων:** the evening rising of the Kids (i.e. the moment in the celestial calendar when they appear on the horizon at sunset) in late September marked the onset of rough weather and is associated with the perils of sailing (Theocr. 7.53–4; cf. Kidd on Arat. 158). Callimachus instead mentions the moment of their setting in December (cf. Kidd on Arat. 682), just as Hesiod (*WD* 619–22) focuses on the setting of the Pleiades as the moment at which storm winds make the sea particularly dangerous. **ναυτίλε:** a variation of the more typical epigrammatic address to the road-traveling passerby (i.e. ὁδίτης).

LIV. Callimachus AP *7.451 (9 Pf., 41 GP)*

An epitaph for Saon. The poem draws on a common epitaphic form in which the dead person is said to "lie here." For the verb conventionally used in such contexts, κεῖται, the speaker substitutes a different euphemism, and then, in the pentameter, departs from the epitaphic narrative to explain why he has done so: one should not say that good men have died.

1[261] τῆιδε "here." **Ἀκάνθιος:** several places were called Acanthus, including cities on the Athos peninsula in Chalcidice, near Memphis on the Nile, and on the Cnidian Chersonese.

1–2[261–2] ἱερὸν ὕπνον | κοιμᾶται: the representation of death as sleep is found already in Homer (*Il.* 11.204 κοιμήσατο χάλκεον ὕπνον) and is common in Hellenistic poetry (cf. Theocr. 22.204, Mosch. 3.104, Pos. *373*, Ogle 1933). The collocation ἱερὸς ὕπνος hints at a divinely sanctioned reward for good behavior (cf. Carphyll. AP 7.260.7–8 ἀπήμονα τὸν γλυκὺν ὕπνον | κοιμᾶσθαι χώρην πέμψαν ἐπ᾽ εὐσεβέων). **μὴ λέγε:** commands addressed either to the gravestone itself (*CEG* 429) or to its reader (*CEG* 865) are sometimes found in inscribed epigrams. Here the speaking voice explains and preemptively answers objections to the description of

death.   τοὺς ἀγαθούς: for the treatment of the dead person as part of
the community of good men, cf. *CEG* 489.1 τοὺς ἀγαθοὺς ἔστερξεν Ἄρης.

LV. Callimachus AP 7.521 (12 Pf., 43 GP)

The tomb asks the passerby to carry news of Critias' death. The poem is
modeled on Asclep. 31 Sens (cf. LIII) and, like it, mentions the dead man's
homeland, his parents, and finally his name in the last verse; the traditional information provided by epitaphs is thus disclosed slowly, obliquely,
and in the reverse of the expected order. Here the speaker is the tomb
rather than the deceased, though revelation of his identity is postponed
to the final words. Unlike that of Asclep. 31 Sens, the tomb contains a
body, and the poem plays on the contrast between the imagined mobility
of the addressee in the opening words and the fixed position of the dead
man in the final verse: by omitting the explicit apostrophe of the passerby
and reference to the tomb found in the first verse of its model, it sets up
a poignant contrast between the parents' location in Cyzicus, specified in
the first word, and the unspecified location (ὧδε) of their dead son, whose
name is deferred; the physical separation of Κύζικον and Κριτίην mirrors
the unbridgeable distance between the dead man and his homeland. The
intended recipients of the news, moreover, will be left in the dark about
the cause of his death, and told only that the tomb detains him elsewhere.

1[263] Κύζικον ἦν ἔλθῃς: the postponement of the conjunction mirrors
that at Asclep. 31.2 Sens εἰς Χίον εὖτ’ ἂν ἵκῃι.   **ὀλίγος πόνος:** that the
semantic range of the noun includes both "labor" and "grief" prepares for
the implicit contrast between the alleged ease of finding the parents and
the emotional pain the parents will experience.

2[264] ἀφανὴς οὔτι "by no means obscure," an emphatic litotes. The con-
spicuousness of Critias' family contrasts with his now perpetual invisibil-
ity.   **γάρ:** the postponement of the particle beyond second position in
its clause is facilitated by the logical cohesion of the two preceding words.

3–4[265–6] The assonance of ἐ- in the hexameter and the alliteration of
τ at the head of the pentameter and (especially) of κ/χ in the reported
message may have a pathetic effect similar to that in LVII (where cf. introductory n.).   **ἀνιηρόν . . . ἔπος** "a grievous message." The report will
be a source of pain for the parents, but the language also suggests the
irritation that bad news arouses toward the messenger (cf. Soph. *Ant.* 277
στέργει γὰρ οὐδεὶς ἄγγελον κακῶν ἐπῶν).   **ἔμπα** "nevertheless," the Attic
equivalent to ἔμπης.   **λέξαι:** aorist active infinitive used as imperative,

with solemn effect; cf. 223–4n. **τὸν κείνων . . . Κριτίην** "their son, Critias." The Ionic form of the proper name is appropriate to a man from Cyzicus. **ὧδ' ἐπέχω** "detain here" (cf. LSJ ἐπέχω IV), a development of the common use of the simplex ἔχω by tombstones speaking in the first person (cf. Asclep. *41.1 Sens); the tomb both contains Critias' body and prevents him from returning to Cyzicus.

LVI. Callimachus AP 7.271 (17 Pf., 45 GP)

A lament for Sopolis, lost at sea. The speaking voice of the cenotaph expresses regret for the invention of ships, which led to Sopolis' death. The poem resembles inscribed and fictive epitaphs in which the speaker is an individual mourner (cf. IV introductory n.), but here the speaker forms part of the community of mourning passersby (2 στένομεν, 4 παρερχόμεθα); inscribed epigrams spoken by the deceased or by the tomb commonly address travelers in the plural.

The opening contrafactual wish recalls the beginning of Euripides' *Medea*, where the Nurse observes that had the *Argo* not been built and sailed to Colchis, Medea would not have reached Greece, but that as things stand she is stricken with grief. Whereas the Nurse's monologue focuses on the woes of an individual who ultimately survives her immediate suffering, the epigram underscores the connection between the creation of ships in the mythical past and the destruction of Sopolis in the present. The evocation of the past is reinforced by the Homeric phraseology that runs throughout the epigram (cf. 1, 3nn.).

The two couplets are carefully balanced. In each, the end of the hexameter and the ensuing pentameter describe mourning of the community; each pentameter concludes with a first-person plural verb. The first part of the two hexameters sets up a formal opposition between the ships in the contrafactual wish of the first couplet and the reality of the location of Sopolis' corpse (which like a ship is carried on the sea) in the second; this opposition is underscored by the phonetic resemblances of νέκυς (3) and νέες (1) in the same position in the verse.

1[267] Cf. Eur. *Med.* 1–8 "Would that the hull of the Argo had not sailed through (εἴθ' ὤφελ' Ἀργοῦς μὴ διαπτάσθαι σκάφος) the dark Symplegades to the land of the Colchians and that the pine had not fallen, cut, in the glens of Pelion . . . For my mistress, Medea, would not have sailed (οὐ γὰρ ἂν δέσποιν' ἐμὴ . . . ἔπλευσ') . . ." **ὤφελε μηδ' ἐγένοντο** "would that (ships) had not even come to exist," a capping of the Euripidean Nurse's wish that a specific ship had not gone to Colchis, though the phrase also plays with the idea of the *Argo* as the first ship, without which there would not be others. The third person singular ὤφελε is here used with the indicative instead of the more usual infinitive (Smyth §1781) to introduce a counterfactual prayer, as if it were εἴθε or εἰ γάρ. A similar construction with first singular ὄφελον is a common feature of the *koine* (e.g. NT 1 Cor. 4.8).   **θοαὶ νέες**: a standard Homeric collocation, which in the nominative plural always appears in epic in the form νῆες . . . θοαί (*Il.* 10.309, etc.). Callimachus changes the form of the noun and alters the word order, but retains the Homeric position immediately preceding the bucolic diaeresis (for νέες in this position, cf. e.g. *Il.* 2.516).

2[268] Σώπολιν: a common name of real individuals, though in context "savior of the City" helps explain the communal mourning described in the poem.

3[269] νῦν δ′: after a contrafactual condition, the phrase regularly amounts to "but as it is," but here the temporal force remains active as well.   **εἰν ἁλί**: at *Od.* 1.161–2, Telemachus asserts that his father's bones are either rotting on the mainland or being tossed by the waves (ἀνέρος, οὗ δή που λεύκ᾽ ὀστέα πύθεται ὄμβρωι | κεῖμεν᾽ ἐπ᾽ ἠπείρου, ἢ εἰν ἁλὶ κῦμα κυλίνδει).   **που** includes both "I suppose" and "somewhere," and reflects the necessity of being cautious in such contexts; cf. *Od.* 1.161–2, above.   **φέρεται νέκυς**: a variation of the Homeric νέκυν φέρον (*Il.* 17.735, 746).   **ἐκείνου**: Sopolis himself.

4[270] οὔνομα: the name inscribed on the tomb.   **κενεὸν σῆμα παρερχόμεθα**: perhaps related to Perses *194* κενεὸν σῆμα περισχόμενοι, occupying the same position in the poem but with the dead man's parents rather than the larger community as subject.

LVII. Callimachus AP 7.453 (19 Pf., 46 GP)

An epitaph for Nicoteles, the young son of Philippus. The pathos of burying a child is traditional (e.g. *CEG* 709.3–5 Εὔκλειτον, τὸμ πρῶτ[ο]ν δὴ κατετύψατο μήτηρ | ὀκτωκαιδεχετῆ παῖδα καταφθίμενον | δωδεχετῆ δὲ μετ᾽ αὐτὸν ἀνέκλαυσεν Θεόδ<ω>ρον), but Callimachus handles the theme with economy, nuance, and sympathy. The single couplet is unified by reiteration of π and κ sounds and by the placement of the names of the father and his dead son at line end. The pathos is enhanced by the juxtaposition of παῖδα and πατήρ at the medial caesura of the hexameter and by the postponement of the boy's name until after the parenthetic description of him as Philippus' "great hope."

1[271] δωδεκέτη τὸν παῖδα: cf. *8*1n. ἀπέθηκε: both ἀποτίθημι and its cognate noun ἀποθήκη occasionally refer to burials (*GVI* 298, D.C. 73.5.3, Luc. *Cont.* 22), but the verb more commonly means "store up," and some of the point lies in the implicit contrast between Philippus' conception of his son as a commodity saved for the future and the termination of that hope with the burial.

2[272] τὴν πολλὴν ἐλπίδα reflects the perspective of the father, who had hoped to benefit from his son in years to come. For the idea, cf. Aesch. *Ch.* 776 Ὀρέστης ἐλπὶς οἴχεται δόμων, *GVI* 720.2 Εὔτυχος, ἡ γονέων ἐλπίς.

LVIII. Callimachus AP 7.317 (4 Pf., 51 GP)

A brief dialogue with Timon. This figure, the subject of a number of epigrams (*AP* 7.313–20), is probably the archetypal misanthrope frequently mentioned in Athenian comedy (cf. Ar. *Lys.* 808 with Henderson ad loc.) rather than the Sceptic Timon of Phlius (as suggested by White 1994: 145–6, Clayman 2009: 149). Timon is explicitly named in two epigrams (Zenod. *AP* 7.315, Hegesipp. *AP* 7.320), but in the others the identification of the misanthropic speaker rests on the biographical tradition or on the lemmata of the Anthology (Leon. or Antip. *AP* 7.316, [Call.] *Epigr.* 3, Ptol. *AP* 7.314, adesp. *AP* 7.313). In this latter group (as also in Hegesippus), the speaking voice is that of the deceased, who commands a passerby to move on without greeting him or asking his name (cf. Fantuzzi in Fantuzzi and Hunter 2004: 302–6, 327–8); these epigrams play upon the conventional invitation for passersby to stop and greet the deceased or to learn something about him (e.g. x). Callimachus' poem may be read as a successor to other dialogue-epigrams on Timon in which the passerby is ordered not to speak. Here the interlocutor does not seek the usual identifying information, but instead inquires about the afterlife; Timon's response reveals his character.

1[273] οὐ γὰρ ἔτ' ἐσσί "for you are no longer alive." He is thus in a position to have an informed opinion on the relative merits of life and death, but the parenthesis also calls attention to the paradox of conversing with a person who no longer exists; cf. Fantuzzi in Fantuzzi and Hunter 2004: 327, Tueller 2008: 115. τί: i.e. πότερον "which of two," a usage found occasionally in prose (e.g. Xen. *Cyr.* 1.3.17, NT Matt. 27.21). σκότος: the darkness of death, and thus metonymically of the Underworld itself (e.g. Eur. *Hec.* 1, Aesch. *Eum.* 72). φάος: a common metonymy for "world of the living," e.g. Soph. *Phil.* 415 μηκέτ' ὄντα ... ἐν φάει. ἐχθρόν:

cf. Eur. *Hipp.* 354–5 "I will not endure living. I look upon the day as hateful, and on the light as hateful" (οὐκ ἀνέξομαι | ζῶσ'· ἐχθρὸν ἦμαρ, ἐχθρὸν εἰσορῶ φάος).

2[274] That death should be more abhorrent than life is hardly surprising, but the specific reason is. **πλείονες**: playing on the well-established use of οἱ πλείονες "the majority" as a euphemism for the dead (e.g. Ar. *Eccles.* 1073, *Suda* π1735 πλειόνων· τῶν νεκρῶν).

LIX. Callimachus AP 7.525 (21 Pf., 29 GP)

A fictive epitaph for the poet's father. In structure and language, the epigram is closely related to Call. *Epigr.* 35, a fictive self-epitaph. Despite the epitaphic features (including the address to the passersby), the unnamed first-person speaker focuses not on himself, but on the activities of his father and son, both named Callimachus. By contrast, in *Epigr.* 35, Callimachus refers to himself as "son of Battus," so that in their language and form (cf. 1, 2, 3–4nn., Scodel 2003) the two epigrams function as a unit covering all three generations. The poem emphasizes the continued success of the speaker's family line, culminating in the ability of the son's poetry to transcend criticism (cf. 3–4n.). The final couplet is transmitted in corrupt form (cf. 5–6n.), but seems to explain the claim that Callimachus has sung "things greater than envy" (cf. 3–4n.).

The Ionic dialect (3 κεν, κοτε, 4 βασκανίης), which is at odds with Battus' Doric ancestry and provenance, is that of the *Aetia*, to which the poem is connected.

1[275] παρὰ σῆμα φέρεις πόδα: φέρεις πόδα reverses the Homeric πόδες φέρον (*Il.* 6.514 etc.).

2[276] ἴσθι: the command "know!" is an epigrammatic trope; e.g. Call. *Epigr.* 60.2 ἴστε . . . παρερχόμενοι, *CEG* 742 πᾶς [δ' ἐ]λθὼν . . . ἴστω.

3–4[277–8] The military and poetic activities attributed to the speaker's father and his son, respectively, mirror those claimed in Archil. fr. 1 εἰμὶ δ' ἐγὼ θεράπων μὲν Ἐνυαλίοιο ἄνακτος | καὶ Μουσέων ἐρατὸν δῶρον ἐπιστάμενος. **εἰδείης . . . κεν** picks up ἴσθι in the preceding line, but turns the meaning of the verb in a new direction: the reader would know who both men were, since they both achieved prominence. **ὅπλων** "troops" (LSJ II.4). **κρέσσονα βασκανίης:** at Call. fr. 1.17 the poet refers to his literary rivals as a "destructive race of Envy (Βασκανίης ὀλοὸν γένος)." The assertion (or hope) that the poet's work will not be harmed by envy, even (or especially) after his death, is a closural device (e.g. Call. *h.* 2.105–12, Ov. *Am.* 1.15.39–42, Stat. *Theb.* 12.818–19) closely related to the wish for a favorable reception at the conclusion of the *Homeric Hymns* and other poems (Bundy 1972).

5–6[279–80] As transmitted in the manuscripts of the Anthology, the text is almost identical to Call. fr. 1.37–8, but with ἄχρι βίου instead of μὴ λοξῶι at the head of the final pentameter and a less significant variation between ὄθματι and ὄμματι. The lines involve interpretative difficulties: (a) οὐ νέμεσις has been thought disconnected from what precedes and obscure in context; and (b) ἄχρι βίου, "while alive," seems redundant in the same clause as πολιούς, which makes the same point that those favored by the Muses while young remain so in old age, and is odd in a poem recording the poet's epitaph. Pfeiffer deleted the lines as an interpolation. Faraone (1986) argues that ἄχρι βίου originally appeared at the opening of the hexameter, whence it was displaced by οὐ νέμεσις under the influence of Call. fr. 1.37. The text printed here assumes that in 6 ἄχρι βίου has wrongly displaced μὴ λοξῶι (found in the equivalent position in fr. 1.38) as an intrusive gloss that summarizes the content of the couplet, i.e. the Muses favor the poet even in old age and thus "as long as he is alive." At the opening of the couplet, οὐ νέμεσις serves as a comment on the speaker's claim to have transcended βασκανία (see 3–4n.): such a boastful assertion need not generate divine anger, since the poet was favored by the Muses throughout his life. Cf. Livrea 1992.   **οὐ νέμεσις** "there is no ground for blame"; the phrase is used to explain an action or situation that would cause anger (cf. Harder 2012: II.84), as at *Il.* 3.156–7, Call. *h.* 3.64–5.   **ἴδον** "looked upon"; cf. Asclep. *34.1 (= Pos. *126.4) with Sens's note.   **ὄμματι:** the rare ὄθματι, which occurs in the same relative position at fr. 1.37, may be preferable.   **ἀπέθεντο** is a gnomic aorist.

LX. Callimachus apud Ath. 7.318b–c (5 Pf., 14 GP)

Dedication of a nautilus shell to Arsinoe-Aphrodite. Shells of various sorts were offered to Aphrodite in her sanctuaries, and she was frequently depicted in association with them in ancient art. Arsinoe II was worshipped at a temple on Cape Zephyrium (cf. 1 Ζεφυρῖτι) as Aphrodite Euploia, protectress of seafarers, including the victims of shipwreck, and as patroness of love and marriage (cf. *391–3*n., Gutzwiller 1992, Bing 2002–3, Lapini 2004). The poem, like several other Hellenistic epigrams, seems to combine both aspects of the god. The speaking object itself is a dead nautilus (genus *Argonauta*), which has been brought to Egypt from Ceos as a first offering by a virtuous young woman. Its identity emerges slowly: the very name of the creature, prominently placed at the head of the second couplet and only explained in the ensuing relative clause, where its movement is described in nautical language borrowed from Aristotle, is initially ambiguous (cf. 3–4n.). After successfully navigating the seas in the past, the shell has come ashore, an event described in language evocative of shipwreck. At the same time, the nautilus mentions the prior use of its θαλάμαι as a nest. The word may refer to the hold of a ship, but it also evokes θάλαμος, bedchamber, and Gutzwiller (1992) plausibly suggests that Selenaea is to be imagined as making the offering in hopes of a successful marriage.

The poem celebrates in a light manner how the royal house aids the movement of goods and people to Egypt (cf. Stephens 2005: 230, 245–6). At Pos. 39.4–5 AB the speaker addresses a sailor, ναυτίλος, as the principal beneficiary of Callicrates' construction of Arsinoe's temple at Zephyrium (θήκατο Καλλικράτης, | ναυτίλε, σοὶ τὰ μάλιστα). Here, a ναυτίλος travels throughout the Eastern Mediterranean in order ultimately to arrive in Egypt and becomes a "plaything" (παίγνιον) of the queen; Selenaea has similarly come to Alexandria from Smyrna.

1[281] κόγχος ἐγώ: *sc.* ἦν. κόγχος is here used generically for "mollusc," referring in this context to the living animal as well as its shell. **παλαίτερον . . . νῦν**: the opposition between the past and present conditions of the speaker is developed in the main body of the poem (cf. 7, 8, 9–10n.). Adverbial παλαίτερον = "long ago" (cf. D.H. 11.36.2 οὐ νῦν πρῶτον ἀλλὰ παλαίτερον ἔτι) is better than the transmitted παλαίτερος, which effaces that opposition.

2[282] ἄνθεμα πρῶτον: the epigram marks a moment of transition in Selenaea's life (cf. XLIV introductory n.); perhaps she may be imagined to have just reached the age of marriage.

3[283] ναυτίλος . . . ἐπέπλεον "(I) used to sail the sea as a 'sailor'." Sailors were among the principal beneficiaries of Arsinoe-Aphrodite's cult at Zephyrium (cf. *393*), but the ναυτίλος here turns out to be a Paper Nautilus, a cephalopod known by several names, including ναυτίλος, ποντίλος, and ὠιὸν πολύποδος ("Octopus' Egg"); cf. Arist. *Hist. anim.* 525b20–1. The position of the nominative, which belongs grammatically within the relative clause, is emphatic (see introductory n.). **εἰ μὲν ἀῆται**: i.e. ἐὰν ἀῆται (nom. pl. of ἀήτης) ὦσι (cf. Arist. *Hist. anim.* 622b13, below); for the omission of ἄν, cf. *67–8n.*

4[284] τείνας . . . προτόνων "stretching my sail from my own stays."
Sailing imagery appears in the description of the creature in Aristotle's
Historia animalium (622b6 ἐπιπλεῖ γὰρ ἐπὶ τῆς θαλάττης, 12–13 "Whenever
there is some wind, it uses (its webbing) as a sail, and lets down two of its
tentacles beside it in place of rudders"; cf. Prescott 1921). Callimachus
varies the language and develops the imagery: for Aristotle's "tentacles"
(δάκτυλοι), Callimachus substitutes the nautical term πρότονοι, "cables."

5[285] Γαληναίη: an epicizing doublet of Γαλήνη, "calm at sea," here personified as a goddess (cf. Hes. *Th.* 244).   λιπαρὴ θεός: in the sense
"bright, radiant," the adjective is applied to a goddess at Hes. *Th.* 901
λιπαρὴν Θέμιν (cf. Bacchyl. 7.1), but it can also suggest the oily sheen on a
calm sea (Theocr. 22.19 λιπαρὴ . . . γαλήνη). Callimachus here combines
both uses.   οὖλος ἐρέσσων "rowing quickly." This use of the predicate
nominative οὖλος is an extension of the adverbial use of the neuter singular οὖλον (*Il.* 17.756, 759, cf. *LfgrE* οὖλον), which some ancient scholars
interpreted as "quickly." Callimachus elsewhere adopts the adverbial neuter plural in passages describing movement (*h.* 1.52, 3.246–7).

6[286] ἴδ' ὡς τὤργωι . . . συμφέρεται "look how the name agrees with the
action." The text is problematic. If Schneider's emendation is correct, the
expression plays on ecphrastic passages in which the viewer is asked to
note the resemblance of an image to its subject (e.g. Nossis *173*).

7[287] ἔστ' "until."   ἔπεσον "I was cast ashore," in sharp contrast to
emphasis on methods of navigating the sea in the two preceding couplets.   παρὰ θῖνας: Homer has the singular παρὰ θῖνα, always in this position of the verse.   Ἰουλίδας: Iulis was one of the principal cities of Ceos,
and the word, here adjectival, is tantamount to "Cean" (cf. Call. fr. 67.5).
The island was important to the Ptolemies and may have played a role in
the conflict with Antigonus in 277–265 (Hammond and Walbank 1988:
284); its main harbor, Coresia, was renamed Arsinoe after the queen's
death (Call. fr. 75.74, Asper 2011: 158).   ὄφρα γένωμαι probably
implies that the nautilus' landing at Ceos was fated rather that it intended
to beach itself; cf. Call. *h.* 3.108–9.

8[288] περίσκεπτον: probably "seen from all sides," "admired," rather
than "worth seeing" (*pace* LSJ) or "amazing" (an otherwise unattested
meaning attributed to the adjective here by Didymus II.3 fr. 5, pp.
184–5 Schmidt). Now fully removed from the water, the shell may be
viewed *in toto* by Arsinoe. The adjective occurs in Homer in the phrase

περισκέπτωι ἐνὶ χώρωι (*Od.* 1.426, 10.211, 253, 14.6); ancient critics differed on whether it meant "seen from all sides" or "whence one can see all sides." **παίγνιον**: the object's intended function is emblematic of the playful tone of the poem as a whole. Aphrodite, like her son Eros, could be playful (e.g. Theocr. 15.101 χρυσῶι παίζοισ᾽ Ἀφροδίτα), often in ways far less benign to humans; cf. 743–4n.

9–10[289–90] The ἀλκυών is the kingfisher, *Alcedo ispida*, but ancient accounts of the bird are a mixture of fact and pseudoscience (cf. Dunbar on Ar. *Birds* 251). From the erroneous belief that the birds nested in the days around the winter solstice, fair weather during the winter came to be known as "the Halcyon Days" (Ar. *Birds* 1591–5 with Dunbar's note, Arist. *Hist. anim.* 542b4–16). The association of the halcyon's roosting with windless calm (Theocr. 7.57–8, Ael. *NA* 1.36) makes the shell's assertion that the bird will no longer lay eggs in it because "I am ἄπνους" a humorous oxymoron. **μηδέ . . . ὡς πάρος**: Callimachus varies the conventional epitaphic idea that the deceased can no longer participate in his or her past activities (e.g. Anyte *AP* 7.215.1–2, *CEG* 95, 680.6–9) by focusing not on the shell but on the bird who used it as an egg depository. **ἐν θαλάμηισιν** "in my recesses"; but θαλάμη plays on multiple images active in the passage, since it may refer to the "holds" of ships (cf. LSJ II) and to cavities of the body (LSJ I.2), as well as to the nests or lairs of animals (cf. *Od.* 5.432, its sole Homeric occurrence). **ἄπνους**: here "without breath, lifeless" but also implying "without wind," and so resuming the distinction drawn in 3–6. **νοτερῆς . . . ἀλκυόνος**: the name ἀλκυών was (falsely) explained by lexicographers as "breeding at sea" (ἅλς + κύειν; cf. *Et. gen.* α501), and νοτερῆς "wet" is thus virtually a gloss; cf. 220n. λυγρῆι ὄρνιθι.

11[291] δίδου χάριν "give favor"; cf. Thgn. 1303.

11–12[291–2] οἶδε . . . ἐσθλὰ | ῥέζειν: Selenaea's proper behavior includes the present offering; for the language, cf. *SGO* 03/02/62.5–6 ἐσθλὰ μὲν εἰπεῖν | [ἐσθ]λὰ δὲ καὶ ῥέξαι πάντας ἐπισταμένους. **Σμύρνης . . . Αἰολίδος**: the phrase (cf. Mimn. fr. 9.6 θεῶν βουλῆι Σμύρνην εἵλομεν Αἰολίδα) represents the city in terms appropriate to its Aeolian settlement. It was transformed into an Ionian city by conquest (Hdt. 1.150, Paus. 5.8.7), and after its destruction by the Lydians existed only as a village until refounded by Antigonus and Arsinoe's first husband Lysimachus (Str. 14.1.37). Its excellent harbor (as evidenced by its prior name Ναύλοχον, "Anchorage"; cf. Steph. Byz. σ238) helps explain why Selenaea's origin would be viewed with favor by a goddess who protects sailors.

LXI. Callimachus AP 6.351 (34 Pf., 22 GP)

Dedication of an oak branch to Heracles. The poem is modeled on inscriptions in which a dedicated object addresses the divine recipient. It proceeds in a conventional manner as far as the first word of the pentameter, at which point Heracles interrupts; readers will retrospectively understand the speaker-divisions only when they reach ποῖος. In dialogue poems, it is usual for the voice of the viewer to question the monument; here the relationship is reversed, and the divine recipient interrogates the dedicator. The contrast between the elevated language – including novel high-style epithets and a phrase adapted from Homer – and the simple, rustic speaker, an oak branch (probably a club, given the speaker's focus on beast-killing), humorously contributes to the characterization of both speakers: the branch as an overenthusiastic admirer of Heracles' exploits, and Heracles as an impatient and laconic recipient.

1[293] The high-style accumulation of epithets is characteristic of hymnic prayers.   τίν is the Doric form of the dative second person pronoun (σοι, τοι), appropriate in the mouth of a Cretan speaker (cf. LXXV introductory n.), though the form is elsewhere used by Callimachus in a variety of dialectal contexts (e.g. fr. 24.3, *h.* 3.90, *Epigr.* 33.1).   λεοντάγχ' "lion-strangling," in reference to Heracles' killing of the Nemean Lion; the adjective appears only here.   ὦνα < ὦ ἄνα. The vocative ἄνα is reserved for gods.   συοκτόνε: first here. The epithet surprisingly reduces Heracles' accomplishment, since Eurystheus' insistence that the hero capture rather than kill the Erymanthian Boar (e.g. A.R. 1.126–9; [Apollod.] 2.5.4) was precisely what made the task difficult (e.g. D.S. 4.12.1); Hygin. *Fab.* 30 reports that Heracles killed the boar but does not specify when he did so.   φήγινον ὄζον: modeled on the Homeric φήγινος ἄξων (*Il.* 5.838).

2[294] In contrast with the elaborate compounds with which the god is addressed in the hexameter, Heracles interrupts the speaker after the first word of the pentameter, and the rest of the line comprises a rapid series of single-word questions and answers.   θῆκε – "τίς;" – Ἀρχῖνος may initially have been read as θῆκέ τις Ἀρχῖνος; the division of speakers is revealed in retrospect.   ποῖος; "which one?" (cf. Herodas 6.48, Pherecr. fr. 155.20–1). Archinus is a common name, and further specification is needed.   ὁ Κρής: Cretans could be terse (cf. LII, Pos. 372), but here the dedicator is considerably more verbose than the honorand.   δέχομαι: the impatient Heracles preempts the conventional request that he receive the offering.

XLII. Callimachus AP 6.149 (56 Pf., 25 GP)

Dedication of a bronze rooster celebrating an athletic victory. The bird provides the essential information about the dedication in indirect speech attributed to the dedicator, but he claims that he cannot personally vouch for it. Callimachus thus playfully distances his speaker from the simple declarations characteristic of inscribed epigram and calls attention to the fact that they are artificial creations subject to false claims. That the epigram itself is a literary fiction contributes to the humor: when the speaker eventually claims to trust Euaenetus, he explicitly puts his faith in a figure invented by the poet.

The speaker's uncertainty gains point from the proverbial tendency of athletes to overstate their accomplishments (e.g. Aesop 33 Perry). Interpretation of the epigram, however, depends on how one reconstructs its imagined circumstances. Critics generally assume that the bird has been dedicated in honor of a victory in a cockfight, but the poem, unlike real epigrams celebrating athletic victories, does not explicitly name the event. Whether Euaenetus won a victory of his own in another event or as the owner of the winner in a cockfight affects how ἰδίης is to be understood: in the latter case, the adjective will be pointedly ironic, since the winner was in fact the bronze bird's real-life doublet; in the former, the speaker professes genuine uncertainty about a victory in which neither he nor a real rooster played any part. For further discussion, see Meyer 1993: 166–7, 2005: 196–8, Tueller 2004: 309–10, Sens 2019: 324–5.

1–2[295–6] φησὶν . . . οὐ γὰρ ἔγωγε | γινώσκω: the opposition is like that at Il. 4.374–5 ὡς φάσαν οἵ μιν ἴδοντο πονεύμενον· οὐ γὰρ ἐγώ γε | ἤντησ᾽ οὐδὲ ἴδον· περὶ δ᾽ ἄλλων φασὶ γενέσθαι; cf. Il. 23.469–70 οὐ γὰρ ἐγώ γε | εὖ διαγιγνώσκω. For the imputed claim, cf. CEG 673.3–4 "they say ([φ]ασί) that (his relatives) set it up in exchange for the race and property he leaves behind." With the speaker's epistemological hesitation contrast epigrams in which the speaker instructs the audience about what it needs to "know" (e.g. 276). ὅ με στήσας "the man who dedicated me." Εὐαίνετος: "Easily Praised" suits a man celebrating a victory. νίκης ἀντί με τῆς ἰδίης: for the ambiguity, cf. introductory n. For the position of με, cf. 5n. ; the first unit of indirect statement introduced by φησί is νίκης ἀντί. For ἰδίης, cf. CEG 844.10–11 αἱ δὲ ἴδιαι | νῖκαι τρίς τε ἑκατὸν καὶ χίλιαι, Zen. II 59, on the proverb Ἀρκάδας μιμούμενος: "for they had no victories of their own (οὐδεμίαν ἰδίαν νίκην) but fought for hire on behalf of others."

3[297] ἀγκεῖσθαι "am dedicated"; cf. 207–8n. χάλκειον ἀλέκτορα: roosters were regularly depicted on Panathenaic prize amphorae (see Popkin

2012: 216–21), where they may be generic symbols of victory, as in the case of a bronze jumping halter engraved on both sides with a rooster (Miller 2006: 64, 65 Fig. 119). The bird was famous for its pugnacity and is thus a fitting gift for athletic patron-deities. On cockfighting and its significance, see Csapo 2006–7.   **Τυνδαρίδηισι**: the Dioscuri, Castor and Polydeuces, who were renowned as sportsmen and commonly treated as patrons of athletes (Pi. *Nem.* 10.51, Call. *h.* 5.24–5 with Bulloch's note, Theocr. 22.24).

4[298] A carefully structured, alliterative line, of which both halves have words beginning first with π and then with φ.   **Φαίδρου . . . Φιλοξενίδεω**: the speaker implies that Euaenetus' genealogy makes him trustworthy (cf. πιστεύω). It is unclear whether Φιλοξενίδεω is to be understood as a patronymic adjective ("son of Philoxenus") or a proper name ("[son] of Philoxenides"), but in either case it is significant in the context of a dedication to the Dioscuri, who were associated with hospitality (e.g. Simon. *PMG* 510, Theocr. 22.132–4) and represented as granting athletic prowess to individuals who treated them and their descendants well (e.g. Pi. *Olymp.* 3.34–41, *Nem.* 10.49–51).

LXIII. Callimachus AP 12.102 (31Pf., 1 GP)

The speaker explains his attitude about love: the pleasure lies in the pursuit. The poem is a "paratactic simile" in which the vehicle consists of an illustrative example without any conjunction; cf. Bernsdorff 1996, Hunter 2006: 108–9. The analogy between the speaker's personal desire and a hunter gains resonance from the common depiction of the god Eros as a hunter armed with bow and arrows. As a reflection on the speaker's amatory views, the poem finds parallels in the *Theognidea* (e.g. 1267–70). That it is addressed to a named male companion is important: ἢν δέ τις εἴπηι (3) suggests that the relationship of the speaker and Epicydes is like that of the hunter and his anonymous advisor, and Epicydes may be imagined as a companion who has observed (perhaps in the context of a symposium) that the speaker has finally captured the attention of a prospective lover. The harsh conditions experienced by the hunter in pursuit of his quarry resonate against amatory epigrams in which the speaker complains about or promises to endure bad weather as he waits outside his hoped-for lover's door (e.g. XVII). Here the speaker reflects on his own amatory tendencies dispassionately; the implication is perhaps that the speaker once underwent such conditions in pursuit of the person he now ignores. The poem was reworked at Hor. *Sat.* 1.2.105–8, Ov. *Am.* 2.9.9; cf. Hunter 2006: 109–11.

1[299] ὠγρευτής: i.e. ὁ ἀγρευτής. The image of the lover as hunter is first found in Ibyc. *PMG* 7 and is developed in subsequent literature (e.g. Xen. *Mem.* 3.11.6–16, Men. fr. 312, Lyc. *Alex.* 102–5) including epigram (cf. Asclep. 22.1 Sens, where Eros himself is still εὐθήρατος). See Murgatroyd 1984, Barringer 2001: 70–124. **ἐν οὔρεσι:** mountains are conventionally treated as especially wild places, good for hunting (cf. *208*).

1–2[299–300] πάντα . . . πάσης: the hunter (and implicitly the lover) is indiscriminate. The repetition of the word in masculine and feminine forms suggests that both sexes are among the lover's targets. **λαγωὸν | . . . δορκαλίδος:** hares and gazelles were timid creatures; the implication is that the speaker's targets were initially just as shy. The collocation here finds a parallel in the simile of *Il.* 10.360–4, where Odysseus and Diomedes are compared to hunting dogs pursuing "a hind or a hare" (361 ἢ κεμάδ᾽ ἠὲ λαγωὸν ἐπείγετον). Ancient critics debated whether the Homeric *hapax legomenon* κεμάς there referred to a young deer or a gazelle (Ap. Soph. p. 97.33 Bekker, *DΣ Il.* 10.261, *EM* κ503), and the use of δορκαλίς here may be a subtle gloss endorsing the latter position (but cf. *Od.* 17.294–5). The change of construction (λαγωὸν | . . . ἴχνια δορκαλίδος) is a typically Callimachean *uariatio* (though gazelles are perhaps more likely to be tracked by their footprints than hares). **διφᾶι:** a Homeric *hapax legomenon* at *Il.* 16.647 (also in a simile), of catching cuttlefish. **δορκαλίδος:** δορκαλίς is a rare diminutive of δορκάς, "gazelle."

3[301] στίβηι . . . κεχρημένος "enduring [LSJ χράω C.III] the frost and snow." στίβη is attested previously only in two passages of the *Odyssey* (5.467, 17.25), both describing the conditions experienced by Odysseus; at *Hec.* fr. 260.64–5 (fr. 74.23–4 Hollis), Callimachus describes the "frosty predawn" (στιβήεις ἄγχαυρος) as the time when the hands of robbers are "in pursuit of prey" (ἔπαγροι).

4[302] τῆ "here," elsewhere usually followed by an imperative or the logical equivalent, and in this case suggesting "take it!" **βέβληται** "has been struck," appropriate both to a hunter's striking of his prey and to the metaphorical "shots" that inspire love. **οὐκ ἔλαβεν:** timeless aorist (Smyth §1932), reflecting the paradigmatic nature of the utterance.

5–6[303–4] The speaker's position runs contrary to the proverbial idea that it is foolish to ignore what is at hand in pursuit of other things; cf. Hes. fr. 61 νήπιος, ὃς τὰ ἑτοῖμα λιπὼν ἀνέτοιμα διώκει, Pi. *Pyth.* 3.21–3 "there is among men a most foolish race, which, shunning what is nearby, seeks that which is far off, hunting in vain (μεταμώνια θηρεύων) with unfulfilled hopes." **χοὐμὸς Ἔρως:** i.e. καὶ ὁ ἐμὸς Ἔρως. Eros is here a personification of the speaker's own desire (cf. Walsh 1990: 12–13), whereas at Asclep. 22.1 Sens οὑμὸς ἔρως is tantamount to "my beloved." **τὰ μὲν . . . | οἶδε:** the language of flight and pursuit is common in the erotic tradition (e.g. Sappho, fr. 1.21, Anacr. *PMG* 417.2, Mimn. *PMG* 717.2, Theocr. 6.17 καὶ φεύγει φιλέοντα καὶ οὐ φιλέοντα διώκει, 11.75 τί τὸν φεύγοντα διώκεις;). οἶδε indicates disposition ("is wont to"); cf. ἐπίσταμαι at Archil., fr. 23 West ἐπ]ίσταμαί τοι τὸν φιλ[έο]ν[τα] μὲν φ[ι]λεῖν[, | τὸ]ν δ᾽ ἐχθρὸν ἐχθαίρειν τε [κα]ὶ κακο[. **τὰ δ᾽ ἐν μέσσωι κείμενα:** i.e. "what is readily available"; cf. Pl. *Rep.* 8.558a ἀναστρεφόμενον ἐν μέσωι, Headlam on Herodas 6.81. **παρπέταται** "flies past," here appropriate to the movement of the winged god Eros.

LXIV. Callimachus AP *12.43 (28 Pf., 2 GP)*

A "priamel" (cf. xiv introductory n., Henrichs 1979) in which a list of things the speaker dislikes sets up his praise of an attractive boy. More often in priamels, an enumeration of desirable objects culminates in something even more appealing. The poem inverts the treatment of amatory matters in Sappho, fr. 16, where the speaker uses others' preferences to emphasize her own view that what one loves is most beautiful (κάλλιστον); here the speaker rejects popular things but discovers that what he finds beautiful (καλός) is already claimed. The epigram also draws from a poem of Theognis, in which a female speaker criticizes sexual behavior of which she disapproves (579–82 ἐχθαίρω κακὸν ἄνδρα, καλυψαμένη δὲ πάρειμι, | σμικρῆς ὄρνιθος κοῦφον ἔχοντα νόον· | ἐχθαίρω δὲ γυναῖκα περίδρομον, ἄνδρά τε μάργον, | ὃς τὴν ἀλλοτρίην βούλετ᾽ ἄρουραν ἀροῦν). Here, the wit hinges on the speaker's embarrassment in the last couplet: the punctuation and text of 5–6 are disputed, but on any reading they reveal that, despite the speaker's rejection of things popular with others, his amatory tastes are not unique to him.

The speaker's elitism in 1–4 is couched in language and imagery elsewhere used of poetry. The opening line expresses distaste for "cyclic" poems, which are regularly criticized in the Homeric scholia for repetition and misuse of words (cf. Cameron 1995: 396–9); images of travel and of water appear in the corpus in programmatic statements in which Callimachus distinguished his refined and novel work from that of others (e.g. fr. 1.25–8, *h.* 3.108–12). But although the speaker's loathing for the commonplace aligns him with Callimachus' broader programmatic posture, he is a persona separable from the poet himself, and the humor depends on the ironic conclusion: rather than being a simple manifesto of literary exclusivity, the epigram turns the poet's posture elsewhere to a new purpose.

The structure of the poem underscores the reversal in the final couplet. Each couplet is a freestanding syntactical unit, and each has a clear sense-pause after the bucolic diaeresis of the hexameter. In the first two couplets, the clause following the diaeresis introduces a new but related idea: the speaker's aversions are put first positively (1 ἐχθαίρω, 3 μισέω) and then negatively (1–2 οὐδὲ κελεύθωι | χαίρω, 3–4 οὐδ᾽ ἀπὸ κρήνης | πίνω). These couplets share a word- and syntax-break after a first-foot spondee in the hexameter. Such parallelisms set the final couplet in stark relief; there the new thought introduced after the bucolic diaeresis marks the speaker's humiliation. So, too, the repetition of sounds in the first two couplets (1–4n.) anticipates the various "echoes" of the last.

Several elements of the epigram's diction appear to be features of everyday discourse (cf. 1–4nn.), and their use to express loathing for all things common may be ironic; cf. 5–6n.

1–4[305–8] form a balanced unit with first-person verbs occupying the opening of every verse and both hexameters ending with a clausula beginning with οὐδέ. ἐχθαίρω is picked up phonetically by (οὐ) χαίρω, just as the disyllabic verbs (μισέω, πίνω) that open the two verses of the second couplet are linked by the vowel of their first syllable.   τὸ ποίημα τὸ κυκλικόν: the poems of the so-called "Epic Cycle," i.e. early epics other than those that ancient critics ascribed to Homer. The adjective is widely used in this sense in ancient criticism (cf. Fantuzzi 2015: 416–29), and although the secondary, more general, connotation "ordinary, commonplace" is defensible (Blumenthal 1978), the primary sense is active here.   κελεύθωι | ... φέρει: in the *Aetia* prologue (fr. 1.27–8), Apollo recommends that the poet avoid the "broad highway" (οἶμον ... πλατύν) and instead seek κελεύθους | [ἀτρίπτο]υς. The road less traveled is also deployed metaphorically to represent other sorts of intellectual originality; cf. Parmen. 1.50, and the dictum λεωφόρους ὁδοὺς μὴ στεῖχε (cf. Arist. fr. 197).   τίς: i.e. ἥ(τις); cf. *187–8*n.   ὧδε καὶ ὧδε "this way and that."   περίφοιτον "who gets around," here reworking Thgn. 581 γυναῖκα περίδρομον. The verb φοιτάω is regularly used of visiting a lover (e.g. Lys. 1.15), and the adjective picks up the reference to travel in the preceding couplet (κελεύθωι; cf. Thgn. 599 οὔ μ᾽ ἔλαθες φοιτῶν κατ᾽ ἀμαξιτόν), taking the earlier image of the meandering highway in a new direction.   οὐδ᾽ ἀπὸ κρήνης | πίνω "I do not drink from the public spring" (for discussion, see Fabiano 1997). The use of κρήνη is modeled on Thgn. 958–61, where the speaker contrasts the pristine state of a spring from which he used to drink with its current muddied condition. Elsewhere Callimachus associates his own refined poetry with pure spring water in contradistinction to bigger, muddier bodies of water (*h.* 2.108–12; cf. Harder 2012: II.99–101 on fr. 2.1). **σικχαίνω πάντα τὰ δημόσια** "I'm revolted by everything popular," a "summarizing foil" of a sort common in priamels (Bundy 1986: 66, Race 1982: 109). The verb is cognate with σικχός, used of those who feel revulsion at everything (Arist. *Eud. Eth.* 1234a6); though the verb was perhaps used by Euphorion (fr. 21.3), its other attestations are from Hellenistic and Imperial prose (e.g. Polyb. 38.5.7). It is rejected by Phryn. p. 307 Rutherford (cf. Moeris β38) as un-Attic (= βδελύττομαι), and it may be a feature of colloquial discourse rather than an exquisite rarity; if so, its use is ironic in context. δημόσιος is "owned or used by the people" and thus "popular, generally available."

5–6[309–10] The speaker, having enumerated things he loathes, starts to express his appreciation of a boy called Lysanies, but even as he finishes speaking, he imagines another man claiming Lysanies for himself. Certainty about text and interpretation is elusive. ἠχώ could be either nominative or accusative and is thus syntactically ambiguous. The principal approaches are:

(a) Λυσανίη, σὺ δὲ ναίχι καλός – "καλός" – ἀλλὰ πρὶν εἰπεῖν | τοῦτο σαφῶς Ἠχώ, φησί τις ἄλλος ἔχειν (adopting Petersen's emendation of P's ἔχει): "Lysianes, yes, you are beautiful – 'beautiful . . .' – but before Echo can say this [i.e. repeated καλός] clearly, some other person says that he has him" (cf. Pelliccia [forthcoming]).

(b) Λυσανίη, σὺ δὲ ναίχι καλός, καλός – ἀλλὰ πρὶν εἰπεῖν | τοῦτο σαφῶς, Ἠχώ φησί τις "ἄλλος ἔχει": "Lysianes, yes, you are beautiful, beautiful – but before I can say this clearly, some Echo says, 'another holds him'." An echo thus repeats the speaker's words in chiastic order and distorted form (ναίχι καλός ~ ἄλλος ἔχει; see below). Such an echo depends on the collapsing of the sounds represented by ε and αι, which remained distinct in the speech of educated Greeks in Egypt into the middle of the third century (cf. Horrocks 1997: 68, 107–11; the collapsing of ει and ι was more widespread in this period); the phonetic play would thus make the phrase resonate ironically against the rejection of common things. On this interpretation, the adverb σαφῶς explains the distortion: the speaker has not yet expressed himself clearly before Echo repeats a contorted facsimile of his words (Pfeiffer *et al.*).

(c) Λυσανίη, σὺ δὲ ναίχι καλός, καλός – ἀλλὰ πρὶν εἰπεῖν | τοῦτο σαφῶς Ἠχώ, φησί τις "ἄλλος ἔχει": "Lysianes, yes, you are beautiful, beautiful – but before Echo can say this clearly, someone says, 'another holds him'") (Cahen, Mair).

(a), adopted here, has several advantages. Like (c), it makes the echo the repeated καλός, which readers retrospectively understand to be uttered not by the speaker but by Echo, the subject of εἰπεῖν: such a repetition conforms to the practice of ancient echoes, which typically reiterate the final word of the immediately preceding utterance (e.g. Ar. *Thesm.* 1065–97, Gauradas *APl* 152, Ov. *Met.* 3.380–92). Unlike (b) and (c) it does not require that τις ἄλλος, which elsewhere is consistently treated as a single unit, be divided between two clauses. In this case, the geminated καλός, a normal feature of such contexts (cf. below), retrospectively emerges as the referent of τοῦτο and the word that Echo cannot clearly utter before an anonymous other person speaks. These advantages outweigh the difficulty posed by the diminished significance that σαφῶς has on this interpretation.

There may be multiple echoes, as often in passages in which Echo appears. φησί τις ἄλλος ἔχειν suggests that what the anonymous other actually says is "ἔχω," and some of the point may reside in the contrast between Ἠχώ and the first-person verb implied by the end of the poem: before Echo herself can clearly repeat the last word of the speaker's praise of Lysanies, another competing voice lays claim to the boy in language suggesting the name "Echo." None of this excludes a distorted echo of ναίχι καλός in ἄλλος ἔχει<ν> (see below).

On any reading, the speaker is revealed to be not alone in his attraction to Lysanies. On this point, the resemblance of the passage to Call. *Epigr.* 29.3–4 (see below) is perhaps significant, since there the speaker hopes that his aesthetic judgment will be unique to him, precisely to avoid the sort of competition the speaker of the current poem experiences. In whatever way the couplet is punctuated, the prominence of Echo, a being who can only repeat the words of others and does so indiscriminately, stands at odds with the speaker's fastidiousness in the previous two couplets.   σὺ δέ: in pointed contrast to vulgar things for which Callimachus expresses his distaste.   ναίχι καλός . . . ἄλλος ἔχειν: cf. Call. *Epigr.* 29.3–4 καλός ὁ παῖς, Ἀχελῶιε, λίην καλός, εἰ δέ τις οὐχί | φησίν – ἐπισταίμην μοῦνος ἐγὼ τὰ καλά, where the fact that Achelous is notoriously amorous may be at issue. The verbal connection between the passages may lend special point: here, the speaker is in fact not the only one who recognizes what is good. Repetition lends emphasis, and for this reason sometimes appears in other sympotic assertions of beauty (e.g. adesp. *AP* 12.130.1), but here the second καλός is subsequently to be reinterpreted as spoken by Echo.   φησί τις ἄλλος ἔχειν: the speaker's embarrassment resembles that of the narrator of Asclep. 4.3–4 Sens, where his partner's undergarment is inscribed φίλει με | καὶ μὴ λυπηθῆις ἤν τις ἔχηι μ᾽ ἕτερος.

LXV. Callimachus AP 12.118 (42 Pf., 8 GP)

A reveler seeking access to his beloved defends himself for his behavior. In the background are epigrams in which the speaker represents himself as standing outside a closed door and commenting on the powerful compulsion that has led him there (cf. 3n.). Here, the speaker, present at the house (2 ἥκω) of the boy to whom he previously led his κῶμος (cf. xvii introductory n.), reflects on and defends his behavior, even while insisting on its relative tameness (cf. 5–6n.). His words thus implicitly form part of an ongoing conversation in which Archinus has accused him of behaving unjustly; the implication is perhaps that Archinus has unfairly misunderstood the situation (Livingstone and Nisbet 2010: 74–7). Some of the point derives from the hyper-rationality with which the speaker lays responsibility on forces outside his control; the final couplet plays on philosophical discussions that seek to define and categorize types of wrongdoing (5–6n.). At the same time, his claim that erotic and alcohol-induced compulsion (3 ἠνάγκασαν) make his fault venial is slyly undercut by the artificiality of his language, which is highly alliterative (e.g. 1 μυρία μέμφου) and contains a series of jingles and plays on words (2 ἄκων ἥκω, προπέτειαν ἔα, 4 εἴα τὴν προπέτειαν ἐᾶν, 5–6 ἐφίλησα | τὴν φιλήν); these features contribute to locating his defense in the tradition of epideictic apologias (e.g. Gorgias, Hel. 7–8, 12).

In addition to being preserved in the Anthology, the epigram was written out on the wall of a house on the Esquiline in Rome (Ep. Gr. 1111); see Hunter 2019b.

1–2[311–12] ἑκών . . . ἄκων: these words express a person's relationship to a deed or experience or, more precisely, the question whether he accepts it as his own (cf. Rickert 1989, Sealey 1994: 94–5).   **ἐπεκώμασα** "led a κῶμος to your house," with the preverb suggesting aggression as well as movement; cf. Ar. Ach. 980.   **προπέτειαν** "rashness," "temerity"; cf. Dem. 21.38 "the one who struck . . . had three excuses: drink, eros, and ignorance . . . Polyzelus made the mistake of striking out of anger and impetuousness (προπετείαι) of manner before he thought about it."   **ἔα:** present imperative of ἐάω. To "allow" the speaker's rashness is to overlook it and thus forgive it.

3[313] ἄκρητος καὶ ἔρως μ᾿ ἠνάγκασαν: cf. 73–4, Asclep. 14.3 Sens, Men. Sam. 340–1 πολλὰ δ᾿ ἐξεργάζεται | ἀνόητ᾿ ἄκρατος καὶ νεότης.   **ὧν . . . αὐτῶν:** though αὐτῶν adds little to the sense, it creates an assonance in keeping with the jingles in the clausulae of other lines.   **ὁ μέν:** i.e. Eros.

4[314] εἷλκεν "was dragging me on"; cf. 73, Headlam on Herod. 2.9. τήν
. . . ἐᾶν: the text is uncertain. Dressel's correction is based on the traces of
the poem in a Roman wall painting (*Ep. Gr.* 1111); P's σώφρονα θυμὸν ἔχειν
probably originated as a gloss.

5–6[315–16] The speaker has engaged in none of the raucous behav-
iors typical of other literary comasts; he has not even begged admit-
tance.   οὐκ ἐβόησα: by contrast, the drunken excluded lover of Asclep.
14.5 Sens shouts out his complaints (cf. Fantuzzi 2004: 214–15).   τίς ἤ
τίνος: i.e. "my name or my father's," by which a visitor seeking admission
would identify himself (cf. Ar. *Clouds* 134, Pl. *Charm.* 154a).   ἐφίλησα | . . .
φλιήν "I kissed the doorpost."   εἰ τοῦτ' . . . ἀδίκημ', ἀδικέω: cf., e.g.,
Eur. fr. 272b (Heracles) νῦν δ' οἶνος ἐξέστησέ μ'. ὁμολογῶ δέ σε | ἀδικεῖν, τὸ δ'
ἀδίκημ' ἐγένετ' οὐχ ἑκούσιον. As he raises the question of whether his harm-
less behavior constitutes an injustice, the speaker's language humorously
subverts serious philosophical discussions of what constitutes right and
wrong action (e.g. Arist. *Nic. Eth.* 1135a19–20 "justice and unjust action
are distinguished by willingness and unwillingness").

LXVI. *Callimachus* AP *12.134 (43 Pf., 13 GP)*

The speaker points out to an unnamed addressee the signs that "the stranger"
is in love. Several Hellenistic poems show a lover's condition revealed by his
behavior and becoming the subject of discussion or interrogation by a third
party (cf. Cairns 1977; for the enumeration of symptoms of love, cf. already
Sappho, fr. 31). Reflections on the impossibility of hiding one's feelings of
love appear in comedy (e.g. Antiph. fr. 232), but the specific model of the
poem is Asclepiades xx, in which Nicagoras' behavior illustrates the claim
that drinking exposes the truth. As in that poem, the imagined setting is
the symposium, at which the speaker addresses an unnamed fellow guest; as
there, the enumeration of symptoms of love moves from the alleged lover's
behavior to a "pathetic fallacy" (cf. 87–8n.) having to do with the behavior
of his garland. Whereas in Asclepiades wine explicitly leads to exposure,
here the role played by drinking is implicit. Asclepiades' Nicagoras is represented as a liar; Callimachus' poem plays on the conventional idea that
love is a hidden wound, and the anonymous stranger's wound is both physically invisible and, through his silence, hidden from his fellow symposiasts.
Whereas Asclepiades' poem opens with an aphorism about the revelatory
power of wine, Callimachus' speaker begins with his realization that his
fellow guest is carrying a secret wound and ends with an aphorism emphasizing his cleverness as a detective (cf. Call. *Epigr.* 30), while simultaneously
revealing his own identical condition. The conventional motif of following

in the tracks of another similarly minded person both asserts his authority as a poet writing about love and calls attention to the literary "theft" of a predecessor's work. See further Giangrande 1968: 120–2, Landolfi 1984; Fantuzzi in Fantuzzi and Hunter 2004: 338–49.
  The dialect is Ionic (cf. 3, 4nn.), as in the Asclepiadean model.

1–2[317–18] The passage recalls the Phaeacian banquet where Alcinoos recognizes Odysseus' suffering (*Od.* 8.93–5, 532–4 ἔνθ' ἄλλους μὲν πάντας ἐλάνθανε δάκρυα λείβων· | Ἀλκίνοος δέ μιν οἶος ἐπεφράσατ' ἠδ' ἐνόησεν | ἥμενος ἄγχ' αὐτοῦ, βαρὺ δὲ στενάχοντος ἄκουσεν). The allusion casts the speaker as "an ideally knowing and sympathetic participant in the symposium," like the paradigmatically good host Alcinoos (Bing 2009: 220). Odysseus' heroic pain is recast as erotic pathos.   ἕλκος ἔχων ... ἐλάνθανεν: love's wounds are invisible (cf. Asclep. 8.1–2 Sens τραῦμα | μὴ σαφές), at least to an inexperienced viewer. The speaker has only just realized a condition that he and others previously could not see or understand.   πνεῦμα "a sigh."   διὰ στηθέων: the location of the lungs; cf. [Theocr.] 25.237 στηθέων ὅθι πνεύμονος ἔδρη.   ὡς ... εἶδες; whether an indirect question, with the main verb in hyperbaton ("did you see how . . .?"; cf. Call. fr. 384.31 οὐδ' ὅθεν οἶδεν ὁδεύω) or an exclamation, with an embedded parenthetic question ("How he . . .! Did you see?"), the apostrophe implicates an anonymous companion (and the reader) in the discovery enacted in the epigram.   ἀνηγάγετο "brought up, drew."

3[319] τὸ τρίτον ... ἔπινε: probably a reference to the third round of drinks rather than the third of the toasts that customarily opened the symposium (cf. Olson–Sens on Archestr. fr. 59.1).   φυλλοβολεῦντα "shedding their petals." At *88*, Nicagoras' garland falls from his head; cf. Theocr. 7. 63–4. The popular belief that the dissolution of a garland meant that its wearer was in love (cf. *87–8*n.) is represented by a verb that usually denotes trees dropping their leaves (e.g. Arist. *Gen. an.* 783b11). The contraction ευ < ε + ο is here an Ionic feature; cf. Asclep. *85* (ἀρνεύμενον).

4[320] τὠνδρός: Ionic crasis of τοῦ ἀνδρός (Attic τἀνδρός).   ἐγένοντο χαμαί "ended up on the ground."

5[321] ὤπτηται: third person singular perfect passive of ὀπτάω (lit. "roast"); the verb is used of the heat of desire already at Soph. fr. 474.3; cf. Ar. *Lys.* 839, Theocr. 7.55 with Gow.   μέγα δή τι: the expression is adverbial, with τι (like δή) adding emphasis (cf. *87–8*n.), and probably colloquial.   μὰ δαίμονας: an emotional exclamation marks the speaker's statement of the specific cause of the wound.   οὐκ ἀπὸ ῥυσμοῦ:

ῥυσμός is Ionic = ῥυθμός. The expression is not precisely paralleled elsewhere and its meaning is not entirely clear, but ἐν ῥυθμῶι and μετὰ ῥυθμοῦ
mean "in step" (often with a verb of movement), so that it may mean "out
of rhythm," i.e. not according to a regular pattern and thus "at random":
the speaker is not making a wild guess but recognizes the evidence of
lovesickness.

6[322] εἰκάζω "I make a guess."   φωρὸς δ' ἴχνια φώρ ἔμαθον: the
speaker implicitly admits that he shares the stranger's hidden condition.
The idea is proverbial (*Epimerismi Homerici* χ30, p. 744 Dyck; cf. the iambic
line preserved at Arist. *Eud. Eth.* 1235a8–9 ἔγνω δὲ φώρ τε φῶρα, καὶ λύκος
λύκον), like English "set a thief to catch a thief."

LXVII. Callimachus AP 9.507 (27 Pf., 56 GP)

On Aratus and his debt to Hesiod. Aratus' didactic epic, *Phaenomena*, married technical astronomical material to a form modeled on Hesiod's *Works
and Days*. It was composed at the court of Antigonus Gonatas probably
some time after 276 (Kidd 1997: 4–5) and exerted a powerful influence
on Hellenistic and, later, Roman poetry; it is here treated by Callimachus
as a model of refined composition (cf. 1–3n.) The epigram evokes features of inscribed epitaphs, including the initial copulative sentence and
the final *envoi* (χαίρετε), which has hymnic resonance but may also be read
against epitaphs in which the speaker bids the deceased or the monument
farewell (e.g. *CEG* 530). More immediately, the poem is related to "book-
tag" epigrams in which the speaker is represented as a work of another
author (e.g. Asclep. 28 Sens), but it plays on them by postponing the
author's ethnic and name until the second couplet – so that the impression left by the first word that the poem will treat a Hesiodic work is initially misleading (cf. 537–8n.).

The obscurity of the opposition of ἔσχατον and μελιχρότατον compli-
cates interpretation, since the meaning of this determines what the poet
is claiming about the relationship between Aratus and Hesiod (cf. 1–3n.).
The second-century Stoic philosopher Boethus of Sidon (*Vita Arati* 11, p.
12.15–18 Martin) allegedly claimed that Aratus' affiliation to Homer is
demonstrated by the fact that his πλάσμα (variously understood as "invention," "substance," or "style"; cf. Hunter 2014: 259–60) is greater (μεῖζον)
than Hesiod's, and it seems clear that the epigram, however understood,
participates in an ancient discussion about the extent to which the
Phaenomena may be understood as Hesiodic.

The epigram treats the *Phaenomena* in terms that Callimachus and other
Hellenistic poets use to describe refined poetry. The insistence on the

work's λεπτότης in the final couplet also probably signals a recognition of the Aratean acrostic λεπτή at *Phaen.* 783–7 (cf. 4n.), especially in light of the treatment of the *Phaenomena* as a text to be decoded; in this context, the word-play ῥήσιες Ἀρήτου (4) embodies the verbal dexterity celebrated in the epigram.

1[323] Ἡσιόδου ... ἄεισμα ... τρόπος "The theme and style are Hesiod's," but this meaning emerges only in retrospect, since the opening words might initially be taken to mean that the work at issue is a Hesiodic poem. At Call. fr. 1.3, ἄεισμα refers to epic "song," but here it and τρόπος seem to refer to content and style, respectively, and the meaning "theme, content" is suggested by the comparable use of ἀοιδή in this sense (LSJ 4).

1–3[323–5] οὐ ... ἀπεμάξατο: a difficult passage which has been variously understood. The interpretation adopted assumes that the correct reading is ἀοιδόν, that it refers to Hesiod, and that the adjective ἔσχατον means "complete," so that the point of the opposition is that Aratus imitated the best parts of Hesiod rather than his poetry as a whole: "but I daresay that the man from Soli has not imitated the complete poet, but the sweetest of his verses." The opposition thus picks up and delimits the meaning of the opening phrase, with τὸν ἀοιδόν, "singer, poet," personifying the cognate ἄεισμα, "poem, song," and τὸ μελιχρότατον τῶν ἐπέων defining the meaning of τρόπος: although the content of the didactic *Phaenomena* is Hesiodic, its style is selectively so.

An alternative is to take τὸν ... ἔσχατον as referring to Homer, so that the poem claims stylistic affiliation of the *Phaenomena* to Hesiod rather than to Homer. This approach is facilitated by reading ἀοιδῶν (Scaliger, now with ancient support from *P.Oxy.* 4648), so that the phrase means "best of poets" (for ἔσχατος in a positive rather than a negative sense, cf. Pi. *Olymp.* 1.113) or "ultimate mode of poets," i.e. Homeric epic (cf. Hunter 2014: 258): "but I daresay that the man from Soli has imitated not the ultimate of songs, but the sweetest of verses."　**ὀκνέω μή:** the fear clause hedges off the speaker's claim ("I wonder whether," "I daresay that"; e.g. Pl. *Phaedr.* 257c, Xen. *An.* 2.3.9), perhaps in order to avoid implying that he is criticizing any part of the Hesiodic corpus as less "sweet" (cf. Hunter 2014: 295, who interprets the passage differently).　**τὸ μελιχρότατον | τῶν ἐπέων:** sweetness is a metaphor for literary quality already in Hesiod, whose treatment of the Muses and their poetry (e.g. *Catalogue of Women* fr. 1.1, *Th.* 39–40; cf. Hunter 2014: 288–9) as sweet is here explicitly applied to his own work. For μελιχρός as a hallmark of refined poetry cf. 344, Call. fr. 1.16.　**ἀπεμάξατο** "took the impression of," i.e. "imitated" (< ἀπομάσσω).　**χαίρετε:** exhortations for the dead person or the tomb to fare well are standard in funerary epigrams; that connection may be in the background here, but the salutation also evokes the addresses to Zeus and the "sweet" Muses in the proem of the *Phaenomena* (15–17 χαῖρε, πάτερ . . . χαίροιτε δὲ Μοῦσαι | μειλίχιαι μάλα πᾶσαι). λεπταί: the adjective, properly "peeled, fine," is associated with intellectual refinement as early as Aristophanes (e.g. *Clouds* 359), and in Hellenistic poetry describes finely wrought poetry (cf. *344*). Lines 783–7 of the *Phaenomena* form an acrostic ΛΕΠΤΗ, in which the first word of 783 is also λεπτή. Callimachus' application of the term to Aratus' poetic program finds parallels in Ptol. *SH* 712.4 ὅ γε λεπτολόγος σκῆπτρον Ἄρατος ἔχει, Leon. *AP* 9.25.1–2 Ἀρήτοιο . . . ὅς ποτε λεπτῆι | φροντίδι δηναιοὺς ἀστέρας ἐφράσατο.

4[326] ῥήσιες, Ἀρήτου: ῥῆσις "speech" puns on the poet's name, which suggests ἄρρητος "unspoken"; Aratus uses ἄρρητον to pun on his name in line 2 (cf. Jacques 1960, Bing 1990, 1993). Here the verbal play is emphasized by the lengthening of the first syllable of Ἀρήτου; the use of epicizing η rather than α in the second syllable appropriately reflects the theme of the poem, the influence of archaic epic on Aratus. As a whole, the expression recalls the Hesiodic dyad ῥητοί τ' ἄρρητοί τε (*WD* 4), and thus embodies the stylistic relationship between the poets.   **σύμβολον ἀγρυπνίης** suggests Aratus' night-time star-gazing as well as his burning of the midnight oil; for the phrase, cf. adesp. *AP* 9.689.2 ἑῆς σύμβολον ἀγρυπνίης; Leon. Alex. *AP* 6.328.2 σύμβολον εὐεπίης. σύμβολον is used of weather signs in ancient scholarship on the *Phaenomena* (e.g. Σ Arat. 1021), though not in the poem itself; if the word is correct, Callimachus implicitly represents the *Phaenomena* as a text to be decoded just as Aratus' poem decodes the celestial signs, and the noun looks back to λεπταί | ῥήσιες, Ἀρήτου and its implicit "decoding" of Aratus' language. Other readings are possible, however: P's σύντονος ἀγρυπνίη, "intense sleeplessness," is defended by Cameron 1995: 379 as underscoring the intensity of the poet's surprising nocturnal work; Stewart 2008 suggests σύντομος ἀγρυπνίη "abbreviated sleeplessness," in which the adjective would suggest stylistic refinement (cf. *253*n.).

HEDYLUS

According to Athenaeus (7.297a), Hedylus was from Samos or Athens, wrote a work that recounted the fate of Glaucus, and was the son of the female poet Hedyle, author of a *Scylla*; his association with Samos or Athens could suggest that he was related to cleruchs who occupied Samos *ca.* 365–322 (so Gutzwiller 1998a: 171). An epigram on a dedication to

Arsinoe-Aphrodite Zephyritis suggests that he spent time in Alexandria. Though he is often dated to the early part of the third century, there is some reason to place him slightly later. A notice in the *Etymologicum genuinum* (α551) reports that a Hedylus commented on the epigrams of Callimachus, and though this Hedylus is usually thought to be different from the poet, the possibility that he might be the same person finds some support from passages in which Hedylus plays with Callimachean aesthetic terminology and with that of the *Aetia* in particular (cf. *329*n., LXX introductory n.). Several epigrams clearly respond to poems by Asclepiades (cf. LXIX, LXX introductory nn.); *AP* 5.161 is ascribed alternatively to Hedylus or Asclepiades (= Asclep. *40); for Hedylus and the so-called *Soros*, see p. 68.

Athenaeus claims that Hedylus told the story of Glaucus' suicide; the poem in which he did so could have been an epigram or a narrative poem. Five epigrams (including *AP* 5.161) are ascribed to him in the Anthology, and eight more are cited by Athenaeus. Several show the strong influence of comedy and poke fun at the incompetence of professionals, the gluttony and bibulousness of symposiasts, and other misbehavior.

Hedylus' language is varied, and words from divergent stylistic registers and generic backgrounds are frequently juxtaposed.

LXVIII. Hedylus ap. Ath. 11.497d (4 GP)

On a gold rhyton dedicated in the temple of Arsinoe-Aphrodite Zephyritis. Rhyta were conical vessels, often in the shape of animals, pygmies, or other humans or gods. In this case, the figure is the Egyptian dwarf-god Bes, apparently holding a trumpet (σαλπίζει, κώδωνος). Chamaeleon fr. 9 notes that rhyta were used μόνοις τοῖς ἥρωσιν, a comment that seems to mean that they were used only in commemorations of heroes (so Thompson 1973: 8). Metal rhyta typically had a spout; ceramic rhyta lacked spouts and were used as drinking cups (the account given by Dorotheus ap. Ath. 11.497e seems confused); cf. Thompson 1973, esp. 1–33. The vessel described here is of the former type, but with an unusual feature: it has been designed by Ctesibius so that Bes's trumpet sounds when wine emerges from the spout.

The poem plays on the features of sympotic and dedicatory epigrams: the address to drinkers initially suggests a sympotic occasion, but the words that follow reveal that they are spectators at the temple of Arsinoe at Zephyrium (cf. LX introductory n., *391–3*n.). Athenaeus claims that Ptolemy II endowed statues of Arsinoe with rhyta rather than cornucopiae (Ath. 11.497b–c). Although the context presumed in the epigram cannot be known, the repeated exhortation for a group of young drinkers to make themselves present to witness and honor an object in Arsinoe's temple suggests an address to celebrants of a rite in her honor (cf. Ar. *Frogs* 372–81; Bulloch on Call. *h.* 5.1–32). If so, the sound made by the Nile during the Niloa (7–8) links the celebrations of that divine river and of Arsinoe (see below).

The poem is constructed in ring composition, with the language of the final couplet mirroring that of the first (cf. 9–10n.), and with the second and penultimate couplets featuring Egyptian divinities represented as musicians. The central couplet opposes war to partying, a contrast emphasized by the use of two forms of the same noun. The figures of Bes and the Nile are described in language evocative of poetic composition. The clausula of 3 shares a striking point of contact with the prologue of Callimachus' *Aetia*, but implicitly redefines λιγὺς ἦχος as a brash trumpet blast rather than a light chirping; that one poem looks directly to the other is probable, and the most likely explanation is that Hedylus is adapting Callimachean esthetic terminology to a new end; cf. Sens 2015.

Luck 1968: 402 n. 1 suggests that the epigram parodies the sort of explanations offered by tour-guides at the temple of Arsinoe-Aphrodite; others see it as a parody of dedicatory inscriptions (Stephens 2005: 246). The tone is lighthearted, but there is little reason to see parody in the strict sense. The appearance of Bes on a rhyton is analogous to the use of pygmies on such vessels and is not inherently absurd, though the poem seems to play on the relationship between size and volume as well as on the opposition of wine and water: in pouring wine, a dwarf produces a loud sound analogous to that of the flooded Nile. The poem appears to contain several forms characteristic of the later *koine* (5 σύνθεμα, 9 εὕρεμα), as well as the prosaic ἱεραγωγοῖς (7), alongside more elevated compounds like φιλοζέφυρος (1) and εὔδιος (2).

1[327] ζωροπόται "drinkers of undiluted wine." Heavy drinking was common among the Macedonian elite (cf. Asclep. *44 with Sens's note) and may have special resonance in a poem celebrating a Macedonian queen.   καὶ τοῦτο: the conjunction locates the rhyton among a series of other objects, and the phrase as a whole implicitly places the poem celebrating it in a broader tradition of dedicatory epigram; cf. *17*n.   φιλοζεφύρου: i.e. Zephyritis; cf. *385–8*n.

2[328] εὐδίης: the adjective may be used of persons and gods in the sense "mild, gracious," but here it refers specifically to Arsinoe-Aphrodite's role as protectress of sailors at sea and bringer of fair weather (Pos. 39.2, 119.5–6 AB).   ἴδετ': exhortations to "look" at an object are characteristic of ecphrastic epigrams; e.g. *25, 173*.

3[329] ὀρχηστὴν Βησᾶν: from the New Kingdom on, the Egyptian dwarf-god Bes was associated with music, dancing, and wine, and he is commonly represented dancing or playing an instrument, especially the double aulos, lute, or tambourine; cf. Dasen 1993: 55–83, esp. 77–80.   **ὅς λιγὺν ἦχον:** cf. Call. fr. 1.29 οἳ λιγὺν ἦχον; see introductory n.

4[330] σαλπίζει: Bes is represented as blowing a trumpet (cf. 6 κώδωνος). The verb contributes to the subversion of the values and imagery of the *Aetia* prologue: in Aristophanes' *Frogs* (966, 1042), from which Callimachus drew much of his aesthetic terminology, the loud sound of the trumpet (e.g. *Il.* 18.219) was associated with Aeschylus' bombastic poetry rather than the sort of fine sounds Callimachus endorses. The σάλπιγξ was associated with sacrifices in Egypt and elsewhere (cf. Call. fr. 75.61 Ζεὺς ἐπὶ σαλπίγγων ἱρὰ βοῇ δέχεται, Pollux 4.86 ἔστι δὲ . . . καὶ ἱερουγικὸν [*sc.* σάλπιγμα] ἐπὶ θυσίαις Αἰγυπτίοις τε καὶ Ἀργείοις καὶ Τυρρηνοῖς καὶ Ῥωμαίοις) and would have special point if the poem is imagined as celebrating a ritual occasion.   **κρουνοῦ πρὸς ῥύσιν οἰγομένου** "when the spout is opened for pouring," cf. LSJ κρουνός 4. πρὸς ῥύσιν etymologizes ῥυτόν. The basic meaning of κρουνός, "spring," prepares for the reference to waters of the flooded Nile (7–8). At Call. *h.* 2.111–12, Callimachus associates his poetry with a trickling spring in opposition to the rushing Euphrates: here, by contrast, the sound of the "spring" and of a river are likened to each other.

5–6[331–2] The guttural alliteration (χρυσέου δὲ γέγωνεν | κώδωνος κώμου) may evoke the brash sound of the trumpet.   **πολέμου:** the usual function of a trumpet blast is to signal the start of battle.   **σύνθημα . . . σύνθεμα** "signal": if the text is correct, the well-established form σύνθημα is conjoined with the newer form σύνθεμα, otherwise first attested in the later *koine* and rejected as a proper Attic form by Thomas Magister p. 332.2, but analogous to εὕρεμα in 9; collocations of different forms of the same word are common in Hellenistic poetry. Athenaeus transmits the unmetrical σύνθημα in 6, however, and it remains possible that a different word has been displaced; Jacobs emends to σύμβολα, but the plural is less welcome.

7–8[333–4] ". . . just like the ancestral song, dear to sacrifice-bearing initiates, which the Lord Nile invented from his divine waters." The reference is apparently to the sound of the water of the Nile rushing into a Nilometer (a structure designed to measure the height of the river), and the sacrifice-performing initiates are probably the participants in a festival celebrating its flooding; see Kenny 1932: 190–1, Bonneau 1964: 361–420.

The sound of wine poured from Ctesibius' rhyton is thus compared to that produced by another piece of engineering, though in this case one in which the sound is made by inrushing rather than outrushing liquid.   ἄναξ . . . θείων: as a personified deity, the Nile was associated and ultimately identified with Osiris (cf. Fraser 1972: 1.263), and commonly connected to Isis, with whom Arsinoe was identified (Bonneau 1964: 242–74, Fraser 1972: 1.239–43).   εὗρε μέλος: the Nile is represented as a poet; cf. *334*.   Κτησιβίου: Ctesibius of Alexandria, inventor of a number of hydraulic and pneumatic devices, including the water-pump and the water-organ (cf. West 1992: 114–18), worked in Alexandria during the reign of Ptolemy II; see Orinsky, *RE* IX.2 2074–6, Kenny 1932.   εὕρεμα: the word links Ctesibius' invention to the Nile's musical "discovery" in 8. The form, a variant of the more common εὕρημα, is first attested in the Hellenistic *koine* and is condemned as un-Attic by Phryn., *Ecl.* 420 (cf. Hdn. *De pros. cath.* 1.353.9–10).

9–10[335–6] These verses pick up the language of 1–2: 1 ~ 9 τοῦτο, 2 ~ 10 δεῦτ(ε), 1–2 κατὰ νηὸν . . . Ἀρσινόης ~ 10 νηῶι τῶιδε παρ' Ἀρσινόης.   ἀλλά: the particle is common in commands and exhortations to mark "a transition from arguments for action to a statement of the action required" (Denniston 14).

LXIX. *Hedylus* AP *5.199 (2 GP)*

Dedication of clothing by a woman after sex at a symposium. The poem combines elements from sympotic and amatory epigram, on the one hand, and dedications, on the other. It begins as an account of an event occurring at the party, though the language leaves the precise meaning initially ambiguous (1–2n.); only in the second couplet does it become clear that a dedication is being recorded. The narrative is a sequel to Asclepiades XX, on Nicagores' lovesickness, and redeploys elements of it: both poems open with οἶνος and mention προπόσεις and love, but in XX, Nicagores' mendacity is revealed by his frequent toasts, whereas here his toasts are deceptive and successful; and while in Asclepiades wine leads Nicagores to nod his head, here alcohol contributes to Aglaonice's post-coital sleep (see Giangrande 1968: 151–2).

The epigram is constructed in such a way that the loss of Aglaonice's virginity seems initially to be the welcome (cf. 2 ἡδύς) result of verbal seduction by Nicagores (whose name may suggest rhetorical facility) at a symposium, but it is slowly revealed to be the result of violence (Pretagostini 2000). The second couplet is framed as a dedication of λάφυρα, a word normally used of military spoils, and thus initially seems to represent Aglaonice as a sexual conqueror, but in the final couplet these spoils are defined in terms that treat her as the victim. The precise items dedicated are named only in the final couplet. The movement from seduction to violence is reflected in the distorted mirroring of the first couplet by the last: 6 ὕπνου corresponds to 1 κατεκοίμισαν, but the verbal persuasion suggested by 1–2 προπόσεις . . . δόλιαι is replaced in the final line by σκυλμῶν.

Though the lemma claims that Aglaonice was a hetaera, παρθενίων in the central couplet reveals that the dedication commemorates the loss of her virginity; her role at the party remains unclear. Dedications upon the loss of virginity do not appear to have been standard practice, and the poem may be understood as a variant of dedications of clothing to Artemis by women who have successfully given birth. At [Theocr.] 27.55–6, a girl complains that the sexually aggressive Daphnis has torn her girdle, which he in response characterizes as a first offering to Aphrodite; cf. Hdt. 2.181.4–5.

1–2[337–8] οἶνος . . . προπόσεις . . . ἔρως: cf. *85–6* οἶνος . . . ἐρᾶν . . . προπόσεις. The sequence suggests a progression in which drinking led to professions of love and finally sex. The hexameter seems initially to represent Aglaonice's sleep as the product of alcohol alone; the link between drink and sleep is commonly mentioned in sympotic contexts (e.g. Thgn. 470). Only in the pentameter do enjambed αἱ δόλιαι and ἔρως reveal that the occasion involved other events.   **κατεκοίμισαν:** contrast *87* ἐνύστασε, where Nicagores nods his head drunkenly. That sleep often stands as a metaphor for death (cf. *261–2n.*) initially leaves open the possibility that Aglaonice has died.   **Ἀγλαονίκην . . . Νικαγόρεω:** a man whose name denotes his skill with words has overcome a girl whose own name means "splendid Victory."   **αἱ δόλιαι:** contrast Asclep. *86*, where Nicagores' many toasts (αἱ πολλαὶ . . . προπόσεις) reveal his true emotional state.   **ἔρως . . . Νικαγόρεω:** the expression is ambiguous, since the dependent genitive might be either subjective ("Nicagores' eros") or objective ("eros for Nicagores"). For whom the experience was "sweet" is equally unclear.

3–4[339–40] ἧς πάρα . . . | κεῖνται "by whom [i.e. Aglaonice] . . . are dedicated."   **μύροις:** perfumed oil was regularly distributed to guests at symposia (cf. Olson–Sens on Archestr. fr. 60.3) and also widely used in erotic contexts (cf. Ar. *Lys.* 938–47, *Eccles.* 525 οὐχὶ βινεῖται γυνὴ κἄνευ μύρου).   **ἔτι . . . μυδῶντα:** i.e. the dedication was made just after the event it commemorates.   **παρθενίων . . . πόθων:** the adjective may be either subjective ("a maiden's desire") or objective ("desire for a maiden"); contrast the unambiguous uses at Asclep. *34.4* = Pos. *126.4*

AB, Leon. *AP* 6.202.1–2.   λάφυρα: commonly used in dedicatory contexts of spoils taken from a defeated enemy, e.g. Aesch. *Ag.* 577–9, *SEG* XI 1212a Συρακόσ[ιοι ἀπὸ] Ἀκραγαντίνων λάφυρα. Here, by contrast, it refers to the clothes taken from the dedicator.

5[341] σάνδαλα ... μίτραι: the items, the first not particularly intimate and the second more so, are listed in the order in which they would have been removed in preparation for sex; cf. Ar. *Lys.* 950.   μαλακαί ... μίτραι: expressions in which the adjective is separated from its noun by a nominal phrase in apposition occur occasionally in Greek (Archil. fr. 196a.49–50 νέον, ἥβης ἐπήλυσιν, χρόα, Aesch. *Ag.* 119, *Eum.* 302) and become popular in Latin poetry (e.g. Virg. *Ecl.* 1.57); see Solodow 1986. The erotically charged adjective μαλακαί is pointed in a description treating women's clothing as if it were armor stripped from an enemy.   μαστῶν ἐκδύματα "items stripped from her breasts." ἔκδυμα is elsewhere attested only in the scholarly tradition (e.g. Zen. II 95 λεβηρὶς δέ ἐστι ... ἔκδυμα τοῦ ὄφεως).

6[342] σκυλμῶν: cognate with σκύλλω ("tear, rend"), and appropriate to sexual violence and the forceful tearing of Aglaonice's clothes from her body. The noun (common in LXX) comes to be virtually equivalent to ὕβρις, with which it is sometimes paired (e.g. *P.Tebt.* 790.11 μεθ᾽ ὕβρεως καὶ σκυλμοῦ).   μαρτύρια: that dedicated objects might testify to an event finds a parallel at e.g. *CEG* 798.1–2 μνᾶμα ... <καὶ> μάρτυρα νίκας | ... μ᾽ ἔστασαν, but in conjunction with σκυλμῶν the word suggests testimony in a criminal matter.

LXX. Hedylus ap. Ath. 11.472f–3a (5 GP)

An exhortation to drink. The poem seems to respond to Asclep. 16 Sens, which opens with an address to the poet, who is apostrophized by name; here the corresponding apostrophe comes in the last line. The poem self-referentially calls attention to its place in a broader literary tradition. After opening in a manner evocative of sympotic elegy and lyric (e.g. Thgn. 763, 1042, Alc. frr. 346, 352), the speaker reflects on his own exhortation, explaining that in drinking he might be able to produce refined poetry (ἔπος). The second couplet, in which he asks an unnamed addressee to drench him with wine and command him to "play," rewrites initiation scenes in which a poet is given water to drink (cf. 3–4n.). On this reading, the final clause can be understood as the product of the initiation imagined in the previous verse, and an embodiment of the values inscribed in the first couplet.

The aesthetic terminology of 1–2 is identical to that used by Callimachus to describe the refined poetry he admired and aimed to produce. At the same time, the privileging of wine as a source of inspiration may participate in a discussion about the proper quantity of wine to drink at the symposium, as well as about the relationship of wine and water to different poetic forms. The later reception of Callimachus associated him with water-drinking, and he seems to have connected water with poetry in his *Aetia* and hymns (cf. *646*n.). The distinction drawn between his ἀοιδαί and sympotic poetry (i.e. epigram) in *Epigr.* 35 shows, however, that for him the distinction between water-drinking and wine-drinking was generically determined: although some passages of Callimachus connect water to ἀοιδαί (esp. *h.* 2.105–12), wine was for him the appropriate vehicle for the production of epigram. None the less, in the *Aetia*, the poetic persona advocates moderate consumption of wine at symposia (fr. 178.11–12), whereas this epigram playfully celebrates drunkenness as the source of inspiration (cf. *AP* 13.29). Hedylus seems elsewhere to associate wine with the aesthetics advocated in the *Aetia* prologue (cf. *329*n.), probably in response to a perceived Callimachean association of refined composititon with water. See Sens 2015, 2016.

1[343] νέον: cf. *141–2*n.   παρ' οἶνον "in a drinking party."

2[344] εὕροιμ' ἄν . . . ἔπος "find something to say," but also "create a poem"; cf. *334.*   λεπτὸν . . . μελιχρόν: the collocation recurs at *32–5* (of the poetry of Aratus) and, with λεπταλέος in place of λεπτός, at fr. 1.16, 24.

3–4[345–6] In asking his companion to soak him with wine, the speaker casts his addressee in the role of an inspiring deity like the Muses who initiate Hesiod by giving him a draught of the Hippocrene in Hellenistic versions of their encounter (cf. *646*); this detail, not found in Hesiod's own version in the *Theogony*, probably has Callimachean roots (cf. Sens 2015).   κατάβρεχε "drench," in the common metaphorical sense "give me large quantities to drink."   κάδοις: large jars, said by Hero Mechanicus (*Geom.* 23.63) to be equivalent to half an amphora, for transporting or storing wine.   Χίου: Chian wine was very highly regarded (cf. Olson–Sens on Archestr. fr. 59.17).   παῖζε, | Ἡδυλε: by embedding a common form of sympotic exhortation (e.g. Amphis fr. 8.1 πῖνε, παῖζε) in a direct command, the epigram highlights its engagement with the literary tradition: the speaker imagines himself in dialogue with an unnamed companion speaking the traditional language of the symposium.   μισῶ ζῆν: exhortations to drink are often justified by the need to enjoy life while one can (e.g. Sens 2016). Here, the speaker takes the *topos* in a new direction: a sober life is unpleasant.   ἐς κενόν: the expression, common in Hellenistic prose (esp. LXX, NT), implies "without purpose" and "without effect," but may also suggest the speaker's dread of an empty wine jar.

HERACLITUS

A single epigram is attributed to Heraclitus in the Anthology, as part of a clear sequence of poems from Meleager's *Garland*. It seems likely that its author is the Halicarnassian poet honored by Callimachus (LI). Nothing certain is known about his life or other work; Swinnen (1970) suggests that he may be the Heraclitus mentioned in inscriptions as a Ptolemaic proxenos.

LXXI. Heraclitus AP *7.465 (1 GP)*

An epitaph for Aretemias, who died in childbirth. The poem is divided into two equal parts, each directed to a passing stranger (3 ὁδοιπόρε, 5 ξεῖν') but very different in their use of voice. In 1–4, the speaker is not the deceased or her tomb, as usual in such contexts, and is hard to distinguish from the poet (cf. Hunter 1992). In context, the γράμμα to be deciphered (3–4) is simultaneously the imaginary inscription and the poem itself, and the emphasis on the freshness of the grave (1, 2nn.) which attracts the speaker's attention stands as a self-reflexive comment on the epigram's novelty (cf. *343*). The second part enacts the process of reading: the words of the poet merge seamlessly into an embedded epigram of a traditional type (e.g. *CEG* 483) in the first-person voice of the deceased. The dead woman, whose otherwise unattested name, Aretemias, may be meant to suggest her virtuous character, describes her life in a straightforward and restrained way that reveals her excellence and role as a wife (7–8).

1[347] ἀρτίσκαπτος "freshly dug"; not elsewhere attested.   μετώπων "brow"; the "face" of the grave-marker is personified as wearing garlands (of people, cf. *Anacreont.* 18.6–7 στεφάνους δότε οἷς πυκάζω | τὰ μέτωπα, Ach. Tat. 1.1.7).

2[348] φύλλων "leaves," probably of myrtle (cf. Eur. *El.* 324, 512), from which funerary garlands were made.   ἡμιθαλεῖς: i.e. "half-wilted," and still recent; only here.   στέφανοι: for the garlands in funerary rites, cf. *104*n.

3–4[349–50] "Deciphering the writing, traveler, let's look at the stone to see whose smooth bones it says it covers," i.e. ἴδωμεν τίνος λευρὰ ὀστέα ὁ πέτρος φατὶ περιστέλλειν. The complex, interlaced word order foregrounds the process of discernment and interpretation required of the reader. διακρίναντες entails both "distinguishing" the writing from the garlands covering the grave and "deciphering" it, though the latter sense is not exactly paralleled elsewhere. The aorist participle denotes action simultaneous with the main verb (cf. Smyth §1872c2). λευρά "smooth" (cf. *72*n.), a variation of the conventional epithet of bones, λευκά (e.g. *Il.* 16.347). περιστέλλειν: in its ordinary sense "clothe" the verb picks up the commonplace idea of the earth cloaking the deceased (cf. *127*n.) but transfers it to the stone.

5–6[351–2] Aretemias summarizes her identifying information in a rapid, asyndetic series of clauses (cf. *CEG* 707 Ἀντιφῶν πατήρ μ' ἔφυσεν, Ἀτθὶς ἦν χώρα πά[τ]ρα | ὄνομα Ἀπολλόδωρ[ος]), with enjambment between the verses. The syntactical simplicity of these clauses, the first two consisting of two words each, the second two of four words each, contrasts with the complexity of 3–4. Εὔφρονος: a speaking name ("Kind") reflecting the harmony of Aretemias' marriage. ὠδίνων οὐκ ἄμορος: the litotes (cf. Pi. *Nem.* 6.14) is a "brave understatement" (Hopkinson) but also reflects Aretemias' pride in the social status she has attained by having children.

7–8[353–4] As often in real epitaphs, the dead woman's principal concern is for her husband. δισσά: *sc.* τέκνα. τὸ μὲν λίπον ἀνδρί: cf., e.g., *CEG* 576.3–4 ἃ ποθ' ὑπ' ὠδίνων στονόεντι κατέφθιτο πότμωι | ὀρφανὸν ἐμ μεγάροις παῖδα λιποῦσα πόσει. ποδηγὸν | γήρως "as a foot-guide for his old age"; for the genitive, cf. Lyc. *Alex.* 385 λαμπτῆρα . . . τὸν ποδηγέτην σκότου "a lamp, guide through the dark." ἀνδρί . . . πόσιος: of these words for "husband," the former reflects the physical and emotional component of marriage, the latter its legal status; the implication is that these two are in alignment (contrast Soph. *Trach.* 550–1 ταῦτα οὖν φοβοῦμαι μὴ πόσις μὲν Ἡρακλῆς | ἐμὸς καλῆται, τῆς δὲ νεωτέρας ἀνήρ). Hunter (1992) suggests that πόσιος might hint at the other meaning of πόσις, "drink," and evoke the sympotic connotations of the wreaths mentioned in 1–2. μναμόσυνον: referring not to the preservation of the memory of the deceased, as is typical in epitaphs, but to Aretemias' recollection of her still-living husband. That the child will remind her of him suggests their resemblance and so implicitly demonstrates her fidelity.

NICIAS

Nicias, of whom eight epigrams are preserved in the Anthology (a ninth, *AP* 11.398, is implausibly ascribed to him by Pl), is almost certainly the physician and poet addressed by Theocritus as an admired friend and a resident of Miletus (XCIV, Idylls 11, 13, 28.6–7). Σ^vet. Theocr. 11, p. 240 Wendel calls him an epigrammatist from Miletus and an associate of the physician Erasistratus. The epigrams share a number of connections to the works of Anyte (e.g. *357n.*); these more probably reflect Nicias' engagement with Anyte's epigrams than the other way around (cf. Sens 2006; contra Bernsdorff 2001: 110–17). Three of his poems purport to be dedications. The rest treat aspects of nature and the rural landscape; the literary self-reflexivity of at least some undermine the case for their being inscriptional. Homeric language is frequently reworked, and even those poems that seem most traditional are linguistically creative (cf. Cairns 2016: 279–80).

LXXII. Nicias AP 6.127 (2 GP)

A dedication of a weapon or armor in the temple of Artemis by a retired soldier. Epigrams recording a retiree's dedication of the tools of his trade are very common in the Anthology and probably reflect an occasional real-life practice (cf. Rouse 1902: 70–1). Here the object, which speaks in the first person, is never directly identified, but its feminine gender suggests that it is a shield (ἀσπίς). The gender suits a resident in Artemis' temple, though there is also a contrast between the speaker's long experience in war and the songs of maidens to which it now listens. The essential information, including the names of the dedicator and the divine recipient, is reserved for the second couplet; in the first, the speaker seems to treat its location among choruses of maidens as a surprising event (cf. *46*n.).

1–2[355–6] "It turns out that I too, having escaped Ares' hateful conflict, was destined to listen to choruses of maidens." μέλλον ἄρα acknowledges a reality that the speaker had not previously expected (cf. Denniston 36). For καί, cf. *17*n.   στυγερὰν . . . Ἄρηος: in Homer, Ares himself is στυγερός, cf. *Il.* 2.385, 18.209.   ποτε "eventually."   ἐκπρολιποῦσα: cf. *Od.* 8.515 κοῖλον λόχον ἐκπρολιπόντες.   χορῶν παρθενίων: choruses of virgins played an important part in the cults of a number of divine figures, including Artemis.

3[357] Ἀρτέμιδος περὶ ναόν: the prepositional phrase suggests the movement of the chorus around the temple (cf. Call. *h.* 3.240 περὶ . . .

ὠρχήσαντο); Nicias probably borrows from Anyte *AP* 6.312.3 θεοῦ περὶ ναόν, of children teaching a goat to give them rides in the temple precinct.

4[358] λευκὸν . . . γῆρας: a tragic collocation (Soph. *Ajax* 624, Eur. *HF* 910); cf. Simias *230* πολιῶι γήραϊ. **κείνου:** i.e. Epixenos.   **γῆρας ἔτειρε μέλη:** an allusion to *Il.* 4.313–15, where the damage done by old age (ἀλλά σε γῆρας τείρει ὁμοίϊον) explains why Nestor's limbs (γούναθ') are no longer mobile.

LXXIII. Nicias AP 6.270 (3 GP)

A thanksgiving dedication of Amphareta's head coverings to Eileithyia; cf. xliv introductory n. The first couplet names the deity, the dedicator, and the dedicated objects; the second provides an explanation of the gift. An apparently Doric dialect patina is overlaid on diction that evokes or varies Homeric language; there is an allusion to a contextually relevant passage of the *Iliad* in which the mourning Andromache throws off her head coverings (cf. 3–4n.).

1[359] κρήδεμνα . . . καλύπτρα: usually treated as synonyms by ancient critics (cf. Llewelyn-Jones 2003: 28–32) but here distinguished, with καλύπτρα probably denoting the fine veil that covers the face and κρήδεμνα a covering for the head, back, and shoulders.   **ὑδατόεσσα καλύπτρα:** the adjective suggests "flowing" as well as "translucent"; at Theocr. 28.11, Nicias' wife is said to weave ὑδάτινα βράκη. The phrase varies the Homeric λιπαρὴν . . . καλύπτρην (e.g. *Il.* 22.406; cf. A.R. 3.445, *Od.* 1.334 λιπαρὰ κρήδεμνα), where the adjective (lit. "oily") has a similarly extended sense.

2[360] Amphareta has placed her headdress and veil on the cult statue of Eileithyia. That some items of clothing dedicated in celebration of the birth of a child were used to clothe the cult statue is reflected in the inventory lists for Artemis' sanctuary at Brauron (cf. Wise 2007: 221), and in Pausanias' claim (7.23.5–6) that the statue of Eileithyia was veiled at Aegium.   **τεᾶς . . . ὑπὲρ κεφαλᾶς:** the placement of the possessive adjective finds parallels in direct addresses to gods elsewhere in Hellenistic poetry (e.g. Asclep. *36.1 Sens = Pos. *128.1 AB σὴν . . . παρ' ἠιόνα, Call. fr. 18.9 σὴν . . . κατ' αἰσιμίην, 260.36 τεόν ποτε . . . θυμόν).   **κεῖται ὑπὲρ κεφαλᾶς:** an inversion of the Homeric formula στῆ δ' ἄρ' ὑπὲρ κεφαλῆς; ὑπὲρ κεφαλᾶς is in a traditional verse-position (cf. Mimn. fr. 5.6, Tyrt. fr. 11.26). κεῖται is not simply equivalent to ἀνάκειται: the garments have been placed upon the statue's head.

3[361] ὡς σὲ ... ἐκαλέσσατο "since it was to you that she appealed with a prayer." οἱ: dative; probably "(throw away) to her benefit" rather than narrowly with the preceding word ("grievous to her").

3–4[361–2] λευγαλέας ... λοχίων "the grievous doom of birth pangs," i.e. death in childbirth. κῆρες with defining genitive is modeled on Homeric κῆρες ... θανάτοιο (Il. 2.302, etc.). The tone of ὠδίνων ... λοχίων, in which the adjective contributes little additional meaning, is elevated (cf. Eur. Ion 452, Euph. fr. 11.11–12 Powell). ἀπ' ... τῆλε βαλεῖν recalls Il. 22.468 τῆλε δ' ἀπὸ κρατὸς βάλε δέσματα ["headdresses"] σιγαλόεντα (of Andromache in grief), where βάλε was Aristarchus' reading for the vulgate χέεν. With κῆρας as object, the phrase varies expressions such as κακὰς δ' ἀπὸ κῆρας ἄλαλκε (Thgn. 13), κακὰς ἀπὸ κῆρας ἀμῦναι (Thgn. 767).

POSIDIPPUS OF PELLA

Posidippus of Pella is named as an epigrammatist (τῶι Ποσειδίππωι τῶι ἐπιγραμματοποιῶι Πελλαίωι) in an inscription from Thermon from 264 or 263 BCE (IG IX².1 17.24) and is probably the man mentioned with a certain Asclepiades in a Delphic proxeny inscription from 276/275 or 273/272 (FD III 3.92). His epigrams celebrating the foundation of the Pharos lighthouse (late 280s) and the temple of Arsinoe-Aphrodite (before the death of Arsinoe in 270 or 268) suggest that he had achieved prominence in Alexandria by the late 270s. He remained active until at least 252 (cf. Thompson 2005: 278–9).

The epigrams preserved in the Greek Anthology are mostly sympotic and erotic; a few are funerary or ecphrastic. Epigrams transmitted by other means, however, reveal a diversity masked by Meleager's selection. A papyrus now in Milan containing a collection of over a hundred of his epigrams, most previously unknown, provides precious information about the poet and his role in Alexandria. The epigrams are probably all by Posidippus: the only two known from other sources are by him, and individual epigrams are separated only by a line (*paragraphos*) without the authorial ascriptions found in some other multi-authored anthologies. Stylistic comparison between the epigrams preserved on the papyrus and those in the Anthology is of limited utility for the question of authorship: Meleager's selection probably offers only a partial picture of the poet's range (see below).

The poems on the papyrus are organized by genre into groups, which are given titles. These include dedicatory (ἀναθηματικά) and funerary poems, though the latter are subdivided among three sections (ἐπιτύμβια, sepulchral epigrams; ναυαγικά, cenotaphic poems; τρόποι, "character" epigrams, apparently illustrating different personality types). There are also other types, some poorly attested in the Anthology: descriptions of gemstones (λιθικά); accounts of bird-omens (οἰωνοσκοπικά); ecphrastic epigrams on statues (ἀνδριαντοποιικά); celebrations of equestrian victories (ἱππικά); and treatments of miraculous cures (ἰαματικά). The collection, apparently copied within a few decades of the last datable epigram, shows signs of artful arrangement both within and among sections. It also participates in the construction and propagation of the image of the Ptolemaic court: a number of epigrams directly honor members of the family for their achievements, for the benefits they bestow as deified royalty on Greeks in Egypt, and for their patronage of the arts; others do so by implication. Some, including those on engraved gems and those on statues, may be productively read as self-reflexive comments on Posidippus' poetic program (cf. Introduction section 4e).

Posidippus' sympotic and erotic epigrams share a number of links with epigrams by Asclepiades. For the most part, these reflect engagement by Posidippus with Asclepiades rather than the other way around, but assessment is complicated by uncertainties about the authorship of six epigrams, whose ascriptions name both poets as alternatives. Only one poem from the Milan papyrus clearly reworks a passage of Asclepiades (see 417–19n.).

Posidippus' epigrams are stylistically variable. His diction is sometimes less straightforward and more highly ornamented than that of Asclepiades and Callimachus (cf. Magnelli 2007: 170–1). The stylistic diversity of the Milan poems, which some scholars have found less polished than those in the Anthology, casts light on Meleager's preferences and their influence on modern taste. The poems on the papyrus are on average longer than those selected by Meleager. Both groups have similar metrical qualities, sharing with most other epigrammatists a preference for dactyls, especially late in the hexameter, and a disregard for "Tiedke's Law" (Introduction section 4h[i]). Like Asclepiades, Posidippus allows some violations of other "Callimachean" metrical norms; these are slightly more frequent in the larger corpus of the Milan papyrus (cf. Magnelli 2007: 181). Both parts of the corpus are notable for allowing a substantial amount of enjambment between distichs; cf. Fantuzzi 2002.

LXXIV. Posidippus *131 AB (AP 7.170 = 21 GP)

Three-year-old Archianax falls into a well. The epigram is attributed to Posidippus in Pl, but in P it is copied twice, once with an ascription to Posidippus and again with an ascription to Callimachus. It plays on the euphemistic language of epitaphs in order to manipulate readers' sympathies. Its opening is constructed in such a way that readers share the mother's urgent desire to know whether she has saved his life (4), but the multivalent language of the final couplet avoids complete resolution: the reaction of the mother, who knows the answer, is omitted, and the language and the evocation of the Hylas story hint poignantly at an alternative outcome in which the boy has not died (cf. Tueller 2016: 231–2). The final couplet would, however, suit a gravestone with a relief of mother and child.

An epitaph from Notion on a boy who died under similar circumstances (*SGO* 1 03/05/04) uses the epigram as a model; see Hunter 2019a.

1[363] παίζοντα: a pathetic detail.

2[364] εἴδωλον . . . κωφόν: i.e. his reflection; cf. Eur. *Med.* 1162 ἄψυχον εἰκώ.   ἐπεσπάσατο "drew (him) in." The regular use of the verb of substances absorbing liquid is here reversed: the reflection in the water draws him in (cf. Sens on Asclep. *36.4 = Pos. *128.4 AB).

3[365] διάβροχον "wet through."   ἥρπασε: this verb more often refers to the sudden snatching of the deceased by death (e.g. *143*).

4[366] ". . . looking to see if he had any bit of life left."

5[367] Νύμφας . . . οὐκ ἐμίηνεν: the slippage between the literal use of νύμφαι of the goddesses of springs and the metonymic meaning "water" (e.g. Nic. *Ther.* 623) makes the phrase ambiguous: it may mean either that the boy did not die in the well and defile the goddesses or that, because his mother pulled him out, his corpse did not corrupt the water. The reference to nymphs in this context evokes the story of Hylas, pulled into the water by a spring-nymph or nymphs who had fallen in love with him (cf. A.R. 1.1221–39, Theocr. 13.43–54).   ὁ νήπιος suggests not just youth but thoughtlessness.

5–6[367–8] ἐπὶ γούνοις | ματρός "on his mother's lap"; cf. *Il.* 22.500 ἐπὶ γούνασι πατρός, of Astyanax, and especially Theocr. 13.53 Νύμφαι μὲν σφετέροις ἐπὶ γούνασι κοῦρον ἔχοισαι, of Hylas. γούνοις is an otherwise unattested variant of γούνασι, generated by back-formation from genitive γούνων, common at line end in Homer (e.g. *Il.* 1.407).   τὸν βαθὺν ὕπνον: βαθύς is common of real sleep (e.g. Arist. *Prob.* 876a24–5) but not elsewhere used of the sleep of death. The definite article and the expectations generated by genre suggest that the phrase refers to death, though τόν could point to "the kind of sleep that is appropriate to a three-year-old"

(Tueller 2016: 232).   ἔχει responds to the verb of the indirect question in 4.

LXXV. Posidippus 102 AB

An epitaph for a laconic Cretan; cf. Call. LII, to which it seems related. The poem appears in the section of the Milan papyrus labeled τρόποι, a group of funerary epigrams that seem to illustrate different character types. The speaker is initially presented as a simple misanthrope like Timon (LVIII) or Hipponax (XXVIII); only in the final line does he reveal that his taciturnity reflects the discretion of a man buried away from his homeland. The poem's dialect is an important part of its characterization. Two forms, ἥασατ(ε) and Φιλάρχω, show phonology characteristic of the subset of "more severe" Doric dialects (cf. Introduction section 4g), of which Cretan was one; the forms thus fit the ethnic identity of the speaker. There are also Ionic forms, conceivably suggesting a foreigner's attempt to avoid exposing his status; cf. Sens 2004.

1–2[369–70] The speaker wonders why the passerby has done exactly what epitaphs conventionally request; e.g. CEG 28 ἄνθρωπε, ὅ<ς> στείχεις καθ' ὁδὸν φρασὶν ἄλ<λ>α μενοινῶν | στῆθι καὶ οἴκτιρον. The series of questions resembles the Homeric τίς πόθεν εἰς ἀνδρῶν; (e.g. Od. 1.170) and tragic queries such as Eur. Ion 257–8 τίς δ' εἶ; πόθεν γῆς ἦλθες; ἐκ ποίας πάτρας | πέφυκας; Cf. GVI 1904.15–16 ἦν δ' ἐρέηι, παροδεῖτα, τίς ἢ τίνος, ἦν ὅδε κεύθει | τύμβος.   **ἔστητε** "did you stop?"   **οὐκ ... ἰαύειν:** irritation about the interruption of figurative "sleep" is a topos in epitaphs for misanthropes; cf. 450n.   **ἥασατ᾿:** aorist of ἐάω.

3[371] παρὰ σῆμα: cf. 275, Pos. 61.1 AB ἴσχε πόδας παρὰ σῆμα.

4[372] ὀλιγορρήμων "taciturn"; only here.   **ὡς ἂν ἐπὶ ξενίης** "as (one would be) in a foreign land"; cf. Pos. 94.2–3 AB ἐπειγόμενος | ὡς ἂν ἐπὶ ξείνης καὶ ὁδοιπόρος, Smyth §1766a. Taciturnity is prudent for foreigners: cf. Apostol. 12.21d "it is better for a stranger to stay silent (σιγᾶν) than to cry out."

LXXVI. Posidippus 100 AB

Zeno regains his long-lost sight shortly before dying. The poem appears among the ἰαματικά, describing miraculous cures, but unlike others from the section, makes no reference to the agency of a god and hints only obliquely at incubation, in which a patient seeking a cure spent the night in a temple, usually of Asclepius (cf. Renberg 2016). The epigram evokes the language and themes of funerary epigram, and plays upon the intersection of three closely related phenomena – sleep (1n.), death, and blindness: Zeno, on the verge of falling into the permanent sleep of death, has his sight restored, but his subsequent death ends his living sight and allows him to "see" Hades, the Unseen. Readers' initial expectations are thus temporarily disappointed: after the specification of Zeno's age, they will naturally expect information about a death, which is deferred by the surprising news of briefly restored vision (cf. 3n.).

1[373] ἡνίκ᾽ ἔδει: the nature of the compulsion on Zeno is not initially clear; that his destined sleep is death is revealed later.   τὸν ἥσυχον ὕπνον ἰαύειν: the sleep of death, but also in context initially suggesting the practice of incubation, which could be used to treat blindness; e.g. *IG* IV².1 121.33–41, Ar. *Wealth* 400–14. ἥσυχος is not elsewhere found in euphemisms for death, but is unsurprising of sleep (e.g. Anacr. *PMG* 431.2).

2[374] πέμπτον ἐπ᾽ εἰκοστῶι . . . θέρει "for twenty-five years"; for θέρος in this sense, cf. *IMEGR* 39.4.

3[375] ὀγδωκονταέτης: cf. *39–40*n. Zeno lived to extreme old age.   ὑγιὴς γένετ᾽: the phrase occurs regularly in cure inscriptions from Epidaurus (e.g. *IG* IV².1 121.47–8, 122.18–19, 124.7) and in the Hippocratic corpus.

3–4[375–6] ἥλιον . . . βλέψας: if the lacuna in 4 is correctly supplemented, the phrase is richly resonant. δίς means that Zeno sees the sun only twice – i.e. two days – more, but it is also appropriate to a man who had vision in two periods of his life. The language plays on the common metaphorical use of ἥλιον βλέπειν to mean "live" (e.g. Eur. *Med.* 1327, Men. fr. 599.1).   τὸν βαρὺν . . . Ἀίδην picks up 1 τὸν ἥσυχον ὕπνον. βαρύς, used of "grim" Hades in some slightly later funerary epigrams (e.g. *SGO* 05/01/40.1, 08/06/11.3), is very common of literal sleep and of the metaphorical sleep of death (e.g. Theocr. 22.204).   εἴδ᾽ Ἀίδην: an oxymoron playing on the folk etymology of Hades as the "Unseen" (ἀιδής).

LXXVII. Posidippus 33 AB

Aristoxenus dies in battle after dreaming he will marry Athena. The poem, found in the section of the Milan papyrus containing omen-epigrams (οἰωνοσκοπικά), incorporates epitaphic elements into a narrative about the grandiose and self-destructive misinterpretation of a prophetic sign. Aristoxenus takes his dream literally, and his delusion leads him to die fighting an entire enemy phalanx and to contend with the gods. The epigram plays with the conventional representation of death as sleep, with the literal and figurative senses of divine names, and with the *topos* of the marriage to death. The poem is divided into two movements marked by 1 ἐνύπνιον and 5 ἀνεγρόμενος. Each couplet covers a different aspect of the story: the first summarizes the dream and Aristoxenus' reaction; the second recounts the dream; the third his waking response; the fourth its consequences.

1–2 [377–8] μεῖζον . . . μεγάλων: Aristoxenus' foolishly ambitious response to a dream "greater than his station," i.e. promising greater things than he had a right to expect, evokes and violates Pittacus' sage advice that it is better to marry at one's own level; cf. [Aesch.] *Prom.* 887–90 σοφός ἦν ὅς πρῶτος . . . διεμυθολόγησεν | ὡς τὸ κηδεῦσαι καθ' ἑαυτὸν ἀριστεύει μακρῶ, with Σ ad loc.; at Call. *Epigr.* 1, a man wondering whether to marry a woman πλούτωι καὶ γενεῆι κατ' ἐμέ or one who has surpassed him (προβέβηκε) is advised to stay in his lane (τὴν κατὰ σαυτὸν ἔλα). Ὡρκάς: i.e. ὁ Ἀρκάς (so written in the papyrus). Arcadians commonly served as mercenaries in the Hellenistic period. They were an ancient people (cf. the Delphic oracle ap. Hdt. 1.66.2, A.R. 4.263–5 with Hunter's note) whom some considered unsophisticated (Philostr. *VA* 8.7.12; cf. Dover on Ar. *Clouds* 398); the ethnic designation may thus have a mocking point apart from its suitability to a warrior; cf. Dickie 1996: 332–3. **μεγάλων . . . ὠρέγετο** "he aspired to greatness" (e.g. Plut. *Alcib.* 14.8, D.S. 18.60.1).

3 [379] Ἀθήνης γαμβρός: an impossible status (cf. *HHAphr.* 7–8), to which it is hybristic to aspire. Artemidorus (1.80) observes that dreaming of intercourse with Athena, Artemis, or Hestia always portends death. **ἐν Διὸς οἴκωι**: of Ptolemy's posthumous assumption to Olympus at Theocr. 17.17–18 καί οἱ χρύσεος θρόνος ἐν Διὸς οἴκωι | δέδμηται.

4 [380] εὕδειν . . . πάννυχος varies the Homeric εὗδον παννύχιοι/παννύχιον εὕδειν (e.g. *Il.* 2.2, 24, 61). The phrase may suggest an extended night of sexual activity (Thgn. 1063), but here ultimately predicts the eternal sleep of death (cf. 261–2n.). **χρυσείωι . . . ἐν θαλάμωι** recalls Mimn. fr. 11a.2 χρυσέωι κείαται ἐν θαλάμωι; cf. Asclep. *36.2 Sens = Pos. *126.2 AB Κύπριδος χρυσέων ἐρχόμενοι θαλάμων.

5 [381] ἦρι δ' ἀνεγρόμενος: cf. A.R. 2.1228 ἦρι δ' ἀνεγρομένοισιν εὐκραὴς ἄεν οὖρος, on the morning after Peleus has reminded the Argonauts of their martial prowess (cf. 1222). **δήιων . . . φάλαγγι**: Aristoxenus imagines that with the support of his divine patron he will, like an epic hero (e.g., *Il.* 13.145–54), be able to handle an entire enemy battle-line alone.   προσέμισγε "he tried to engage with."

6[382] Probably "believing that he had the spirit of Athena in his breast" rather than "inasmuch as he had …," but playing on the idea that gods can endow a warrior with θυμός in order to destroy him; cf. *Il.* 16.689–90, of the foolish (686 νήπιος) Patroclus deluded by Zeus, "who easily takes away victory, whenever he himself rouses a warrior to fight; it was he who then sent spirit into Patroclus' breast (θυμὸν ἐνὶ στήθεσσιν ἀνῆκεν)." **ἐν φρενὶ θυμὸν ἔχων:** cf. Hes. *Th.* 239 Εὐρυβίην τ' ἀδάμαντος ἐνὶ φρεσὶ θυμὸν ἔχουσαν. Early epic uses the plural φρεσί in similar expressions.

7[383] τὸν . . . ἐρίσαντα: to imagine oneself worthy of a marriage not even a real god could attain was a provocative act (cf. Theopomp. *FGrH* 115 F 31, Rhianus fr. 1.14 μνᾶται δ' εὔπηχυν Ἀθήνην, of a man who errs by contending with the gods). **μέλας . . . Ἄρης** "grim Ares"; cf. *11–12*n. The phrase is not a banal personification of war (cf. Aesch. *Ag.* 1511) but makes concrete the image in θεοῖς ἐρίσαντα. **κατεκοίμισεν:** here metaphorical, mirroring the literal sleep with which Aristoxenus' misfortune began.

8[384] The evocation of 3 by sound and sense (ᾤχετο ~ ᾤετ', ψευδὴς νυμφίος ~ Ἀθήνης γαμβρός, εἰς Ἀΐδεω ~ 3 Ὀλυμπίου ἐν Διὸς οἴκωι) underscores the irony: instead of rising to the home of Zeus on Olympus and marrying Athena, Aristoxenus descends to the underworld home of Hades, where he will experience a different sort of sleep.   **ψευδὴς νυμφίος** "a false groom," in that he "marries" only in the euphemistic metaphorical language of death; young men are sometimes said to experience marriage in Hades, though less often than girls are. The phrase serves the same function as do paradoxical collocations in which a noun is modified by a cognate alpha-privativized adjective; e.g. Eur. *Hec.* 612 νύμφην τ' ἄνυμφον παρθένον τ' ἀπάρθενον, Soph. *El.* 1154 μήτηρ ἀμήτωρ.

LXXVIII. Posidippus 116 AB (12 GP = P.Louvre *7172* [P.Firmin-Didot])

On the foundation of the temple of Arsinoe-Aphrodite by Callicrates, admiral of the Ptolemaic navy. The epigram appears in a fragment of a multi-genre, early second-century anthology of texts from the Serapeum at Memphis; it is there juxtaposed with another epigram of Posidippus (115) celebrating the construction of the Pharos lighthouse by another Alexandrian official, Sostratus of Cnidus. Both emphasize the benefits and security that the Ptolemaic building program provides to vulnerable Greeks, and show that "Egypt is not a barbarian land" or "a mere Macedonian possession; it is a civilized, cultured, and celebrated place, peopled by Ptolemaic Greeks" (Obbink 2004: 22, 2005: 106).

The founder of the temple, Callicrates of Samos, son of Boiscus, was commander of the Ptolemaic navy from the 270s to the 250s, and the first priest of the cult of Alexander and the Savior Gods, inaugurated in Alexandria in 272/271. He also dedicated a temple of Isis and Anubis at Canopus. Two other epigrams by Posidippus commemorate his dedication of the temple at Zephyrium by addressing an audience of prospective worshippers (39, 119) who will benefit from the "fair sailing" provided by the goddess; cf. Introduction section 3. All three epigrams enact the creation of the cult and provide instructions for worshipping Arsinoe (cf. Ambühl 2007: 280–2). This one opens by specifying the temple's location in a way that suggests its centrality in the new coastal landscape. Thereafter it gives the titles by which the occupant will be called, in the process performing the act of naming that it recounts (ὠνόμασεν . . . ἀκουσομένην): a general reference to the windiness of the locale (ἀνεμώδεα) is followed by a more specific identification of the prevailing breeze as Zephyr, and by the revelation that Arsinoe-Aphrodite will henceforth be known by a cult title derived from it. Finally, it identifies the groups who should come to worship there and who will benefit from the new goddess's patronage.

That Arsinoe is addressed as queen as well as identified with Aphrodite suggests that this epigram was composed before her death in 270 or 268.

1–4[385–8] These lines locate the temple at the midpoint between two of the best-known and most important landmarks of the Egyptian coast, the famous island of Pharos, a place of shelter for ships already in Homer (*Od.* 4.358–9), and the westernmost mouth of the Nile at Canopus, which also served as a port. It thus has a central place among other harbors; cf. 10n.   **Φαρίης ἀκτῆς** "the coast of Pharos"; Pharos is low-lying (115.3–4 AB).   **Κανώπου:** perhaps more likely a noun than an otherwise unattested adjective.   **ἐν περιφαινομένωι κύματι χῶρον:** i.e. from its position on the promontory, the temple appears to be surrounded by water. The expression plays on *HHAphr.* 100, where Anchises promises the disguised Aphrodite that he will construct an altar for her ἐν σκοπιῆι, περιφαινομένωι ἐνὶ χώρωι: Callicrates actually does so.   **πολυρρήνου Λιβύης:** here, as often, Libya is a synecdoche for the north coast of Africa (e.g. Hdt. 1.46.2, Call. fr. 228.51). Its richness in sheep was well known (e.g. *Od.* 4.85–6). The thematic form of the adjective is a rarity (only at *Od.* 11.257 in the Homeric poems, which otherwise have πολύρρην).   **χηλήν:** here a strip of land creating a breakwater (LSJ ii 2);

the island of Pharos is so called at Pos. 115.4, but there may be special point in the use of the word (literally "hoof") in proximity to a reference to sheep. Ἰταλὸν ζέφυρον: Italy, source of the westerly Zephyr, is represented as the western boundary of the world. The wind (associated with Boreas at *Il.* 9.5) is here represented as blowing from the northwest.

5–6[389–90] βασιλίσσης | . . . Ἀρσινόης Κύπριδος: cf. LX introductory n. The benefits to be provided by divine Arsinoe are concretely connected to the policies of the royal court. **Ζεφυρῖτιν ἀκουσομένην** "who will be called by the cult-title Zephyritis," a vital piece of information for the prospective worshippers named in the following verses.

7–9[391–3] Arsinoe-Aphrodite's patronage of young Greek girls and sailors reflects her dual role as patron of marriage and protectress of those at sea. Though sailors were notorious for frequenting prostitutes in ports, they are here united with pure girls by the goddess's protection. **ἁγναὶ . . . θυγατέρες:** i.e. unmarried girls. Sacred laws at the entrances of sanctuaries often prescribe that those who enter must be pure in specific ways (e.g. by abstaining from sex); cf. Robertson 2013. The language is perhaps mimetic of ritual; cf. *336*, Call. *h.* 2.8 οἱ δὲ νέοι μολπήν τε καὶ ἐς χορὸν ἐντύνασθε. **ἁλὸς . . . ἄνδρες:** an inclusive description covering fishermen, merchants, and members of the Ptolemaic navy. **ὁ . . . ναύαρχος:** Callicrates' professional responsibility for the fleet, emphasized also at 39.4 and 119.4 AB, gives him a vested interest in providing safety for those at sea.

10[394] παντὸς κύματος εὐλίμενον "as shelter from every wave." The shelter provided by the temple from waves of every sort (including both literal ones and those on the metaphorical journey over the sea of love toward successful marriage) links it to the physical harbors of 1–2.

LXXIX. Posidippus 36 AB

Dedication of a linen object to Arsinoe; cf. XLIV introductory n. The poem illustrates the proper interpretation of and response to a divine sign (Ambühl 2007: 283); as the first of the ἀναθηματικά, it establishes a thematic bridge to the immediately preceding group of omen-epigrams (οἰωνοσκοπικά); contrast LXXVII.

Arsinoe appears to Hegeso in a dream-epiphany as a warrior fresh from fighting but still feminine and appealing. She is simultaneously cast as a participant in Ptolemaic foreign policy and as a patron of an individual

Macedonian girl; the specification of Hegeso's virginity perhaps implies an interest in marriage (cf. Bing 2009: 246–7). The geographic and ethnic details of the poem suggest an integrated, cosmopolitan world in which an object made from an indigenous Egyptian material in the Greek city of Naucratis is brought to Arsinoe's temple by a Macedonian girl (Stephens 2005: 236–7).

The gift, apparently a strip of white linen, resembles a Macedonian royal diadem, and on the Pithom Stele, a hieroglyphic inscription of the deeds of Ptolemy II, Arsinoe is described as "wearer of the white crown" in the entry for Year 12 of Ptolemy's reign (274/273). The precise ideological and historical significance of the object here is not wholly clear, however; cf. Stephens 2005: 236–40.

The poem is structured in ring composition, in three movements. The first and final couplet together (1 σοι ~ 7 σοι, 2 βύσσινον . . . βρέγμ' ~ 7 λευ<χ>έανον κανόνισμα, 2 ἄγκειται ~ 8 θῆκε) identify the donor, the recipient, and the dedicated object; the two central couplets narrate the background. Each section is marked by a second-person pronoun referring to Arsinoe (1, 3, 7). The first three couplets each contain a direct address to the goddess (Ἀρσινόη . . . φίλη . . . Φιλάδελφε).

The gift is described in unfamiliar, abstract diction, and the tone of the poem as a whole is elevated.

1[395] διὰ στολίδων "through its folds."   **ἀνεμοῦσθαι** "for blowing through" (epexegetic), an oblique reference to the breezes associated with Arsinoe-Aphrodite's temple at Zephyrium (cf. *385–8*n.).

2[396] βύσσινον . . . βρέγμ': apparently a straight (cf. 7n.) linen object, perhaps a head scarf, an otherwise unparalleled sense of βρέγμα (ordinarily "front of the head"). There may also be a hint at a (false) derivation from βρέχω, "wet," in reference to the fluidity of the object (cf. *359*n.) or to the fact that it will be used to wipe away the goddess's sweat (3n.). Linen was commercially grown in Egypt for trade on the international market.   **ἀπὸ Ναυκράτιος**: Naucratis was a Greek city and center of commercial activity about 70 miles south of Alexandria on the Canopic branch of the Nile.

3[397] γλυκὺν ἰδρῶ: Arsinoe continues to smell sweet after battle; cf. the athletic, feminine Athena at Call. *h.* 5.23–8.

4[398] ὀτρηρῶν: the adjective was originally associated with slaves, and its use of divine labors is bold; it was variously understood as meaning "quick," "manly," "active," "effective," "trusty," and "fearful" (Hsch. 01515, Σ *Od.* 1.109). **παυσαμένη καμάτων**: the phrase appears in the same verse-position in Leon. *AP* 6.289.8, of women dedicating their equipment on retirement from wool-working; Posidippus instead applies it to the divine recipient.

5–6[399–400] identify Arsinoe's toils as military. Her epiphany in arms suggests an active role in Ptolemaic military and foreign policy (cf. *IG* II³.1 912); the idea is reinforced by Φιλάδελφε. Her participation in warfare locates her among a series of Macedonian queens (e.g. Olympias, Eurydice, and Cynane) who fought in battle. Aphrodite, with whom the deified Arsinoe was identified at Zephyrium, was sometimes depicted in arms, and Athena was regularly so represented.   **ὡς ἐφάνη⟨ς⟩**: i.e. sweating from exertion.   **Φιλάδελφε**: the title was probably used even before Arsinoe's death, when Ptolemy II formally established a cult of Arsinoe Philadelphus (cf. Fraser 1972: 1.217 with 11.367).   **δούρατος αἰχμήν** varies the Homeric δουρὸς | αἰχμή (*Il.* 6.319–20) and is here a synecdoche for the entire spear.

7[401] **λευ⟨χ⟩έανον** "white-woven," a hapax formed like οἰέανος (A.R. 3.646) and εὐέανος (Mosch. 4.75).   **κανόνισμα**: literally "product of using a ruler," a rare word (elsewhere only in Phanias *AP* 6.295.3), here referring to a straight piece of cloth and perhaps suggesting the skill with which it was produced.

8[402] **παρθένος**: cf. *391–3*n.   **Μακέ[τη**: the dedicator's ethnic background, emphasized by its final position, contributes to the implicit appeal for the Macedonian Arsinoe's favor; cf. *404*n. and, for similar rhetoric, *291–2*n.

LXXX. *Posidippus 87 AB*

On an Olympic chariot victory by Berenice I. This and the following epigram, appearing in succession at the end of the ἱππικά, are linked by theme. Both evoke a famous inscription (*CEG* 820 = *AP* 13.16) by Cynisca, daughter of Archidamas II, sister of Agesilaus II, and victor at Olympia in 396 and again in 392. That poem accompanied a statue group representing Cynisca, her charioteer, and her team (Paus. 5.12.5, 6.1.6), and celebrated her status as the first woman to win the event: "My forebears and brothers were kings of Sparta, but I, Cynisca, winning with a chariot of swift-footed horses, set up this image, and I assert that I am the only woman in all Greece to have taken this crown." Posidippus' epigram explicitly treats Berenice as eclipsing the glory of her Spartan predecessor. As one of the few Greek states led by a hereditary dyarchy, Sparta was a model from the old Greek world for Macedonian kingship (cf. Pi. *Pyth.* 1.62–6, on the foundation at Aetna). Much as in the archaic period Alexander I claimed Argive origins for the Argead line in order to justify his participation in the Olympic Games (Hdt. 5.22.1–2), the linkage between Berenice and the Spartan princess implies continuity between the old and new worlds and marks the legitimacy of Ptolemaic rule. That Cynisca received heroic honors after her death makes her a fitting antecedent and model for Berenice, who was posthumously deified in 268 (cf. Fantuzzi 2005: 253–68).

The Doric dialect typical of the ἱππικά which celebrate victories at Olympia matches the local dialect of the place, but also contributes to the broader affiliation between the Spartan Cynisca and the Macedonian Berenice; cf. Introduction section 4g, Sens 2004, Hunter in Fantuzzi–Hunter 2004: 375–7.

1[403] π[ῶλοι] ἔθ᾽ . . . ἐοῦσαι: i.e. before they were depicted as statues, with the underlying ecphrastic point that the chariot-team itself has been transformed into art.

2[404] Π[ι]σᾶ[τ]αι: residents of Pisa, the area that included Olympia. Μακέτας: the proud focus placed on the Macedonian origins of the royal family here (cf. 78.14 AB) locates the Ptolemaic victories in a line of successful Olympic competitions by earlier Macedonian kings, and so suggests the legitimacy of the family as successors to Alexander the Great and his ancestors; cf. Fantuzzi 2005: 251–2. ἀγάγομ[ε]ς στέφανον "we brought the crown."

3[405] [πο]λυθρύλητον "much chattered about." θρυλέω, from which the adjective is formed, connotes babbling, confused speech; the compound is somewhat derisive. -ητον, initially written by the scribe and then mistakenly altered to hyper-Doric -ατον, is the correct Doric form for an adjective formed from a verb in -έω.

4[406] χρόνιον "longstanding." κῦδος ἀφειλόμεθα: i.e. by nullifying Cynisca's claim to be the only female Olympian victor. There is an allusion to *Il.* 22.18 μέγα κῦδος ἀφείλεο, spoken by Achilles to Apollo, who has just pointed out the difference between his divinity and Achilles' mortality: the phrase corresponds to and caps λαβεῖν στέφανον at the conclusion of Cynisca's epigram (*CEG* 820.4), and suggests Berenice's superior status.

LXXXI. Posidippus 88 AB

On Olympic victories won by Berenice I, Ptolemy I Soter, and their son, Ptolemy II Philadelphus; cf. LXXX introductory n. In addition to engaging with the Cynisca epigram, the poem draws on the encomiastic, and more specifically epinician, trope that excellence runs in families. The speaker is not the victorious queen but her son, and whereas Cynisca had defined herself in relation to the male members of her family, Ptolemy focuses on the ἀρετή of both sides of his family, culminating in his mother's victory, which implicitly benefits her son.

1–2[407–8] "My parents and I are the only three dynasts to win Olympian victories with our chariots." Emphasis on uniqueness and priority (πρῶτο[ι] . . . καὶ μόνοι) is an encomiastic convention (cf. Arist. fr. 673). The Ptolemaic boast is broader than Cynisca's (CEG 820.3–4 μόναν δ' ἐμέ φαμι γυναικῶν . . . λαβεῖν στέφανον). βασιλῆες . . . καὶ γονέες καὶ ἐγώ recalls CEG 820.1 βασιλῆες ἐμοὶ πατέρες καὶ ἀδελφοί but converts Cynisca's reference to her royal line into an assertion of familial athletic aretē.

3–4[409–10] "I, by Berenice the son of Ptolemy, sharing his name, Eordaean offspring, am one of them, and two are my parents." The lines explain, in chiastic order, 2 καὶ γονέες καὶ ἐγώ, with variation of prosody (γονεῖς, γονέες). ὁμώνυμος reinforces the picture of continuity and resemblance. Ἐορδαία: an area of central Macedon, birthplace of Ptolemy I, which Ptolemy II, though in reality born on Cos, claims as his own.

5–6[411–12] These lines function as a priamel in which the great glory of father and son serves as foil for the superior achievement of the mother. πρὸς . . . κλέος "I add my renown to the great renown of my father," a heroic ideal; cf. Il. 6.446 ἀρνύμενος πατρός τε μέγα κλέος ἠδ' ἐμὸν αὐτοῦ. εἷλε . . . ἅρματι picks up the language of Cynisca's boast in CEG 820.3–4 μόναν δ' ἐμέ φαμι γυναικῶν [cf. γυνά] | Ἑλλάδος ἐκ πάσας τόνδε λαβεῖν στέφανον. τοῦτο μέγα: the terse ending (cf. Call. Epigr. 6.4) avoids claims to uniqueness or priority; despite Cynisca's earlier victory, Berenice's victory is a major accomplishment.

LXXXII. Posidippus 63 AB

On a statue of Philitas (cf. pp. 121–2) by Hecataeus. The poem is the second epigram in the thematically unified ἀνδριαντοποιικά, of which the lacunose first epigram opens by instructing readers to "imitate these works" (62.1 μιμήσασθε τάδ᾽ ἔργα), a phrase that may be taken to refer both to the statues treated in the subsequent poems and the epigrams describing them. The section plays on the analogy between statues and the epigrams in which they are described, and implies that both share similar aesthetic qualities (cf. Gutzwiller 2002a, Sens 2005: 209–16), including novelty, precision, refinement, and a tension between grandeur and sublimity on the one hand and λεπτότης on the other (Prioux 2007: 109–11; cf. Porter 2011).

This epigram develops the analogy. Hecataeus and Philitas are described in similar terms, the former as precise in the finest details and committed to capturing Philitas' true appearance, the latter as "having the greatest care" (5 ἀκρομέριμνον), a reference to Philitas' notorious poetic perfectionism (cf. adesp. *FGE* 134); the juxtaposition of the adjective with a reference to Hecataeus' artistry (5 ὅληι . . . τέχνηι) links the activities of sculptor and poet. At Theocr. 7.39–48, Simichidas adduces Philitas as a model of the literary skill to which he aspires, and he claims to despise those who seek to produce grand structures or compete against Homer; the implication is that good poets, including Philitas, do not do so. In this respect Hecataeus, who represents his subject as he is without adding girth or height, resembles Philitas, who was associated with thinness through the refinement of his poetry (λεπτότης, for which cf. *323–5*n.) and consequently sometimes represented as physically slender. The epigram thus asserts both a sculptural and a poetic program: both Hecataeus and Philitas were similarly refined, and so by implication is Posidippus' account of their work.

Hermesianax (fr. 7.75–8) mentions a statue of Philitas dedicated by the Coans. Whether this epigram refers to the same statue is not clear, but it seems likely that Posidippus has Hermesianax' account in mind (1n.); cf. Prioux 2007, Hardie 1997.

1–2[413–14] "Hecataeus precisely formed this bronze to be identical to Philitas in every respect, down to the last detail." κατὰ πάνθ᾽ Ἑκαταῖος probably looks to Hermes. fr. 7.77 περὶ πάντα Φιλίταν at line end; the allusion helps assimilate the artist Hecataeus to his subject (cf. above). For the critical language, cf. D.H. *Dem.* 13, ὅλος ἐστὶν ἀκριβὴς καὶ λεπτὸς καὶ τὸν Λυσιακὸν χαρακτῆρα ἐκμέμακται εἰς ὄνυχα.   ἀ]κριβής refers to the artist's precision in representing specific details (Pollitt 1974: 123) and is a mark of his refinement and skill (cf. Arist. *Nic. Eth.* 1141a9–11).   ἄκρους . . . εἰς ὄνυχας "to the tips of his toenails," i.e. "from head to toe": Hecataeus pays attention to the smallest detail. An obscure aphorism attributed to Polyclitus observes that the job is hardest "for those for whom clay reaches the nail" (Plut. *Mor.* 86a χαλεπώτατον τὸ ἔργον οἷς ἂν εἰς ὄνυχα ὁ πηλὸς ἀφίκηται; cf. *Mor.* 636c); cf. Prioux 2007: 34–42.

3[415] καὶ με]γέθει κα[ὶ σα]ρκί "in height and body type"; cf. *177–8*n. Here the two nouns correspond to the features implied by the adjectives in the phrase μείζονα καὶ πάσσονα in passages where Athena beautifies Odysseus (e.g. *Od.* 6.230): by contrast, Hecataeus makes no improvements to Philitas' form (cf. 4n.) by augmenting his famously frail frame (Hermes. fr. 7.77–8, Ael. *VH* 9.14; cf. Cameron 1991, Bing 2009: 14–15). The final epigram of the ἀνδριαντοποιικά (70 AB) seems to oppose the "fleshy" (σάρκινα) works of Polyclitus to Lysippus' sculptures, treated in the opening poem as the epitome of modern style.   **διώξας:** i.e. "having sought to capture"; cf. Pi. *Isthm.* 3/4.21 ὑμετέρας ἀρετὰς ὕμνωι διώκειν (where the usage derives from the image of the chariot of song).

4[416] ἀφ᾽ ἡρώων . . . ἰδέης: Hecataeus' unwillingness to apply idealized, heroic qualities to his subject suits Hellenistic poets' broader interest in humble individuals and their occasional treatment of traditional heroes in less than heroic terms.

5[417] τὸν ἀκρομέριμνον "the most careful man"; cf. Dion. Cyz. *AP* 7.78.3 ἄκρα μεριμνήσας, of Eratosthenes. The adjective, a hapax, picks up by sound and meaning the language of 2 (ἀ]κριβὴς ἄκρους) and suggests exacting artistic toil and precision similar to that of Hecataeus.

5–7[417–19] ὅλ[ηι κ]ατεμάξατο . . . ἔοικεν: a reworking of Asclepiades' description of Lysippus' statue of Alexander at 47–9, where a similar phrase occupies the same relative positions, also shortly followed by χάλκεος. In that poem, Alexander transcends the limits of humanity and challenges Zeus; here the subject is explicitly human, in contrast with the deified Ptolemy of 9–10.   **πρ]έσβυν:** Hellenistic poets regularly represent earlier authors as old men to suggest their priority in the tradition as well as their antiquity and prestige (cf. 8 ὁ γέρων, *501*, Leon. *APl* 306.1, 307.1, Call. fr. 75.76, Hunter 2001: 250). The representation of older, non-idealized subjects was also common in Hellenistic art.   **ἀληθείης ὀρθὸν [ἔχων] κανόνα** "having the straight yardstick of truth." Posidippus defines the standard for artistic creation as the accurate, unadorned representation of physical appearance (Gutzwiller 2002a: 47–8). The phrase is probably borrowed from Timo of Phlius *SH* 842.2, who highlights the subjectivity of his view (cf. 1 ὥς μοι καταφαίνεται εἶναι) while insisting on its truthfulness (cf. Prioux 2007: 45–6). κανόνα reframes the proper standard for the creation of sculpture in the "Canon" of Polyclitus, where the artist proposed a set of ideal, numerical proportions. The nature of "truth" in art was the subject of considerable controversy (Pollitt 1974: 125–38, Stewart 2005). That art can produce and distort truth is as applicable to literature as it is to statuary; cf. Hes. *Th.* 22–34, Theocr. 7.44 πᾶν ἐπ' ἀλαθείαι πεπλασμένον . . . ἔρνος (cf. introductory n.), Call. fr. 75.76 πρέσβυς ἐτητυμίηι μεμελημένος.   **αὐδήσ]οντι δ' ἔοικεν**: though uncertain, the supplement depends on the structural and verbal parallelism with *49* and is supported by the importance of the imagined voice of an object as a marker of its realism in other ecphrastic contexts (cf. *92*, A.R. 1.763–4).   **ὅσωι ποικίλλεται ἤθει** "with so much character is he artfully depicted." Σᴬ *Il.* 18.590 (ἐν δὲ χορὸν ποίκιλλε περικλυτὸς ἀμφιγυήεις) understands ποίκιλλε there to refer to Hephaestus' artistic precision (ἐγκατεσκεύασε δὲ ἐπιμελῶς); an ancient account of Sophocles' artistry connects it to characterization (*Vita Sophoclis* 20 ἠθοποιεῖ τε καὶ ποικίλλει καὶ τοῖς ἐπινοήμασι τεχνικῶς χρῆται).

8[420] ἔμψυχ]ος: cf. Theocr. 15.82–3 ὡς ἔτυμ' ἑστάκαντι καὶ ὡς ἔτυμ' ἐνδινεῦντι, | ἔμψυχ', οὐκ ἐνυφαντά.

9–10[421–2] complement 1–2, naming Hecataeus and Philitas; here Ptolemy and Philitas frame the couplet (cf. 2 ἔπλασε ~ 10 ἄγκειται, 1 τόνδε ~ 9 ὧδε). Unlike Hermesianax, Posidippus does not specify the community in which the statue is set up but instead focuses on the divine king's patronage, which is represented as a source (cf. ἐκ) of artistic creation and serves a role played elsewhere by the Muses; cf. Belloni 2008. Ptolemy was tutored by Philitas and, like him, was born on Cos (*Suda* φ332); the final specification of the poet's ethnicity may hint at a further reason for the king's support.

The printed text assumes no change of speaker. Scodel (2003) suggests ἄγκειμ]αι, in which case the couplet contains the words that Philitas is to speak. On this reading, the embedded speech would differ from others imputed to statues, which generally embody or reflect on some aspect of the representation (e.g. *50*).   **θεοῦ . . . βασιλῆος:** cf. 5–7n., *389–90*n. As a god and king, Ptolemy differs from the humble Philitas, but the implication is probably that the characterization is as accurate as Hecataeus' depiction of his subject is. Cf. the treatment of Ptolemy as ἡμίθεος at Theocr. 17.135–6 and of Hieron as a hero at Theocr. 16.80–1 ἐν δ' αὐτοῖς Ἱέρων προτέροις ἴσος ἡρώεσσι | ζώννυται.   **Μουσέων εἵνεκα** implies both "in honor of the Muses" and "because of his literary ability" (cf. "Simon." *AP* 7.25.1–2, of Anacreon, τὸν ἄφθιτον εἵνεκα Μουσέων | ὑμνοπόλον).   **Κῶιος ἀνήρ:** cf. Simon. fr. 19.1, of Homer, Χῖος . . . ἀνήρ.

LXXXIII. Posidippus 65 AB (APl 119 = 18 GP)

On a bronze statue of Alexander by Lysippus; cf. xii introductory n. The epigram is transmitted via the Anthology but also appears in a multi-author Hellenistic anthology preserved on a papyrus (*SH* 973) and among the ἀνδριαντοποιικά. Its conceit is that the sculptor has so accurately captured the king's appearance that the speaker understands why the Persians fled from him. Like lxxxii, the epigram analogizes the character of the artist to that of his subject.

In the Milan Posidippus, the poem has a Doric coloring lost in the later tradition. The spoken dialect of Lysippus' homeland Sicyon was Doric, and the speaker is thus represented as part of the same linguistic community as the sculptor he addresses; cf. Introduction section 4g.

1[423] πλάστα "sculptor." The vocative in -ᾱ (also in 2 τεχνίτᾱ) as opposed to -ᾰ might be a Doric feature.   θαρσαλέα: Lysippus' courage contrasts with the flight of the Persians in 4; it lies in his innovative approach and in his ability to produce a fierce portrait without fleeing. "Boldness" was also an important (ethically ambiguous) attribute of Alexander; cf. 47n., adesp. *APl* 121.1–2.   χείρ: used in ecphrastic contexts of the skill of artists, especially in producing accurate likenesses of their subjects (cf. Headlam on Herodas 4.72, Pos. 7.3, 14.2, 62.3, 67.2 AB), but here deployed more boldly in apposition to the artist himself.

2[424] δάϊε: apparently "skilful" (< *δάω; cf. Epicur. fr. 183 Usener δαῖως), but also evoking the standard use of δήϊος, "hostile," as an epithet of fire (e.g. *Il.* 9.347). Both suit the creator of a statue with a fiery glance.   πῦρ . . . ὁρῆι "has a look of fire," as at e.g. *Od.* 19.446 πῦρ δ' ὀφθαλμοῖσι δεδορκώς. ὁρῆι is Doric present indicative (Buck §41, Introduction section 4g).

3[425] ὅν . . . ἔθευ: "which you set down over the form of Alexander"; the statue gives the impression that Lysippus has used as a model the king's actual form, rather than the wax-covered clay molds used in ancient bronze-casting (cf. Mattusch 1996: 20–6).   οὔ τί γε "not in any way at all" (cf. Pl. *Phaedo* 81d, Arist. *Phys.* 258b22), implicitly correcting (γε) contrary views. The rejection of the conventional idea that the Persians were cowardly (cf. Hall 1988: 123–5, Briant 1989) elevates both the vanquished foe and Alexander's conquests.

4[426] συγγνώμα: sc. ἐστί: "it is forgivable," a prosaic usage (cf. LSJ c).   βουσὶ . . . λέοντα evokes Alexander's leonine appearance, which only Lysippus was said to be able to capture (Plut. *Mor.* 335b); it gestures at Homeric passages comparing warriors to lions attacking cattle: e.g. *Il.* 5.161, 12.293 λέονθ᾽ ὡς βουσίν.

LXXXIV. Posidippus 15 AB (20 GP)

On the image of a chariot on a snake-stone seal. The poem is preserved by Tzetzes and in the λιθικά of the Milan papyrus. Epigrams on highly wrought miniature gems, little attested before the discovery of the papyrus, play on the original material context of epigram as a form designed for inscription on stone. Several of them focus on the engraver's skill in producing an elaborate image on a tiny surface, and so may be understood as self-reflexive comments on the poet's own production of a refined, miniature artifact (see Schur 2004, Elsner 2014). The λιθικά have also been read in political terms: the stones derive from many places in Alexander's former empire, and the section as a whole constitutes a map of Ptolemaic imperial ambitions (Bing 2005) that treats the sources of the dynasty's wealth as coterminous with Alexander's domain. Some poems have a background in technical literature; this epigram shares points of contact with an account of the fantastic stone attributed to the Hellenistic geologist Sotacus by Pliny, *NH* 37.158 (cf. 3–5, 7–8nn., Smith 2004: 112–17); it also plays on the belief that the stone magically improved vision (Ptol. Chenn. ap. Phot. *Bibl.* 150b.20–2).

The poem describes a work of art on a stone which was alleged in a probably near-contemporary work to have been impossible to carve (7–8n.); the artistry is thus doubly marvelous. It also suggests the capacity of ecphrasis to make an image visible verbally: here, the image carved in the stone is only visible when expressed in secondary form, and the viewer's experience is defined by what he cannot see at first glance (6). In this context, the double entendre involved in ψεύδει χειρός (5) is programmatically significant.

1[427] οὐ ποταμὸς κελάδων perhaps plays on λιθικά which specify rivers as the source of their gems (e.g. 7.1–3, 16.1 AB). ποταμὸς κελάδων is a Homeric phrase (*Il.* 18.576; cf. Theocr. 17.92, of rivers under Ptolemaic control).   ἐπὶ χείλεσιν "against its banks"; but the noun's literal sense "lips" fits the focus on the snake's head in the next clause.

1–2[427–8] δράκοντος | ... κεφαλή: the mythical snake-stone was thought to have derived from a serpent's brain (Pliny, *NH* 37.158).   εὐπώγων: snakes are often described as bearded (e.g. Nic. *Ther.* 443), perhaps in reference to the fact that some expand their neck in a defensive posture.

3–5[429–31] The claim that the stone resembles a fingernail with white marks fits Sotacus' description of it as white and translucent (ap. Pliny, *NH* 37.158).   πυκνὰ φαληριόωντα "densely streaked with white." The phrasing is modeled on *Il.* 13.799 κυρτὰ φαληριόωντα, of waves.   ἅρμα: the image perhaps hints at the method of acquiring the stone: those hunting the snakes that produced it allegedly traveled in chariots (Sotacus ap. Pliny, *NH* 37.158; cf. Gutzwiller 1995: 388).   κατ᾽ αὐτοῦ "down into it."   ὑπὸ Λυγκείου βλέμματος "with the aid of vision like Lynceus"; more usually, the artist's hand is the means of production (see next n.). Lynceus, son of Aphareus, who possessed such extraordinary sight that he could even see underground, is here an analogue for the artist who carved below the surface of the stone an image invisible from above.   ψεύδεϊ χειρός: the primary meaning is "a mark on the fingernail," in reference to the size and color of the stone; the phrase also evokes the capacity of artistry (χείρ; cf. 423n.) to produce realistic falsehood (ψεῦδος).   ἀποπλασθέν "when formed as an image," i.e. in the impression formed from the seal.

6[432] κατὰ πλάτεος "on its surface."   οὐκ ἂν ἴδοις προβόλους: the viewer's failure to see "projections" (because the image is in relief) contrasts with the carver's supernatural vision.

7[433] ἧι "for which reason."   θαῦμα . . . μέγα: the greatness of the speaker's amazement contrasts with the smallness of the object.

7–8[433–4] μόχθου . . . οὐκ ἐμόγησε is a significant *figura etymologica*: despite his toil (μόχθου) on the object, the carver did not strain (ἐμόγησε) his eyes.   τὰς ἀτενιζούσας . . . κόρας "his intently staring pupils."

LXXXV. Posidippus 139 AB (AP 12.131 = 8 GP)

A cletic hymn to Aphrodite. The wit depends on the subversion of the elevated form and diction by the revelation that the speaker is a widely available hetaera. The dialect is inconsistent: the repeated Doric relative pronouns in the opening couplet followed by a pair of Ionic forms (Συρίης, ἥ) in the second part may contribute to the point. With the text as transmitted, Doric forms of the relative pronoun referring to the goddess and suiting the elevated, "choral" opening contrast with the Ionic form of the relative referring to the hetaera.

1–2[435–6] Invocation of a god by reference to multiple cult sites is a conventional hymnic feature; e.g. Ar. *Lys.* 833–4, Theocr. 15.100–1, Men. Rh. p. 334.26–32 Spengel. Cyprus, Cythera, and Syria are mentioned more often as Aphrodite's cult sites than is Miletus (cf. Theocr. 7.115–16), which became a Ptolemaic possession in 279 and may have political resonance here.   ἐποιχνεῖς "visit" (cf. Hsch. ε5483); a rare verb otherwise restricted to lyric contexts (Bacchyl. 10.1, Aristonous, *Paean to Apollo* 11–12).   καλὸν . . . δάπεδον: a high-style periphrasis; cf. e.g. Eur. *Hel.* 207–8 ἱππόκροτα . . . δάπεδα.

3[437] ἔλθοις ἵλαος: the purpose is never explained, but it is reasonable to infer that the speaker seeks the goddess's assistance with someone with whom she has become enamored (e.g. Sappho, fr. 1).

4[438] οἰκείων . . . προθύρων "the doors of her house"; there is perhaps an obscene double entendre ("from her own genitalia"; cf. Asclep. *35.2 Sens = Pos. *127.2 AB εὐίππων . . . ἐπὶ προθύρων, Henderson 1991: 137).

LXXXVI. Posidippus 135 AB (AP 12.45 = 5 GP)

The speaker urges the Erotes to shoot him. The poem combines elements from two of Asclepiades' epigrams addressing the Erotes: in one, they assume Zeus's role; in the other, they are represented as thoughtlessly destructive children who remain unaffected by the speaker's suffering. Here, by contrast, the speaker sarcastically represents their victory as a grand conquest that will change their status among the gods; in reality, he poses no challenge and the gods will not benefit from defeating him.

1[439] ναὶ ναὶ . . . Ἔρωτες: borrowed from Asclep. 17.5 Sens, where the speaker urges the Erotes to shoot him with thunderbolts rather than arrows. The repetition ναὶ ναὶ is ironic encouragement.

1–2[439–40] σκοπὸς . . . | κεῖμαι "am set up as a target."   εἷς ἅμα πολλοῖς: Posidippus makes explicit the iniquity implicit in other epigrams where plural Erotes attack an individual; cf. *83–4*n.

2[440] ἄφρονες: i.e. the Erotes would be "foolish" to spare the speaker and pass up the opportunity for glory. Posidippus restores the ordinary meaning of ἄφρων, which Asclepiades uses in the unusual sense "heedless."

2–4[440–2] ἢν . . . ἰοδόκης "For if you defeat me, you will become famous archers among the immortals for controlling large quivers," playing on the typical Hellenistic representation of the Erotes as small children armed with miniature weapons. Since Eros/the Erotes conventionally have power even over Zeus, the idea that shooting the speaker will alter their reputation is absurd; the larger point of μεγάλης is that it will have taken numerous arrows to bring him down. With ὀνομαστοί contrast the representation of Eros as an "unspeakable" (ἄφατον) evil at A.R. 3.129. The lines rework Asclep. *83–4*.   **δεσπόται**: as at Soph. *Phil.* 262 Ἡρακλείων δεσπότης ... ὅπλων.

LXXXVII. Posidippus 138 AB (AP 12.120 = 7 GP)

A pledge to resist Eros: the speaker will use reason to reject love while he is sober. The depiction of Eros as an armed combatant appears early in Greek and is developed in Hellenistic and Roman literature (cf. Murgatroyd 1975). The speaker's defiance resembles the combativeness of other lovers who speak too freely or behave recklessly when drunk (e.g. Anacr. *PMG* 396). Readers may therefore initially expect that the speaker is inebriated; the second couplet reveals that he is not. The wit derives from the contrast between the speaker's broad resistance and his subsequent acknowledgment that it will be temporary: the common association of erotic epigrams with the symposium and the conventional idea that love is all-powerful (Soph. *Ant.* 781 Ἔρως ἀνίκατε μάχαν) suggest that his sobriety will not last long.

The epigram finds a counterpart in another in which Posidippus privileges the symposium over Stoic philosophy (123 AB). It has been understood as a comment on Stoicism's ability to overcome passion (Gutzwiller 1998a: 162), but Posidippus may be playing with contemporary philosophical ideas more broadly (Fantuzzi in Fantuzzi and Hunter 2004: 345, Prauscello 2006: 517 n. 34).

1[443] εὐοπλῶ "I am well armed." Another military verb, θωρήσσομαι (literally, "put on armor"), can have the metaphorical sense "get drunk" (cf. Ar. *Ach.* 1134–5 with Olson's note); possibly the metaphor extended to other words in the same semantic range, and if so, the verb contributes to the initial impression that the speaker is fortified with wine rather than reason.   **οὐδ᾽ ἀπεροῦμαι** "and I will not give up the fight"; cf. Plut. *Lyc.* 22.5, *Pomp.* 23.4, of soldiers and leaders desisting from battle.

2[444] θνητὸς ἐών: concessive; i.e. though fighting as a mortal against a god.   **μηκέτι**: Eros has attacked the speaker on earlier occasions, perhaps successfully.   **πρόσαγε** "approach."

3[445] ἄπαγ᾽ ἔκδοτον "lead me away in surrender"; cf. lyr. adesp. fr. 1.12–14 Powell Κύπρις | ἔκδοτον ἄγει με χὠ | πολὺς Ἔρως παραλαβών. Contrast 2 πρόσαγε.

3–4[445–6] νήφω ... λογισμόν: for the connection between sobriety and rational decision-making, cf. Epicur. *Menoec.* 132 νήφων λογισμός, Plut. *Mor.* 656c (summarizing Arist. *Prob.* 871a11–13) "it is characteristic of the sober man to make rational decisions (κρίνειν τὸν λογισμόν) well and in accordance with reality." Line 4 picks up 1 in ring composition, and τὸν παραταξάμενον πρὸς σὲ λογισμὸν ἔχω in 5 defines what the speaker means by εὐοπλῶ. **παραταξάμενον** "arrayed," a military term (e.g. Thuc. 1.29.5 παραταξάμενοι ἐναυμάχησαν).

THEOCRITUS

Theocritus seems originally to have been from Syracuse and to have begun his literary career by the late 280s or early 270s. An appeal to Hieron of Syracuse for patronage (poem 16) probably dates to about 275. A connection to Alexandria is suggested by several poems directly praising Ptolemy II Philadelphus, his wife Arsinoe, and his parents (14, 17), and by others honoring the Dioscuri (22) and Heracles (24), who were important for Ptolemaic self-representation. The bulk of Theocritus' extant corpus consists of thirty-one "idylls" (the last preserved only in a papyrus fragment), short, highly refined poems mostly composed in dactylic hexameter, though 28–31 are in Aeolic meters. His works are generically diverse and innovative; they include hymns, encomia, and narrative poems on mythological subjects ("epyllia"), but the most innovative and influential of them are hexameter "mimes" set in the countryside or the city and consisting of dialogues or monologues by herdsmen, laborers, or city-dwellers of relatively low social standing. The refined and often elevated diction and meter of these poems contrast with the humble status of their speakers, whose words sometimes resonate ironically against literary models. The so-called "bucolic idylls" are written in an artificial poetic dialect overlaying Doric on epic morphology. These imagine an idealized countryside in which humans and the natural world are closely intertwined; the tranquility of this rural landscape contrasts with the lovesick anguish frequently experienced by its herdsmen, who seem more preoccupied with the composition of song than with pastoral duties. Though the bucolic idylls share common elements and themes, these are not yet treated as basic expectations of the genre, as they are in later pastoral. These poems sometimes seem to comment self-reflexively on their genre and its creation, and indeed some non-bucolic idylls assume the existence of bucolic poetry and its themes (e.g. Theocr. 22.27–74). This is equally true for some of the epigrams ascribed to Theocritus.

Twenty-two epigrams are appended to the Ambrosian manuscripts of Theocritus. These poems also appear in the Anthology, some with ascriptions to other poets; a number of epitaphs are assigned to Leonidas in *AP* 7, apparently as the result of an error leading to the mis-ascription of an entire series (Gow 1952: II.525–7). The Anthology includes several others ascribed to Theocritus, and one without attribution appears in a sequence of epigrams bearing his name. Meleager does not mention Theocritus in his prefatory poem, and the epigrams included in the Anthology probably derive from a later collection.

In the Ambrosian manuscripts, the epigrams are organized by theme and form three groups: those with bucolic themes; epitaphs and dedications; and those in non-elegiac meters (cf. Gutzwiller 1998a: 41–5; Rossi 2001: 367–70). The boundaries between these sections are permeable: both the "bucolic" and the non-elegiac groups include epigrams that manipulate the conventions of sepulchral and dedicatory epigram in sophisticated ways. That fact is relevant for the question of authenticity; *Suda* θ166 locates the epigrams among the poems that "some ascribe" to Theocritus. At least one poem seems to reflect a post-Theocritean approach to bucolic themes (cf. Rossi 2001: 138–9), but for most there is no reason to exclude Theocritean authorship. Their style, form, and content are typical of epigrams from the early third century. XCIV is almost certainly genuine.

LXXXVIII. *Theocritus 19 Gow (AP 13.3 = 13 GP)*

An epitaph for Hipponax. The choliambic meter, closely associated with Hipponax in antiquity (e.g. Call. fr. 191), assimilates the speaker to the poet. The epigram plays on fictive epitaphs for misanthropes by depicting Hipponax not as indiscriminately hostile (contrast XXVIII), but as a discerning judge of character and capable of kindness toward the deserving. It has been argued that Theocritus is participating in a broader debate about Hipponax by casting him in a positive light (cf. Rossi 2001: 299–301), but other depictions are not necessarily critical. Theocritus in any case articulates a nuanced vision of iambic abuse, which is directed only at those who deserve it (Rosen 2007: 470–1).

1[447] μουσοποιός: see *485*.

2[448] εἰ μὲν πονηρός: *sc.* ἐσσί.

3[449] κρήγυος . . . παρὰ χρηστῶν: it is more common for forms of the same word to be used in similar contexts; e.g. *CEG* 547 Ἄττις ἦν χρηστὸς καὶ χρηστῶ[ν ἐξεγ]εν[ήθη], Fehling 1969: 218–19. κρήγυος is here "good," though some ancient scholars believed it meant "true" in its single

Homeric occurrence (*Il.* 1.106), and Hellenistic poets use it in both senses. It was associated with Ionic speech, especially in choliambs (cf. Phoenix 6.4, Herodas 4.46, Call. fr. 193.30); and it suits the voice of the Ionian Hipponax' tomb; it may have been used by him. χρηστός, commonly applied to the deceased in epitaphs (cf. *457–8*n.), is here transferred to the passerby.

4[450] θαρσέων: cf. Leon. *135* ἀτρέμα, an adverb literally meaning "without trembling" (< τρέμω "tremble [with fear]") but implying "without making a disturbance." **ἀπόβριξον** "nod off." Elsewhere, passersby are cautioned against, or scolded for, awaking a "sleeping" misanthrope (cf. *135–6*, Zenod. or Rhianus *AP* 7.315). Σ *Od.* 9.151 derives βρίζειν, falsely, from βαρὺ ἵζειν, "sit heavy," or μετὰ βορὰν ἵζειν, "sit after eating," and its conjunction with καθίζευ is thus perhaps a *figura etymologica*.

LXXXIX. Theocritus 15 Gow (AP 7.658 = 7 GP)

An epitaph for Eurymedon, who claims that he can judge a passerby's character from his reaction to the tomb. Epitaphs sometimes urge the traveler to "know" something about the tomb or its occupant (cf. 277, "Simon." *APl* 2.1–2 γνῶθι Θεόγνητον προσιδὼν τὸν Ὀλυμπιονίκαν | παῖδα), and many insist on the high moral character of the deceased. Here, the dead man will be the one to acquire knowledge, though the implication is that Eurymedon is good and thus deserving of a special greeting. In contrast with epigrams in which the passerby is asked to greet the deceased or utter certain words (e.g. *IMEGR* 10.16 "χαῖρε λέγοις "κούφη δ' ἀμφιπέλοιτο κόνις," "Erinna" *AP* 7.710.3, Damag. *AP* 7.355.2), here the speaker notes that only some will be wise enough to do so. Moreover, although it is conventional for travelers to wish that the dust might lie lightly on the deceased, here the discerning passerby recognizes that the tomb in fact does so. The point thus depends on the reciprocal relationship between the passerby and the deceased: the former's ability to recognize the latter's character reveals his own.

1[451] τι νέμεις ... πλέον "you grant some greater honor (to)" (cf. Eur. *Hec.* 868, [Xen.] *Ath. Pol.* 1.4).   **ὁ δειλός** "the coward," and thus, more broadly, "the bad man."

2[452] ὡσαύτως ἴσον "just the same amount"; ἴσον contrasts with 1 πλέον.

3–4[453–4] If the traveler can make distinctions between good and bad, he will congratulate the tomb for lying lightly on Eurymedon.   **ἐρεῖς:** i.e.

whenyourecognizeEurymedon'smeritoriouscharacter.   **Εὐρυμέδοντος:**
at Theocr. *AP* 7.659 (7 Gow) a certain Eurymedon is said to have a seat
"among divine men" and to be the son "of a good father."   **κεῖται . . .**
ὑπὲρ κεφαλῆς: cf. *360*n. For the application of κοῦφος to the tomb rather
than the soil, cf. *SGO* 08/05/01.8.   **τῆς ἱερῆς . . . κεφαλῆς:** a similar
expression occurs already in an inscribed epitaph from the fourth century; cf. *SEG* XLI 226.1 = ΣΗΜΑ 2361.1 226 τὴν ἱερὴν κεφαλὴν . . . ἔχει γῆ.

XC. Theocritus 20 Gow (AP 7.663 = 11 GP)

On a monument dedicated to a Thracian wet-nurse by her former charge.
The theme is traditional: epitaphs erected in honor of nurses by those for
whom they cared appear among fourth-century inscriptions (*CEG* 534,
571; cf. Rossi 2001: 305–13) and Hellenistic literary epigrams; in particular, this poem resembles Call. *Epigr.* 50, an epitaph recording burial honors given a Phrygian wet-nurse by a boy called Mikkos; cf. Diosc. *AP* 7.456.
Whereas Callimachus' poem is in elegiac couplets, here a Phalaecian (see
XCV introductory n.) alternates with an "Archilochian asynartete" (four
dactylic feet plus a trochaic tripody, with colon break between them: – ⏔
– ⏔ – ⏔ – ⏔ | – ⏑ – ⏑ – ×) to produce an epodic structure in which the
shorter verse precedes the longer (cf. Introduction section 4h[iii]).

The epigram implies a monument on which the honorand's name
appeared apart from the verse epitaph (e.g., in the form Κλείτα χρηστή μα:
3–4nn.). Nothing excludes its having been composed for inscription,
but it is probably a fiction inspired by other poems on the relationship
between nurses and their wards. The content is neatly partitioned: the
first couplet records the dedications; the second its consequences for
Clita's posthumous renown, which her name ("Famous") suits.

1[455] μικκός: an affectionate diminutive of μικρός, often used of children
(e.g. Aesch. fr. 47a.813), here perhaps reflecting what the nurse called
the boy when he was young (cf. Call. *AP* 7.458.2) rather than indicat-
ing his age at the time of her death.   **Θρᾷσσαι:** trisyllabic (cf. Herodas
1.1). Thracian slaves, commonly used as domestic workers (cf. Theocr.
2.70, Olson on Ar. *Ach.* 273), are often addressed simply by an ethnic
designation. That the word is here not a proper name becomes clear only
at the end of 2.

2[456] ἐπὶ τᾶι ὁδῶι "alongside the road" (LSJ ἐπί B.I.1); similar specifications of place, usually with παρά and ἐγγύς, are common in epitaphs
(e.g. *CEG* 16, 39, 74, 167, 171a = 727). τᾶι ὁδῶι is scanned as a cretic,

with the article unshortened before the initial vowel of the next word; this has an analogy in Theocritean hexameters (e.g. 4.22), where long monosyllables sometimes do not stand in hiatus before a word beginning in a vowel. The cretic instead of a fourth dactyl was a feature of archaic Archilochians (Hephaest. p. 50.4–5 Consbruch) but is found only here in Hellenistic examples of the meter.   κἠπέγραψε Κλείτας "and inscribed it with Clita's name." The verb is ordinarily used of prose rather than verse inscriptions in the Hellenistic period; the implication is that the (probably fictional) stele contained the extra-metrical inscription Κλείτα(ς) in the nominative or genitive.

3[457] ἕξει τὰν χάριν "will receive gratitude" (Eur. *Hec.* 830) rather than the more common sense "be grateful"; cf. Call. *Epigr.* 50.4 ἡ γρηῦς μαστῶν ὡς ἀπέχει χάριτας.   γυνὰ ἀντί scans as three syllables; the middle syllables experience crasis or aphaeresis ("prodelision").

3–4[457–8] ἀντὶ . . . ἔθρεψε "in exchange for the nurturing she provided the boy." Attraction of the relative pronoun (properly ἅ, internal accusative of ἔθρεψεν) into the case of its antecedent (τήνων).   τί μάν; "How could that not be the case?", a common elliptical use (cf. Denniston 332–4); more probably a lively rhetorical question by the same speaker than an interruption by a second person.   χρησίμα καλεῖται "she will be called 'useful'." The future passive καλεῖται (for the middle in a passive sense, cf. e.g. Soph. *El.* 971) is used as at *CEG* 24 κόρη κεκλήσομαι αἰεί. Whether or not one imagines that Clita was called χρησίμα in an extra-metrical inscription (cf. 2n.), the epigram – and its fictional monument – ensures that she will be so called even in death. The more common adjective in epitaphs is χρηστός (cf. 475–8n.): the speaker focuses on Clita's beneficial services rather than on her character.

XCI. [Theocritus] 25 Gow (Automedon AP 7.534 = Automedon 12 GP = Alexander Aetolus fr. dub. 25 Magnelli)

An epitaph for the trader Cleonicus, who drowned while sailing out of season. The poem is similar in theme to LIII, though the advice, which mirrors Hesiod's (1–2n.), is placed at the beginning rather than the end. Its position has generic consequences: recommendations made at the opening of epigrams sometimes occur in sympotic contexts, and urge the enjoyment of the present moment since life is short; at the end of the first couplet, a reflection on the brevity of life is converted into a reason for behaving with caution. In the remainder of the poem, the pathos of

Cleonicus' death is tempered by the speaker's implicit contempt for his commercial activity, and perhaps by the final play on words.

The epigram is not transmitted in the Theocritean manuscripts, and Planudes writes only the first couplet with an ascription to Theocritus. P says the epigram is Αἰτωλοῦ Αὐτομέδοντος. Automedon, author of twelve epigrams in the *Garland* of Philip, is alleged to be from Cyzicus (*AP* 11.46), not Aetolia; some have followed Jacobs in assuming that the original attribution was to "Alexander Aetolus or Automedon." There is in any case nothing that excludes a third-century date.

1–2[459–60] A reworking of the instructions given at Hes. *WD* 618–30, where prospective sailors are advised to put up their ships during winter and wait for seasonable sailing.   **ἄνθρωπε:** so at the opening of epigrams, e.g. *CEG* 28 ἄνθρωφ' ὃς στείχεις.   **περιφείδεο** "preserve," a rare compound (A.R. 1.620, Isyllus 26); the speaker treats life as a commodity to be risked cautiously, in implicit contrast to Cleonicus' hasty pursuit of profit.   **παρ' ὥρην:** i.e. outside the sailing season, ignoring Hes. *WD* 630 αὐτὸς δ' ὡραῖον μίμνειν πλόον εἰς ὅ κεν ἔλθηι, 641–2 ἔργων μεμνημένος εἶναι | ὡραίων πάντων, περὶ ναυτιλίης δὲ μάλιστα.   **καὶ ὥς:** i.e. even if one avoids sailing out of season.

3[461] δείλαιε: see *465*n. **λιπαρὴν Θάσον** "wealthy Thasos." Thasos had gold mines (Hdt. 6.46–7) and was famous for its wine (Archestr. fr. 59.15), which was traded in distant markets in the fourth and third centuries (Tzochev 2016).

4–5[462–3] ἠπείγευ: Cleonicus' haste leads him to ignore the danger. **Κοίλης . . . Συρίης:** the collocation regularly refers to the entirety of Syria except Phoenicia, but here it might refer more specifically to southern Syria below the Eleutheros river, as subsequently in Seleucid documents of the second century; cf. Cohen 2006: 27–41. **ἔμπορος . . . ἔμπορος:** the epanalepsis (cf. *467*n.) suggests surprise that Cleonicus has risked his life for financial gain (cf. *257*n.).

5–6[463–4] δύσιν . . . συγκατέδυς: chiastic, with the first and last words corresponding and Πλειάδος αὐτήν mirrored by αὐτῆι Πλειάδι. The morning setting of the Pleiades (i.e. the date when they appear to sink below the horizon just before daybreak) marked the start of astronomical winter and the end of sailing season (cf. *259–60*n., Aratus 265 with Kidd's note).   **δύσιν . . . αὐτήν** "at the time of the very setting of the Pleiades." The singular is commonly used for the constellation as a group. **ποντοπορῶν:** ποντοπορέω is a Homeric hapax at *Od.* 11.11 (ποντοπορεύω at *Od.* 5.277, 7.267). αὐτῆι Πλειάδι "along with the Pleiades themselves." The singular Πλειάς sometimes stands for the entire constellation when it refers to the time of its heliacal rising; cf. Asclep. *42.1 with Sens's note. The comitative dative with αὐτός (Smyth §1525), here reinforced by συν- (συγκατέδυς), varies expected usage, since the construction is more typically applied to ships and sailors in descriptions of naval misfortunes (e.g. Xen. *HG* 6.2.35, A.R. 2.749, Theocr. 22.18 αὐτοῖσι ναυτῆσι).

XCII. *Theocritus 6 Gow (AP 9.432 = 22 GP)*

An address to Thyrsis, who has lost a young goat to a wolf. The epigram blends linguistic and thematic elements found in bucolic idylls (cf. 1, 3, 5–6nn.) and in epitaphs, including those on pets and other dead animals (cf. v introductory n.) and cenotaphs in which the body of the deceased is absent. Its symmetrical structure emphasizes the parallel responses of the human and animal worlds to a death: the first and last couplets are linked by language (1 ~ 5 τί τὸ πλέον, 2 ὀδυρόμενος ~ 6 οἰχομένας) and by the idea that mourning is futile; 5–6 engage in the "pathetic fallacy" that the natural world is experiencing grief parallel to Thyrsis' (1–2), while 3–4 report the death in elevated, even tragic, terms.

1[465] ἆ δείλαιε: a variation of the Homeric ἆ δειλέ (e.g. *Od.* 14.361). Inscribed epitaphs often begin with expressions of sympathy directed at the deceased or a family member (e.g. *CEG* 591.9–12). **Θύρσι:** the name of a herdsman and master singer in Theocr. 1. **τί τὸ πλέον** "what is the use?" [double closing quote] (cf. *61*). For the idea, cf. Philemon, fr. 77, esp. 6–7 ἐάν τε κλάῃς ἄν τε μή, πορεύεται. | τί οὖν ποιεῖς πλέον; **κατατάξεις** "turn (your eyes) to liquid": cf. *66*n. The compound, used of melting snow in a simile describing Penelope's tears at *Od.* 19.204–5, occurs of lovesickness at Theocr. 7.76, 11.14.

2[466] διγλήνους: a stylistically elevated hapax, functionally equivalent to "two," since the second element is otiose in context. **ὦπας** "eyes."

3[467] οἴχεται ... οἴχετ᾽ ἐς Ἀίδαν: tragic language, as at Theocr. 4.26–7, where the coming demise of Aegon's cattle is treated in the language of human death (βασεῦνται καὶ ταὶ βόες ... | εἰς Ἀίδαν). The repetition (epanalepsis), here adding pathos, is a marked feature of Theocritus' style (cf. Dover 1971: xlv). **ἁ χίμαρος** "the young she-goat," slightly older than a kid; the article points to a specific animal recognizable in Thyrsis' flock, as at Theocr. 1.6. **τὸ καλὸν τέκος:** the narrator speaks as if the kid were Thyrsis' own child.

4[468] τραχύς "savage." χαλαῖς: perhaps "jaws" rather than "claws," since wolves seize with their mouths; the evidence is problematic for that sense, however, and it may be unnecessary to expect biological precision (cf. [Opp.] *Cyn.* 3.313 ὀνύχεσσιν ἔμαρψεν). Theocritus may have misunderstood the use of the word at Eur. *Hec.* 90–1 ἔλαφον λύκου αἵμονι χαλᾶι | σφαζομέναν and *Phoen.* 1025 χαλαῖσί τ᾽ ὠμοσίτοις, where it probably means "claws" (cf. Mastronarde on *Phoen.* 1025, Gregory on *Hec.* 90) but could be interpreted as "jaws" (cf. Σ ad loc.). ἀμφεπίαξε "grabbed hold of," Doric aor. of ἀμφιπιέζω. The compound is otherwise unattested, but the uncompounded verb means "seized" at *Il.* 16.510 χειρὶ δ᾽ ἑλὼν ἐπίεζε βραχίονα and Theocr. 4.35 ἄγε πιάξας, of a herdsman bringing a bull from the mountains.

5–6[469–70] The sounds made by Thyrsis' dogs (a natural response to a wolf) are interpreted as an act of mourning matching the human lamentation in the first couplet. αἱ δὲ κύνες κλαγγεῦντι: the verb is third person singular present indicative of the otherwise unattested κλαγγέω. Xenophon distinguishes between κλαγγή and ὑλαγμός, "barking," of dogs (e.g. *Cyn.* 4.5, 6.17), and the verb may connote "making a wailing cry" rather than "bark," in which case the animals' reaction matches their human owner's (cf. 2 ὀδυρόμενος). τήνας | . . . οἰχομένας: reversing Theocr. 4.15–16, of a neglected calf, τήνας μὲν δή τοι τᾶς πόρτιος αὐτὰ λέλειπται | τὠστία; both passages evoke the language of epitaph. τήνας is Doric genitive singular = (ἐ)κείνης. ὀστίον οὐδὲ τέφρα "neither bone nor ash." οὐδέ with the second element of a negated pair sometimes implies an omitted οὐ before the first; cf. Denniston 194. The implication is that Thyrsis would have honored his goat with human funeral rites if its body was available: the Greeks buried the bones with the cremated ashes of a dead person (D Σ *Il.* 4.99); cf. *64*.

XCIII. Theocritus 1 Gow (AP 6.336 = 5 GP)

Rural offerings to the Muses and Apollo. Gow, citing epigrams accompanying frescoes in a house on the Via Stabiana in Pompeii, thought the poem accompanied an image (cf. Gow 1952: 11.527, *GPh* 11.527–8). The demonstratives (1, 5), however, are as appropriate to the voice of a herdsman within a bucolic poem as to that of a viewer of a representation; the epigram is a generic experiment in which dedicatory features are integrated into a rustic scene playing on the conventions of Theocritean bucolic.

The diverse models for the poem's language include Sappho, Anacreon, and tragedy; there are several thematic and linguistic connections with Theocritus' bucolic idylls. It may plausibly be read as a programmatic assertion of the poet's literary ancestry and influences (cf. Gutzwiller 1998a: 43, Rossi 2001: 125–9).

1–2[471–2] τὰ ῥόδα . . . ταῖς Ἑλικωνιάσιν: for the connection of roses to the Muses, cf. *187–8*n., Sappho, fr. 55.2–3 βρόδων | τὰν ἐκ Πιερίας. δροσόεις too has Sapphic ancestry (cf. fr. 71.8, 95.12, Simon. *PMG* 519.52.5, Eur. *Tr.* 833). The goatherd of Lycophronides *PMG* 844.1 offers dedications of roses and other plants.   **κατάπυκνος:** a prosaic adjective describing the dense mat formed by thyme.   **ἐκεῖνα:** "bucolic" speakers similarly use the demonstrative to describe their landscape; cf., e.g., Theocr. 1.1–2 ἁ πίτυς, αἰπόλε, τήνα | . . . μελίσδεται, 7–8 τὸ καταχὲς | τῆν᾽ . . . καταλείβεται . . . ὕδωρ.   **κεῖται:** "has been offered" (i.e. ἀνάκειται).

3[473] μελάμφυλλοι δάφναι: cf. Anacr. *PMG* 443 †μελαμφύλλωι δάφναι χλωρᾶι τ᾽ ἐλαίαι τανταλίζει†.   **τίν:** see *293*n.   **Πύθιε Παιάν:** this invocation of Apollo is otherwise attested only in a magical papyrus (*PGM* 3.250–1, 259).

4[474] Δελφὶς . . . πέτρα: a tragic periphrasis (cf. Soph. *OT* 464, Eur. *Andr.* 998, *Ba.* 306) for Delphi.   **τοῦτό τοι ἀγλάισε:** probably "gave this to you as an adornment," with the verb used as in *carm. pop. PMG* 851b.1 Page σοί, Βάκχε, τάνδε Μοῦσαν ἀγλαΐζομεν. The close juxtaposition of the second person dative pronoun τοι with τίν in the preceding verse is supported by the identical variation at Call. fr. 24.3–5 τὶν δ᾽ ὦνα γέλως ἀνεμίσγετο λύπηι | εἰσόκε τοι τρίπολον νειὸν ἀνερχομένωι | . . . ἀνὴρ ἀβόλησε; cf. *GVI* 1859.7. The verb might have the secondary, botanical sense attested by Hsch. α595 ἀγλαΐζει· θάλλει (cf. Antiph. fr. 294), in which case the meaning would be "made this plant grow for you," but the point is essentially the same. τοῦτο refers to the laurel, though the noun to be supplied is not obvious.

5[475] βωμὸν . . . αἱμάξει: i.e. will be sacrificed; e.g. Lyc. *Alex.* 992, Steph. Byz. ε92.   **κεραὸς τράγος:** cf. *25*n., Theocr. 1.4.   **ὁ μαλός** "the white one." The specification is typical of the way in which animals are identified in bucolic poetry (e.g. Theocr. 4.20 ὁ ταῦρος ὁ πυρρίχος, 5.99; of white goats, Theocr. 3.5, 5.147 οὗτος ὁ λευκίτας ὁ κορυπτίλος). μαλός is otherwise attested in the compounds μάλουρις (Call. *h.* 6.110, Hsch. μ207) and μαλοπάραυος (Hsch. μ204).

6[476] Similarly, a cow eats the shoots of an olive tree at Theocr. 4.44–5 τᾶς γὰρ ἐλαίας | τὸν θαλλὸν τρώγοντι.   **τερμίνθου:** the terebinth or turpentine tree. Apollo was worshipped as Termintheus at Carian Myous (cf. Lyc. *Alex.* 1207), which was controlled by Miletus (for the importance of which, cf. *435–6*n.) in the Hellenistic period.

XCIV. Theocritus 8 Gow (AP 6.337 = 1 GP)

On a wooden cult-statue (ξόανον) of Asclepius commissioned by Nicias. The poem commemorates a dedication in thanksgiving for the god's patronage, but its focus is on the commissioning and artistry of the object; in this sense, it combines features of both dedicatory and ecphrastic epigrams.

The poem plays on the reciprocal relationships between Nicias and Asclepius and between Nicias and the sculptor Eetion: Nicias, who was a poet as well as a physician (above, p. 168), has benefited from the god's patronage in his medical art and is in turn a generous contributor to his cult; this relationship is emphasized by the ring composition of 1–3 (cf. 3n.). Through the god's benefaction, he can afford to pay the sculptor generously for an expensive artifact, into which the sculptor pours all his own skill: the ambiguous language of 5 calls attention to the analogy between Eetion's skill as a sculptor and Nicias' as a physician, and the analogy is underscored by the parallel placement of the datives Νικίαι and Ἠετίωνι in 3 and 5.

In focusing both explicitly (5–6) and by implication (3) on Nicias' resources and his lavish spending, Theocritus teases him for his wealth, as he does at the end of poem 11. The shift from the grand, epic language for Asclepius' arrival and Nicias' devotion (1–3) to the technical language of contracts (5) contributes to the playful tone.

1–2[477–8] Beginning in the late fifth century, the cult of Asclepius spread rapidly through the Greek world; for the theme of the god's arrival, cf. Isyllus 65–6, 73, Aston 2004: 21–2. The prospect of friendship with Nicias is tendentiously represented as the motive for the establishment of the Milesian cult, which must have predated him.   **ὁ τοῦ Παιήονος υἱός**: i.e. Asclepius, son of Apollo. Παιήων was originally a distinct god (Hes. fr. 307), but the name came to be used of both Apollo and Asclepius himself (cf. Headlam on Herodas 4.1).   **ἰητῆρι νόσων ἀνδρί**: elevated phrasing with parallels in the description of Asclepius himself at *HH* 16.1–2 ἰητῆρα νόσων Ἀσκληπιὸν ἄρχομ' ἀείδειν | υἱὸν Ἀπόλλωνος τὸν ἐγείνατο δῖα Κορωνίς (cf. Pos. 97.1 AB ἰητήρια . . . νούσων) and *Il.* 11.514 ἰητρὸς . . . ἀνήρ.   **συνοισόμενος** "to be together in friendship" (cf. Hdt. 4.114.4).

3[479] It is left unclear whether Nicias' daily propitiation is the cause of Asclepius' arrival or its consequence.   **ἐπ' ἦμαρ** "daily"; cf. *Od.* 18.137. Hellenistic inscriptions attest to daily offerings (*OGIS* 332, Nilsson 1945: 64), but the point is probably to emphasize Nicias' zeal and his resources.   θυέεσσιν "offerings of incense," an epic form (*Il.* 6.270, 9.499, A.R. 1.353, 860).   ἱκνεῖται "beseeches," a common sense of the verb, with the idea of movement picking up Asclepius' arrival in 1 (ἦλθε) and so suggesting their reciprocal relationship.

4[480] ἀπ᾽ εὐώδους . . . κέδρου: the sweet smell of the cedar (from which ξόανα were regularly carved; cf. Paus. 8.17.2) marks the quality and value of the offering (cf. Arist. *Econ.* 1353b26).   γλύψατ᾽ "arranged to have carved."

5–6[481–2] The lines are an elaborate development of the (typically brief) indications of the name of the artist sometimes found in inscribed epigrams (e.g. *SGO* 06/02/05.4–5 ἁ δὲ τέχνα | Θοινίου) or, more frequently, appended separately below dedications.   Ἠετίωνι: the artist cannot be identified securely with the Eetion of Amphipolis whose statue is the speaker of Call. *Epigr.* 24, and his probable dates do not align with those of the mid fourth-century sculptor or painter mentioned at Pliny, *HN* 34.19.   χάριν γλαφυρᾶς χερός "in gratitude for (Eetion's) refined skill." The phrase overtly refers to Eetion's artistic ability and suggests the elegance of the finished product (cf. *423*n.), but it is equally applicable to Nicias' medical practice ("in gratitude for his (medical) art").   ἄκρον ὑποστὰς | μισθόν "having promised him the highest payment," an unusual detail (though cf. "Simon." *FGE* 63) which suggests Nicias' beneficence and good judgment (cf. Theocr. 16.22–33), while slyly teasing him for his wealth (cf. Theocr. 11.81 with Hunter's note). Physicians were notorious for charging high fees, and Asclepius himself was faulted for his greed (Pi. *Pyth.* 3.54–60, Wickkiser 2013: 627–31). ὑφίστημι with an accusative is regularly used in the technical language of contracts and agreements.   πᾶσαν ἀφῆκε τέχνην: cf. Himerius 68.4 "(Phidias) didn't always sculpt Zeus, or forge Athena in weapons, but he exerted his artistry (ἀφῆκε τὴν τέχνην) on other gods."

XCV. *Theocritus 22 Gow* (AP *9.598 = 16 GP*)

On a statue erected by the people of Rhodian Camirus in honor of their townsman Peisander, author of the epic *Heracleia*. Peisander's poem, said to date to the seventh or sixth century or earlier (cf. *Suda* π1465), consisted of two books and recounted some of Heracles' labors, including his killing of the Nemean Lion and encounters with the Lernaean Hydra, the Hind of Cyrneia, and the Stymphalian Birds (cf. Huxley 1969: 100–5). The regard in which it was held in the Hellenistic period is shown by Peisander's inclusion in the Alexandrian canon of epic poets; Clement of Alexandria, by contrast, claims that the *Heracleia* was wholly plagiarized from Peisinus of Rhodian Lindus (*Str.* 6.2.25). The date at which Camirus erected a statue in Peisander's honor is unclear, but is likely to be Hellenistic and may have been conceived as a response to Peisander's treatment of the Ptolemies' alleged ancestor Heracles (for civic commemorations of local poets, see Wallis 2016: 34–81, Rossi 2001: 92–8). There would then be an implicit analogy between Peisander's honorific treatment of Heracles, whose divine lineage is underscored in the first line, and the island's recognition of Ptolemy I, honored as a god and called Σωτήρ, "savior," by the Rhodians in thanksgiving for his role in relieving Demetrius' siege (D.S. 20.100.2–4). At the same time, Peisander's treatment of Heracles mirrors the poet's honorific treatment of him elsewhere (cf. 17.20–7, 24 *passim*).

The poem is composed in two parallel movements, the first recounting Peisander's treatment of Heracles (1–5), the second the Camirans' subsequent commemoration of the poet (6–8). These are linked by the juxtaposition of accusative object and nominative subject in 1 and 6 (τὸν τοῦ Ζανὸς ὅδ' ὑμὶν υἱὸν ὡνήρ ~ τοῦτον δ' αὐτὸν ὁ δᾶμος). Such juxtapositions are typical of inscriptions commemorating the erection of honorific portraits (Ma 2013: 24–30); but because the poem delays both Peisander's name and the main verb until 3–4, who ὅδ' . . . ὡνήρ in 1 is and what he is doing to Heracles are not initially clear. The epigram thus sets up a parallelism between sculpture and poetry and blurs the boundaries between them (cf. Wallis 2016: 188–92). It also implicitly reflects on Theocritus' poetry and its merit: its final line recognizes the posthumous honors that poets can attain even centuries later, and so emphasizes the continued vitality of the past in the present.

The Doric dialect matches the language spoken at Rhodes; although the predominant coloring of the *Heracleia* was Ionic, Peisander seems to have included Doric forms (cf. fr. 12 Bernabé, Huxley 1969: 104). Unlike Theocritus' epigram for Hipponax, the meter differs from that used by its honorand: it is in stichic Phalaecians (oo – ◡◡ – ◡ – ◡ – ×, where oo represents the "Aeolic base," i.e. – ×, × –, or ◡◡), elsewhere used in combination with other meters in Theocritus' epigrams (xc, *AP* 7.663; cf. Call. *Epigr.* 38); *SEG* xxxix 1334 is a learned, late third-century, inscription in stichic phalaecians from Pergamum (cf. Kerkhecker 1991, Lehnus 1996).

1[483] τὸν τοῦ Ζανὸς . . . υἱόν: Heracles' descent from Zeus, though a standard feature of his mythology, was emphasized in official Ptolemaic documents (e.g. *OGIS* 54, linking Ptolemy II through his father's line to "Heracles, son of Zeus"). **ὑμίν:** i.e. the implied readers of the epigram and of the *Heracleia*.

2[484] Both epithets evoke the killing of the Nemean Lion, which as the first of Heracles' labors must have been related early in the *Heracleia.*   **λεοντομάχαν:** attested only here; cf. λεοντάγχ(α) in 293.   **ὀξύχειρα:** the primary sense is "dextrous," in reference to the fact that Heracles killed the lion using only his hands, but the word commonly has the negative sense "quick with the fists," "rash" (e.g. Lys. 4.8 ὀξύχειρ λίαν καὶ πάροινος, Nicom. fr. 1.33 ὀξύχειρ κοὐκ ἐγκρατής) and here playfully gestures at more negative depictions of Heracles as an ill-mannered and intemperate glutton and drunkard (e.g. Ar. *Frogs* 503–33). Strabo claims that the *Heracleia* was the first poem to represent Heracles wearing the lion-skin and carrying a club (15.1.9; cf. *Suda* π1465); Megaclides says that this outfit was first attributed to Heracles by Stesichorus and associates it with bandits (ap. Ath. 12.512e–f; cf. Rossi 2001: 332–3).

3[485] πρᾶτος . . . μουσοποιῶν: interest in the person to introduce a particular feature into literature is a component of a broader ancient concern with "first discoverers" that is reflected in a number of fourth-century catalogues of inventions and that was a prominent feature of Hellenistic scholarship (cf. Kleingünther 1933, Arnott on Alexis, fr. 27.1–2, Rossi 2001: 88–9). The insistence on Peisander's primacy may respond to a competing view of its originality (cf. introductory n.).   **ἐπάνωθε** "from the past"; cf. Theocr. 7.5.

4[486] συνέγραψεν: the word appears in ancient biographies of writers and can apply to compositions in both verse and prose; e.g. *Suda* α1916 (of Anacreon) συνέγραψε παροίνιά τε μέλη καὶ ἰάμβους; cf. κ227, of Callimachus' *Pinakes*, "records of those who shone in all forms of learning and of what they composed (συνέγραψαν)."

5[487] χώσσους ἐξεπόνασεν . . . ἀέθλους "and he recounted all the labors that Heracles completed," not "and he specified the number of the labors that H. completed." Elsewhere in Theocritus, ἐκπονέω is used of the composition of poetry (7.51).   **εἶπ':** often of poets; e.g. Ar. *Peace* 1096, Pl. *Phaedo* 112a.

6–8[488–90] "The people set up this man himself, making him bronze, many years and months later; I tell you this so that you may know it clearly." It is common in Greek inscriptions for statues to be treated as if they were the individuals they represent; cf. Mednikarova 2003. αὐτόν evokes the ecphrastic commonplace that the statue has thoroughly and accurately depicted its subject (cf. *173*n.), despite being made of bronze (cf. Theocr. *AP* 9.600.3–4 χάλκεόν νιν ἀντὶ ἀλαθινοῦ | . . . ἀνέθηκαν); cf. Tueller 2008:

179–80.   ὁ δᾶμος: i.e. of Camirus.   ὡς σάφ' εἰδῆις: whether the phrase is a parenthetic comment on the speaker's claim ("I tell you this so that you know it clearly"; cf. Theocr. 15.91 ὡς εἰδῆις καὶ τοῦτο, Κορίνθιαι εἰμὲς ἄνωθεν), or explains the Camirians' purpose in erecting the statue ("they set it up so that you might know him clearly," where the second person would be generalizing) is grammatically ambiguous, though the former fits the ecphrastic context well: the speaker assures his audience that the Camirians have captured Peisander in his entirety; cf. xcvi introductory n.   ποήσας: the verb with short first syllable (whether or not the iota was written) was characteristic of Attic drama and the Hellenistic koine but absent from early epic. It results from treating the original iota of ποιέω as a glide ("internal correption"; cf. Olson–Sens on Archestr. fr. 1); once so perceived, the letter was easily omitted.   πολλοῖς μησὶν ὄπισθε κἠνιαυτοῖς: the inclusion of μησίν adds little in the case of a statue dedicated centuries after Peisander's death; perhaps the phrase is merely a generic expression for "a long time"; cf. [Gal.] Def. med. 19.389.12–14 Kühn χρόνιον νόσημά ἐστι τὸ μεταβάλλον . . . ἐν μησὶ καὶ ἐνιαυτοῖς.

XCVI. Theocritus 17 Gow (AP 9.599 = 15 GP)

On a statue of Anacreon. The poem blends aspects of funerary and ecphrastic epigrams. The opening couplet addresses a passing ξένος and asks him both to pay attention to an artifact (cf., e.g., GVI 1254.1–2 δέρκεο τὰν ἀρίσαμον, ὁδοιπόρε, τὰν Βερενίκας | εἰκόνα τᾶς μελέας, ἂν τάφος οὗτος ἔχει) and convey information about it to his own homeland, as in epitaphs in which the deceased asks the passerby to bring news of his death to his family (e.g. LV). Subsequent couplets engage more directly with the ecphrastic idea that an artifact has almost fully represented a person, but transfer it to the mouth of the passerby, whose hypothetical reported speech in 3–4 lacks only one piece of information in order to provide a complete picture of the poet.

The allegedly complete description of Anacreon is in fact partial. Anacreon was a popular subject for Hellenistic poets, who emphasize his interest in sympotic and erotic matters. Two ecphrastic epigrams by Leonidas (APl 306, 307) invite consideration of an unspecified image of the poet, drunk, missing one sandal, and singing of boys. This epigram, by contrast, provides no information about the appearance of the image and focuses on a small subset of the interests that the Hellenistic scholarly and literary traditions connect with him. The final assertion that a comment about the poet's interest in boys is all that is necessary to complete the depiction of him resonates playfully against ecphrastic descriptions that emphasize the verisimilitude of an image (cf. Bing 1988: 121, Rossi 2001: 284–5, Prioux 2007: 16–18).

The poem is composed of couplets consisting of an iambic trimeter without resolutions (cf. Leon. *APl* 307, on Anacreon) followed by a Phalaecian hendecasyllable (xcv introductory n.), a meter used by Anacreon (*PMG* 397); the effect is to produce a couplet in which the first verse is one syllable longer than the second, and in which the iambic rhythm of the second half of the Phalaecian echoes the basic alternation of heavy and light syllables in the previous verse. The Doric dialect (cf. 1, 2nn.) distinguishes the voice of the speaker from that of Anacreon and other natives of Teos, who spoke Ionic (cf. Ar. *Thesm.* 163).

1[491] θᾶσαι: cf. 25, Leon. *APl* 306.2 (on Anacreon) θάεο. The Doric form (Attic/Ionic θέασαι) of the aorist middle imperative is metrically guaranteed.

2[492] σπουδᾶι "seriously, attentively," though the ordinary epic sense "in haste" may lie in the background, evoking epitaphic addresses acknowledging the haste of the passerby and asking him to delay his journey only briefly (e.g. *37*).   **λέγ' . . . ἔνθηις:** cf. 265–6. ἔνθηις is the Doric equivalent to ἔλθηις, but neither it nor ἐπάν, for which most witnesses have the Ionic equivalent ἐπήν, is metrically guaranteed.

3[493] ἐν Τέωι: Anacreon's birthplace (e.g. Hdt. 3.121.1, Ar. *Thesm.* 161).

4[494] "most extraordinary of earlier poets" (lit. "if there was anything extraordinary of earlier poets"). Here εἴ τι περισσόν, in which the adjective is neuter in agreement with τι (cf. especially Theocr. 7.4–5), is functionally equivalent to a superlative.   **ὠιδοποιῶν:** only here; for Anacreon as composer of ὠιδαί, cf. Crit. 88 B 1.1–2 τὸν δὲ γυναικείων μελέων πλέξαντά ποτ' ὠιδάς | ἡδὺν Ἀνακρείοντα Τέως εἰς Ἑλλάδ' ἀνῆγεν, *Suda* α1916 "his life was directed at love for boys and women and at songs (ὠιδάς)."

5–6[495–6] These lines play on the idea that the absence of speech is all that keeps an image from being entirely realistic: here it is the speech of the viewer, and the focus is on the accuracy of the description rather than the accuracy and truthfulness of the artistic representation.   **προσθείς:** cf. 91–2n. ποτέθηκ'.   **τοῖς νέοισιν ἄδετο:** Anacreon's interest in young men is an important feature but not the exclusive focus of his biography in Hellenistic epigrams (cf. Leon. *APl* 306.7–8, Diosc. *AP* 7.31.1, *SGO* 08/01/47), which often also mention his bibulousness.   **ἐρεῖς ἀτρεκέως** "you will describe accurately." The phrase recalls epic uses of the adverb followed by a verb of speaking (e.g. *Il.* 2.10, 10.413), but ἐρεῖς evokes the ecphrastic *topos* of imagining what a hypothetical viewer would "say" in

response to an image (e.g. Theocr. 1.42, Herodas 4.32–4).   ὅλον τὸν
ἄνδρα: cf. 92, 413–14n.

DIOSCORIDES

Dioscorides flourished in the latter half of the third century. Several of
his roughly forty extant epigrams have to do with Alexandria (XCVII, *AP*
6.290, *AP* 11.363). At least some points of contact between his epigrams
and those of Damagetus, Rhianus, and Antipater of Sidon are likely to be
the product of engagement with his work by those poets.

The epigrams cover a range of themes and creatively rework traditional
forms and topics. Several erotic epigrams, though (*pace* Fraser 1972: 598)
not so different from some poems by Asclepiades (6 Sens) and Posidippus
(*127 AB = Asclep. *35 Sens) in their "extravagant voluptuousness of
expression" and "highly sensuous vocabulary rich in compound adjectives,"
are explicitly obscene where his predecessors rely on innuendo; on these,
see Iordanoglou 2003. A series of mock epitaphs for poets together constitute a cycle offering a mini-history of drama (cf. XCVII, CII introductory
nn.). These combine features of funerary epigram with material drawn
from the scholarly tradition (cf. Acosta-Hughes and Barbantani 2007: 439–
40), and treat the older style of archaic and archaizing poets as innovative;
contrast LXX. Several epigrams deal with the cult of Cybele (cf. C introductory n.), and some others treat stories about Spartans (XCVIX, CI); both
groups include poems incorporating dedicatory material in a wider narrative or dialogic context. There are also ecphrastic and satiric epigrams.

Some poems are written in the Ionic *koine*, others in Doric. Dioscorides'
metrical practices, though less restrictive than Callimachus', resemble
those of most Hellenistic epigrammatists in observing "Callimachean"
norms for the hexameter, especially in the latter half of the verse (cf.
Introduction section 4h[i], Magnelli 2007: 181). Galán Vioque 2001 contains a full-scale commentary on the corpus.

XCVII. Dioscorides AP 7.708 (24 GP)

A mock epitaph for Machon, author of comedies in Alexandria in the
first part of the third century. The poem belongs to a cycle of five epigrams constructing a history of the theater (Fantuzzi 2007a); the others
treat Thespis, Aeschylus (CV), Sophocles, and Sositheus. Athenaeus preserves fragments of Machon's comedies and substantial sections of his
book of Χρεῖαι, humorous anecdotes in iambic trimeter featuring para-
sites, hetaerae, and other characters typical of comedy; see Gow 1965,

Kurke 2002. This epigram is modeled on Simias xlviii, urging ivy to grow on the tomb of Sophocles in recognition of his literary excellence (εὐμαθίη). The reworking of a theme earlier applied to an Athenian playwright enacts the contents of the poem, which argues that Machon's contribution lies in recreating elements from Attic Old Comedy. Machon's interest in the oldest comedy mirrors Dioscorides' focus on early drama (cf. cii introductory n.); the poem celebrates the reuse of ancient elements in a novel context. The final lines set up an equivalence between Egypt and the cultural capital of the classical period, and so establish Alexandria as the heir of a still living (cf. 1–2) tradition of comedy that originated in Athens.

1[497] κωμωιδογράφωι: a technical term used in the scholarly tradition (e.g. Σ^vet. Ar. *Clouds* 296), though κωμωιδ(ι)οποιός is more common (Pl. *Ap.* 18d, *Phaedo* 70c, etc.). **κούφη κόνι**: epitaphs often express the wish that dust might lie "light" on the deceased (e.g. *IMEGR* 10.16), and the address (cf. Zenod. or Rhianus *AP* 7.315.1 = Rhianus fr. incert. 76.1 Powell ψαφαρὴ κόνι) implicitly assumes that this wish has come true for Machon.

1–2[497–8] τὸν . . . φέροις: cf. *231–2*n. The image is that of the earth awarding (φέροις) a prize of victory to Machon. φιλάγων occurs only here. **ὑπὲρ τύμβου ζῶντα**: the juxtaposition of the prepositional phrase and participle emphasizes the vitality of the ivy and, since the plant is a symbol of victory, the continued flourishing of Machon's poetry even after his death.

3[499] κύφωνα: a playful double entendre. κύφων literally refers to a wooden collar for criminals and was used as a term of abuse ("good for nothing") befitting Machon's own abusive manner (cf. *Suda* κ2800, Σ Ar. *Wealth* 476), but it was also an article of women's clothing (Posidipp. Com. fr. 45), a meaning subsequently confirmed by παλίμπλυτον and picked up by 4 ἠμφίεσας. **παλίμπλυτον** "rewashed."

3–4[499–500] τι . . . λείψανον: the precisely interlaced (ABABA) word order shows an artifice that suits the focus on τέχνη here. **ἠμφίεσας** "you cloaked"; cf. *506*n.

5–6[501–2] Machon's imagined response (ἐρεῖ) is directed at Athens. It anticipates and rejects the criticism that Machon is derivative by adducing the spontaneous growth (πέφυκε) of bitter Attic thyme on the banks of the Nile, but also asserts Egypt's (occasional) competitiveness even in a genre

particularly associated with Athens. See introductory n.   ὁ πρέσβυς:
cf. *417–19*n.   ἐρεῖ: cf. *49, 418–19*.   Κέκροπος πόλι: the periphrasis for Athens finds close parallels in Attic drama of the classical period,
including Aristophanes (fr. 112.1 ὦ πόλι φίλη Κέκροπος; cf. *Clouds* 300–1,
Wealth 772–3, Eur. *Hipp.* 34, *Ion* 1571); it is thus especially appropriate in
Machon's claim to sharing features with Old Comedy.   ἔστιν ὅτ᾽ "sometimes" (Smyth §2515), a crucial qualification: Machon is a member of a
select group.   ἐν Μούσαις: suggesting "in the Museum"; cf. Herodas
8.72.   δριμὺ . . . θύμον: i.e. comedy. Thyme, sometimes described as bitter (Hp. *Nat. Mul.* 7.330.8 Littré) – the Attic variety was especially so (Arist.
Prob. 925a9) – was associated with Attic style (Luc. *Hist. Conscr.* 15, Quint.
12.10.25). δριμύ may imply that Machon's work includes some of the harsh
personal abuse found in Old Comedy (Σ^{vet.} Ar. *Clouds* 64 δριμέα . . . καὶ
ἀστεῖα τὰ τῆς κωμωιδίας σκώμματα, Gabathuler 1937: 87–90) or obscene
and scatological jokes, which were characteristic of fifth-century comedy
but not of later periods (Konstantakos 2015, esp. 33–6). It is less likely
that Machon has combined formal features of Old Comedy (choral songs,
polymetry) with the content of New Comedy. Further discussion in Webster
1963: 537–43, Gow 1965:4–5, Fantuzzi 2007a: 120, 2007b: 494–5.

XCVIII. *Dioscorides* AP 7.76 (33 GP)

The tomb of Philocritus, a retired sailor, is flooded by the Nile so that his
body is lost at sea. The poem is related to epigrams in which a drowned
man complains about the location of his tomb in proximity to the sea
(e.g. Asclep. 30 Sens), and to those in which sailors survive the sea but
die paradoxically on land (cf. XXIV); here Philocritus dies uneventfully
on land only to end up as though shipwrecked. The change in his fortunes is illustrated at the structural level by ring composition, with the first
and last couplets corresponding in language and theme: 5 καὶ ζωὸς μὲν
ἔφευγε πικρὴν ἅλα restates the opening ἐμπορίης λήξαντα Φιλόκριτον, while
the remainder of each couplet describes Philocritus' "tombs," the first
in the earth and the second in the water. The final clausula of the first
and the last hexameter opens with a temporal adverb (1 ἄρτι δ᾽ ~ 5 νῦν
δέ), 5 καλυφθείς reframes the action of 2 ἔκρυψε, and 6 ναυηγὸν . . . τάφον
corresponds to ξείνωι and τάφωι in comparable positions in 2. The central
couplet narrates the disruption of Philocritus' first grave.

1–2[503–4] The lines contain a compressed chronological account in
which the moment of Philocritus' death is left implicit: having retired
(λήξαντα) from trading, he had just begun farming (ἀρότρου | γευόμενον)

when he (died and) was buried at Memphis.   ξείνωι: Philocritus settled in Memphis as an expatriate, but the word also prepares for his subsequent reburial at sea, since in epigrams shipwrecked sailors are regularly said to be washed up and buried on foreign shores (e.g. Leon. *AP* 7.661.3).   Μέμφις: for the personification of the city in which a person is buried, cf. *245–6*n.   ἔκρυψε τάφωι: this and similar collocations occur frequently in epitaphs; e.g. *CEG* 528.2, 607.

3[505] Νείλοιο πολὺς ῥόος: a variation of the more common Hellenistic expression μέγας ῥόος (e.g. Call. *h.* 2.108 Ἀσσυρίου ποταμοῖο μέγας ῥόος).   ὕδατι λάβρωι: a Homeric collocation (*Il.* 16.385 λαβρότατον . . . ὕδωρ; cf. 15.625, 21.270–1, A.R. 2.594 κύματι λάβρωι), but here the etymological connection with λαμβάνω is pointed.

4[506] τὴν ὀλίγην βῶλον "his small piece of earth," i.e. his grave; the same expression is used of a tomb at Leon. *AP* 7.656.1, but here the noun, with its basic sense "clod," picks up the reference to the dead man's time as a farmer (cf. ἀρότου).   ἀπημφίασε "disrobed," a development of the commonplace that someone who has been buried is "cloaked in earth"; cf. *127–8*n.

5 [507] πικρὴν ἅλα: the standard term for "salt water," though here suggesting the bitterness of death at sea.

6[508] ναυηγὸν . . . τάφον "a shipwrecked (sailor's) tomb," i.e. in water.

XCIX. Dioscorides AP 7.229 (30 GP)

A Spartan father sheds no tears as he buries a brave son. The poem is one of a number of epigrams on the reaction of Spartan parents to their sons' actions in war, including several in which a Spartan mother kills a child who has failed to show valor. These regularly end with the mother repudiating her son's behavior; here, the father's endorsement of it similarly reveals his Spartan character. A set of oppositions emphasizes the symmetry between father and son. Lines 1 and 4, at the beginnings of the two halves of the six-line epigram, name the son and father respectively, with 4 ἐπὶ πυρκαϊῆς matching 1 ἐπ' ἀσπίδος. ἄδακρυς at the end of the last hexameter poignantly echoes ἄπνους at the end of the first. Finally, the first words of the poem, naming the son's home village, Pitana, correspond with the final word Λακεδαιμόνιον, which reframes Spartan identity as ethical rather than merely geographical.

The dialect of the poem, despite its Spartan theme, is transmitted as predominantly Ionic, with the exception of the opening words τὰν Πιτάναν. The epigram is the model for Aus. 24 Green.

1[509] τὰν Πιτάναν: accusative of motion. Pitana was a village (κώμη) on the banks of the Eurotas.   **Θρασύβουλος:** a common Spartan name (though the local dialect form would be Θρασύβωλος) appropriate for a man who has shown bold resolve in battle.   **ἐπ᾽ ἀσπίδος:** the son has lived up to the code famously embodied in the demand of Spartan mothers that their sons return from war either carrying their shields or on them (cf. Plut. *Mor.* 241f ἢ ταύταν ἢ ἐπὶ ταύτας, Stob. 3.7.30, Sen. *Suas.* 2.8, Val. Max. 2.7 ext. 2).   **ἤλυθεν:** the form, guaranteed by meter, is typical of epic/Ionic, though it appears occasionally in literary Doric (e.g. Pi. *Pyth.* 3.99).   **ἄπνους:** cf. *289*.

2[510] πρὸς Ἀργείων: for the traditional enmity between Sparta and Argos, cf. CI.

3[511] δεικνὺς πρόσθια πάντα: the boy never turns his back to the battle, so that all his wounds (2 ἑπτά) are in the front.

3–4[511–12] ὁ πρέσβυς | παῖδ᾽: the juxtaposition, at the midpoint of the poem, emphasizes the gravity of the father's loss in old age; cf. *229–30*n.

5–6[513–14] Tynnichos' refusal to lament his son represents an extreme version of the commonplace that those who have died courageously in battle are blessed rather than unfortunate; e.g. Hdt. 1.30.4–5.   **κλαιέσθωσαν:** third person plural present imperative passive ("let . . . be lamented"). Medio-passive imperatives in -σθωσαν appear in Attic prose first in the fourth century (e.g. Xen. *Cyn.* 4.11, Pl. *Laws* 6.760a) and become a feature of the Ionic *koine* in the third century; cf. Abbenes 1990.   **ἄδακρυς:** that Tynnichus does not cry is both a mark of restraint (cf. Plut. *Agis et Cleom.* 43.7, where the public display of tears is treated as un-Spartan) and a reflection of his pride in his son's death on Sparta's behalf (cf. Plut. *Mor.* 241c οὗ . . . αὐτὸν ἕνεκεν ἔτεκον, ἵνα ὑπὲρ τᾶς Σπάρτας ἀποθάνηι, τοῦτό μοι συνέβη).   **τὸν καὶ ἐμὸν καὶ Λακεδαιμόνιον:** perhaps playing on a tradition of poems in which Spartan mothers disown their children; cf. Asclep. *48 with Sens's note, Tymnes *AP* 7.433.8 τὸ μὴ Σπάρτας ἄξιον οὐδ᾽ ἔτεκον.

C. Dioscorides AP 6.220 (16 GP)

A gallus, an emasculated priest of Cybele, is followed into a cave by a lion, but divine inspiration leads him to beat his kettledrum, and the beast runs away. The lengthy narrative culminates in an "embedded" dedication of both cave and instrument. At sixteen verses in length the poem is longer than most Hellenistic epigrams in the Anthology, and until the final dedication it is indistinguishable from narrative elegy. Several Hellenistic epigrams describe this encounter ("Simon." *AP* 6.217, Alc. *AP* 6.218, Antip. *AP* 6.219, Ant. *AP* 6.237) and others refer to the behavior of Cybele's adherents (e.g. Hermes. fr. 8, Leon. *AP* 6.281, Rhianus *AP* 6.173; cf. Call. frr. 193.34–6, 411 Pf., Alex. Aet. *AP* 7.709.3), including two by Dioscorides (*AP* 9.340, 11.195). Although the goddess's rites were known and practiced already in fourth-century Athens (cf. Dem. 18.260, *IG* II/III³.4 1337), greater familiarity with the Near East in the Hellenistic period seems to have led to increased literary interest in them, perhaps stimulated by the publication around 300 BCE of a detailed discussion by a certain Timotheus (cf. Bremmer 2004). Hermesianax (fr. 8) tells the story of Attes, a Phrygian by birth and unable to bear children, who moved to Lydia, introduced the mysteries of Cybele there, and was killed by a boar sent by Zeus (for the alleged link between this story and Herodotus' account of the death of Atys, son of the Lydian Croesus, on a boar-hunting expedition, cf. Bremmer 2004); the movement of Attes from Phrygia to Lydia and the discreet phrasing with which his inability to procreate is described resemble features of Dioscorides' narrative (cf. 3n.). The encounter between gallus and lion may have Near Eastern roots (West 1969: 117–18), but the form it takes in Hellenistic epigrams may be inspired by Leon. *AP* 6.221, where a lion enters a farmstead to escape rough weather and the residents pray to Zeus for protection; when the lion leaves without harming them, they dedicate an artistic representation of the episode to the god (for the relationship of this poem to "Simon." *AP* 6.217.1–2, cf. Bonsignore 2013–14: 215–17). For the relationship of this and other Hellenistic epigrams on the theme to Catull. 63, see Harrison 2005, Harder 2005.

Cairns (2016: 97–101) argues that the detailed geography of the poem suggests it was produced to advertise and explain the origin of a specific sanctuary of the Magna Mater on the road between Pessinous and Sardis, but the poem's complex literary affiliations and the fact that Dioscorides composed several epigrams featuring galli make it unlikely that it served this pragmatic function. Fantuzzi (2019) argues that it engages with Hellenistic discussions of the value of the music associated with Cybele: although the inspiration of the goddess is represented as savage (3 ἄγρια), the poem ultimately treats her music as powerful and salvific. Speech and sound feature prominently, as does "wind," both metaphorical and literal (2, 4, 9).

1[515] Σάρδις: Ionic accusative plural (cf. Hdt. 1.15).   Πεσσινόεντος: Pessinous, on the border of Phrygia and Galatia to the north of the River

Sangarius, was the principal site of the cult of Magna Mater (cf. Str. 12.5.3).

2[516] Wild hair-shaking was a characteristic behavior of galli in ancient poetry (cf. Diosc. *AP* 9.340.3, Call. fr. 193.34–6, Leon. *AP* 6.281.6, Rhianus *AP* 6.173.2, adesp. *AP* 6.51.8).   ἔκφρων μαινομένην: the juxtaposition emphasizes the gallus' maddened state. μαινομένην is a transferred epithet, properly describing the man's condition but grammatically applied to his hair; cf. Antip. *AP* 6.219.2 λυσσομανεῖς πλοκάμους.   ἀνέμοισι: here literal "winds," but anticipating later references to divine inspiration.

3[517] ἁγνός "chaste," a discreet allusion to castration; cf. Hermes. fr. 8 οὐ τεκνοποιός (see next n.).   Ἄτυς: the name, which was borne by members of the Lydian royal family (Hdt. 1.7.3, 34.2, 94.3, 7.27.1, 74.1), here evokes Attis/Attes, Cybele's divine consort whose name was used by priests at Pessinus.   θαλαμηπόλος: the word, originally used of female attendants, here refers to a priest in charge of the cave consecrated to Cybele, generally identified in Greek with the Mother of the Gods, Rhea; cf. Nic. *Alex.* 7–8 Ῥείης . . . θαλάμαι τε καὶ ἐργαστήριον Ἄττεω, explained by the scholia ad loc. as sacred underground places dedicated to Rhea.

3–4[517–18] ἄγρια . . . θευφορίης "The savage inspiration of his harsh divine possession was cooled." The emphasis on the harshness of the experience discreetly points to the self-mutilation performed by galli.   ἐψύχθη . . . πνεύματα: playing on the basic sense of ψύχω, "blow," and its common extended sense "cool." πνέω and its cognates are commonly used of divine possession (e.g. Hes. *Th.* 31).   χαλεπῆς . . . θευφορίης: as applied to an emasculated and thus chaste gallus, the apparent reworking of Call. *Epigr.* 30.4 χαλεπῆι δ' ἤντεο θευμορίηι, of a lover reduced to skin and bone by desire, is perhaps ironic.

5[519] στείχοντος: modifying 3 αὐτοῦ.   κάταντες: the cave slopes downward from its mouth.

6[520] νεύσας "diverging," an unusual sense (more usually, "nod").   βαιόν: adverbial, qualifying ἄπωθεν.

7[521] τοῦ: object of ὤρουσε (cf. LSJ ὀρούω I.2).

7–8[521–2] ἀνδράσι . . . | θαρσαλέοις: i.e. *even* for brave men, by contrast with the emasculated gallus.   δεῖμα "source of fear"; cf. Soph. *Phil.* 927,

Eur. *HF* 700 δείματα θηρῶν.   **γάλλωι:** the term "gallus," first appearing
in the third century, was associated by Greek authors with the Phrygian
river Gallus and the eponymous king Gallus who was castrated in an
ecstatic frenzy at the wedding of his daughter (cf. Call. fr. 411, Bremmer
2004).   **οὐδ' ὀνομαστὸν ἄχος** "an indescribable source of grief"; the
phrase resembles *Od.* 19.260, 597, 23.19, where οὐκ ὀνομαστήν means
"unmentionable." Whereas the reaction of a brave man can be described
as "fear," no suitable word exists to express the abject terror of the gallus
(though it is in fact called δέος in 9).

9[523] The reinspiration of the gallus and the consequent change in his
fortunes occur at the poem's midpoint.   **ἄναυδος . . . δέους ὕπο:** the
gallus' fearful silence develops the theme of speechlessness implicit in 8
οὐδ' ὀνομαστόν.   **αὔρηι** "inspiration"; cf. 4 πνεύματα.

10[524] ἐς τὸν ἑὸν τύμπανον: the *Suda* (τ1167) cites this line to illustrate
the rare use of masculine τύμπανος rather than neuter τύμπανον.

11[525] οὖ . . . μυκήσαντος "and when it made a deep bellowing sound"
(genitive absolute), in contrast to the gallus' silence. μυκάω, "bellow,"
is properly used of cattle lowing, and though its extended use includes
the roar of lions (Nonn. *Dion.* 42.148–9) and other sounds (cf. e.g. *Il.*
20.260), it may evoke the many encounters between lions and cattle in
epic. The implication is perhaps that the drum had an oxhide skin.

12[526] ἐλάφων . . . ὀξύτερον: cf. *639–40*n.

13[527] βαρύν: the reiteration of the word (cf. 11 βαρύ) might suggest the
reverberation of the kettledrum.   **οὐ μείνας** "not tolerating."   **ἀκοαῖς**
"in his ears," with βαρύν.   **ἐκ δ' ἐβόησεν:** *sc.* Atys; for the phrase cf. A.R.
3.631. The unmarked change of subject calls attention to the suddenness
with which Atys' voice returns when the lion flees; cf. *161*n.

14–16[528–30] The final three verses contain an elaborate "embedded" dedicatory epigram, spoken by the gallus in the present tense
and thus imitating the act of dedication.   **Σαγγαρίου:** the Sakarya
river in Phrygia, which features prominently in the Phrygian account of
Cybele's rites as they are recounted by Timotheus.   **χείλεσι** "banks," as
often.   **θαλάμην:** i.e. the cave, now dedicated by Atys as a shrine (cf.
3n.) to Cybele.   **ζωάγρια** "(as) a reward for saving my life," a rare
Homeric word (*Il.* 18.407, *Od.* 8.462; cf. Call. fr. 516).   **λαλάγημα:**
i.e. the kettledrum (abstract for concrete). The noun, lit. "chattering,"

may be inspired by Alex. Aet. *AP* 7.709 λάλα τύμπανα (λάλα Meineke: καλά MSS). It is a *hapax legomenon* formed from λαλαγέω, more typically used of the prattling of humans (Pi. *Olymp.* 2.97) and the chirruping of insects and birds (Theocr. 5.48, 7.139). It would be more appropriate for the cymbals of the galli (cf. Eryc. *AP* 6.234.5) than for the deep-sounding (βαρὺ ... βαρύν) drum.   **ἀντίθεμαι:** i.e. ἀνατίθεμαι.

CI. Dioscorides AP 7.430 (31 GP)

Two Argives survey the aftermath of a battle. The epigram participates in a debate about the Battle of Thyrea (mid-sixth century) between the Argives and the Lacedaemonians. According to Herodotus (1.82.4–6, 8), 300 men from each side fought to the death, and when the fighting was over, two Argives and one Spartan were left; the Argives, Alcenor and Chromius, returned to Argos on the assumption that only they had survived, whereas the Lacedaemonian survivor, Othryades, stripped the Argive corpses and returned to his camp. A dispute arose about who had won, since the Argives claimed they were represented by a greater number of survivors, the Spartans that their opponents had fled the field. The poem is one of several epigrams on the battle ("Simon." *AP* 7.431, Nic. *AP* 7.526, Chaerem. *AP* 7.720, 721, Damag. *AP* 7.432, Gaet. *AP* 7.244). "Simonides" and Nicander support the Spartans, but Dioscorides' poem, in rejecting the claim made by Herodotus that Othryades returned to his camp and remained at his post and by showing the Argives present at the site in the immediate aftermath of the fighting, seems to endorse the Argive position (Cairns 2016: 306–13).

That the poem is meant as a dialogue is strongly suggested by the asyndeton at the head of 5 and 7. Some editors mark a change of speaker before ἆ πρόπατορ Ζεῦ (9), but this is unnecessary and removes significant structural symmetry: one Argive speaks the opening and concluding four verses, the other the central distich. The dialogic form is consonant with some aspects of the poem's diction, which includes several elements resonant of tragedy (cf. 7–8n.).

The poem enacts the process of reading and making sense of a dedicatory inscription. Cf. cxxvi introductory n., Herodas 4.21–4. Here, the opening queries are answered in chiastic order by 7–10, which pick up the language the first two couplets (3 ὑφ' αἵματος ~ 8 αἵματος, 2 πέλτα Δωρίς ~ 7 ἐπ' ἀσπίδος). Without quoting the actual inscription, the Argive reader paraphrases the essential information contained in it: the name of the dedicator, Othryades; the intended recipient, Zeus; and the reason for the dedication (cf. 10n.).

1–2[531–2] The paired opening questions and the phrase καθᾶψεν | ἔντεα resemble Antim. *AP* 9.321.1–3 (= fr. [205].1–3 Matthews), on the Spartan Aphrodite in armor: τίπτε μόθων ἄτλητος Ἐνυαλίοιο λέλογχας, | Κύπρι· τίς ὁ ψεύστας στυγνὰ καθᾶψε μάταν | ἔντεα; – but the relative chronology, like the identity of that poem's author, remains uncertain.   **νεοσκύλευτα:** a neologism. The stripping of corpses forms part of the story told by Herodotus (1.82.6 σκυλεύσας τοὺς Ἀργείων νεκρούς).   **τῷ . . . ἀναγράφεται;** "Whose Dorian shield has been inscribed?"; cf. Introduction section 4e. The present is here used as a vivid equivalent of the expected perfect. The severe Doric form τῷ (= τοῦ = τίνος) is appropriate for either Lacedaemonian or Argive speakers (Introduction section 4g).   **πέλτα Δωρίς:** the adjective would suit both Spartan and Argive shields and does not identify the side to which the shield belongs. The πέλτη was properly a light shield of Thracian origin that would have been inappropriate for a hoplite battle in the mid-sixth century (cf. Xen. *Mem.* 3.9.2), though light infantry armed with it (peltasts) were a feature of Hellenistic armies; cf. Fischer-Bovet 2014: 137–8.

3[533] πλάθει "is flooded" (πλήθει), perhaps implying an image such as that at A.R. 3.1391–2, where furrows are said to have filled (πλήθοντο) with the blood of the Earthborn; cf. *Il.* 21.218, Eur. *HF* 1172.   **Θυρεᾶτις . . . ἄδε:** *sc.* γᾶ.   **λοχιτᾶν:** both Sparta and Argos had λόχοι, "companies" (λοχίτης of Argives at Aesch. *Ag.* 1650, *Ch.* 768), though here the word may evoke Herodotus' claim (1.82.8) that Othryades ultimately killed himself out of guilt, τῶν οἱ συλλοχιτέων διεφθαρμένων.

4[534] χἀμές = καὶ ἁμές; the Doric form of the pronoun (Buck §119) is metrically guaranteed.   **τοι** = οἱ.

5–6[535–6] "Search every fallen corpse, to make sure that no one left still alive has made a false claim to glory on Sparta's behalf."   **δεδουπότα:** cf. *Il.* 23.679 δεδουπότος Οἰδιπόδαο, where ancient scholars debated whether the participle was used catachrestically to mean "having died" or referred to a suicidal leap. Here it means "having fallen in battle" (cf. *Il.* 13.426); some Hellenistic poets used the verb in the sense "die" without implying a martial context (cf. A.R. 1.1304, 4.557, Lyc. *Alex.* 492).   **ἔτ' ἔμπνους** "still alive" (e.g. Eur. *Phoen.* 1442, fr. 936).   **λειπόμενος:** passive, as in 4; cf. Hdt. 1.82.4 ὑπελείποντο ἐξ ἀνδρῶν ἑξακοσίων τρεῖς.   **κῦδος ἔλαμψε νόθον** "made his glory shine false(ly)"; cf. Pi. *Nem.* 8.34 "[Misrepresentation] does violence to the illustrious (τὸ . . . λαμπρόν) and upholds (ἀντείνει) the rotten glory (κῦδος . . . σαθρόν) of the obscure." ἔλαμψε is transitive (e.g. Eur. *Hel.* 1131 ἀστέρα λάμψας), and the phrase as a whole is based on the intransitive use in expressions such as λάμπει . . . κλέος (Pi. *Olymp.* 1.23).   νόθον: i.e. illegitimate.

7–8[537–8] "Hold your step. For here on the shield the victory of the Spartans is proclaimed with Othryades' dried blood."   ἴσχε βάσιν: the speaker has found the perpetrator and there is no need to continue searching. There may be a reminiscence of orders to stop addressed to passersby in epitaphs; cf. 25n. βάσις is characteristic of tragedy (cf. Olson–Austin on Ar. *Thesm.* 968) and appropriate to the dialogic form.   φωνεῖται: passive. For the idea, cf. Aesch. *Sept.* 434 (of the torch depicted on Capaneus' shield) χρυσοῖς δὲ φωνεῖ γράμμασιν, "πρήσω πόλιν."   θρόμβοις αἵματος: lit. "clots of blood," i.e. dried blood; the collocation is common in the medical writers, but cf. also Aesch. *Ch.* 533 θρόμβον αἵματος, Antiph. fr. 55.8.   Ὀθρυάδα: genitive singular. The speaker has read Othryades' name on the inscription.

9[539] χὠ τόδε μοχθήσας "And the one who accomplished this with toil," answering the initial question.   σπαίρει: cf. 5 ἔμπνους.   ἃ πρόπατορ Ζεῦ: a variation of the more common invocation of Zeus as πάτερ (*Il.* 1.544, etc.). Othryades has dedicated the shield to Zeus (cf. [Plut.] *Parall. min.* 306b), to whom the speaker refers as the father of the eponymous founder of Argos and thus his figurative ancestor.

10[540] στύξον "reject with loathing." The request reverses the more usual prayer for a god to accept an offering favorably (cf. 294n.).   ἀνικάτω . . . φυλόπιδος: as spoken by the Argive, the phrase must carry the unusual sense "strife that was not won by the man who claims victory." Its literal sense "strife that had no victor" self-referentially suits combat whose outcome remained controversial. Othryades may be imagined to have asked the god to accept the armor as σύμβολα νίκης. φύλοπις is markedly epic in color.   σύμβολα: i.e. the ἔντεα. For the expression, e.g. 326n., Call. fr. 59.7 Pf. νίκης σύμβολον Ἰσθμιάδος.

CII. Dioscorides AP 7.411 (21 GP)

On Aeschylus' innovations in the manner, language, and staging of tragedy. The epigram's first phrase links it closely to Diosc. *AP* 7.410, which purports to represent the work of Thespis and his invention of tragedy; it initially gives the impression that this poem's subject will be the same. Only in 3 does it emerge that the focus will not be on the texts indicated by the demonstratives of 1–2 but on Aeschylus' development of them.

The poem's account of the development of tragedy from insignificant amusements broadly mirrors late classical and early Hellenistic accounts (cf. 5n.), and the diction recalls that of the biographical and literary-historical tradition (cf. 1–2, 3nn.). But the representation of Aeschylus and his work more specifically evokes the treatment of him in Aristophanes' *Frogs* (for this play's effect on the subsequent treatment of Aeschylus, see Hunter 2009), though it modifies the opposition there between the archaizing Aeschylus (cf. *Vita* 5, where he is said to view archaizing, heroic grandeur as a desideratum) and the innovative Euripides, by treating Aeschylus as simultaneously archaic (6n.) and innovative (5n.).

This engagement with Aristophanes raises the question as to what literary values underlie the poem. In the second couplet, Aeschylus' words are implicitly compared to the content of inscribed epigram, and evoke the inherent contrast between the refinement and limited scope of the epigram and the grand style of its honorand. Moreover, the praise of Aeschylean grandeur appears to be at odds with the values expressed in the prologue to Callimachus' *Aetia*, where the contrast between Callimachus' refined poetry and the bombast of his rivals is couched in language and imagery deriving from the opposition between Euripides and Aeschylus in the *Frogs*. The epigram also appropriates and inverts the critical language of Call. *h.* 2.108–9, where the copious but dirty Euphrates contrasts with the limpid spring representing the poet's own work.

1–2[541–2] The association of the earliest tragedy with rural games (παίγνια) and revelry (κώμους) reflects an evolutionary view of the genre resembling Aristotle's statement that as a consequence of its "satyric" origins, it began with μικροὶ μῦθοι and λέξις γελοία but was ultimately made serious (*Poetics* 1449a19–21). See further Glucker 1973, Fantuzzi 2007a, Nervegna 2017.   **Θέσπιδος . . . τοῦτο** recalls epigrams that begin by announcing "this is the tomb-/grave-marker of so-and-so," but here the referent of the demonstrative is tragedy as a genre; for the fiction that the epigram marks a volume of poetry, cf. Asclep. 28.1 Sens Ἠρίννας οὗτος πόνος.   **εὕρεμα** evokes the Hellenistic interest in identifying the first inventors of individual forms (cf. *485*n.; for Thespis as inventor of tragedy, cf. Σ Dion. Thrax p. 475.20–1 Hilgard, Clem. Alex. *Str.* 1.16.79).   **ἀν' ὕλαν:** a Hellenistic line end (Theocr. 1.116, A.R. 4.1338, Nic. *Ther.* 499), here perhaps playing on the use of the noun in reference to literary "material."   **παίγνια . . . τελειοτέρους:** Aeschylus' elevation of tragedy is couched in terms evoking biological maturation, beginning with child's play and becoming more fully adult (for τελειοτέρους in this sense, cf. Aesch. *Ag.* 1504).   **τούσδε:** cf. 1 τοῦτο.   **τελειοτέρους** "so as to be more fully formed," predicate with 3 ἐξύψωσεν. The question as to whether Aeschylus "perfected" tragedy is implicit in the comment of the ancient *Vita* endorsing the view that Sophocles was a "more perfect" tragic poet (ὁ τελεώτερος τραγωιδίας ποιητὴς Σοφοκλῆς; cf. Quint. 10.1.66–8), but adding that perfection was easier in the wake of Aeschylus.

3[543] ἐξύψωσεν "elevated to stylistic grandeur"; cf. Arist. *Poetics* 1449a20–1 ἀπεσεμνύνθη, Ar. *Frogs* 1004 πρῶτος τῶν Ἑλλήνων πυργώσας ῥήματα σεμνά. The compound is novel, but the simplex elsewhere refers to "sublime" style (ὕψος); cf. Longin. 14.1 with Russell's discussion on pp. xxx–xlii.

3–4[543–4] ὁ ... καταρδόμενα "the one who inscribed words not cut with a chisel, but as though drenched/swept downstream in a torrent."   **μὴ σμιλευτά ... | γράμματα:** an idea drawn from Ar. *Frogs* 819, where σμιλεύματα ... ἔργων are mentioned as a Euripidean technique against Aeschylus, is here reimagined as an epigraphic metaphor (see introductory n.). A σμιλή is a chisel of the sort used for cutting inscriptions (cf. Arnott on Alexis fr. 223.8), χαράσσω was the *uox propria* for cutting letters on stone, and Aeschylus is represented as a stonecutter grandly updating Thespis' "invention." Cf., in an inscriptional context, *CEG* 777.ii.3 χαράγμασι Μουσῶν.   **χειμάρρωι δ' οἷα καταρδόμενα:** the language entails both that Aeschylus' words are grand and sweeping, not finely hewn – though the sense ("washed downhill") is not elsewhere attested for κατάρδω (ordinarily "irrigate") – and that they are like inscribed letters "made obscure by the flood," i.e. as though under (or worn by) water; for inscribed letters that are difficult to make out precisely, cf. Thuc. 6.54.7. Comparison of poetic language to flowing water is traditional (cf. Pi. *Olymp.* 10.9–10), but the more specific image of the grandiloquent poet as a raging torrent resembles the characterization of Cratinus at Ar. *Knights* 526–8, probably picking up Cratinus' own self-assessment (fr. 198). At Ar. *Frogs* 1005 Aeschylus is said to have "sent forth a spring" (κρουνὸν ἀφίει).

5[545] τὰ κατὰ σκηνήν "things having to do with the stage," a very general way of referring to the playwright's contributions, which were described variously by Aristotle (*Poetics* 1449a15–18) and in the subsequent biographical tradition (cf. Them. *Or.* 26.316d, *Suda* αι357, *Vita Aesch.* 14 τὴν ... σκηνὴν ἐκόσμησεν).   **μετεκαίνισεν:** a novel coinage, perhaps picking up the prefix of μεταβαλεῖν at Arist. *Poetics* 1499a20, of the development of tragedy (Glucker 1973: 87–8).   **στόμα:** the personification is common in Hellenistic poetry, e.g. 559, Theocr. 7.37 ἐγὼ Μοισᾶν καπυρὸν στόμα, [Mosch.] 3.72.   **πάντων:** i.e. "in every respect."

6[546] δεξιόν: of Aeschylus at Ar. *Frogs* 1121 (cf. 762); Dover (on Aristophanes' *Frogs*, pp. 13–14) argues that the adjective was already becoming obsolete as an evaluative term in the late-fifth century; if so, it may have an archaic flavor here.   ἀρχαίων . . . ἡμιθέων: in treating Aeschylus as one of the ancient heroes, the phrase links him with the "heroic" manner, subject matter, and dramaturgical practices for which he was known; cf. Ar. *Frogs* 1030–44, *Vita Aesch.* 5 ἀρχαῖον εἶναι κρίνων τὸ μεγαλοπρεπές τε καὶ ἡρωϊκόν.

CIII. Dioscorides AP 5.55 (5 GP)

A sexual encounter with Doris. Lines 1–2 provide a narrative summary, culminating in the assertion that the speaker has become immortal; the final couplet explains that claim by treating the climaxes of Doris and the speaker in language evoking religious practice. The poem offers an eroticized account of Doris' body that focuses first on her buttocks and legs, then her eyes and breasts. Although the speaker initially represents himself as the active partner (1 διατείνας), Doris subsequently assumes the active role, before being represented again in passive terms (8 ἐξεχύθη).

The poem belongs to a tradition of epigrams on sexual encounters, and picks up the horse-riding imagery of Asclep. 6 Sens; unlike that and similar poems (e.g. Asclep. *35 Sens = Pos. *127 AB), however, it makes the sexual character explicit before introducing the metaphor of horse-riding. The principal archaic model is the "Cologne Epode" of Archilochus (fr. 196a), describing a sexual encounter with a young woman. Lines 1–2 recall Archil. 196a.42–3 παρθένον δ' ἐν ἄνθε[σιν | τηλ]εθάεσσι λαβών, while 7 ἀπεσπείσθη λευκὸν μένος seems related to the speaker's account of his ejaculation at Archil. fr. 196a.52 [....]ον ἀφῆκα μένος (where λευκ]όν is a likely supplement). In Archilochus, however, the girl is a virgin; here she appears sexually adept. Moreover, in Archilochus the speaker suggests that the pair might find pleasure "outside the divine thing" (15 παρὲξ τὸ θεῖον χρῆμα), i.e. in acts other than vaginal intercourse; here the language anticipates the culmination of their intercourse as an apotheosis (1–2n.; cf. 5–7n.). Finally, in Archilochus the focus is on the speaker's own orgasm; here the climax is mutual.

1–2[547–8] The couple's position, the precise meaning of διατείνας and ἀθάνατος γέγονα, and the relationship of ὑπὲρ λεχέων to ἄνθεσιν ἐν χλοεροῖς are initially unclear.   **ῥοδόπυγον** "rosy-buttocked," a novel epithet formed on the model of ῥοδοδάκτυλος, the epithet of Dawn, and ῥοδόπηχυς, used especially of nymphs and other divine figures in epic and elsewhere. This association prepares for the metaphorical deification in 2; for the attributive adjective establishing a theme developed subsequently, cf. e.g. Asclep. 20.1 Sens Δόρκιον ἡ φιλέφηβος.   **ὑπὲρ λεχέων**

"on the bed" (cf. Colluth. 375 ὑπνώουσαν ὑπὲρ λεχέων). **διατείνας:** both literally "stretching her apart" and metaphorically "straining her to the utmost." **ἄνθεσιν ἐν χλοεροῖς:** the meadow is a common place for sexual encounters in literature (cf. Bremer 1975, Henderson 1976), but here the flowers imply Doris' sexual appeal in a general way (cf. e.g. Solon, fr. 25.1 ἔσθ' ἥβης ἐρατοῖσιν ἐπ' ἄνθεσι παιδοφιλήσηι); the language may also suggest an obscene double entendre (cf. Archil. 196a.23–4 σχήσω ἐς ποη[φόρους | κ]ήπους, Sandin 2000: 345; cf. 67–8n.). The botanical image picks up the first element of ῥοδόπυγον. **ἀθάνατος γέγονα** develops an idea already implicit in Sappho, fr. 31.1, where the proximity of the anonymous man to the object of the speaker's interest makes him seem like a god.

3–6[549–52] These lines reveal the sexual position to be the κέλης, in which the woman mounts the man. Nautical and equestrian images are often intertwined in sexual contexts; in a literal sense, κέλης could refer either to a trace horse or to a type of ship (cf. Henderson 1991: 164–5). **ὑπερφυέεσσι . . . ποσσίν** "with her very long legs." The focus on Doris' πόδες (here, as often, referring to the entire leg) prepares for the foot-racing imagery. **μέσον:** i.e. at the midpoint of the body (cf. Henderson 1991: 156). The word for "middle" occurs in the center of the verse, straddled (cf. διαβᾶσα) by ὑπερφυέεσσι . . . ποσσίν; the rhyme at caesura and line end emphasizes the symmetry. **ἤνυσεν . . . δόλιχον** "she completed Aphrodite's long race without deviating from the course." For the sexual metaphor, cf. e.g. Anacr. *PMG* 417.4 ἡνίας δ' ἔχων στρέφοιμί σ' ἀμφὶ τέρματα δρόμου, Asclep. 6.5 Sens ἀκέντητος τελεόδρομος. ἀκλινέως suggests single-minded focus on the task at hand. A δόλιχος is properly a lengthy foot-race: the sexual act lasted a long time. **ὄμμασι νωθρὰ βλέπουσα** "with a languid look in her eyes." Cf. Anacr. *PMG* 417.1 (of a girl represented as a mare) λοξὸν ὄμμασι βλέπουσα. Doris' look stands in contrast to the energy implied by what precedes, but νωθρός is sometimes used of horses (e.g. Ael. *NA* 15.24) and is appropriate in a metaphorical equine context.

5–6[551–2] τὰ . . . πορφύρεα: probably a reference to Doris' nipples, used synecdochically for her breasts. On this reading, τά seems initially to refer to her eyes and is subsequently clarified only two lines later; some scholars, however, take the phrase to mean "eyes." **ἠύτε πνεύματι φύλλα:** the epic conjunction ἠύτε and the theme of the simile evoke the numerous Homeric comparisons of humans to leaves (e.g. *Il.* 2.468, 6.146–51); for the wind, cf. Bacchyl. 5.65–7 οἷά τε φύλλ' ἄνεμος . . . δονεῖ, A.R. 3.968–71.

7[553] ἀμφισαλευομένης "as she is made to move up and down on me"; cf. Asclep. 6.4 Sens κοῦφα τινασσομένης. The verb is common in nautical contexts, and here Doris is treated as a boat tossed by the tide (cf. 562n.) as she sits astride (ἀμφι-) the speaker.   ἀπεσπείσθη . . . ἀμφοτέροισιν "was poured for both of us," as if a libation to deified figures, picking up the "apotheosis" mentioned in the first couplet, rather than "in both our cases." Both partners achieve orgasm (cf. Asclep. 1.3–4 Sens); some believed that women also ejaculated; cf. Arist. *Gen. anim.* 727b33–4, [Hp.] *Genit.* 7.474.16–17 Littré. ἀποσπένδω ordinarily denotes pouring wine, frequently in the context of religious rites, but here refers to the lovers' mutual climax and picks up the mock-divine depiction of Doris and the metaphorical apotheosis of the speaker in 1–2.

8[554] παρέτοις . . . μέλεσι "with her limbs slack" picking up 3 ὑπερφυέεσσι . . . ποσσίν. παρίημι, from which πάρετος is derived, is sometimes used in nautical contexts (cf. Ar. *Knights* 436 τοῦ ποδὸς παρίει, "slacken the rope!"), and the adjective is appropriate to the seafaring metaphor (cf. next n.).   ἐξεχύθη "was spread out (on the bed)" (cf. A.R. 2.902, of sails), but the basic sense ("was poured out") continues the idea of pouring out liquid (ἀπεσπείσθη).

CIV. Dioscorides AP 5.138 (2 GP)

The speaker burns with love for Athenion as she sings of the burning of Troy. Her name would suit a hetaera (cf. 1n.), and the occasion may be understood as a symposium at which she provides entertainment. Like some lyric poems, the epigram applies heroic themes and language to erotic experience, drawing a parallel between Troy, destroyed by the intervention of Athena, and the speaker, ruined by a woman called "Little Athena"; it thus assimilates the speaker's account of his own suffering to heroic narrative. This parallelism is structurally reinforced by correspondences between the couplets. The clausula of 1 ἐν πυρὶ πᾶσα is picked up by ἐν δ' ἑνὶ φέγγει in the corresponding place in 3; lines 2 and 4 open with an enjambed word and conclude with parallel expressions with the first-person verb in final position (2 κἀγὼ κείνηι ἅμ' ἐφλεγόμαν ~ 4 καὶ Τρῶες κἀγὼ ἀπωλόμεθα).

Crinag. AP 9.429 has a similar theme (Nauplius' fires inspire the speaker's); cf. Iordanoglou 2003: 77–8.

1[555] Ἵππον . . . ἦισεν "sang (the story of) 'The Trojan Horse'," with the first word of the epigram signaling the subject (and perhaps title) of Athenion's recitation, as the opening word regularly does in epic. ἦισεν, "sang," suggests the performance of an epic or lyric narrative, and the remainder of the epigram implies a poem about the Horse like that recommended by Odysseus at *Od.* 8.492–5. The contracted form of the aorist is not attested in epic or lyric.   Ἀθήνιον: the name, formally a diminutive of Ἀθήνη, evokes Athena's role in the construction of the Horse. Female names in -ιον are frequently associated with hetaerae, but are not restricted to them.   ἐμοὶ κακόν: the personal pronoun can be retrospectively understood not only with ᾗσεν (cf. *Od.* 1.1 ἄνδρα μοι ἔννεπε) but also with κακόν, appropriate both to the Trojan perspective on the Horse (ἵππον) and to the speaker's assessment of his response to it.

1–2[555–6] πᾶσα | Ἴλιος recalls the Homeric enjambment ἅπασα | Ἴλιος (*Il.* 22.410–11). Feminine Ἴλιος rather than neuter Ἴλιον is almost universal in Homer.   ἐφλεγόμαν: metaphorical, as often (e.g. *82*). The Doric form of the first singular imperfect passive is at odds with Ionic κείνῃ and is not persuasively explained by the fact that Hellenistic scholars recognized the existence of Doric forms in epic; if it is correct, there may be an evocation of lyric narrative.

3[557] οὐ δείσας . . . πόνον "though I did not fear the decade-long labor of the Achaeans." The speaker momentarily pauses to reflect on his narrative: his emotional state was generated not by fear for the fate of Troy, but by ἔρως (cf. Iordanoglou 2003: 85–6, 2009). Editors have offered various alternatives to the participle, but the text is probably sound.

3–4[557–8] ἐνὶ φέγγει | τῶι τότε "on that single day" (cf. LSJ φέγγος 1d), in contrast with the decade-long war (cf. Eur. *Or.* 656–7 μίαν πονήσας ἡμέραν . . . μὴ δέκ' ἐκπλήσας ἔτη), but also suggesting "in that blaze" (LSJ 2). Whereas epic routinely emphasizes the distance between the present and the heroic past (e.g. *Il.* 9.558–9 ἀνδρῶν | τῶν τότε), here the expression effaces the temporal gap between the Trojans and the speaker, who shares their experience.   ἀπωλόμεθα: erotic hyperbole, though the claim that the speaker has already "died" plays on the common type of epigram in which the speaker is the deceased.

CV. Dioscorides AP 5.54 (7 GP)

Guidance on having sex with a pregnant woman. The speaker's authoritative posture mimics Hesiodic didactic, and the epigram's structure, with a universal prohibition introduced by μήποτε followed by an explanatory γάρ-clause and finally a contrasting (ἀλλά) positive recommendation, condenses features found at Hes. *WD* 388–404. The admonitory voice is also reminiscent of sympotic elegies offering instructions on proper behavior. At the same time, the poem probably evokes lost treatises on sexual positions like the notorious work of Philaenis (cf. Aeschrion *AP* 7.345, Diosc. *AP* 7.450, Archestr. T 4 with Olson–Sens's note); it may be a Hellenistic reconfiguration of prose didactic material (cf. Aratus' *Phaenomena* and Nicander's *Theriaca* and *Alexipharmaca*).

The last couplet recalls a tradition of texts in which the speaker claims to prefer boys over women (e.g. Thgn. 1367–8, Pi. fr. 123. 4–9, Eur. *Cycl.* 583–4, Seleuc. p. 176 Powell, Asclep. *37 Sens = Pos. *134 AB). Here, however, the issue is limited to a particular circumstance, and the distinction between heterosexual and homosexual ἔρως is elided: sex that produces children and sex with boys are both potential sources of pleasure; see further Goldhill 1995: 114–15, Iordanoglou 2003: 111–28.

The epigram applies elaborate imagery and language to coarse subject matter. Its argument is neatly divided into three units that correspond to individual couplets: the first cautions the audience what not to do, the second explains the reasons, and the third gives a positive recommendation. The first and third are verbally linked by 2 τερπόμενος ~ 5 τέρπεο and 2 παιδογόνωι ~ 6 ἀρσενόπαιδα (cf. 6n.).

1[559] γαστροβαρῆ "pregnant," only here, on the analogy of adjectives such as γυιοβαρής.   **ἀντιπρόσωπον** "face to face."

2[560] παιδογόνωι . . . Κύπριδι: i.e. "sex that leads to childbirth," in contrast with ὁ ἀρσενόπαιδα Κύπριν (where Κύπριν means "sexual partner" rather than "sex").

3[561] μεσσόθι: the word's position at the head of the central couplet mirrors its meaning; cf. *549–52*n.   **μέγα κῦμα:** the Homeric phrase used in a Homeric verse-position plays on the double significance of κῦμα as "wave" (thus setting up the nautical imagery of 4) and "fetus" (= κύημα; cf. LSJ κῦμα 2).   **οὐκ ὀλίγος πόνος** "a great deal of toil" (litotes). The use of πόνος plays on its common application to childbirth (cf. Aesch. fr. 99.7–8) and to the experience of sailors in storms and shipwreck (e.g. *HH* 33.17, Eur. *Or.* 343).

4[562] ". . . as she is rowed and you are tossed by the swell." The image of sex as a sea voyage in which the man is an oarsman and the woman the vessel is common (cf. Ar. *Eccles.* 37–9, 1091, Pl. Com. fr. 3.4; Henderson 1991: 161–6). For σαλευομένου, cf. *502*. The line falls neatly into grammatically parallel and metrically identical halves, the first treating the woman and the second the man (cf. Hes. *Th.* 704).

5[563] πάλιν στρέψας "turning her around."   ῥοδοειδέι ... πυγῆι: cf.
547–8n.   τέρπεο: present middle imperative.

6[564] ἄλοχον, related to λέχος, forms a ring with 1 πρὸς σὸν λέχος. The
poem assumes that a pregnant woman with whom a man would have sex
would be his wife.   ἀρσενόπαιδα Κύπριν: cf. 2n. The context demands
the sense "a male lover," but the phrase also plays on Aphrodite's status
as a mother "with a male child." The formal reversal of 2 παιδογόνωι (in
which παῖς supplies the first rather than last element, as here) mirrors the
physical reversal of the positions (πάλιν στρέψας): the addressee should
not have sex in the manner that produces παῖδες, but in the manner one
has sex with παῖδες.

EUPHORION

According to the *Suda* (ε3801), Euphorion was born in Euboean Chalcis
during the 126th Olympiad (276–272); studied in Athens; was supported
by Nicaea, wife of Alexander son of the Euboean dynast Craterus; and
subsequently went to the court of the Seleucid king Antiochus III the
Great (reigned 222–187), who put him charge of the public library in
Antioch. His personal connection to Athens (Helladius ap. Phot. *Bibl.*
279, p. 532b) seems to be reflected in his literary interest in Attica (cf.
below); Theodoridas (CXVII) claims that he was buried there as an initiate
in the Eleusinian mysteries (the *Suda* places his burial in Syria), though
that poem was probably composed as a joke during Euphorion's lifetime.

In addition to two epigrams preserved in the Anthology, Euphorion
wrote numerous hexametric poems, including curse poems (*Thrax, Curses
or Cup-thief, Chiliades*), local Attic history (*Mopsopia*), an encomium (*The
Greater Hippomedon*), and a number of other works named after individuals. His poetry is recherché and often difficult: his diction is replete with
learned glosses, unusual forms, and neologisms, and he often includes
obscure myths or tells familiar ones in novel ways; cf. Magnelli 2002:
5–56, Lightfoot 2010: 191–9. He adheres to most of the Callimachean
restrictions on word-end in the verse (cf. Introduction section 4h[i]), but
his hexameters are markedly more spondaic than those of most contemporary poets.

Euphorion's epigrams show traces of his interest in unusual diction,
novel morphology, and learned local geographical references, but their
language is not difficult to comprehend. Their interest resides in the complexity beneath their superficial simplicity, and in their innovative play
with narrative voice and form.

CVI. Euphorion AP 7.651 (2 GP)

A cenotaph for Polymedes in the land of the Dryopes. In the first and last couplets two types of tomb are set in contrast: first, a grave surmounted by a tree or a grave-marker, and later an empty mound, which is, somewhat surprisingly, revealed as the speaker (cf. Bruss 2005: 130–2). In epitaphs the speaker usually professes not to know where the body is, but here the central couplet locates the corpse with precision, while the false tomb is placed in a vaguely specified land once visited by the deceased.

1[565] τρηχὺς ἔλαιος: the passage is related to a fragment of Rhianus' *Messeniaca* (fr. 55 Powell) πάρ τε τρηχὺν Ἐλαιὸν ὑπὲρ δρυμόν τε Λύκοιο, where Ἐλαιόν refers to the town; if Euphorion is the borrower, the allusion might point to a Messenian location of the Dryopes (6; see 5–6n.). For the marking of a tomb with wild olive, cf. A.R. 2.842–3. **ἐπ᾽ . . . καλύπτει:** tmesis (cf. Hes. *Th.* 798 κακὸν δ᾽ ἐπὶ κῶμα καλύπτει). **κεῖνα** plays on the more typical use of deictic ὅδε in inscriptional epigrams; the speaker represents the bones as distant from him.

2[566] κυάνεον may imply the metaphorical sense "grim" (e.g. Hes. *Shield* 249) but is also appropriate in its literal sense, since letters on ancient grave stelai were painted in a variety of colors, including blue; cf., in a funerary context, *RECAM* II 338 γράμμασι κυανέεσσι (Roman Imperial period). **γράμμα λαχοῦσα πέτρη:** cf. Alc. *AP* 7.429.2 γράμμα λέλογχε λίθος. More often, λαγχάνω denotes the lot that has befallen the deceased (e.g. Eur. fr. 360.33, Phal. *219*, *CEG* 24.2 ἀντὶ γάμου παρὰ θεῶν τοῦτο λαχοῦσ᾽ ὄνομα, 147, 172).

3–4[567–8] "These [*sc.* bones] the Icarian wave beats against the shore of Doliche and steep Dracanus." Dracanus was a hill in the northeast of the island of Icarus, which was originally called Doliche. The learned topographical reference may play on *HH* 1.1, where Dracanum and Icarus are juxtaposed as distinct places. For the structure of line 3, cf. *Il.* 2.573 οἵ θ᾽ Ὑπερησίην τε καὶ αἰπεινὴν Γονόεσσαν. **κροκάλαις:** literally "pebbles" and thus "shore," a rare noun (before the Hellenistic period, only at Eur. *IA* 210); there is a contrast between the word in its literal sense and 2 πέτρη.

5–6[569–70] "In exchange for Polymedes' hospitality, I, the empty earth, was heaped up in the thirsty pasture-land of the Dryopes." The cenotaph has been built by someone the dead man once hosted. **ἀντὶ . . . ξενίης:** a variation of the more common trope that the deceased lies in a foreign land (ξείνη). **Πολυμήδεος:** the name of the deceased; the Byzantine lemmatist of the Anthology claims that the cenotaph is anonymous, and some editors have preferred Saumaise's πολυκήδεος.   ἡ κεινὴ χθών: κεινή is "empty," i.e. without a body. Hellenistic hexameters ending in a monosyllable usually have bucolic diaeresis and a dactylic fifth foot (e.g. 539), but Euph. fr. 418.17 βουφόντης λίς and the common Homeric line end εὐρεῖα χθών make Reiske's emendation κενεή unnecessary; cf. Magnelli 2002: 79.   ὠγκώθην "I was heaped up"; the verb and its by-forms are used in the sense "bury" in Euripides (Ion 388, Or. 402) and appear with some regularity in Hellenistic funerary contexts (cf. Alex. Aet. fr. 3.33 with Magnelli's note).   Δρυόπων . . . βοτάναις: the Dryopes were said to have been expelled from their ancient homeland in central Greece (between Malis and Phocis) by Heracles and the Malians, and to have settled in Messenia, the Argolid and Euboea, and on Cythnus and Cyprus (cf. Finglass 2012: 40–2); the reference to their territory thus does not directly locate the tomb.   διψάσιν: i.e. "dry"; cf. A.R. 1.1147–8 ἀνέβραχε διψάδος . . . | ἐκ κορυφῆς. The botanical coloring of βοτάναις picks up the reference to the olive at the opening of the poem.

MNASALCES

Mnasalces is named as the author of eighteen epigrams; one other is doubly ascribed to him or Leonidas (AP 6.110). Two additional epigrams appear in an organized collection along with four of his known epigrams in P.Köln v 204 (cf. Gutzwiller 1998a: 31). Little is known of his life, except that he was from Sicyon (Ath. 4.163a, Str. 9.142); he may be honored in a decree from Oropos (IG VII 395 = I.Oropus 17). He seems likely to have been a contemporary or near-contemporary of Theodoridas, whose mock epitaph for him (AP 13.21) makes best sense if he was still active.

Mnasalces' extant poems are all funerary and dedicatory; though CVIII could have been composed for inscription, most are obviously fictive and experimental with those genres in various ways. Anyte's influence is particularly marked, but they also engage with epigrams by Asclepiades, Nicias, and others; the depiction of the bucolic world in CIX gains particular point if it was produced against the backdrop of Theocritean bucolic. See further Bernsdorff 2001: 122–3.

CVII. Mnasalces AP 7.171 (8 GP)

An epitaph for Poemandrus. The theme of the poem – that birds are now safe to rest on a plane tree where the dead man used to fowl – is related to that of Call. *Epigr.* 62, where Cretan goats are said to be safe from weapons dedicated in the temple of Artemis. The opening couplet plays on epigrams in which the speaker invites a traveler to rest in a rural *locus amoenus*, with the bird's wings taking the place of the traveler's tired limbs (cf. 1, 2nn.). The epigram as a whole juxtaposes peaceful bucolic "rest" with death through the parallel position of ἀμπαύσει and ὤλετο at the heads of the two couplets.

1[571] ἀμπαύσει . . . θοὸν πτερόν: cf. Anyte *APl* 228.1 ξεῖν', ὑπὸ τὰν πτελέαν τετρυμένα γυῖ' ἀνάπαυσον.   **καὶ τᾶιδε:** cf. *17*n. καί.   **θοὸν πτερόν:** by which the fowler would have caught the bird in the past; cf. *608*n.   **ἱερὸς ὄρνις:** cf. *609*(n.), where the phrase describes a captured blackbird and prepares for a particular allusion to Alcman; if the two passages are related, Mnasalces' poem, in which it has no such allusive function, might be thought the later.

2[572] ὑπὲρ . . . πλατάνου: a variation of the conventional focus on the area *under* a plane tree; the bird, sitting on the tree, takes the place of the resting traveler in epigrams such as Hermocr. *APl* 11.1 ἵζευ ὑπὸ σκιερὰν πλάτανον.   **ἀδείας:** the tree is "sweet" – a key term in the bucolic *locus amoenus* (cf. Theocr. 1.1–3) – for the pleasure it provides to the bird and other visitors through its shade, its scent, or the sound of its leaves.

3[573] Ποίμανδρος ὁ Μάλιος: the rarely attested name, suggesting "Herdsman," befits the occupant of the rural setting here imagined; the ethnic might be a play on the word for sheep (properly μῆλον in Doric but sometimes appearing with hyper-Doric ᾱ in MSS).

4[574] ἰξὸν . . . χευάμενος: cf. *589–90*n.

CVIII. Mnasalces AP 7.242 (7 GP)

An epitaph for men who have died for their country in conflict. The poem touches with great elegance on several of the commonplaces of public memorials: that the deceased perished as liberators; thereby won praise; and should serve as examples for others. The words are ordered artfully (1–2n.), with attention to phonetic effects (3n.), and with the last verse picking up the first in ring composition (1 οἵδε πάτραν ~ 4 τούσδ'. . . ὑπὲρ πατρίδος); conventional expressions are varied in subtle ways (1–2n.). Nothing excludes it from having been designed for a real communal grave.

1–2[575–6] The structure of both verses mimics their content: other than the initial pronoun, the hexameter is chiastically ordered (ABCBA), with the noun δεσμόν and its adjective πολύδακρυν surrounding ἐπ᾽ αὐχένι like a bond on a neck; in the pentameter δνοφερὰν . . . κόνιν surrounds a verb meaning literally "put around." **πολύδακρυν . . . δεσμόν:** the adjective is common in epic (e.g. *Il.* 17.544); the noun is used as at *CEG* 789.5–6 βαρὺν ἀπὸ δεσμὸν ἑλόντες | φρουρᾶς Λοκροῖσιν τεῦξαν ἐλευθερίαν. **ῥυόμενοι** "while fighting to protect," standard language in public epitaphs for the war dead (e.g. *CEG* 131.4; cf. "Simon." *AP* 7.442.2, "Aesch." *AP* 7.255.1–2). **δνοφερὰν . . . κόνιν:** a variation of archaic collocations of the adjective with γῆ/γαίη (Hes. *Th.* 807, Thgn. 243). The epithet is used of grief at 2. **ἀμφεβάλοντο** "they put on," as if the earth were an item of clothing (cf. *127–8*n.); a variation of expressions with ἔννυμι; cf. "Simon." *AP* 7.251.2 θανάτου ἀμφεβάλοντο νέφος.

3[577] The line (for which cf. *Il.* 6.446 ἀρνύμενος πατρός τε μέγα κλέος ἠδ᾽ ἐμὸν αὐτοῦ) is assonant. **ἀλλά τις ἀστῶν:** cf. Archil. fr. 13.1–2 (of civic grief) κήδεα μὲν στονόεντα, Περίκλεες, οὔτε τις ἀστῶν | μεμφόμενος θαλίῃς τέρψεται οὐδὲ πόλις. ἀλλά often introduces exhortations and commands at the end of speeches, where it marks the transition from the reasons for action to the action required; cf. Denniston 13–15.

4[578] Cf. *3–4*n.

CIX. Mnasalces AP 9.324 (16 GP)

On a syrinx dedicated in a sanctuary of Aphrodite. The poem resembles a group of epigrams (e.g. Leon. *AP* 9.320, *APl* 171) in which the speaker wonders about the apparent inappropriateness of a dedication. In particular, it shares a close formal and verbal resemblance to an undated epigram attributed to a certain Antimachus (*AP* 9.321) on a dedication of armor to Aphrodite; that epigram similarly opens with a series of questions, cites the elements appropriate to the goddess, and concludes with a set of commands. Here the speaker, who represents himself as located within the precinct (1 ὧδε), expresses surprise that the instrument has abandoned its pastoral home; in attributing agency to the syrinx, the poem omits the role played by the shepherd, who is mentioned only obliquely and may be supposed to have fallen in love and, abandoning his pastoral duties, offered the instrument to Aphrodite, like the shepherd of Lycophronides *PMG* 844, who, distracted by love, dedicates his equipment to a god.

The epigram may be read against Hellenistic bucolic poetry and the pervasive presence of erotic suffering in Theocritus' idealized landscape (cf. above, p. 191). The speaker's insistence on a stark divide between the worlds of the shepherd and of Aphrodite are, for the reader of bucolic, humorously tendentious. The speaker's pejorative characterization of the shepherd's Muse as ἀγρία, however, is more likely to be ironic and playful than to represent hostility on the part of the poet. Instead the epigram, and especially its final restriction of the "rustic Muse" to the mountains, exploits tensions characteristic of contemporary pastoral poetry, including the tension between its rustic subject matter and its elegant language and between the calmness of nature and the turmoil of its residents (Sens 2006: 165; cf. Fantuzzi 2016: 285–6).

1[579] ἁ σῦριγξ: addresses in which the article plus the nominative takes the place of a vocative often mark the speaker's social superiority or are peremptory in tone (Sansone 1993: 205).   **τί τοι** "why, I ask you . . . ?" (cf. Denniston 545); τοι appeals for the addressee's attention.

1–3[579–81] ὧδε . . . ὧδε . . . ὧδ': the emphatic epanalepsis is a bucolic mannerism (*467*n.) and thus ironic in context.   **Ἀφρογένειαν** "to (the sanctuary of) Aphrodite." A Hellenistic name for the goddess (first attested here; cf. *683*, Mosch. *Eur.* 71, Bion fr. 11.1) emphasizing her connection to the sea by birth and thus the incongruity of an instrument designed for the mountains in her precinct.   **ὀρούσας** suggests eagerness on the part of the personified syrinx.   **ἀπὸ ποιμενίου χείλεος:** i.e. from the shepherd who used to play it; cf. Theocr. 1.129 ἐκ κηρῶ σύριγγα καλὸν περὶ χεῖλος ἑλικτάν, "Pl." *AP* 9.823.4, Alc. *APl* 226.

3–4[581–2] The speaker defines the world of the syrinx by its physical features (πρῶνες . . . ἄγκεα), but that in which he resides by emotions (Ἔρωτες | . . . Πόθος). **οὐ . . . οὔτ'** (= οὔτε . . . οὔτε) is common in poetry (cf. Denniston 509–10).   **ἔθ'** "any more," i.e. "here."   **πάντα . . . Πόθος** "love and desire are all there is"; cf. Theocr. 14.47 Λύκος νῦν πάντα.   **Ἔρωτες:** cf. *82*n.   **ἁ . . . ἀγρία Μοῦσ'** suggests "rustic" song, but the adjective also implies "uncultivated, unsophisticated" in contrast with the more urbane world of the speaker.   **ἐν ὄρει:** the conventional home of shepherds (Theocr. 3.46; cf. Sens on Theocr. 22.36) and the locus for bucolic composition (e.g. Theocr. 7.51).   **μενέτω:** the text is uncertain. Pl's νέμεται is possible, but an imperative finds some support from "Antim." *AP* 9.321.5–6 κάθες . . . ἴθι (cf. introductory n.); the emendation μενέτω is suggested by P's μένεται, though νεμέτω "let the rustic Muse drive her flocks," with the verb used absolutely (e.g. *Od.* 9.233), would make a neat bookend to the opening reference to the syrinx; cf. Call. fr. 112.5 τῶι Μοῦσαι πολλὰ νέμοντι βοτά.

RHIANUS

The scholar-poet Rhianus seems to have lived in the second half of the third century. The *Suda* (ρ158) reports that he was originally from Crete, though some traced him to Messene, probably by conjecture from his work (see below). The *Suda* further records that he started as an overseer of the palaestra and a slave but became a grammarian, and that he was a contemporary of Eratosthenes. Neither his role in the wrestling school nor his servile status can be confirmed; the former claim may derive from epigrams that reflect an interest in well-oiled young men. That he worked in Alexandria at some time is likely. In addition to epigrams, he produced critical editions of the Homeric poems; the fragments preserved in the scholia are particularly focused on matters of diction. He wrote substantial epics, including a *Heracleiad* in fourteen books; a treatment of Achaean history, the *Achaiika*; and the *Messeniaka*, on the Second Messenian War. The last likely narrated a night raid by Aristomenes (cf. *FGrH* 265 F 42), perhaps modeled on that of Odysseus and Diomedes in *Iliad* 10; like the *Iliad*, it treated only part of the war. Rhianus' engagement with Homeric themes finds a complement in his style and diction, which seem more straightforwardly epic than those of poets like Callimachus; its novelty is marked less by the invention of new words and forms than "by the conscious choice of words and style and by delicate allusions" (Pfeiffer 1968: 149). Ten epigrams are unambiguously ascribed to Rhianus, and another (*AP* 7.315) is alternatively ascribed to him or to a certain Zenodotus. Some are dedicatory and sympotic, but the most notable are Rhianus' pederastic poems, which play on the contrast between epic language and erotic content. The literary models for these are wide-ranging and include epigrams by Leonidas, Callimachus, and Asclepiades (e.g. *605–6*n., Cameron 1995: 299).

CX. *Rhianus* AP *6.173 (7 GP)*

A dedication of hair by Achrylis upon retirement from service to Cybele. The links between the epigram and Diosc. c, on a dedication by a gallus, seem more likely to reflect reworking by Rhianus than the use of the epigram as a model. Unlike Dioscorides and other epigrams on priests of Cybele, Rhianus represents the cooling of Achrylis' madness as the end of long professional service to the goddess; the epigram thus belongs to a group recording the dedication of tools on retirement; cf. cxxxii introductory n. Both the dedicator's name and the feminine forms that run through the poem suggest that Achrylis is female, but if, as is possible, 3 γαλλαίωι Κυβέλης ὀλολύγματι refers to her cry rather than that of male co-celebrants, the epigram may play with gender by using female forms to refer to a castrated priest, as perhaps in Call. fr. 761 γάλλαι μητρὸς ὀρείης φιλόθυρσοι δρομάδες, | αἷς ἔντεα παταγεῖται καὶ χάλκεα κρόταλα, and subsequently in Catullus' Attis poem (63).

1[583] Ἀχρυλίς: no Greek names beginning in Ἀχρ- are attested, though other female names in -υλις are. Emendation to the plausible Greek name Ἀρχυλίς (e.g. D.S. 14.52.5 Ἀρχύλος) is, however, perhaps not necessary in the case of a Phrygian. **θαλαμηπόλος:** see *517*n. **περὶ πεύκας:** perhaps "among the pine trees," which played an important part in the rites of Cybele and Attis and were particularly connected with the castration of the latter (cf. Lancelotti 2002: 84–5, 89–90, Bremmer 2004), rather than "among the torches."

2[584] Cf. Eur. *Bacch.* 455–6 (of Dionysus) πλόκαμος . . . | γένυν παρ' αὐτὴν κεχυμένος. Unbound hair is a conventional attribute of Cybele's worshippers (cf. *516*n.). It is ἱερός because it is to be dedicated to the goddess (cf. 5). **πολλάκι:** epigrams often emphasize the regularity with which an object was used before its owner retired and dedicated it (e.g. Mnasalces *AP* 6.125.3–4, 128.3).

3–4[585–6] A difficult phrase which might mean "adding (δοῦσα) the sound from her mouth, unpleasant on the ears, to the cries of Cybele's galli" or "with the cry of a gallus of Cybele, giving to the ears the unpleasant sound from her mouth"; see introductory n. The passage is closely connected to *527*, where the literal sense of βαρύν seems more naturally to fit the sound of a kettledrum than it does the ecstatic cries of a celebrant here. For the aorist participle δοῦσα, here also used in an unusual sense, cf. δοὺς ἀνέμοισι τρίχα in *516*. **γαλλαίωι:** first here. **ἀπὸ στομάτων:** cf. *238*n.

5[587] δικλίδι "door." The word was originally an adjective modifying πύλαι, θύραι, and the like; in the Hellenistic period it served as a noun in both singular and plural (cf. Asclep. 12.1 with Sens's note). The reference is probably to a mountain cave (cf. the note on ὀρείηι below), and the humor lies in the application of a term suited to domestic architecture to a rural dwelling. **ὀρείηι:** Cybele is often so described (e.g. Eur. *Hipp.*

144, *Hel.* 1301–2 ὀρεία . . . μάτηρ . . . θεῶν, Call. fr. 761) and although the position of the word favors taking it with δικλίδι rather than θεῆι, it logically applies to both the goddess and her home.

6[588] θερμόν: of the "heat" of divine possession; contrast 517–*18*n.   λύσσης represents the priest's ecstatic state as a negative, destructive force.   ἀνέπαυσε πόδα: i.e. ceased her frenzied leaping; for the expression, cf. *Od.* 23.298 παῦσαν ἄρ' ὀρχηθμοῖο πόδας.

CXI. Rhianus AP 12.93 (3 GP)

Boys are like a maze. The speaker addresses an unnamed second person, who is imagined as a participant in the erotic viewing that the poem describes; second-person verbs (2, 7, 8) thus implicate the reader in a community of ἐρασταί (cf. Fountoulakis 2013: 295–6). The first couplet contains a generalized observation (1–2) that is balanced by a farewell to the boys in the last (11–12). The central section offers three exempla, the first two occupying a single couplet each (3–4, 5–6), the last two couplets (7–10). The epigram thus represents a simplified and miniaturized "Catalogue of Boys," reflecting a form more elaborately attested in Phanocles' elegiac Ἔρωτες ἢ καλοί and the Ἠοῖοι of Sosistratus or Sosicrates of Phanagoreia (*SH* 732; cf. Cameron 1995: 382), which recounted homoerotic myths. The first two exempla are introduced in parallel language (3, 5 τῆι . . . τῆι) that suggests the formulaic repetitions of catalogue poetry; there is variation at the opening of the third (ἥν). Each of the individual sections of this catalogue is metrically unified by enjambment, with a sense-pause after each one. Though the speaker expresses desire, he shows no trace of the erotic misery of many epigrammatic ἐρασταί, and despite the opening claim that boys are to be found at every turn, his final wish for their maturation treats the passage of time and their transition from boyhood as positive events rather than as a threat to them (cf. Murgatroyd 1989: 310–13).

   The poem seems to be the model for adesp. *AP* 12.88.3–4; Giangrande (1967: 21) argues that it is the model for *AP* 12.129, attributed to Aratus.

1–2[589–90] The opening generalization is explained by the rest of the couplet and illustrated by the examples given in the body of the epigram; for a similar technique, cf. *85*.   **λαβύρινθος** "maze"; the speaker cannot turn in any direction without encountering an attractive boy.   **ἧι . . . ἄν** "wherever."   **ὡς . . . προσαμπέχεται** reverses the usual representation of the ἐραστής as a hunter (cf. LVIII, 299n.). Fowling is a form of hunting appropriate for boys (cf. Bion, fr. 13.1–2; Long. 3.5–6), who here captivate the speaker. ἰξῶι "birdlime," a sticky substance, commonly made from mistletoe, that was used to capture small birds; cf. *574, 607*, Reed on Bion, fr. 13.5. For the idea that an attractive person was like birdlime for the viewer, cf. Timoth. Com. fr. 2.1 ὁ πτερωτὸς ἰξὸς ὀμμάτων Ἔρως with Kassel–Austin's note. προσαμπέχεται "is held."

3[591] τῆι "on this side." ἄγει: *sc.* "your eye" (ὄμμα).

3–4[591–2] ποτὶ πίονα σαρκὸς | ἀκμήν: a highly compressed expression amounting to "to his body, which is at the height of its richness." ἄνθος: here equivalent to "beauty," as e.g. *HHDem.* 108, Thgn. 994 παῖς καλὸν ἄνθος ἔχων; cf. the common ἄνθος ἥβης. Plucking flowers is a widespread metaphor for sexual intercourse (cf. Bremer 1975). ἀκηράσιον "undefiled," i.e. "unpicked," as at *HHMerc.* 72 (of real meadows). Ancient critics seem to have debated whether the word meant undefiled (< κῆρ) or unmixed (< κεράννυμι) in its unique Homeric occurrence (*Od.* 9.204–5 οἶνον ἐν ἀμφιφορεῦσι δυώδεκα πᾶσιν ἀφύσσας, | ἡδὺν ἀκηράσιον, θεῖον ποτόν).

5[593] χρύσεον ῥέθος "golden face"; cf. Alcm. *PMG* 1.55 ἀργύριον πρόσωπον. The adjective may have the metaphorical sense "valuable," and thus "desirable"; sexual attractiveness is implicit in the conventional description of Aphrodite as χρυσέη (e.g. *Il.* 6.220). Ancient critics treated singular ῥέθος in the sense "face" as an Aeolic usage (cf. Pfeiffer on Call. fr. 67.13, Gow on Theocr. 29.16), but it appears in tragedy (Soph. *Ant.* 529, Eur. *HF* 1204) and in other Hellenistic poetry (e.g. A.R. 2.68, Lyc. *Alex.* 173, 1137, Nic. *Ther.* 165). ὅς τε: "epic" τε following the relative pronoun often appears in clauses denoting permanent or typical states or recurring actions (cf. Ruijgh 1971, Probert 2015: 108–10), but is not directly translatable. The use of the epic phenomenon paradoxically introduces grandeur to the description of the small, charming boy. καθ᾽ ὕψος "in stature."

6[594] οὐρανίη "as high as the sky" (LSJ II) but also suggesting "divine." ἀμφιτέθηλε: cf. *610*n. θαλεραί.

7[595] ἐπὶ Λεπτίνεω στρέψηις δέμας "if you turn (your eye) toward Leptines' body."

8[596] ἀλύτωι δ᾽ ὡς ἀδάμαντι μενεῖς "you will remain as if (fettered) by inescapable adamant," picking up the image of birdlime but also perhaps the language of erotic binding in magical spells; cf. *Supplementum magicum* no. 45.42–5 (late antique) "seize Euphemia and lead her . . . to me, maddened with desire; and bind her with strong, inescapable (ἀλύτοις) bonds of adamant (ἀδαμαντίνοις) in friendship with me . . ."

9[597] ἴχνια κολληθείς "with your feet glued in place," evoking the opening image of birdlime.   τοῖον σέλας ὄμμασιν αἴθει "such brightness does he blaze from his eyes"; σέλας is the direct object of transitive αἴθει, which also suggests the erotic burning experienced by the viewer; cf. Theocr. 2.133–4 Ἔρως . . . σέλας φλογερώτερον αἴθει.

10[598] κὰς νεάτους ἐκ κορυφῆς ὄνυχας: the burning affects the viewer's entire body; for ἐς . . . ὄνυχα, cf. Eur. *Cycl.* 159 (the effects of wine), Asclep. 8.2 (of erotic suffering), *414*. The phrase is a variation of the Homeric ἐς πόδας ἐκ κεφαλῆς (*Il.* 18.353, 23.169).

11–12[599–600] Cf. *18*0n. χαίροις . . . μάκαιρα. The couplet traces the development of the young men from boyhood (παῖδες) through early adulthood (ἥβην) to old age (λευκήν . . . κόμην). Both verses have homoeoteleuton at the beginning and the end; there is internal rhyme at the medial caesura of 12; and the optatival clauses are phonetically and grammatically parallel.   ἐς ἀκμαίην . . . ἥβην "may you reach the prime of your youth."   λευκὴν ἀμφιέσαισθε κόμην "may you cloak yourself in white hair." The good wishes previously expressed now take on a new meaning, since the speaker's hope that they will reach old age is simultaneously a wish that they grow beyond allure (cf. Anacr. *PMG* 358.6–7).

CXII. Rhianus AP *12.121* (*4 GP*)

The Graces encounter Cleonicus. The epic language with which the poem opens and closes evokes divine initiations (e.g. Hes. *Th.* 22–34, Theocr. 7 with Hunter's introductory note) and other encounters between gods (usually disguised) and humans, often on a journey (e.g. *Il.* 24.322–472, *Od.* 7.14–132). In 4 Cleonicus, who wholly embodies "grace," has been turned into a Grace himself, and the wish that he will rejoice "from afar" (5) may be read as inverting prayers for divine figures to approach and bring benefits (e.g. *437*n.). The poem thus plays on the form of a cletic hymn, with an opening vocative followed by an account of Cleonicus' "deification."

Call. *Epigr.* 30 also contains an address to a Cleonicus, the expression ἦ ῥά, and an apostrophe in the final line, but these links do not justify Ludwig's view (1968: 317–18) that Callimachus' poem is a model; cf. Murgatroyd 1989: 307.

1–2[601–2] ἦ ῥά νύ τοι: a Homeric verse-opening (*Il.* 3.183, 10.401). τοι has its full pronominal sense ("to you").   δι᾽ ἀτραπιτοῖο . . . στεινῆς: "narrow" implies that the path is remote and little used. As is traditional in divine epiphanies, the Graces encountered Cleonicus in an isolated and unfrequented spot. ἀτραπιτός occurs a single time in Homer (*Od.* 13.195), who otherwise has ἀταρπός or ἀταρπιτός, and its rarity made it popular with Hellenistic poets (Call. *h.* 4.74, A.R. 4.123, 1173, Pos. 96.2 AB, Rhianus, fr. 1.15).   λιπαραὶ Χάριτες: the Graces are λιπαροκρήδεμνοι ("having bright headbands") in early epic (*Il.* 18.382, *Cypria* fr. 5.3–4). λιπαρός has a variety of connotations, but the opposition between it and αὐχμηρός "dry, withered" (cf. 5–6n. αὐηρήν) at Xen. *Mem.* 2.1.31 suggests that here it should be taken to mean "vibrant with life." Cf. *61*on. θαλεραί.

3[603] ποτὶ . . . ἐπηχύναντο "embraced." ποτί is probably a preverb in tmesis (for the compound, cf. Call. *h.* 1.46) rather than a preposition governing the dative. For the idea, cf. Meleager's reworking at *AP* 12.122.1–2 ὦ Χάριτες, τὸν καλὸν Ἀρισταγόρην ἐσιδοῦσαι | ἀντίον εἰς τρυφερὰς ἠγκαλίσασθε χέρας. In this context the verb evokes the second element of the traditional epic epithet ῥοδόπηχυς (e.g. Hes. *Th.* 246, 251).   ῥοδόεσσιν: cf. *547–8*n. ῥοδόεις is ordinarily a three-termination adjective, but the restriction of adjectives in -όεις to two terminations is common (e.g. Nic. *Ther.* 502, *Alex.* 473, 604). ῥοδέῃσι of the apographa is therefore unnecessary, though it is supported by Musaeus 116 οἷά τε χωομένη ῥοδέην ἐξέσπασε χεῖρα. χέρεσσιν "arms," as often (LSJ I.2).

4[604] "You have been made Grace throughout the whole of your body [lit. 'as big as you are']"; cf. *594*. For the treatment of an attractive person as the god whose qualities he or she embodies, cf. Ibyc. *PMG* 287, where an attractive man is treated as Eros, and Call. *Epigr.* 51, where Berenice is a fourth Grace. Whether or not one capitalizes χάρις, the larger point is that Cleonicus' encounter with the Graces is a sort of apotheosis in which he himself joins their number.

5–6[605–6] The boy's sexual appeal is a fire that will burn those who come near him (cf. CIV). That the speaker is at risk because he is "dried up" with old age reverses an idea in Asclep. *41 Sens, where the speaker sympathizes with those who came into contact with the courtesan Archeanassa when she was younger and even more capable of burning them.   μάλα χαῖρε: in the same metrical position, also with nominative φίλος for vocative, at *Od.* 8.413 καὶ σύ, φίλος, μάλα χαῖρε, θεοὶ δέ τοι ὄλβια δοῖεν.   πυρός: with ἆσσον. The separation of the word from ἀνθερίκην at the end of the next verse matches the distance he seeks.   ἕρπειν:

cf. 37n. παρέρπων.   αὐηρήν . . . ἀνθερίκην "dry asphodel-stalk," used
metaphorically for one who has gone beyond the prime of youth, as e.g.
Asclep. *46.3–4 "who would say that dry stalks (αὐχμηράς) are better than
corn-ears?" Both words are unusual. αὐηρήν, if it is not a corruption of
αὐχμηρήν, serves as a doublet of αὐαλέος on the analogy of such pairs as
διψηρός/διψαλέος. ἀνθερίκην could be emended to ἀνθέρικα or, less plausibly,
ἀνθρακιήν (Renehan 1964: 375–6), but should probably be retained as a
feminine doublet of ἀνθέριξ, which is elsewhere masculine.   ἆ φίλος: cf.
41–2n. ἆ expresses strong emotions of a variety of sorts, and the apostrophe reflects the speaker's complex feelings for Cleonicus, whom he both
desires and urges to keep at a distance. Eustathius (1.133.34 Stallbaum)
cites Od. 3.375 in the form ἆ φίλος οὔ σε ἔολπα κτλ., and it is conceivable
that Hellenistic uses of the expression (Leon. AP 9.318.2, Parth. fr. 2.12)
evoke that Homeric variant.

CXIII. Rhianus AP 12.142 (10 GP)

The speaker wishes to be captured by Dexionicus. The poem is composed
in two thematically linked movements of three verses (cf. 2 κόσσυφον
~ 5 κόσσυφος, 3 ἀναστενάχων ἀπεκώκυεν ~ 6 καὶ φθογγὴν καὶ γλυκὺ δάκρυ
βάλω). The first recounts Dexionicus' capture of a blackbird, the second
the speaker's wish to become a bird so as to be captured in the same
way. The poem seems initially to be about fowling and would fit a dedicatory epigram after a successful hunt; the second half comes as a surprise,
and plays on the commonplace representation of courtship as a hunt (cf.
LXIII). The lover is typically analogized as the hunter or treated as the
victim of Eros' weapons (cf. Barringer 2001: 86–9). Here, by contrast, an
ἐραστής wishes to be caught by Dexionicus so that he can plead his case,
lamenting and weeping like a captured bird, in close proximity to him
(Murgatroyd 1989: 303–4).

Fowling was a common activity of boys. That the speaker is considerably
older than Dexionicus is also suggested by the epigram's literary affiliations. It transforms a passage of Alcman (PMG 26) in which the speaker,
addressing a group of maidens, asks to become the bird called the κηρύλος
so that he can fly with the females of his species. Antig. Car. Mir. 23 introduces that fragment by observing that, when those birds become old,
the females take them on their wings and carry them (φέρουσιν αὐτοὺς αἱ
θήλειαι ἐπὶ τῶν πτερῶν λαβοῦσαι). The fragment's precise meaning and the
relationship of its context to Antigonus' claims are uncertain, but Rhianus
may be both reversing the gender of the addressee and evoking a now-lost
wish in Alcman's poem that the girls lay hold of him.

1[607] ἴξωι: see 589–90n.   ὑπὸ χλωρῆι πλατανίστωι: cf. *Il.* 2.307 καλῆι ὑπὸ πλατανίστωι, 572n. In this verse position ὑπὸ χλωρῆι has a model in the Homeric line end ὑπὸ χλωρὸν δέος εἷλεν (*Il.* 8.77, etc.).

2[608] κατὰ πτερύγων "by its wings from above." Birdlime could be smeared on a perch so that a bird's feet became stuck, or applied to a cane that was extended out and then down onto the bird's wings, as here.

3[609] ἀναστενάχων: cf. *Il.* 23.211, Bion, *Ep. Ad.* 80.   ἀπεκώκυεν: a rare compound (elsewhere at Aesch. *Ag.* 1544).   ἱερὸς ὄρνις: the blackbird is not elsewhere so described, but the adjective prepares for the evocation of Alcman in 5; the point may be that from the speaker's perspective, the captured bird seems to be the possession of a god. For the expression, cf. *571*, Call. fr. dub. 803 Πειρήτιδος ἱερὸς ὄρνις.

4[610] ὦ φίλ᾽ Ἔρως: the speaker appeals proleptically to his friendly relationship to Eros.   θαλεραί "burgeoning" with charm and beauty; cf. *601–2*n. λιπαραὶ Χάριτες and descriptions of attractive young people as shoots (θάλος) of the gods of love or of the Graces (e.g. Ibyc. *PMG* 288; cf. above, introductory n., Philox. *PMG* 821, Hedyl. *AP* 6.292.3–4, Sens on Asclep. 34.2).

5[611] εἴην ... κόσσυφος: cf. introductory n. The wish for metamorphosis so as to be close to a beloved is an erotic *topos*; e.g. *PMG* 900, 901, Theocr. 3.12–14. Here the speaker's wish to become a bird is not for escape (as commonly in tragic choruses, cf. Barrett on Eur. *Hipp.* 732–4), but for constraint. Thrushes and blackbirds frequently appear together in Greek literature, though here καί ... καί separate two distinct possibilities (= "or"); cf. Denniston 292.

5–6[611–12] ὡς ἂν ἐκείνου | ... δάκρυ βάλω: the phrase reworks 79–80.   καὶ φθογγὴν καὶ γλυκὺ δάκρυ βάλω: cf. 3 ἀναστενάχων ἀπεκώκυεν. The phrase is a zeugma: although δάκρυ(α) βάλλω is a common poetic expression for "cry" (e.g. Eur. *Hipp.* 1396), the verb is not normally used with nouns denoting sound as object (though forms of ἵημι are regularly so employed, e.g. Eur. *Hipp.* 418). γλυκὺ δάκρυ evokes the idea, first and most famously expressed by Sappho (fr. 130.2), that Eros is bittersweet.

CXIV. Rhianus *AP 12.38 (1 GP)*

On the beautiful buttocks of Menecrates. The wit depends on the contrast between style and content. The opening line is couched in epic language and recalls scenes in which the Horae and Graces endow young people, especially women, with beauty (cf. 1–2n.). That the addressee is buttocks, as is revealed in the pentameter, is humorously bathetic. The deflation is reinforced in the second couplet, in which the buttocks are the recipient of divine favor – or perhaps deified – and responds to the speaker's queries; the boy's name is delayed until the end. The buttocks' response might be understood as taking the form of a fart, as in passages treating farts as divine utterances (*HHMerc.* 295–6, Ar. *Knights* 638–42).

1–2[613–14] For similar scenes in which the Horae and Graces adorn a person, cf. Hes. *WD* 73–5 with West on 75, *Cypria* fr. 4.1–2 εἵματα μὲν χροΐ ἕστο, τά οἱ Χάριτές τε καὶ ῟Ωραι | ποίησαν καὶ ἔβαψαν ἐν ἄνθεσιν εἰαρινοῖσιν, Theocr. 1.150, Asclep. *34 Sens = Pos. *126 AB.   **κατὰ ... ἔλαιον:** the expression overlays the language of *Od.* 18.188 κατὰ γλυκὺν ὕπνον ἔχευεν on the word order of *Il.* 17.619, *Od.* 15.527 κατὰ δ' ἡνία χεῦεν ἔραζε.   **ἔλαιον:** a surprise at line end, where a word denoting physical beauty or charm might have been expected. Instead, the Hours and Graces pour olive oil on Menecrates as if preparing him for athletic competition; the implication is perhaps that the speaker has seen the boy naked and glistening with oil at the palaestra (cf. Theocr. 2.79). At Call. fr. 7. 13–14 the poet asks the Graces to wipe their hands, anointed with oil, on his elegies.   **κνώσσειν:** insomnia is a conventional symptom of lovesickness (e.g. Phanocl. fr. 1.5, Thomas 1979: 195–205). The verb is a Homeric hapax (*Od.* 4.809).   **οὐδὲ γέροντας:** even old men, ordinarily past the point of sexual desire (cf. Pl. *Rep.* 329a–d), are affected. For the idea, cf. Archil. fr. 48.5–6 ἐσμυριχμένας κόμην | καὶ στῆθος, ὡς ἂν καὶ γέρων ἠράσσατο, Long. 3.13.3, Ov. *Am.* 3.7.41.

3[615] λέξον μοι, τίνος ἐσσί: perhaps playing on epitaphs in which the passerby is imagined as directing an inquiry to the tomb; cf. *369–70*n. **μάκαιρα τύ:** because these buttocks are the recipient of divine favor (cf. 1–2n.).

4[616] κοσμεῖς "decorate, adorn," as if the πυγή were an item of jewelry or clothing.   **ἁ πυγὰ δ' εἶπε:** an unusual intrusion of the voice of a third-person narrator into a dialogue poem, where changes of speaker are normally left unmarked.   **Μενεκράτεος:** the genitive responds to the first of the speaker's questions (5 τίνος).

THEODORIDAS

Of Theodoridas of Syracuse (cf. Ath. 15.699e–f) nineteen epigrams are extant. He also composed a dithyramb, Κένταυροι, of which a single fragment survives (*SH* 739), and a μέλος in honor of Eros (*SH* 741). There are several other short fragments of uncertain provenance (*SH* 742–7), including traces of local dialect forms from Syracuse (*SH* 742) and Tarentum (*SH* 745).

A striking feature of Theodoridas' epigrams is their humorous tone and witty use of language. One (*AP* 13.21) pokes fun at Mnasalces, another (cxvii) at Euphorion. These were probably composed during the lifetimes of those poets. Theodoridas' literary relationship to Euphorion seems to have been competitive. Their epigrams share verbal and thematic points of contact (cf. cxv introductory n., Magnelli 2002: 104–5). If the transmitted form Θεωρίδαν at Clem. Alex. *Str.* 5.8.47.2 is to be emended to Θεοδωρίδαν, Euphorion composed a set of responses (ἀντιγραφαί) to Theodoridas; the sole surviving fragment suggests a disagreement over the meaning of the rare gloss ζάψ. There are also signs of engagement with epigrams of Callimachus (e.g. *AP* 6.224, which reworks LX).

CXV. Theodoridas AP 6.155 (1 GP)

Four-year-old Crobylus dedicates his hair after having it cut for the first time. The epigram, which involves an onomastic joke (1–2n.), may be read as a jocular rewriting of Euphorion's apparently serious epigram on the same theme (*AP* 6.279); the humorous tone is reinforced by the elaborate, comic language of 3–4. The first and third couplets are linked by language and theme (5 Ὤπολλον ~ 1 Φοίβωι, 5 τὸν Κρωβύλον ~ 1 ὁ Κρωβύλος; 5 θείης . . . εἰς τέλος ἄνδρα stands in contrast to 2 κῶρος ὁ τετραετής), while the central couplet recounts an accompanying sacrifice and provides the name of the boy's father.

1–2[617–18] Crobylus' hair has never before been cut and so is the same age as he; there may be an allusion to Call. *h.* 4.297–8 ἥλικα χαίτην | παρθενικαῖς. The couplet is framed by ἅλικες and ὁ τετραετής, the latter providing the specific information left open by the former.   **ὁ Κρωβύλος:** a rare though securely attested proper name, but in context a joke, since κρωβύλος was a way of arranging long hair so that it was bound in a bun behind the head (Thuc. 1.6.3; for a similar joke, cf. Ar. *Wasps* 1267 with Biles–Olson's note), and after αἱ . . . κόμαι it would initially have been so understood ("the hair and the man-bun . . ."). **ἀπὸ . . . | πέξατο** "had cut off" (tmesis). Applied to humans, πέκω (ordinarily "comb") has the sense "cut" only at Euph. *AP* 6.279.1; the phrase thus varies the use of the verb at Call. *h.* 5.31–2 ἀπὸ χαίταν | πέξηται, where it has the expected sense "comb." For a different view, cf. Cairns 2016: 304–5.   **μολπαστᾶι** "the minstrel," an epithet pointing to the god's role as patron of singing and dancing; songs, including those sung by boys, were important in his cult. Pl. *Tim.* 21b mentions songs by boys at the Athenian Koureion (cf. next n.). The word is otherwise unattested in literature but it is glossed "playmate" (συμπαίκτης) at Hsch. μ1581.   τετραετής: there is little detailed evidence for the dedication of hair by young boys, but at Athens, three- or four-year-olds seem to have had their hair cut and offered to Artemis on Koureotis, the second day of the Apaturia, when they were enrolled in their phratries and became citizens (Σ^vet. Pl. *Tim.* 21b, Lambert 1998: 143–89).

3–4[619–20] The grandiose language for the boy's simple sacrifice is almost parodic.   αἰχμητὰν ... ἀλέκτορα "a fighting cock"; cf. Nic. *Alex.* 294 αἰχμητῆισιν ... νεοσσοῖς.   πλακόεντα ... τυροφόρον: πλακοῦς was a generic term for a variety of sweet or savory unleavened cakes. The description of the cake, including the neologism τυροφόρος, is characteristic of elaborate accounts of flatbreads in comic and parodic contexts; cf. Ar. *Ach.* 1125 πλακοῦντος τυρόνωτον δὸς κύκλον, Matro, fr. 1.116–18 with Olson–Sens's note.

5–6[621–2] "Apollo, grant that Crobylus protect his household and possessions as a full-grown man." For the prayer that a boy grow into adulthood, cf. *599–600*n.   χεῖρας ὕπερθεν ἔχειν: cf. Solon, fr. 4.4 Παλλὰς Ἀθηναίη χεῖρας ὕπερθεν ἔχει.

CXVI. *Theodoridas* AP *6.222 (4 GP)*

Dedication of the rib of a fantastic sea-creature. The opening couplet, focusing on the beaching of the creature in rough seas, evokes and distorts the conventions of epitaphs for drowned sailors (cf. 1n.). The epigram thus initially appears to be a fictive epitaph for a beached sea creature (cf. e.g. Anyte *AP* 7.215) and so to play on cenotaphs for drowned sailors; but in the second couplet it unexpectedly becomes a dedication. The identity of the animal, too, is delayed until 3, where it is revealed as a gigantic, shark-like creature rather than a worm. This fictitious animal is discussed by Ael. *NA* 13.23, who reports that it is the largest of sea-creatures and terrifying even when beached on shore; he compares its locomotion to that of an oared boat (νήχονται ... πολλοῖς τοῖς ποσί ... καὶ ἐκεῖθεν οἰονεὶ σκαλμοῖς παρηρτημένοις ... ἑαυτοῖς ἐρέττουσαι). That account, though late, fits the contrast between the "twenty-oared" Iapygian ships and the "many-footed" scolopendra, underscored both by their positions at the opening and close of the epigram and by the fact that ships' oars could be represented as feet (e.g. Lyc. *Alex.* 23 ἰουλόπεζοι).

1[623] μυριόπουν σκολόπενδραν: the noun usually denotes a millipede or a slightly smaller, stinging marine worm (cf. Arist. *Hist. anim.* 505b13–17, 621a9). The implication that a small creature is at issue is consonant with μυριόπους, which is said by Σ Nic. *Ther.* 805–12 to be a type of worm.   **ὑπ' Ὠρίωνι** seems initially to refer to the constellation Orion and its role as marker of weather bad for sailing, but it subsequently emerges as a reference to Mt Orion (cited as a boundary of Iapygian territory by Pseudo-Scylax, *Periplus* 14).

2[624] Ἰαπύγων: residents of southern Italy (modern Apulia), comprising three groups, the Daunians, Peucetians, and Messapians.   **ἔβρασ'** "washed up." The rare verb, which some ancient critics thought lay behind βράσσων at *Il.* 10.226 (cf. Σ^A ad loc.), attracted the interest of Hellenistic poets (A.R. 2.323, Nic. *Alex.* 137, 359), especially Lycophron, who uses it frequently in this sense in the simplex (461) and, more often, in the compound (συν)εκβράσσω (e.g. 66, 377, 396, 717, 749, 1240).

3[625] βλοσυροῦ "terrifying"; cf. Ael. *NA* 13.23 ἐκβρασθεῖσαν μὲν θεάσασθαι οὐκ ἄν τις θρασύνοιτο.   **σελάχευς:** a generic term for sharks and rays.   **ἀνῆψαν** "dedicated" (cf. *Od.* 3.274, Lyc. *Alex.* 853).

4[626] δαίμοσι: unspecified, in imitation of real votive poems in which the divine recipient was unnamed because it was given elsewhere on the monument (e.g. *CEG* 769), or because the location made it obvious (e.g. *CEG* 327, 363). In Antipater's imitation, the dedication is to the δαίμοσι εἰναλίοις Palaemon and Ino (*AP* 6.223.7–8).   **βουφόρτων κοίρανοι . . . εἰκοσόρων:** i.e. owners of large merchant ships; a grand circumlocution for "traders." βουφόρτος is a novel and unique adjective, probably meaning "filled with a lot of cargo," with βου- intensifying (cf. *Suda* β476 πολυφόρτων), rather than "cattle-carrying." εἰκόσοροι are twenty-oared cargo ships (cf. Dem. 35.10, 18).

CXVII. *Theodoridas* AP 7.406 (14 GP)

A mock epitaph for Euphorion (cf. p. 224). The poem formally resembles the many Hellenistic epigrams honoring dead poets, but here the implication that Euphorion was buried in Athens as an initiate in the Mysteries gives way to a sexual joke whose point reaches a climax with the final word, which calls attention to his status as a lover. Dickie (1998: 54–8) argues that the poem is a literal tribute honoring his status as an Eleusinian initiate, but Crates *AP* 11.218.2–4 similarly deploys obscene puns to mock his interest in sex. It is none the less unclear whether the

poem should be understood as hostile toward him or as a mocking tribute
to an admired poet (cf. Cairns 2016: 144–5).

1[627] ὁ . . . ποῆσαι: an ambiguous phrase admitting the positive sense
"the one who knows how to create extraordinary poetry" (cf. Thgn.
769–70 χρὴ Μουσῶν θεράποντα καὶ ἄγγελον, εἴ τι περισσὸν | εἰδείη, σοφίης μὴ
φθονερὸν τελέθειν, Simylus *SH* 728) and also "the one who knows how to
do/create excessive things," whether in reference to overly fussy poetry
or to unusual sexual activity.

2[628] Πειραϊκοῖς . . . σκέλεσιν: the primary reference is to the Long Walls
(σκέλη; e.g. D.S. 13.107.4) connecting Athens to the Piraeus, but the language is also appropriate to the legs of a lover. The adjective, though normal in form (Steph. Byz. π85), is not usually applied to the Walls, and has
here been deployed to evoke the use of πειράω in the sense "attempt to
seduce"; the association of the Piraeus (and other ports) with prostitutes
may also be operative (cf. Ar. *Peace* 165 with Olson's note).   **κεῖται** suits
a corpse and a lover lying in bed.

3[629] μύστηι ῥοιήν seems initially to refer to the ritual importance
of pomegranates: the fruit played an important role in the myth of
Persephone (*HHDem.* 372), and initiates in the Eleusinian Mysteries were
forbidden to consume it. Retrospectively, however, the phrase may be
reinterpreted as referring to Euphorion's sexual activity, here couched
as participation in the "rites" of Aphrodite (cf. the obscene double entendre at Ar. *Ach.* 747, 764 χοίρους μυστικάς). For the sexual implications of
the pomegranate, cf. Ar. fr. 623 ὀξυγλύκειάν τἄρα κοκκιεῖς ῥόαν (parodying
Aesch. fr. 363), where the seeding of fruit is a metaphor for destruction
of a hymen (cf. "cherry" in English).   **μῆλον:** apples are a common
metaphor for breasts (e.g. Ar. *Lys.* 155–6, *Eccles.* 903).   **ἀπάρξαι** "offer,"
in a generalized sense without the more usual implication of a gift of first-
fruits (cf. Jim 2011).

4[630] μύρτον: the myrtle-berry was slang for female genitalia (cf. Hsch.
μ1926).   **ζωὸς ἐών:** a common Homeric juncture (e.g. *Il.* 2.699,
17.153); cf. Tyrt. fr. 10.29–30 ἐρατὸς δὲ γυναιξὶ | ζωὸς ἐών.   **ἐφίλει:** pos-
sible senses include "he loved (them)," "he kissed (them)" and "he was a
lover."

ALCAEUS OF MESSENE

The Greek Anthology contains twenty-two epigrams by Alcaeus;
some are falsely ascribed in the lemmata to "Alcaeus of Mytilene,"

the archaic lyric poet. Fragments corresponding to Alcaeus *AP* 9.588 are preserved in *P.Tebt.* 3.13–20. Porphyry ap. Eus. *Praep. ev.* 10.2.23 records that Alcaeus wrote abusive iambs as well as epigrams, and assigns to him a parodic work attacking the historian Ephorus for plagiarism; that attack probably had some political significance (Momigliano 1942: 57). One poem features the athlete Clitomachus, victorious at Olympia in 216 and 212; another the citharode Pylades, whose activity includes a performance of the *Persians* of Timotheus in 205. An epigram critical of Philip V of Macedon can be dated to the period 197–191; for Alcaeus' relationship to Philip, see CXVIII introductory n. His political poems include several set at a symposium. He also composed erotic, ecphrastic, funerary, and dedicatory epigrams (all probably fictive).

Alcaeus engages in innovative ways with earlier poetry, including epigrammatists such as Asclepiades, Leonidas, and Callimachus (cf. Bonsignore 2013–14: 22–6), and he uses language of various stylistic registers from a range of genres. Like Perses and Anyte, he draws on Homeric language more directly than do Asclepiades and Callimachus, though he rarely reuses it without variation. Alcaeus is strict in his observance of "Callimachean" restrictions on the hexameter; only Meyer's First Law is infringed (cf. Introduction section 4h[i], Magnelli 2007: 181).

CXVIII. Alcaeus AP 9.518 (1 GP)

Zeus is warned to prepare for an assault on Olympus by Philip V. The theme of the epigram – the relationship between a Macedonian king on earth and Zeus on Olympus – has its roots in XII, where a statue of Alexander by Lysippus seems to be about to announce that Alexander holds the earth under his sway but that Zeus should keep Olympus; a similar distinction is drawn by an anonymous epigram celebrating a Thracian victory by Philip, *APl* 6. Both those poems contrast the king's power on earth with Zeus's sway over the heavens. In *APl* 6, however, Philip's glory is said *almost* to have reached the heavens (ὁ δόξα πάλαι θείων ἄγχι βέβακε θρόνου), whereas in Alcaeus, Philip is on the verge of challenging Zeus's sovereignty on Olympus itself.

This fact is important for gauging the tone of the epigram. Elsewhere Alcaeus scathingly attacks Philip (cf. *AP* 7.247, *APl* 5, *AP* 9.519), but some take this epigram as sincere flattery and suppose that it belongs to an earlier period in his career. The epigram does not claim, however, that Philip will be able to conquer Olympus, only that Olympus should prepare for his assault, and its evocation of the doomed Otus and

Ephialtes (cf. 2n.) suggests that his ambitions will meet with failure. It is, moreover, an encomiastic trope that Hellenistic rulers ascend to the heavens on their death, and the final verse may thus be understood as bitingly ironic.

There are points of contact with adesp. *AP* 6.171, on the Colossus of Rhodes (1 ~ *AP* 6.171.1 αὐτῶι σοὶ πρὸς Ὄλυμπον ἐμακύναντο κολοσσόν, 3–4 ~ *AP* 6.171.8 πάτριος ἐν πόντωι κἢν χθονὶ κοιρανία). Most have considered Alcaeus the borrower, but this is uncertain (cf. Jones 2014: 45). Alpheus of Mytilene adapts the epigram in a poem (*AP* 9.526) celebrating, apparently without irony, Roman dominion of the entire world. For further discussion of Alcaeus' relationship to Philip, see Edson 1948, Vertsetis 1988: 132–4, Bonsignore 2013–14: 30–66.

1[631] μακύνου τείχη "raise your walls" rather than "extend your walls." μῆκος is a standard term for height, including that of buildings and walls (e.g. Ar. *Birds* 1130, *IG* ii² 1682), and the verb μηκύνω has this sense at adesp. *AP* 6.171.1 (cf. introductory n.). Olympus is already conventionally μακρός; cf. *Il.* 8.410, 15.193.

2[632] ἀμβατά "accessible" < ἀναβαίνω. The adjective in its context evokes *Od.* 11.315–16, where Otus and Ephialtes are said to have desired to stack Mt Ossa and Mt Pelion on Olympus, ἵν' οὐρανὸς ἀμβατὸς εἴη; they are killed by Apollo. The implication is that a similar fate awaits Philip's arrogance. Cf. Pi. *Pyth.* 10.27 ὁ χάλκεος οὐρανὸς οὔ ποτ' ἀμβατὸς αὐτῶι. **χαλκείας ... πύλας:** cf. *Il.* 1.426 Διὸς ποτὶ χαλκοβατὲς δῶ, 17.425 χάλκεον οὐρανόν.

3[633] χθών ... πόντος: that a ruler controlled both land and sea was a conventional idea in Hellenistic encomia; cf. Theocr. 17.91–2 θάλασσα δὲ πᾶσα καὶ αἶα | καὶ ποταμοὶ κελάδοντες ἀνάσσονται Πτολεμαίωι, Call. *h.* 4.166–8.

3–4[633–4] ὑπὸ σκήπτροισι Φιλίππου | δέδμηται reverses *Il.* 6.159 Ζεὺς γάρ οἱ ὑπὸ σκήπτρωι ἐδάμασσε, where Zeus is explicitly represented as responsible for the territorial conquests of human kings; cf. A.R. 3.353, 395. The σκῆπτρον marks its bearer as a representative of a god (cf. West on Hes. *Th.* 30), and the implication that Zeus's dominion too will come under the scepter of Philip is thus paradoxical. Plural σκῆπτρα for "royal scepter" is especially characteristic of tragedy; cf. Chiasson 1982: 159–60. **λοιπά ... ὁδός:** the ordinary way for Macedonian rulers to ascend to Olympus was to die (cf. Theocr. 17.16–19). The image was much developed by Roman poets; cf. Virg. *Georg.* 1.24–5, 503–4, Hor. *Odes* 1.2.45–9, Ov. *Met.* 15.868–70, and with similar tonal ambiguity, the address to Nero at Lucan, *BC* 1.45–7 *te, cum statione peracta | astra petes serus, praelati regia caeli | excipiet gaudente polo.* The road to Olympus or to the heavens in general is a conventional image; cf. Sappho, fr. 27.12, Hegesander, fr. 9, [Luc.] *Dem. Enc.* 50.

CXIX. *Alcaeus* AP 7.247 (4 GP)

On the dead at the battle of Cynoscephalae. The epigram allegedly irritated the victorious Roman general, T. Quinctius Flamininus, because it awarded credit to the Aetolians in spite of their poor behavior at the conclusion of the battle (Plut. *Flam.* 9). The version preserved in the manuscripts of the Anthology lacks lines 3–4, which are transmitted only by Plutarch. Those verses are not easily explicable as a later addition. More probably, they were in the original version and were subsequently removed by Alcaeus himself in response to Flamininus' displeasure. This alteration would be consonant with the reuse of line 4 in an epigram justifying the invasion of Greece as an act of liberation (*APl* 5). A Latin version (*Epigrammata Bobiensia* 71) is six lines long but does not credit the victory to the Aetolians (for the problem of its textual history and the nature of its model, see Kuijper 1972, Mondin 2011–12, Bonsignore 2013–14: 54–5). Philip V is said (Plut. *Flam.* 9.4) to have composed a distich parodying the opening couplet (ἄφλοιος καὶ ἄφυλλος, ὁδοιπόρε, τῶιδ᾽ ἐπὶ νώτωι | Ἀλκαίωι σταυρὸς πήγνυται ἠλίβατος "barkless and leafless, a crucifix stretching to the sun is fixed here to Alcaeus on this ridge"); another, perhaps related, couplet attacking the poet is preserved as adesp. *AP* 9.520 (cf. Cameron 1995: 100–2).

Formally, the poem resembles epigrams for people who have died at sea and been washed up and left unburied on shore (e.g. XLI introductory n.). Here the unburied dead speak in the conventional language of epitaphs for the mass casualties of battles (cf. 1–2n.); part of the conceit is that the speakers address a passerby not from the tomb, but from the plain on which they lie rotting.

Epic diction and phraseology contribute to the larger distinction between the heroic Macedonian dead and the cowardly Philip. The predominantly epic/Ionic dialect suits the Homeric background; in line 6 θοᾶν, in a context without epic resonance, is an isolated Doricism; the related epigram *APl* 5 has more Doric forms.

1–2[635–6] The Macedonian dead of Cynoscephalae lay unburied until the year 191 (Livy 36.8, App. *Syr.* 16).   ἄκλαυστοι καὶ ἄθαπτοι: a

Homeric phrase, recalling the verse-opening of *Od.* 11.54 ἄκλαυτον καὶ
ἄθαπτον (of the body of Elpenor), a line which Callistratus is said to
have athetized; cf. *Il.* 22.386, *Od.* 11.72 ἄκλαυτον ἄθαπτον. It is uncertain whether Alcaeus wrote ἄκλαυστοι or ἄκλαυτοι: both forms appear in
Homeric manuscripts (cf. Eust. on *Od.* 11.54, 1.399.32-3 Stallbaum); the
former is the vulgate reading.   τῶιδ᾽ ἐπὶ νώτωι | Θεσσαλίας "on this
Thessalian hill." It seems likelier that the phrase was designed as a variation of ἐπὶ τύμβωι, a Homeric clausula (*Il.* 11.371; cf. Thgn. 1203) that
was frequently reused in Hellenistic epigrams (e.g. Perses *AP* 7.445.3,
Antip. *AP* 7.353.1), than that Alcaeus wrote ἐπὶ τύμβωι in order to treat
the place where the dead lie unburied as a sort of figurative tomb. νώτωι
| Θεσσαλίας may phonetically evoke the common Homeric ἐπ᾽ εὐρέα νῶτα
θαλάσσης (*Il.* 2.159, etc.).   τρισσαὶ κείμεθα μυριάδες: though Livy cites
a similar figure (33.10), the number is almost certainly inflated for encomiastic purposes (cf. Plut. *Flam.* 8-9); the effect is to locate the poem in
the tradition of epitaphs honoring victims of major battles such as the one
cited by Hdt. 7.228.1 for the Greeks who died at Marathon (μυριάσιν ποτὲ
τῇδε τριηκοσίαις ἐμάχοντο | ἐκ Πελοποννάσου χιλιάδες τέτορες). Cf. Antip. *AP*
7.246.2, on the Persian dead at Issus (Περσῶν κείμεθα μυριάδες).

3-4[637-8] The couplet resembles the end of an oracle reported by
Pausanias (7.8.9) and Appian (*Mac.* fr. 2). In Pausanias' version, the
Macedonian defeat is attributed to forces from the west and the east:
"You Macedonians who take pride in your Argead kings, Philip's rule
will be both a benefit and a pain for you; for the first Philip will make
you lords over cities and peoples, but the younger one will destroy all
your honor when he is conquered by men from the west and the east"
(δμηθεὶς ἑσπερίοισιν ὑπ᾽ ἀνδράσιν ἠώιοις τε). Appian's version attributes
Philip's defeat only to westerners (δμηθεὶς δ᾽ ἑσπερίοισιν ὑπ᾽ ἀνδράσιν ἐνθάδ᾽
ὀλεῖται). That this version avoids giving credit to easterners (i.e. Attalus'
Pergamene forces) may reflect a desire to avoid irritating a Roman audience. The historical realities that underlie the oracle are uncertain; if it
was really issued before the battle, Alcaeus is probably alluding to its language and content.   δμηθέντες: whatever its relationship to the oracle
received by Philip, the phrase perhaps resonates against *633-4* (of Philip)
χθὼν ὑπὸ σκήπτροισι . . . δέδμηται.   ἠδέ: a markedly epic conjunction.
οὓς Τίτος εὐρείης ἤγαγ᾽ ἀπ᾽ Ἰταλίης: the phrase recurs with καί for οὓς at *APl*
55, on Titus' liberation of the Greeks. It evokes epic relative clauses such
as *Il.* 15.530-1 τόν ποτε Φυλεὺς | ἤγαγεν ἐξ Ἐφύρης, ποταμοῦ ἄπο Σελλήεντος.

5[639] Ἠμαθίηι: properly the area of the central Macedonian plain that
included the capital Pella, but here as often (e.g. Simias, fr. dub. 22.6)

a synecdoche for Macedonia and its king. μέγα πῆμα: a Homeric expression (e.g. *Il.* 3.50, 9.229), mostly in this verse-position.

5–6[639–40] τό . . . ἐλαφρότερον: the brevity with which Philip's flight is described suits its speed and contrasts with the greater focus on the sacrifice of his troops. τό . . . | πνεῦμα means "that famous (κεῖνο) bluster of Philip," but is tantamount to "that bold Philip," a sardonic, high-style periphrasis formed on the model of Homeric expressions such as σθένος Ἰδομενῆος (*Il.* 13.248); the grandiosity of the phrase matches the arrogance attributed to Philip. For πνεῦμα suggesting "spirit, arrogance," cf. the use of πνέω at Pi. *Pyth.* 10.44 θρασείαι δὲ πνέων καρδίαι. Deer are timid animals, and the comparison implies cowardice on Philip's part; cf. *526*. ἐλαφρός was regularly explained as deriving from ἔλαφος, and the etymological figure is thus tantamount to "more deer-quick than quick deer."

CXX. Alcaeus AP 7.55 (12 GP)

On the burial of Hesiod, washed and entombed by the Nymphs and given funeral honors by shepherds. The washing of Hesiod's corpse (1–2) is picked up by the reminiscence of his initiation in the final couplet, with the Nymphs' springs balanced by those of the nine Muses (2 Νύμφαι κρηνίδων . . . ἀπὸ σφετέρων ~ 5–6 Μουσέων | . . . καθαρῶν . . . λιβάδων). Both these couplets depict Hesiod in conspicuously Hellenistic terms, the first casting him as a bucolic/Theocritean figure washed by the Nymphs from the springs of a *locus amoenus*, the second evoking his initiation by the Muses as represented in Callimachus' *Aetia*. The couplets, representing the conclusion and initiation of Hesiod's literary activities, frame his poetic career while suggesting two different if complementary poetic modes.

1–2[641–2] The account of Hesiod's burial includes conventional features of a *locus amoenus*, including shade and spring water (cf. VIII introductory n.) and so suits his characterization as a bucolic poet (see below). The spondaic rhythm of the first hemistich of 2 is solemn. Λοκρίδος: Hesiod is said to have been killed and buried in Locris, at Oeneon (Thuc. 3.96.1) or Oenoe (*Certamen* pp. 224–36 Allen). Subsequently his bones were transferred to Orchomenos (Mnas. *AP* 7.54.1–3, Plut. *Mor.* 162c). ἐν νέμεϊ σκιερῶι: in a different verse position at *Il.* 11.480, a disputed line in which Zenodotus read γλαφυρῶι for σκιερῶι. Νύμφαι: Nymphs associated with springs (*Od.* 17.240, Theocr. 1.22 with Hunter's note) are the patrons and inspirers of poets in bucolic: cf. Theocr. 7.91–3, a passage modeled on Hes. *Th.* 22–3 but with the Nymphs rather than the Muses as inspiring deities (Fantuzzi in Fantuzzi and Hunter 2004:

153–4).   **κρηνίδων**: a rare diminutive of κρήνη, found in earlier literature at Eur. *Hipp.* 208, of a pure spring, and at Call. fr. dub. 751 Pf.

3[643] ὑψώσαντο: the verb may refer to architectural construction (e.g.
IG v.2 268.45) but, along with its compounds, may also be used of the
production of literary grandeur; cf. *543*n. Here it may be read against
ancient attempts to define Hesiod's "sweet" poetry in opposition to the
sublime style of Homer (cf. Hunter 2014: 282–315), a distinction which
the poem confounds.

3–4[643–4] γάλακτι . . . μέλιτι: libations (χοαί) offered to the dead in
literature often include milk; cf. *105*, Aesch. *Pers.* 611, Soph. *El.* 895 with
Finglass's note. This was frequently mixed with a variety of other liquids,
including honey (cf. Eur. *Or.* 115). For ξανθῶι . . . μέλιτι, cf. Simon. *PMG*
88, Emped. 31 B fr. 128.7, Philox. *PMG* 836b.37.   **αἰγῶν**: with γάλακτι;
cf. Hes. *WD* 590 γάλα τ' αἰγῶν.   **ἔρρανᾰν**: i.e. sprinkled a drink offering;
cf. *105*.

5[645] τοίην . . . γῆρυν: i.e. Hesiod's song has the qualities of honey
(cf. μελίγηρυς, e.g. *Od.* 12.187).   **ἀπέπνεεν**: commonly used of smells
but here with special resonance, since the Muses of the *Theogony* inspire
Hesiod by blowing *into* (ἐνέπνευσαν) him their divine voice (31), which he
is now represented as blowing *out* in performance (cf. Pi. *Pyth.* 4.11, of
Medea's prophecy; Diosc. *AP* 7.407.3). The imperfect is appropriate to
Hesiod's composition of numerous poems. Cf., e.g., "Simon." *AP* 7.24.9–
10 δρόσος ἧς ὁ γεραιὸς | λαρότερον μαλακῶν ἔπνεεν ἐκ στομάτων.   **ἔννεα
Μουσέων**: dependent on λιβάδων.

6[646] ὁ πρέσβυς: "Hesiodic old age" was proverbial (*App. prov.* 4.92, *Suda*
τ732, Scodel 1980), but the representation of earlier poets as old men
was also conventional (cf. *417–19*n.).   **καθαρῶν . . . λιβάδων**: a draught
from Hippocrene seems likely to have featured in the poetic initiation in
Callimachus' *Aetia*, but there is no such scene in extant Hesiodic poetry;
in the *Theogony*, the Muses give Hesiod only a branch of laurel. Here the
spring is described in Callimachean terms: cf. *h.* 2.111–12 ἀλλ' ἥτις καθαρή
τε καὶ ἀχράαντος ἀνέρπει | πίδακος ἐξ ἱερῆς ὀλίγη λιβὰς ἄκρον ἄωτον.

CXXI. Alcaeus AP 7.1 (11 GP)

On the death and burial of Homer. A number of cities made claims to
Homer; Ios' claim goes back at least to Bacchylides (fr. 48). The epigram
draws heavily on epic language and imagery (2, 3, 5, 6nn.), but avoids

reusing Homeric diction unchanged. It also plays on the contrast between Homer's banal death and his great reputation, here suggested by his assimilation to his own heroes (3n.). At the same time, by associating him with the Graces as well as the Muses as implicit sources of inspiration, the poem represents poetic composition in Hellenistic rather than Homeric terms and thus retrojects contemporary literary values upon the archaic past (cf. Bolmarcich 2002: 71). cxxiii, by Antipater, is an imitation.

1[647] The verse contrasts Homer's heroic subject matter with his un-heroic death. This is emphasized both by the placement of ἡρώων and Ὅμηρον and by the juxtaposition παῖδες Ὅμηρον. **Ἴωι ἔνι:** the anastro-phe evokes epic (e.g. *Il.* 7.221 Ὕληι ἔνι, *Od.* 9.505 Ἰθάκηι ἔνι). **παῖδες:** according to a story told in the biographical tradition (e.g. *Certamen* 321–39, pp. 237–8 Allen, Paus. 10.24.2), some boys who had been fishing posed a riddle to Homer on the shore of Ios, and having been unable to answer it, he slipped in the mud and died (cf. Levine 2002–3).

2[648] ἤκαχον: transitive ("caused grief"). This Homeric word is play-fully used in a pseudo-epitaphic account of a death. The grief of survi-vors would be more typical, just as in Homer a warrior's death aggrieves the family or larger community (e.g. *Il.* 16.822 δούπησεν δὲ πεσών, μέγα δ᾽ ἤκαχε λαὸν Ἀχαιῶν, *Od.* 15.357). Instead, Homer's grief is the cause of his death.   **ἐκ Μουσέων . . . ὑφηνάμενοι** plays on the literal and extended senses of γρῖφος and ὑφαίνω: the noun is properly a "fishing basket" but metaphorically a "riddle," while the verb may refer not only to actual weaving or to the arrangement of words in speech (e.g. the vulgate read-ing of *Il.* 3.212, where ἔφαινον is a variant) and song (cf. Pi. *Pyth.* 4.275, Call. fr. 26.5 with Harder's note); at Archestr. fr. 16.6–9 an actual fishing basket is described via a riddle. In a literal sense, then, the phrase refers to the boys' fishing, but figuratively they are cast as inspired poets (cf. Hes. *Th.* 94–5 ἐκ Μουσέων . . . | ἄνδρες ἀοιδοὶ ἔασιν) who have bested the poet of heroes with their song; cf. Bonsignore 2013–14: 75–7. For the association of children with poetic composition, cf. *Il.* 18.569–61, Call. fr. 1.5–6.

3[649] The involvement of the Nereids in Homer's funeral rites mirrors the roles played by them and Thetis in lamenting the deaths of Patroclus (*Il.* 18.35–69) and Achilles, the latter mourned also by the Muses (*Od.* 24.47–9, 58–61).   **νέκταρι . . . ἐχρίσαντο:** the gods use nectar and ambrosia, alone or in combination, as unguents to preserve or immortal-ize dead humans (e.g. *Il.* 16.680, Theocr. 15.108, Bion, fr. 1.3 with Reed's note). The choice of nectar rather than ambrosia (perhaps a variation of *Il.* 16.680 χρῖσέν τ᾽ ἀμβροσίηι) reflects the association of the notoriously sweet substance (e.g. *HHDem.* 49, Nossis *AP* 6.275.3–4) with poetic sweetness (cf. *171–2*n., Pi. *Olymp.* 7.7–8, fr. 94b.76). **εἰνάλιαι Νηρηίδες:** the noun and adjective are both Homeric, but their collocation is not.

4[650] ἀκταίηι . . . ὑπὸ σπιλάδι: the phrase continues the assimilation of Homer to a hero, since conspicuous tombs by the sea were a heroic honor (e.g. *Il.* 23.125–6, A.R. 1.585–6; cf. Pearce 1983). Homer was worshipped as a hero in various locations; cf. Clay 2004: 74–6, 136–43. σπιλάς, originally any rock over which the sea crashes, here implies "tomb," as at Antip. *AP* 7.2.3.

5[651] The line evokes *Il.* 13.350 ἀλλὰ Θέτιν κύδαινε καὶ υἱέα καρτερόθυμον, where the subject is Zeus, to whom Homer is here implicitly assimilated. Thetis' privileged place in the description of the *Iliad* reflects the Nereids' priorities. The Homeric *unicum* υἱέα is picked up by Hellenistic poets (cf. Call. *h.* 6.79, *AP* 7.520.3, A.R. 2.803, 4.1493, Rhianus, fr. 66.6). μόθος is an Iliadic word; it is absent from the *Odyssey*, and is otherwise rare and restricted to hexameter poetry.

6[652] Ἰθακοῦ . . . ἔργματα Λαρτιάδεω: a periphrasis for the *Odyssey* that avoids naming Odysseus directly. The expression uses un-Homeric forms of the hero's ethnic and patronymic, for which Homer has Ἰθακήσιος (*Od.* 2.246) and Λαερτιάδης (*Il.* 2.173, etc.). ἔργματα appears first in Hesiod and the Homeric Hymns.

7[653] ὀλβίστη νήσων: contrast *HHAp.* 38 καὶ Χίος, ἣ νήσων λιπαρωτάτη εἰν ἁλὶ κεῖται. **πόντωι** "in the sea."

8[654] The wholly spondaic opening of the pentameter suggests grandeur. **βαιή** "despite its small size." For the contrast between the dimensions of the burial site and the grandeur or physical size of its occupant, cf. Hermes. fr. 7.27–32, Kimmel-Clauzet 2017. The small size of the island that contains Homer matches the brevity of the epigram in which Alcaeus has reworked the language of his epics. **Μουσάων . . . Χαρίτων:** cf. 235–6n. The morphological and prosodic variation Μουσέων . . . Μουσάων appears early (Hes. *Th.* 93–4). **ἀστέρα:** the metaphorical use is common (e.g. Pi. *Pae.* 6.126, Call. fr. 67.8 Pf.), but here the source is perhaps Leon. *AP* 9.24, where the relationship of Homer to other poets is like that of sun and stars (1 ἄστρα . . . 3–4 Ὅμηρος | λαμπρότατον Μουσῶν φέγγος ἀνασχόμενος); cf. Antip. *AP* 7.6.3.

CXXII. Alcaeus AP 12.30 (8 GP)

The speaker reminds Nicander that time is fleeting and he will soon be unattractive. The poem resembles others in which the speaker adduces the *carpe diem* motif to seduce a resistant person (cf. xv introductory n.); here, the speaker's intentions are unmistakable, but his request is left discreetly unstated. That the arrival of body hair marks the end of a boy's desirability as an *eromenos* is implicit already at Thgn. 1327–8 (ὦ παῖ, ἕως ἂν ἔχῃς λείαν γένυν, οὔποτε σ᾽ αἰνῶν | παύσομαι) and becomes a *topos* in Greek epigram, which treats it either as an already present feature that renders a boy unappealing (cf. Tarán 1985: 90–4) or mentions it as an impending outcome, as here.

The basic observation with which the poem opens leads to two injunctions, introduced by ἀλλά and beginning after the bucolic diaeresis of the hexameter; the first of these (1) urges caution for the future, while the second, beginning in the equivalent position of the second hexameter (3), advises action for the present. Adesp. *AP* 12.39 seems to represent the unhappy outcome of a similar situation; cf. 1 ἐσβέσθη Νίκανδρος . . . 4 εἰσὶ τρίχες; cf. Tarán 1985: 95–100.

1[655] κνήμη: as often, the word (literally "shin") stands for the entire "leg."   **Νίκανδρε**: an extremely common name, here perhaps suggesting the boy's current power to "overcome men" and resonating poignantly against his future inability to do so (cf. Tarán 1985: 95).   **δασύνεται** "is getting hairy"; cf. Ar. *Eccles.* 66 and compounds like δασυπώγων, δασύπρωκτος, and esp. δασύπυγος (below).

1–2[655–6] φύλαξαι | . . . λάθῃ "take care that the same thing does not happen to your buttocks without you noticing." ταὐτό is a crasis of τὸ αὐτό.   **πυγή**: cf. *447*. At Σ^vet. Theocr. 5.112/113b, δασύπυγος is paired with ἐνῆλιξ "mature."

3[657] καὶ γνώσηι: the connective suggests that this might be not a future indicative but a rare thematic aorist middle subjunctive (cf. Manetho 2.51 γνώσασθαι), parallel to λάθῃ in the μή-clause. If so, the speaker frames the prospect that the boy will reach maturity without a companion as a contingency rather than a certainty, suggesting that if he grants his favors now, their partnership will continue into the future. In Strato's imitation (*AP* 12.186.6 καὶ τότ᾽ ἐπιγνώσῃ τί σπάνις ἐστί φίλων), where the rhetorical context is somewhat different, the verb is future indicative, and it may be here as well.   **φιλέοντος ὅση σπάνις**: σπάνις may denote an objective lack of something or a subjective desire for it, and the phrase thus allows "how complete is the lack of anyone to love you" and "how great is your (unfulfilled) desire for someone to love you"; cf. Bonsignore 2013–14: 154–5.   ἀλλ᾽ ἔτι καὶ νῦν: i.e. "but even at this late moment," a Homeric clausula (e.g. *Il.* 9.111, 259, 11.790) that suggests the loss of prior opportunities and the need to seize the moment.

4[658] ἀμετακλήτου "which cannot be called back," a prosaic word that perhaps evokes the use of καλέω and compounds in erotic and sympotic contexts (e.g. 56, Asclep. 13.3 Sens); just as it is impossible to retrieve one's youth, so too the boy, once past puberty, will not be sought by lovers.

ANTIPATER OF SIDON

Antipater of Sidon was probably born in the first third of the second century and seems to have died at an advanced age around 100 BCE; in Cicero's *De oratore* (3.194), set at the fictional date of 91, he is treated as a prodigious improviser of epigrams from the recent past. A late second-century Delian inscription containing an epigram by him confirms his connection to Sidon (*Inscr. Dél.* 2549 = 42 GP); Meleager's assertion that he was from Tyre (*AP* 7.428.14) may be a generic reference to his Phoenician background. See Argentieri 2003: 29–33.

Assessment of Antipater's work is complicated by difficulties of ascription. The Greek Anthology contains a number of epigrams by Antipater of Thessalonica, whose work, dating from the second half of the first century, was included in Philip's *Garland*. Forty-six epigrams are specifically attributed to the poet from Sidon, but more than twice that number are ascribed to "Antipater" without ethnic adjective; and for some that are assigned specifically to one or the other, the ethnic may be mistaken. In many cases, the position of a poem within sequences apparently drawn from one or the other *Garland* is a more helpful index than style or content.

Antipater's work is notable for the way it engages with the Greek artistic past. He composed a number of epigrams on earlier poets, especially of the archaic and classical period; some of these appropriate and confound "Callimachean" aesthetic polarities. He imitates a range of earlier poets, especially Leonidas. Rather than broadly innovating on a theme found in a model while gesturing at that model's language and structure, as poets like Callimachus, Posidippus, and other earlier epigrammatists typically do, Antipater often adheres very closely to his models' form and diction. Indeed, he seems to have been interested in variation as a poetic mode. In one series of epigrams, he treats Myron's famous cow from a range of perspectives (cf. CXXVII introductory n.). Another sequence consists of mock epitaphs in which the reader attempts to make sense of images accompanying the tomb; these poems explore the process of interpretation involved in reading epigrams (cf. CXXVI introductory n.).

Antipater's language is highly ornate (Argentieri 2003: 59–67, Magnelli 2007: 173–4). He follows but extends Leonidas' use of elaborate, recherché diction, and he deploys adjectives, many of them novel compounds, abundantly and even superfluously. Repetition of individual words is common, and individual conceits are sometimes reiterated within a poem. In his metrical practice Antipater shares with other epigrammatists a pronounced preference for dactyls and for the feminine caesura. Hexameters with more than two spondees are rare; no verse contains four. He adheres to Callimachean norms, especially in the second half of the verse. He is the first epigrammatist to avoid accented final syllables in the pentameter. See Argentieri 2003: 53–9.

CXXIII. Antipater of Sidon AP 7.2 (8 GP)

On the tomb of Homer. The epigram reworks Alcaeus CXXI, and similarly concludes by contrasting the small size of Homer's resting place with the greatness of his poetry. Here the identification of the island with the epigram is particularly striking: the speaker claims to be the sole heir to Homeric inspiration, and demonstrates this by producing a recast and miniaturized version of the *Iliad*. The final couplet, in which the speaker adduces a story found in Callimachus, sets up an implicit analogy between the epigram itself and the *Aetia*. The recast version of the *Iliad* in 5–8 may thus be read against the backdrop of Callimachus' refusal in the *Aetia* prologue to produce a long poem on kings and heroes.

1[659] μερόπων "mortals"; objective genitive.   Πειθώ "Persuasive Charm" (cf. Σ *Od.* 8.170, of the admiration people feel for the man whom the gods have endowed with speech: "they delight in looking at him διὰ τὴν ἐκ τῶν λόγων πειθώ); there is a suggestion of poetic authority (cf. Aesch. *Ag.* 106).   μέγα στόμα: the expression most obviously refers to the size and grandeur of the Homeric poems, but the evocation of *Il.* 10.8 πτολέμοιο μέγα στόμα πευκεδανοῖο, where the phrase was understood by the D-scholia to refer to the "beginning" of the war, perhaps suggests Homer's primacy in the literary tradition.

2[660] Μαιονίδεω: Homer, thought to be son of Maeon (cf. Hellanicus *FGrH* 4 F 5b–c); the identification of the poet by patronymic alone has a Homeric flavor (e.g. *Il.* 1.223–4), as does the synizesis in the final syllable (e.g. *Il.* 1.1).

3[661] ναοῖτις is extremely rare.   Ἴου σπιλάς: see 650n.

4[662] ἐν ἐμοὶ ... ἔλιπεν "he left his divine breath in me and no other."
Beyond endorsing Ios' claim to Homer's body, the passage tendentiously
asserts that the speaker, and by implication the poem, is sole heir to
Homer's inspired voice.   ἱερὸν ... πνεῦμα: i.e. the inspiration that he
has received from the Muses; cf. Democr. 68 B 18 ποιητὴς δὲ ἅσσα μὲν ἂν
γράφηι μετ' ἐνθουσιασμοῦ καὶ ἱεροῦ πνεύματος, καλὰ κάρτα ἐστίν.

5–8[663–6] Having claimed to be the recipient of Homer's inspired voice,
the speaker gives its own version of the *Iliad*, evoking but varying Homeric
language and diverging on one important detail. The events enumerated
may be read as covering, in order, important moments in the plot, beginning with Zeus's agreement to favor the Trojans (*Il.* 1.528 νεῦσε Κρονίων)
and the resulting strife on Olympus, followed by the Trojan attack on the
Greek ships, and concluding with the death and attempted mutilation of
Hector.   νεῦμα ... παγκρατές: neither the noun nor the adjective is
Homeric.   Αἴαντος ... βίαν: the form of the periphrasis is familiar in
Homer (cf. *Il.* 17.187 Πατρόκλοιο βίη, 18.117 βίη Ἡρακλῆος), though never
used of Ajax.   ναύμαχον: a reference to Ajax' defense of the Greek
ships in the *Iliad*, especially 15.677, where he brandishes a ξυστὸν μέγα
ναύμαχον ἐν παλάμηισι.   τὸν ... δρυπτόμενον "and Hector, torn to his
bones by Achilles' Thessalian horses on the Dardanian plain." The claim
pointedly diverges from the *Iliad*, where the gods protect Hector's corpse
so that Achilles "might not tear him by dragging him" (*Il.* 23.187, 24.21
ἀποδρύφοι ἑλκυστάζων); Lyc. *Alex.* 266–7 similarly asserts that the corpse
was desecrated.   Ἀχιλλείοις ... πώλοις is resonant of tragedy; cf. Soph.
Ajax 41 Ἀχιλλείων ὅπλων, Eur. *Andr.* 1169–70 τὸν Ἀχιλλεῖον | σκύμνον, *IA*
241 Ἀχιλλείου στρατοῦ.   Φαρσαλίσιν: i.e. Thessalian, with reference to
Achilles' home town of Phthia (cf. Eur. *Andr.* 16).   ὀστέα: the accusative indicates extent.

9[667] εἰ ... ἴσθ' ὅτι: the protasis involves an ellipsis ("If (you are both-
ered by the fact that) I, though small, hold one so great, know that
...").   ὀλίγα: cf. 654n. βαιή.

9–10[667–8] κεύθει | ... Ἴκος: probably a reference to Callimachus'
treatment of Peleus' death and burial on Icus in the *Aetia* (frr. 178.24,
185a Harder). The speaker here has information not included in the
Homeric poems, where Odysseus tells the shade of Achilles that he has no
knowledge about the death of his father; cf. Harder on Call. fr. 178.23–
6.   βραχύβωλος: cf. 506n. The adjective is first attested here; contrast

Homeric ἐρίβωλος (i.e. "with large clods"; cf. Hsch. ε5806), referring to
fertility rather than size.

CXXIV. Antipater of Sidon AP 7.34 (18 GP)

A fictitious epitaph for Pindar. The epigram plays on the Pindaric association of poetic composition with other forms of craftsmanship and concludes with an auditory ecphrasis that evokes epigrams describing art. The
poem is connected with Antip. APl 305, lemmatized without ethnic in the
Anthology and attributed to Antipater of Thessalonica by GP but probably
by the Sidonian poet (cf. Argentieri 2003: 166–7); there, the poet is similarly treated as a trumpet and associated with bees. Pindar, whose work
exerted a powerful influence on Callimachus and his programmatic language, is here praised in terms that evoke but confound the Callimachean
opposition between the "light" poetry that he admires and the "heavy"
poetry of his rivals, whom he associates with workers in bronze.

1–2[669–70] Pindar is identified first as an instrument that would have been
made of bronze, then as a bronze worker, and finally by name. The poem
may thus initially appear dedicatory; that it is nominally funerary emerges
at the end of 2.   σάλπιγγα: see 330n.   τὸν ... χαλκευτάν: an elevated,
almost Pindaric, phrase; cf. Nem. 3.4–5 μελιγράϋων τέκτονες | κώμων, Pyth.
3.113–14 ἐπέων κελαδεννῶν, τέκτονες οἷα σοφοὶ | ἅρμοσαν, Crat. 70.2 τέκτονες
εὐπαλάμων ὕμνων.   εὐαγέων: perhaps "pure" (cf. Xenophan. 21 B 1.13–
14 χρὴ ... θεὸν ὑμνεῖν ... μύθοις καὶ καθαροῖσι λόγοις) rather than "well-turned"
(< ἡγέομαι), an unusual sense ascribed to the adjective here by Suda ε3360;
elsewhere perhaps at Leon. AP 6.204.3, of a craftsman's plane. Antipater
appropriates for Pindar's heavy song a quality that Callimachus associates
with his own verse; cf. Cairns 2016: 150–1.   βαρύν is used of the poet/
trumpet in reference to the sound he produces (for βαρύς, cf. 525, 527);
contrast Callimachus' wish to be "the light one" (fr. 1.32).   χαλκευτάν
"bronze smith"; cf. Pi. Pyth. 1.86 "he forged (χάλκευε) his tongue on a true
anvil." In Antip. AP 7.409 (attributed to Antipater of Thessalonica in P
but probably by Antipater of Sidon), the description of Antimachus' verse
as "forged (χαλκευτόν) on the anvils of the Muses" (3) and the claim that
those with a "clear" ear will appreciate it probably respond to Callimachus'
criticism of Antimachus' work as οὐ τορόν (fr. 398).

3–4[671–2] ". . . hearing whose song, you would say that the swarm [i.e.
of bees who famously inspired Pindar] copied it from the Muses in the
marriage chambers of Cadmus." The implicit point is that Pindar's song

appears to the listener to be the Muses'. The passage, which has been variously understood, plays with ecphrastic tropes and develops the language
of craftsmanship introduced in 1–2. The object of ἀπεπλάσατο is Pindar's
song. The couplet is highly compressed and depends on knowledge of the
story that Pindar, who refers to himself as a bee (e.g. *Pyth.* 10.54), began
his career after bees flew upon him while he slept and formed wax against
his lips (Paus. 9.23.2; cf. *Vita Pindari*, p. 1.8–9 Drachmann, Philostr. *Im.*
2.12), an act that serves as a poetic initiation. The story is explicit in
Antip. *APl* 305.3–4. Ancient techniques for bronze-casting involved applying wax to a clay-form; the wax melted as the molten metal was poured
in; cf. *425*n. The bees' activity thus belongs to the same realm as that
of Pindar, a χαλκευτής.   εἰσαΐων φθέγξαιό κεν plays with the ecphrastic
convention of reporting what a viewer would say about an object after
seeing it (cf. *495–6*n.).   ἐν Κάδμου θαλάμοις: i.e. in Thebes, home of
Pindar, though with a specific reference to the Muses' performance at
the wedding of Cadmus and Harmonia. At *Pyth.* 3.88–91, Pindar reports
that those who heard (ἄϊον; cf. εἰσαΐων) that performance were the most
blessed of mortals. The implication is that Pindar's audience is equally
so.   ἀπεπλάσατο: literally, "took an impression of" it in wax.

CXXV. Antipater of Sidon AP 7.218 (23 GP)

An epitaph for Lais. The epigram reworks Asclep. *41 Sens, on
Archeanassa, by featuring a more famous and beautiful hetaera (3n.).
In the model, the speaker could be the dead woman's lover or her tomb
(cf. Thomas 1998); here the speaker is clearly the tomb, but it describes
its occupant in highly eroticized language. Gutzwiller 1998a: 255–7,
pointing to the epigram's insistence on the continued sensuality of the
tomb, reads it as reflecting nostalgia for a past lost with the destruction of
Corinth in 146 (cf. Antip. *AP* 9.151).

The poem is structured around a series of hyperbolic comparisons in the
first three couplets (2 ἁβροτέρην, 4 φαιδροτέρην, 6 πλείονες). The last of these
develops the first, in which Lais is said to be more luxurious than Aphrodite;
the claim in 5 that she is "the mortal Aphrodite," a status usually associated
with Helen, leads to a comparison between the number of suitors each of
the two mortal women attracted. That comparison plays on the ambiguous
representation of Helen as a virtuous bride or a harlot in the literary tradition; it elevates Lais and her customers to a heroic status that is humorously
undercut in the final couplet, where her sexual activity is treated as servile
(13 δούλην). The final point, that Lais's promiscuity has saved Greece from
conflict, entails a humorous comment on Helen: had she been (even) less
chaste, the Trojan War could have been avoided. Cf. Kanellou 2016.

1–2[673–4] ". . . the woman haughty with both gold and purple and with Eros as a companion, more luxurious than tender Aphrodite." The resemblance of the sumptuous clothing and jewelry of courtesans to the attire of the gods prepares for the comparison.   καὶ σὺν Ἔρωτι: Antipater may have known the famous "Sardanapalus epigram" (= Choeril. *SH* 335.4–5) in the form cited by Athenaeus (8.335e), κεῖν' ἔχω ὅσσ' ἔφαγον καὶ ἐφύβρισα καὶ σὺν ἔρωτι [μετ' ἔρωτος *alii*] | τέρπν' ἔπαθον. An allusion would account for the slightly awkward pairing of the phrase with what precedes.   θρυπτομένην entails the same combination of luxurious decadence and haughty conceit (e.g. Ael. *VH* 1.19) denoted by ἁβροτέρην at line end.   ἀπαλῆς: the adjective is common in erotic contexts.

3[675] Λαΐδ' ἔχω: cf. Asclep. *41.1 Ἀρχεάνασσαν ἔχω. At least two famous Corinthian courtesans bore the name Lais, and the many anecdotes about them in fifth-century and later comedy (cf. Strattis fr. 27 with Orth's note, Ar. *Wealth* 179) are inextricably intertwined.   πολιῆτιν: a rare feminine form of epic/Ionic πολιήτης (A.R. 1.867, Pos. 118.1 AB; cf. Eur. *Hipp.* 1126).   ἁλιζώνοιο Κορίνθου: cf. Call. fr. 384.9–10 ἁλιζώνοιο . . . | στείνεος (the Isthmus of Corinth), the only earlier attestation of the adjective. The reference to a woman's girdle is appropriate to the sensualized context.

4[676] Πειρήνης: the famous central fountain of Corinth.   λευκῶν . . . λιβάδων "clear waters"; in a difference sense, cf. A.R. 4.1735 (of milk) λευκῆισιν . . . λιβάδεσσι γάλακτος.

5[677] τὴν θνητὴν Κυθέρειαν: the hyperbolic praise is belied by the generic context; the "mortal" version of the goddess is already dead.

5–6[677–8] ἐφ' ἧς . . . Τυνδαρίδος "over whom there were more illustrious suitors than there were aiming to get Helen as a bride." The application of the Homeric formula μνηστῆρες ἀγαυοί (e.g. *Od.* 2.209) – used only of the suitors of the chaste Penelope – to the promiscuous hetaera humorously elevates Lais's customers to the status of epic nobility and equates marriage with a commercial transaction. ἐφ' ἧς is to be preferred to ἐφ' ἧι for the symmetry it creates with 9 ἧς ἔπι. GP, objecting to the prepositional phrase in a copulative sentence of this sort, proposed μνηστῆρες ἄγερθεν, which would be a reworking of the Homeric μνηστῆρες ἀγήνορες ἠγερέθοντο (*Od.* 17.65), with the substitution of a different epic form of the verb (cf. *Il.* 23.287).

7[679] ". . . reaping the benefit of her favors and purchased sex." The participle modifies Lais's suitors but the structure of the sentence elides the

distinction between them and Helen's suitors, and between the fees paid
to the former and the bride price given to the latter. δρεπτόμενοι evokes
Asclep. 41.3 Sens ἀποδρέψαντες and suggests the act of picking flowers, a
common sexual metaphor (e.g. Pi. *Pyth.* 9.109–11, Aesch. *Supp.* 663–4,
Archipp. fr. 50; cf. *142*). The present participle suggests the ongoing
character of the activity. For χάρις as a generic term for sexual favors, cf.
Henderson 1991: 160. The metonymic representation of sex as Ἀφροδίτην
(e.g. *Od.* 22.444) picks up other references to the goddess throughout
the poem.

8–10[680–2] These lines cap Asclep. *41.3–4 Sens, where Archeanassa is
said to be attractive even in old age; even Lais's corpse and tomb still smell
sweetly of sex. Lais' supposed tomb was still visible on the eastern edge of
Corinth in the time of Pausanias (2.2.4).   καί qualifies τύμβος.   ὑπ'
. . . κρόκωι "is redolent of sweet-smelling saffron." ὑπό + dative is unusual with ὄζω, which is typically accompanied by a genitive alone or as the
object of a preposition.   κηώεντι: a rare epic epithet, generally applied
to bedchambers (*Il.* 3.382, *Od.* 15.99).   ὀστεῦν: i.e. ὀστέον (cf. Leon.
AP 7.480.1, Diosc. *AP* 7.31.1); here, her skull.   ἄσθμα πνέουσι: though
the language is not unusual of smells, the reference to breath suggests
continued life after death.

11–12[683–4] The lamentation of the gods lends Lais the status of a hero
like Achilles, mourned by the Nereids and Muses, or like Adonis (cf. Bion,
Ep. Ad. 25–7).   ἄμυξε κάτα "scratched" her face in grief (cf. Theocr.
6.14 κατὰ δὲ χρόα καλὸν ἀμύξηι); tmesis with anastrophe of the preverb (=
κατάμυξε), a Homeric feature that contributes to the ennobling of Lais.
The second syllable of κατά is treated as heavy before ῥ- as in Homer (e.g.
Il. 21.147).   ῥέθος: see *593n.*   Ἀφρογένεια: see *579n.*   γοερὸν
λύζων "choking out mournful sobs"; cf. Ar. *Ach.* 690 with Olson's note.

13–14[685–6] "If she had not made her bed a common slave of profit,
Greece would have struggled for her sake, as for Helen."   εἰ δ' οὐ: the
Homeric use of οὐ rather than μή in the protasis (e.g. *Od.* 2.274) suits the
reference to the Trojan War.   πάγκοινον: the evocation of Aphrodite
Πάνδημος, who was associated with prostitution (cf. Philemon, fr. 3.8–9)
deflates the grandiose comparisons that precede: Lais is a common pros-
titute.   δούλην . . . κέρδεος: cf. Eur. *Hec.* 865 ἢ χρημάτων γὰρ δοῦλός ἐστιν
ἢ τύχης.   ἔσχε πόνον: an epic collocation (*Od.* 8.529, 13.423).

CXXVI. Antipater of Sidon AP 7.427 (32 GP)

An attempt to interpret the meaning of nine knucklebones on a stele.
The epigram, transmitted as part of a sequence by Antipater on similar

themes (cf. *AP* 7.423–6), reworks Leon. *AP* 7.422, in which the tomb is marked by a single knucklebone thrown on the least valuable roll, called Chios. It does so through a "window" rewriting of Alc. *AP* 7.429, which shares Leonidas as a model (cf. Gutzwiller 1998a: 267–71). In Leonidas the speaker, addressing the dead man by name in familiar terms (4 ἀγαθέ), contemplates two obvious (cf. 3 ἔοικεν) and literal explanations about the dead man's ethnicity and about his gaming habits, but rejects them in favor of the less obvious conclusion that the man died while drunk on Chian wine. Alcaeus deliberates between two ways of understanding a double phi as a symbol for the deceased's name; he first speculates that it could be understood as a mathematical representation for the name Chilias (φφ = 500 + 500) but then changes his mind and concludes that it is a rebus (i.e. a representation of a word by symbols) for Pheidis (i.e. φεῖ δίς); the poem ends with praise for the creator of the riddle.

Antipater combines elements from both poems. His speaker explicitly observes that the monument lacks an inscription, and like Alcaeus', he knows nothing about the deceased; he similarly concludes by praising the conceit of the monument. He draws the theme of gambling from Leonidas, but his speaker's interpretation follows a different course: he first canvasses an allegorical reading in which knucklebone-throws signify the vanity of power and youth, but he ultimately arrives at a literal one in which the symbols provide the basic information expected of an epitaph. In the final couplet, however, the tomb's symbolism adds a further metaphorical dimension in which the knucklebones suggest the randomness of human fate.

The epigram gives voice to the act of interpreting a monument and verbalizes the process involved in making sense of an epigram. The speaker, a passerby looking to identify the deceased by reading an inscription, must instead interpret non-verbal symbols; that these are paradoxically represented as engaging in speech reflects the mediation of the narrator who describes them. Goldhill (1994: 199–201) suggests that the poem analogizes the randomness of human fate, the throwing of knucklebones, and the process of reading and interpreting symbols, "aleatory all." Such an interpretation overstates the randomness of the speaker's interpretation: though his first, allegorical, suggestion is plausible in the abstract, he ultimately opts for one that reflects his understanding of generic expectations.

1[687] ἄ . . . νέκυν "Come, let me see what corpse this gravestone holds." The speaker initially imagines that he will be able to identify the deceased by inspecting the writing on the grave.   στάλα . . . ἔχει is a variation of the more common usage with the tomb as subject. The stele holds the deceased in the sense that it would ordinarily contain his name; there is no need to emend to ἐρεῖ.

2[688] The surface point is that the tomb bears no inscription (γράμμα; cf. Euph. 566), but the line plays on Alc. *AP* 7.429.2, where a double phi, "the only letter" inscribed on the stone (δισσάκι φεῖ μοῦνον γράμμα λέλογχε λίθος), is what the speaker must interpret.　ὕπερθε λίθου is inspired by Leonidas' ὑπὲρ λίθου but appears to have the unusual sense "on the face of the stone" rather than "above" it.

3[689] ἀστραγάλους: knucklebones are commonly found in Greek tombs and were associated with the dead; cf. *84*, Kurke 1999: 288–90.　πεπτηότας "fallen" (i.e. "thrown"); epic perfect participle of πίπτω. The word is as appropriate to dead bodies (e.g. *Od.* 22.384) as to dice and anticipates the analogy established in 13–14.　πίσυρες: gambling with four knucklebones was standard Roman practice; the evidence from the classical and early Hellenistic periods suggests that it was usual for Greeks to gamble with five (Kidd 2017a).

4[690] Ἀλεξάνδρου . . . βόλον: nothing is known about the throw called "Alexander" (cf. Hsch. α2869), though it must have had a high value.

4–6[690–2] μαρτυρέουσι . . . μανύει: forensic language casting the speaker as a juror making sense of testimony.　οἱ δέ: i.e. a second group of four knucklebones.　τὸ τᾶς νεότατος ἐφάλικος ἄνθος "the flower of late youth," a rewriting of the common νέον ἄνθος ἥβης and a gloss on the name of the throw, "Ephebe," which is otherwise unknown. ἐφῆλιξ, elsewhere unattested in literature, anticipates the prefix of ἔφηβον.　εἷς . . . ἀφαυρότερον "one, the Chios, announces a less distinguished outcome." Chios was the name of the lowest-valued face, worth a single point; because of the shape of the knucklebone, it was also least likely to be thrown, and thus particularly unlucky.

7–8[693–4] For the tomb as a messenger, cf. 259–60n. The symbols "speak" in elevated language.　ἀγγέλλοντι: Doric third-person plural present indicative.　ὁ σκάπτροισι μεγαυχής "grandiose in his royal power"; the speaker initially suspects a reference to Alexander the Great.　θάλλων ἥβαι: cf. Pi. fr. 171.1 κατὰ μὲν φίλα τέκν' ἔπεφνεν θάλλοντας ἥβαι.　τέρμα . . . ἔχει "ends in naught"; cf. Eur. *Hec.* 622 ὡς ἐς τὸ μηδὲν ἥκομεν, Hdt. 1.32.1 ἡ δ' ἡμετέρη εὐδαιμονίη . . . ἀπέρριπται ἐς τὸ μηδέν.

9–10[695–6] are modeled on Leon. *AP* 7.422.5–6 "Or are these guesses not even close? . . . yes, I believe, with this one we've come close" (ἢ τὰ μὲν οὐδὲ σύνεγγυς; . . . ναὶ δοκέω, τῶιδε προσηγγίσαμεν). The metaphor of the interpreter as archer shooting straight at his target picks up and reverses the Pindaric image of the poet as bowman, as at *Olymp*. 2.83–5, where Pindar claims to be shooting arrows which speak to those who understand but generally need interpreters. **Κρηταιεύς . . . ὀϊστοβόλος:** Cretan archers and their bows were famous. The rare noun ὀϊστοβόλος sets up a contrast between the speaker's straight shot and the gambler's random throw (βόλον; cf. Leon. *AP* 7.422.4 πλειστοβόλος).

11–12[697–8] The speaker's revised interpretation takes the form of an epitaph providing the identifying information he sought at the beginning of the poem. **ἧς:** see *91–2*n. **λελογχώς:** the verb appears in epitaphs (cf. Alc. *AP* 7.429.2, Euph. *566*), but here the implication of chance is particularly appropriate. **ὤλετ' ἐν ἁλικίαι:** the speaker uses the conventional language of epitaph; cf. *CEG* 662a.2 ἐν ἡλικίαι πνεῦμ' ἔ[λ] ιπεν βιότου.

13–14[699–700] "How well did someone say with unspeaking knuckle-bones the (idea of) the young man dead at random and life's breath gambled!" A reworking of Alc. *AP* 7.429.9–10 αἰνετὸς οὐκ δισσοῖο καμὼν αἴνιγμα τύποιο, | φέγγος μὲν ξυνετοῖς ἀξυνέτοις δ' ἔρεβος, with a form typical of ecphrastic epigrams in which a viewer praises the creation of a realistic image (e.g. Leon. *APl* 182.5–6). **ἄκριτα:** probably implying the arbitrariness of fate, though the ambiguity of the word, whose senses include "without judgment," "at random" (cf. Theodoridas *AP* 7.439.1) or "in a way that it is impossible to judge," "uncertain" (e.g. Thuc. 4.20.2, Arist. *Meteo.* 361b30), ironically undercuts the speaker's confidence in his interpretation; cf. Goldhill 1994: 200. GP suggest "rashly," but see next n. The word plays by sound (though not prosody) on Leonidas' speculation that the deceased marked by the Chios throw has died ἐν ἀκρήτωι, "drunk on unmixed wine." **κυβευθέν** refers broadly to gambling without any reference to a particular game; cf. Kidd 2017b. The point is probably that life is generally like a game of chance (cf. Alexis fr. 35 τοιοῦτο τὸ ζῆν ἐστιν ὥσπερ οἱ κύβοι with Arnott's n.; adesp. epica fr. 4.9–13, p. 79 Powell) rather than that the deceased has engaged in particularly risky behavior. **πνεῦμα** is occasionally so used in inscriptional epitaphs; e.g. *CEG* 662a.2, 646.2 πνεῦμα λιποῦσα. **ἀφθέγκτων . . . ἀστραγάλων:** unlike Alcaeus' symbols, whose interpretation depends on their pronunciation (see introductory n.), Antipater's are silent. **εἶπέ τις:** cf. *247*. The expression encompasses both the monument's creator and the speaker who has interpreted it in words, to whom the mask of anonymity has shifted now that the honorand has been identified.

CXXVII. Antipater of Sidon AP *9.720 (36 GP)*

On Myron's cow; for the theme, cf. xxx introductory n. This and the following four epigrams appear in the Anthology as a sequence, probably deriving, via Meleager's anthology, from a collection of Antipater's epigrams; AP 9.728, ascribed to "Antipater" without ethnic and separated from the others by three anonymous epigrams, may originally have belonged to the same group (cf. Gutzwiller 1998a: 247–50, Argentieri 2003: 140–2). Unlike Posidippus' ἀνδριαντοποιικά (cf. pp. 182–3), which produce the effect of passing through an epigrammatic gallery of different sculptures, Antipater's sequence treats a single work from different perspectives (cf. Gutzwiller 1998a: 246–50, Squire 2010). In each epigram, the relationship of the speaker to his addressee is unique. Individual poems develop and vary themes introduced earlier in the sequence. The first is the most closely modeled on Leonidas' epigram on the cow (xxx), and imagines that a living cow has been captured by the artist; the fourth picks up that idea, but represents the stone and metal that constrain the representation as independent from the artist. Similarly, in the second, the cow advises a calf that the artist has not endowed it with milk, but in the third, the speaker imagines that the statue nurses a calf. As a group, the poems explore the mimetic capacities and limitations of art, including sculpture and epigram.

The first poem plays with the contrafactual form of ecphrastic epigrams that claim that a representation would have fully captured its subject if a feature such as a voice had been added (cf. 92). Here, by contrast, the artist's activity is all that prevents the cow, here endowed with a voice, from joining the herd. As in the Leonidean model, the artist's role is to affix the speaker to a base, but unlike that poem, this epigram leaves unstated whether he was involved in the creation of the image in the first place.

2[702] The hemistichs are symmetrical, with ἄλλαις picked up by βουσίν and the verb νεμόμαν by its subject δάμαλις.

CXXVIII. Antipater of Sidon AP *9.721 (37 GP)*

Myron's cow addresses a confused calf; cf. cxxvii introductory n. The poem emphasizes art's ability to deceive and its limitations: art has not given the cow milk. In asking why the calf approaches and moos, the cow resembles the speakers of epitaphs for misanthropes who urge passersby to move on in silence. At the same time, the poem places the calf in the position of a viewer of art, and its mooing replaces expressions of aesthetic appreciation in ecphrastic contexts.

1[703] ἐς δὲ τί: Jacobs' emendation of transmitted τίπτε avoids a violation of Naeke's Law (Introduction section 4h[i]).

2[704] μαζοῖς: cf. *106*n. μαστόν.   **ἐνέθηκε:** the verb is used of Hephaestus forming scenes on the shield of Achilles (*Il.* 18.541, 550, 561, 607 ἐν δ' ἐτίθει).

CXXIX. Antipater of Sidon AP 9.722 (38 GP)

The speaker urges a cowherd not to disturb the cow, who is or will soon be nursing (cf. 2n.). That the reference is to Myron's statue (CXXVII introductory n.) emerges only from the poem's position in the series. Otherwise, it appears to be a piece of advice from one herdsman to another. The poem casts as a reality what the preceding epigram represented as impossible, but the implication that the sculpture has transcended the limitations of its material form is undercut by the evocation of epitaphs for misanthropes. That the heifer takes the place occupied in those poems by the tomb suggests its artificiality.

1[705] βουφορβέ: a rare word, principally attested in Euripides before the Hellenistic period (cf. *El.* 252, *IT* 237, 265, 462).   **παρέρχεο** evokes addresses to passersby in epitaphs.

2[706] συρίσδῃς: if correct, a rare example of a present subjunctive used prohibitively, but this like most other instances is easily amended (e.g. Eur. *IA* 1143 with Stockert's note), and Boissonade's συρίξῃς may be right.   **ὑπεκδέχεται** "is receiving." GP prefer P's ἀπεκδέχεται, "is awaiting," on the grounds that Myron did not sculpt a calf, but this is hyperrealistic.

CXXX. Antipater of Sidon AP 9.723 (39 GP)

On Myron's cow, who would be pasturing if not bound to the stone. The epigram shares the theme of CXXVII but here represents the physical media that constrain it as at odds with the artist, thus ignoring the reality that it was he who attached it to the stone.

1[707] ἁ μόλιβος: molten lead poured through holes in the feet of bronze statues secured them to their bases; cf. Mattusch 1996.   **κατέχει** is commonly used of the earth containing the body of the deceased in epitaphs (e.g. *670*).   **εἵνεκα ... σεῦ:** i.e. "as a result of your work." The protasis εἰ δὲ μή, i.e. if the lead did not constrain the statue, is implied.

2[708] πλάστα: see *423*n.   **λωτὸν καὶ θρύον** "clover and rush," recalling the plants burned by the banks of the Scamander at *Il.* 21.351 καίετο δὲ λωτός τε ἰδὲ θρύον ἠδὲ κύπειρον.

CXXXI. Antipater of Sidon AP 9.724 (40 GP)

On Myron's cow; cf. cxxvii introductory n. The epigram reworks Erinna xxi, where the point is that the absence of a voice distinguishes representation from reality. The viewer here suspects that this limitation will be transcended; the idea that the cow will moo varies the motif in which a representation of a human seems about to speak (cf. *49–50, 417–19*).

1[709] ἁ δάμαλις . . . μυκήσεται: cf. Herodas 4.32–3 τοὖργον, | ἐρεῖς, λαλήσει.

2[710] οὐχὶ μόνος: *sc.* πλάττει.   **πλάττεις:** the verb is a technical term for the formation of the mold used to craft a statue, but it may also denote the creation of a fiction (LSJ v). -ττ- is a feature of Attic.   **Μύρων:** the name, postponed to final position, may in context evoke the sound of a cow lowing (cf. Phld. *On Poems* 1.106.8, on μυκάομαι as onomatopoeic) and thus effects the vocalization that the speaker anticipates; cf. Squire 2010: 612.

PHANIAS

Almost nothing is known about the life of Phanias, whose work was included in Meleager's *Garland* (cf. *AP* 4.1.54), though his use of an apparently Latin word (Ath. 2.56a, Pliny, *NH* 12.130, 15.6) for olive, δρύππα (Greek δρυπεπής), suggests a date in the second century. The lemma of one poem calls him a γραμματικός. One of the eight extant epigrams is an erotic exhortation, modeled on poems such as cxxii, another a cenotaph; but the majority are dedicatory or para-dedicatory. Like the epigrams of Leonidas, these are characterized by their use of difficult, elaborate language, including many novel compound adjectives and rare nouns, to describe humble objects.

CXXXII. Phanias AP 6.307 (7 GP)

On a barber who has given up his trade to pursue Epicureanism, only to fail at philosophy. The poem seems initially to be one of the numerous epigrams (many by Leonidas) in which the dedications of professional implements by simple working people on the occasion of their retirement are described in elaborate, metaphorical language. At the halfway point of the poem, however, the language becomes more straightforward, as the speaker reports that the barber has almost starved and thus returned to his trade. Beyond ridiculing the barber's failure as a philosopher, the poem pokes fun at Epicureanism. The Garden was open to people of any social standing, and the point is that although life there initially seems attractive for a humble tradesman, its crushing poverty (cf. 1n.) proves intolerable: the epigram thus undercuts the Epicurean dictum "cheerful poverty is an honorable thing" (Sen. *Ep.* 2.6). In antiquity, Epicureanism was caricatured by its critics as being excessively interested in gourmandizing, but here its adherents cannot even gather enough food to survive.

1[711] Εὐγάθης λαπιθανός: whether Εὐγάθης is an otherwise unattested proper name (as printed here) or a predicative adjective (cf. Eur. *HF* 792) having adverbial force ("gladly"), the word suggests a happy disposition appropriate to a man abandoning his trade in order to reside with Epicurus. So, too, λαπιθανός could be understood as a novel adjective or an unattested proper name, but in either case it is probably to be read as a combination of intensifying λα- ("very"; cf. Ar. *Ach.* 220 Λακρατείδηι with Olson's note) and πιθανός ("credulous"; cf. LSJ II); the resulting sense, "excessively credulous," is appropriate for a naïve would-be philosopher.   **ἐσοπτρίδα** "mirror," a unique variant of ἔσοπτρον/κάτοπτρον.   **φιλέθειρον:** only here; presumably the σινδών is "fond of hair" in the sense that it catches it as it falls, but the precise point of the word, one of Phanias' several novel adjectives in φιλ-, is less important than the elevated tone it produces.

2[712] σινδόνα: a napkin placed around the customer's neck and shoulders to catch the cut hair.   **πετάσου φάρσος ὑποξύριον:** a felt cloth cut by the frugal barber from a broad-brimmed hat, apparently to be used as a mat for the razor. φάρσος, "fragment, piece" (e.g. Jos. *Ant. Jud.* 3.126), is generally rare in verse (Nic. *Ther.* 664) but a favorite of Phanias (cf. *AP* 6.297.2, 299.1). The hapax ὑποξύριος seems to mean "under the razor," though it could mean "sheared with a razor," like ὑπόξυρος.

3[713] ψήκτραν δονακῖτιν: a brush or comb with bristles made from reeds; elsewhere a ψήκτρα is a curry comb for grooming horses (e.g. Eur. *Hipp.* 1174).   **ἀπέπτυσε** "rejected" (LSJ 2), instead of the expected verb of dedication.   **λιποκώπους** "without handles," a novel coinage; λιποκόπτους "which have stopped cutting," is possible.

4[714] φασγανίδας "shears," not elsewhere; probably a neologism created on the analogy of the ordinary term for a barber's shears, μαχαιρίδες (cf. Eup. fr. 300).   τοὺς συλόνυχας στόνυχας "points that rob the nails"; a stylistically elevated, riddling periphrasis for some ordinary object, perhaps picks for cleaning the fingernails. The novel adjective creates a jingle with στόνυξ, a very rare poetic noun (Eur. *Cycl.* 401, A.R. 4.1679, Lyc. *Alex.* 486, 795, 1181), denoting anything with a sharp end, including fingertips (Hsch. σ1927).

5[715] ἔπτυσε: i.e. ἀπέπτυσε; it is common in Greek and other Indo-European languages for compounded verbs to be followed by the simplex with the same force as the compound (Watkins 1967, Renehan 1976: 11-27).   ψαλίδας ... θρόνον: the end of the list of barber's implements is more straightforward and unadorned than what precedes. A ψαλίς is a knife used for grooming (Poll. 2.32, 10.140), a θρόνος a barber's chair (Alciphron 3.30.2).

5-6[715-16] Ἐπικούρου | κουρεῖον: the pun depends on the possibility of understanding Ἐπί-κουρος as "after (being) a barber."   ἅλατο (< ἅλλομαι) suggests a hasty, metaphorical leap into a new life.   κηπολόγος "a garden-picker": as a student in Epicurus' Garden (D.L. 10.10), he will live by gathering its produce; picking fruits and vegetables replaces his previous work as a haircutter.

7[717] λύρας ἤκουεν ὅπως ὄνος: i.e. "he understood as much as an ass listening to odes," a proverbial expression to denote uneducated people (Diogen. VII 33, Crat. fr. 247, Eup. fr. 279 with Olson's note, Men. *Mis.* 296, fr. 418).

8[718] λιμώσσων "starving," a prosaic verb that deromanticizes the poverty of the Garden.   στέρξε: in pointed contrast to his earlier abhorrence (ἀπέπτυσε).   παλινδρομίαν: despite his failure as a philosopher, the barber makes a wise choice by returning to his former career (cf. [Luc.] *Asin.* 18 παλινδρομῆσαι μᾶλλον ἢ κακῶς δραμεῖν); whether or not there is a more specific reference to a philosophical precept, the language may evoke the metaphorical use of παλινδρομ- to denote intellectual activity (e.g. Philopon. in Arist. *Analyt. post.* p. 26.13-14 Wallies εἰ γὰρ ἀπὸ τοῦ αἰτιατοῦ ἐπὶ τὸ αἴτιον παλινδρομήσομεν).

SAM(I)US

Meleager in the prefatory poem to his *Garland* mentions a poet called Samius (*AP* 4.1.14), but *AP* 6.116 is ascribed to Samus (Simmius, implausibly, in *Pl*). Since that epigram purports to record a dedication by Philip V, its author was probably the Samus who grew up with Philip, produced a witty parody of Euripides at his expense (Polyb. 5.9.4), and was later killed by him (Polyb. 23.10.9): Meleager may be mistaken about the name, or the text of *AP* 4.1.14 may be corrupt.

CXXXIII. Sam(i)us AP 6.116 (2 GP)

A dedication by Philip V to Heracles. The epigram engages with the Antigonid connection to Heracles, from whom the royal family claimed descent (cf. Edson 1934), and who had a temple in their native Beroea (*I.Beroia* 3), where he was worshipped as a patron of hunting, a favorite pastime of Macedonian royalty (cf. Polyb. 31.29.3–5). In the central couplet, the bull killed by Philip is said to have been "glorying in its hybris" (ὕβρεϊ κυδιόωντα). That term is appropriate to the behavior of unruly animals, but also has negative moral connotations (cf. αὐχήεντα in *AP* 6.114.3); the king is both a hunter and a civilizing force. The killing of the unruly animal is thus analogous to his honorand Heracles' labors, which involved the killing or capture of monstrous creatures.

The stylized language includes two neologisms (ταναιμύκος, Μινυαμάχας) and the rare noun κράντωρ; the verbs σβέννυμι and αὐαίνομαι carry unusual metaphorical senses; the adjective λευρός bears a meaning debated by Homeric scholars; and several other words and phrases are modeled on passages of early epic.

AP 6.114 deals with the same dedication of hide and horns by Philip. There, C's correction of P's τοῦ αὐτοῦ (*sc.* Simias, author of *AP* 6.113) to Ἀμύντου has found favor (Cameron 1993: 11–12, Gutzwiller 1998a: 34–5), but it remains possible that *AP* 6.114 too is by Sam(i)us. The epigrams share several points of contact (cf. 3, 4nn.) but do not cover the same ground: 114 focuses on the horns, 116 on the hide; Heracles is addressed by different epithets in each. Each describes the area of Mt Orbelus where Philip killed the bull using a phrase found in Perses *197–8*, where a dead sailor lies "along the ankle" (παρὰ σφυρόν) of Lesbos, under a sea-washed promontory (ὑπὸ πρόποδι). Whereas here the killing of the bull is placed "under a rough promontory of Orbelus" (Ὀρβηλοῖο τρηχὺν ὑπὸ πρόποδα), in 114 it occurs "beside the ankle of Orbelus" (Ὀρβηλοῦ παρὰ σφυρόν). In both, the phrases in question occur in the same metrical position as in Perses. The division of different phrases from a single poem between two closely related poems is perhaps most easily explained if they are the product of deliberate variation by a single poet.

1[719] A chiastic line, beginning and ending with the divine recipient (σοί) and the dedicator (Φίλιππος) respectively, and with the demonstrative τοῦτο and predicate γέρας framing a pair of vocatives.   γέρας: predicate, "as an honor," e.g. *CEG* 873.1 [Π]αφίαι γέρας εἰκόνα τάνδε.   Ἀλκείδα Μινυαμάχε: Heracles was worshipped as patron of hunting in Macedonia under the cult-title Κυναγίδας (Edson 1934: 228), but Samius here (cf. *AP* 6.114.2 Ἀμφιτρυωνιάδαι) avoids evoking any of his well-known big-game hunting adventures, perhaps to avoid overshadowing Philip's accomplishment (contrast, e.g., LXI). The epithet Ἀλκείδας (first at Hes. *Shield* 112; cf. Call. *h.* 3.145, [Mosch.] 3.117) is explained as a reference to Heracles' mortal grandfather Alcaeus (2.4.5) or as the hero's original name ([Apollod.] 2.4.12). Μινυαμάχος (only here) refers to one of Heracles' earliest adventures, his liberation of Thebes from the Minyae of Orchomenos; cf. [Apollod.] 2.4.11, *RE* vi.433-4.

2[720] ταναιμύκου: the first element of the word, attested only here, probably denotes the long distance over which the bull's bellowing could be heard (and thus its loudness), rather than its duration (cf. [Opp.] *Cyn.* 2.144 ταναηχέτα "far-echoing," Q.S. 12.58 ταναῆι ὀπί).   **λευρόν:** properly "smooth," "level," but some ancient scholars apparently interpreted it to mean "wide" in its unique Homeric occurrence, *Od.* 7.123 λευρῶι ἐνὶ χώρωι. The poet may thus be engaging with a philological debate: either meaning would be appropriate here, but "wide" augments the encomiastic point.

3[721] αὐτοῖς σὺν κεράεσσι "together with its horns"; cf. *HHAp.* 148 αὐτοῖς σὺν παίδεσσι (also at line opening). More often, the comitative dative with αὐτός is used without a preposition (Smyth §1525).   **ὕβρεϊ** "wild behavior"; cf. Hdt. 4.129.2 ὑβρίζοντες ὧν οἱ ὄνοι ἐτάρασσον τὴν ἵππον, Ael. *NA* 10.10 (of elephants) τοῦ σκιρτᾶν καὶ ὑβρίζειν ἐξουσίαι. Treating the noun as trisyllabic avoids a violation of "Naeke's Law" (cf. Introduction section 4h[i]).   **κυδιόωντα:** a variation of *Il.* 6.509 (of a horse).

4[722] ἔσβεσεν "killed"; cf. Leon. *AP* 7.295.8. The verb, which may refer to drying liquids (LSJ 2), is picked up by the similar metaphorical use of αὐαίνομαι ("dry up") in 5.   **Ὀρβηλοῦ:** Mt Orbelus (mod. Lekani), on the border between ancient Macedon and Thrace.   **πρόποδα:** cf. introductory n.

5-6[723-4] Dedicatory epigrams sometimes conclude by asking for divine favor (e.g. *CEG* 761.3-4), but here the request adopts a stance commonly taken by praise poets, who call attention to the danger that virtue and the accomplishments it brings will attract the envy of the gods and thus lead to misfortune (e.g. Pi. *Olymp.* 8.54-5, *Pyth.* 8.71-2, fr. 94a.8-9 παντὶ δ᾽ ἐπὶ φθόνος ἀνδρὶ κεῖται ἀρετᾶς; cf. McGlew 1993: 40–2). The envy of gods and men alike is particularly a danger for royal houses, and the speaker's wish is that none fall on Philip for his success, so that the king and his family may continue to increase Heracles' glory in the future.   αὐαίνοιτο "dry up (and disappear)"; cf. above, 4n., Solon, fr. 4.35.   τεόν: i.e. Heracles'.   κῦδος: contrast 3 κυδιόωντα; the bull's pride gives way to the glory of the Antigonid house.   ῥίζα ... Ἠμαθίας "family [LSJ ῥίζα II] of the Beroean ruler of Emathia," i.e. the Antigonid royal house. Emathia, properly the region between the Haliacmon and Axius rivers (cf. Edson 1934), was sometimes understood as the original name for Macedonia and is here a synecdoche for the kingdom as a whole (cf. Str. 7a.1.11, Hsch. η409–10). The adjective Βεροιαῖος identifies the kingdom as a whole with the place of Philip's birth, Beroea.   κράντορος "ruler"; elsewhere only at Eur. Andr. 508. The reference must be to Philip himself, as at AP 6.114.5–6 πολύολβος | Ἠμαθίς, ἃ τοίωι κραίνεται ἀγεμόνι.

MELEAGER

Meleager was the editor of the *Garland*, which includes over 130 epigrams attributed to him. In a series of fictive self-epitaphs, he claims that he was born in Gadara, moved to Tyre, and spent his old age on Cos (729–30n.). The observation of a lemmatist that he was contemporary with "the last Seleucid" (Seleucus VI Epiphanes Nicator, reigned 96–95) may be guesswork, but roughly fits the likely date of his *Garland*, ca. 100–90 (Cameron 1993: 49–56). In addition to epigrams, he wrote a Menippean satire called *Graces* (728n., Ath. 4.157b), apparently including a discussion of the diet of Homeric heroes; Athenaeus also mentions an unspecified work containing a comparison of bean soup and lentil soup (4.157b) and a prose work called *Symposium* (11.502c). He is called ὁ κυνικός by Athenaeus, and the rejection of national and ethnic difference in AP 7.417.4–5 is at least consistent with a Cynic world-view.

Although the original structure of the *Garland* has been partially disrupted by subsequent editors, it is clear that in it Meleager both juxtaposed his compositions with their models and arranged his own poems into meaningful groups. He thus showcases individual poems' engagement with their antecedents and with his other epigrams (cf. Introduction section 5a, Gutzwiller 1998b, Höschele 2009b).

Meleager was a remarkably versatile poet. Though the majority of the extant epigrams have erotic themes, they play in sophisticated ways with the conventions of many other epigrammatic forms. So, too, they capture complex emotional states with particular nuance and depth, sometimes

transforming the tropes of Meleager's predecessors in ways that suggest
deep emotion rather than ironic distance (cf. Garrison 1978: 71–93).

Meleager's style is variable, and though he often uses relatively straightforward diction, he also writes in a more elevated register. Neologisms
are common, as are novel variations of familiar expressions. Though he
does not adhere to "Callimachean" metrical norms (cf. Introduction section 4h[i]), his prosodic practice is more restrictive than his predecessors' (cf. Page 1963, Magnelli 2007: 180–3): he limits the shortening of
a final long vowel before a word beginning in a vowel (epic correption),
the lengthening by position (both before mute plus liquid and by the
addition of nu-movable), and the elision of -αι.

CXXXIV. Meleager AP 7.419 (4 GP)

An epitaph for himself. This is the last of a series of three closely related
autobiographical epitaphs by Meleager (AP 7.417–19); a fourth (AP
7.421) is a riddle in which he associates himself with Meleager the mythical boar-hunter. The present epigram and the two preceding it tell his
literary autobiography and trace his movement from the Greek cultural
margins in Syria to Cos (cf. Gutzwiller 1998b, Höschele 2009a). Together,
they form a thematically and verbally unified group in which the individual poems provide complementary information. AP 7.417 recounts the
poet's birth in Gadara and upbringing in Tyre and concludes by focusing on his literary activity in old age; in that poem, Meleager defends his
Syrian identity by noting that all share a common cosmos, and "affirms
the possibility of being Greek notwithstanding one's origins" (Höschele
2009a). AP 7.418 mentions Gadara and Tyre and adds that late in life
Meleager became a citizen of Cos; it concludes by focusing on the favor
the Muses bestowed on him in his youth. The present epigram illustrates
the ecumenism of the first by casting the poet as a friendly man capable
of addressing his audience in the various languages of the places he has
lived. The trilingual greeting of the final couplet perhaps gestures at bilingual Greek–Semitic inscriptions throughout the Greek-speaking world,
including on Cos (cf. Fraser 1970, Stager 2005); in any case, it reflects
the experience of people in areas where different ethnic groups live in
close proximity.

1–2[725–6] The lines evoke Leon. *135–6*, but treat the deceased as an
approachable, pious man rather than as an indiscriminately angry wasp
whom passersby must not wake.   ἀτρέμας "without fear"; contrast
*135–6*n.   παρ' εὐσεβέσιν: as often in epigram the deceased is treated
as residing in a privileged part of the Underworld (e.g. Call. *Epigr.* 10.4,

IMEGR 3.4). Here Meleager's piety explains (γάρ) the preceding reassurance. ὁ πρέσβυς: see *417–19*n. εὕδει κοιμηθείς: pleonastic. ὕπνον ὀφειλόμενον: the representation of death as a debt is borrowed from Call. *Epigr.* 16.3–4 ἥ δ᾽ ἀποβρίζει | ἐνθάδε τὸν πάσαις ὕπνον ὀφειλόμενον; the universality of the obligation is here left implicit. Meleager rarely ends a pentameter without a sense-pause; enjambment of the poet's name lends it special emphasis.

3–4[727–8] ὁ . . . Χάρισιν "who sewed together bittersweet Eros and the Muses with the amusing Graces." The image is probably that of joining cloth or yarn, as apparently at Eur. *Or.* 1435, the other ancient attestation of συστολίζω. The verb then evokes the common representation of composition as weaving or sewing. The phrase looks back to σὺν Μούσαις . . . | πρῶτα Μενιππείοις συντροχάσας Χάρισιν in the same relative position in *AP* 7.417, where Χάρισιν refers to Meleager's prose *Graces*; cf. Mel. *AP* 7.421.13–14 Μοῦσαν Ἔρωτι | καὶ Χάριτας σοφίαν εἰς μίαν ἡρμόσαο, where χάριτας suggests both the title and the quality of Meleager's verse (cf. Gutzwiller 1998b). ἱλαραῖς . . . Χάρισιν is a programmatic assertion of the poet's lighthearted approach to lovesickness. γλυκύδακρυν: a variation (cf. Mel. *AP* 5.177.3) of Sappho's epithet for Eros, γλυκύπικρος (fr. 130.1–2), which Meleager takes to mean that the pain of love also brings pleasure; cf. *511–12*n., Asclep. 19.3–4 with Sens's note.

5–6[729–30] The couplet refers serially to the stages of life from youth (θεόπαις) to manhood (ἤνδρωσε) and old age (πρέσβυν ἐγηροτρόφει). θεόπαις: a rare adjective, usually meaning "child of a goddess" (cf. ἱερά; Archestr. fr. 46.2 with Olson–Sens' note, Herodicus *SH* 494.6 θεόπαις Βαβυλών), but here perhaps suggesting "having godlike boys" (compare *CEG* 680.5 τὰν ἁβρόπαιδα πάτραν) and gesturing at Meleager's own childhood; cf. Mel. *AP* 12.56.7–8 (of an attractive boy) ὀλβίστη Μερόπων ἱερὰ πόλις ἃ θεόπαιδα | καινὸν Ἔρωτα νέων θρέψεν ὑφαγεμόνα, where again both senses are open. ἤνδρωσε "made a man." ἱερὰ χθών: unlike many Hellenistic poets, Meleager does not require a hexameter ending in a monosyllable to have bucolic diaeresis. Κῶς δ᾽ ἐρατὴ Μερόπων: the island's name is said to have derived from Cos, daughter of the earthborn Merops (Steph. Byz. κ315), and the Coans were sometimes called Meropes. The mythological background facilitates the personification of the island as a young woman caring for Meleager in his old age.

7–8[731–2] These lines expand on the conventional request that the passerby bid the tomb or the deceased "farewell" (e.g. *GVI* 1342–52) by imagining that he might speak not just Greek but Aramaic and Phoenician as well. In linking ethnicity strictly to language, Meleager ignores the possibility of multilingualism, even as he performs it; cf. Andrade 2014: 305–7. The friendliness of the speaker here forms a frame with the opening couplet (cf. 1–2n.).   εἰ . . . Σύρος: the phrase resonates against Meleager's defense of his Syrian background at *AP* 7.417.5–6, where he asserts that the universe is the shared fatherland of all people. That passage (cf. Zenod. *AP* 7.117.6 εἰ δὲ πάτρα Φοίνισσα, τίς ὁ φθόνος;) has its background in Asclep. 5.3–4 Sens εἰ δὲ μέλαινα, τί τοῦτο;, where the speaker rejects skin color as a criterion for beauty.   ναίδιος: no such greeting is attested in Phoenician inscriptions, and the word may be corrupt; cf. Luz 1988.   τὸ δ' αὐτὸ φράσον "respond in kind," by wishing me well in your native language.

CXXXV. *Meleager* AP *7.196 (13 GP)*

On the song of a cicada in a *locus amoenus*. The epigram draws on models from several genres, including Hesiodic didactic, but it particularly evokes the bucolic landscape. It reverses the more usual representation of the singer as a metaphorical cicada (e.g. Call. fr. 1.33–5) by treating the insect's song in terms usually applied to human musicians; the qualities with which it is endowed, including novelty and playfulness, are among those which Hellenistic poets attribute to their own compositions. The poem falls into two four-line halves, each containing a direct address to the insect; the first address introduces a narrative, the second a request for the production of a novel song.

1–4[733–6] The lines rework the temporal clause defining summer at Hes. *Shield* 393–8 (cf. *WD* 582–4) "when the dark-winged (κυανόπτερος), resounding cicada (ἠχέτα τέττιξ), sitting on a green branch (χλοερῶι . . . | ὄζωι ἐφεζόμενος), begins to sing the summer [i.e. summer's song] for men, the cicada to whom delicate dew is food and drink (ὧι τε πόσις καὶ βρῶσις θῆλυς ἐέρση), and it pours forth its song throughout the morning and day, in the most terrible heat, when Sirius dries the skin." The cicada's song is characterized as an ode (μέλισμα λύρας) and described with elaborate compound adjectives that evoke the stylistic register of lyric, though there are also words from a technical, scientific register; the multiple alliterations (μέλπεις μοῦσαν, πετάλοις πριονώδεσι, κλάζεις χρωτί) perhaps elevate the tone.   ἀχήεις: a variation of the usual epithet of cicadas, ἠχέτης, which was sometimes used as a noun (e.g. Ar. *Peace* 1159, *Birds* 1095).   δροσεραῖς . . . μεθυσθείς "drunk on dewdrops." Cicadas were thought to feed on dew (e.g. Call. fr. 1.33–5). The phrase evokes the Hellenistic debate about whether wine or water is a better source for poetry (cf. Nicaenetus *AP*

13.29 = Asclep. *47 with Sens's n.), but conflates the two ideas by representing the insect as inebriated on water; cf. Antipater Thess. *AP* 9.92.1. For dew as a source of poetic inspiration, cf. Hes. *Th.* 83–4 with West's note.   ἀγρονόμαν "living in the countryside"; the adjective elsewhere has two terminations.   μοῦσαν "song" (LSJ II).   ἐρημολάλον "chattering in isolation"; a novel word. Though in reality cicadas usually sing in choruses, the insect is depicted as an isolated, rustic poet like Hesiod and some bucolic singers.   ἄκρα: adverbial, "atop."   ἐφεζόμενος πετάλοις: the participle is drawn from the Hesiodic models (above), the noun from Alc. fr. 347.1 ἄχει δ' ἐκ πετάλων ἄδεα τέττιξ, itself part of an extended rewriting of *WD* 582–8.   πριονώδεσι κώλοις: in fact, cicadas stridulate via a membrane on their bodies, and not with their legs, but such misrepresentations are not unusual; cf. Hes. *WD* 584 with West's note. πριονώδης, "serrated," belongs to the technical language of biological descriptions (Clytus *FGrH* 490 F 1, Σ Ar. *Birds* 1138, Σ Nic. *Ther.* 71); the short iota of its first element is a Hellenistic innovation (Leon. *AP* 6.204.2, Nic. *Ther.* 52).   αἰθίοπι ... χρωτί "dark skin," a variation of Hes. *Shield* 393 κυανόπτερος.   μέλισμα: first attested as a synonym for μέλος in the bucolic corpus (Theocr. 14.31, [20].28, [Mosch.] 3.55, 92), where the verb from which it derives, μελίσδω, is programmatic for the singing of herdsmen and the sympathetic sounds of nature (cf. Theocr. 1.2 with Hunter's note).

5[737] φίλος: see *41–2*n.

5–6[737–8] τι νέον ... | παίγνιον: a reworking of LXX, where Hedylus urges drinking as a way to produce novel poetry (τι νέον), the product of play (παῖζε; cf. Thgn. 567, Ion fr. 27.7, Sens 2016: 230–1).   δενδρώδεσι Νύμφαις "tree-nymphs"; the adjective more often means "wooded" or "treelike," but cf. Lyc. *Alex.* 830 δενδρώδης κλάδος "tree branch." The Nymphs rather than the Muses are regularly represented as the inspirers of pastoral poetry (e.g. Theocr. 7.148).   ἀντωιδὸν Πανί "singing in response to Pan" (cf. Ar. *Thesm.* 1059). The exchange of song was a conventional feature of bucolic poetry; here the cicada's song is in counterpoint to that of Pan, the inventor of the syrinx.   κρέκων κέλαδον: the alliteration captures the raucous sound of the insect.

7–8[739–40] "so that, having escaped Eros, I may hunt midday sleep, reclining beneath a shady plane tree." The opposition between the calm of the *locus amoenus*, of which the singing of cicadas is a conventional feature (e.g. Pl. *Phaedr.* 230c, Theocr. 7.139), and the erotic turmoil experienced by its residents is a bucolic commonplace.   φυγὼν ... ὕπνον ἀγρεύσω: perhaps reversing the recommendation that threshers φεύγειν τὸ μεσαβρινὸν ὕπνον at Theocr. 10.48, where τὸ μεσαμβρινόν is adverbial. The expression plays on the more common depiction of Love or the lover as a hunter; cf. 299n. **μεσημβρινόν:** noon was the conventional time for encounters with gods and a moment when the silence of other animals made the cicada's song prominent (cf. Ar. *Birds* 1095–6, Pl. *Phaedr.* 258d–9a, Aristophon, fr. 10.6–7). **ὑπὸ σκιερᾶι ... πλατάνωι:** the plane tree is a feature of the *locus amoenus* at Pl. *Phaedr.* 229a–30b, and is common in subsequent idealized landscapes; cf. Hermocr. *APl* 11.1 ὑπὸ σκιερὰν πλάτανον.

CXXXVI. Meleager AP 5.176 (6 GP)

A reflection on the nature of Eros. Some of the wit resides in the emotional self-indulgence of the speaker, who is made to repeat verbatim his opening exclamation about the cruelty of Eros even as he insists that such repetition is counterproductive; the implication is perhaps that he enjoys wallowing in the pain caused by Eros. At the same time, the emphasis placed on the futility of such complaints amounts to a playfully self-reflexive comment about the frequency and conventionality of similar lovesickness in epigram.

The epigram plays on the ambiguous status of Eros in poetry. Initially, the speaker adopts the traditional epigrammatic conception of the god as a young child, but ultimately treats him as embodied fire. The transformation enacts the process of growth that the speaker describes in the second couplet (τρέφεται); cf. 5–6n.

1–2[741–2] Indignant complaints (σχετλιασμοί) about Eros' cruelty were a *topos* in Hellenistic epigram and other Greek poetry (cf. 83–4, LXXXVI, Thgn. 1231, A.R. 4.445–7). The heavy alliteration of π reinforces the idea of repetition. **δεινός ... δεινός:** the epanadiplosis reflects exasperation and enacts the repetition that the speaker is describing. **τί δὲ πλέον:** see 6n. The question resonates against epigrams in which the speaker wonders what benefit Eros will receive from harming him; here, it is the speaker who gains nothing.

3[743] **γελᾶι:** like his mother Aphrodite (e.g. *HHAphr.* 49), Eros often laughs derisively at his victims (e.g. A.R. 3.124, 129, 286).

3–4[743–4] **πυκνὰ κακισθείς | ἥδεται** "he enjoys being reviled repeatedly," as he just has been by the speaker. With few exceptions, Meleager restricts the shortening of a final long syllable before an initial vowel to words ending at the bucolic diaeresis or, as in the case of ἥδεται, to trisyllabic

words in the first foot.   λοίδορα "abusive words."   καὶ τρέφεται: i.e.
"he even grows," playing on the representation of the god as a living boy.

5–6[745–6] A reformulation of the *topos* that Eros burns his victims, and
of the paradox that the fire of love can be generated from Aphrodite, a
goddess traditionally associated with the sea; cf. Asclep. *36.3–4 (= Pos.
*128 AB) with Sens's note. Though the speaker emphasizes the truth of
his genealogy (ἄρα; cf. Denniston 37–8), Eros' parentage was debated:
cf., e.g., Antag. fr. 1, who claims not to know whether the god was born
"under the seas of wide Ocean" or is the son of Aphrodite, Earth, or the
Winds. That Aphrodite was his mother was conventional in Hellenistic
epigram (e.g. Asclep. 21 Sens), but here his personification as fire created
from water evokes cosmogonies in which these were primordial elements
and so hints at an alternative version of the god's place in the development of the universe.   θαῦμα . . . πῶς: cf. *433*. Despite his alleged
condition, the speaker is composed enough to express amazement at a
paradox.   διὰ γλαυκοῖο . . . ἐξ ὑγροῦ "appearing through the grey wave
you bore fire from moisture." Genitives ending in -οιο are relatively rare in
Meleager: γλαυκοῖο lends an epic flavor that suits the content. ὑγροῦ may
readily be understood as a neuter substantive ("moisture"; LSJ A2), but
κύματος could be understood with both prepositional phrases.

CXXXVII. *Meleager* AP 5.192 (57 GP)

Praise for an attractive woman. The poem combines the conventional
funerary address to the passing ξένος with the ecphrastic *topos* in which
the speaker imagines the verbal response to seeing an object; though
their chronology is not certain, poems in which someone speculates that
an artist has seen Aphrodite naked may lie in the background (cf., e.g.,
"Plato" APl 160.4, adesp. APl 162, 168). Here, the subject is a woman
about whom the speaker shares privileged information, but the imagined
response involves a pun dependent on the idea that a letter in her name
could be changed to another one of similar shape; the "ecphrastic"
response thus assimilates the viewing and the reading of letters, as one
would on a stone inscribed with her name.

1[747] ἢν ἐσίδῃς . . . φήσεις: cf. *495–6*n. ἐρεῖς.   Καλλίστιον: a speaking
name, suggesting the woman's superior beauty (i.e. she is καλλίστη).

2[748] "The double letter of the Syracusans has been changed." The symbol
in question is X, which was used in different alphabets to represent either
the aspirated velar stop (*chi*) or the "double" consonant representing the

combination of velar and sibilant (*xi*). διπλοῦν here refers to the latter use
(the proper adjective for "aspirated" being δασύς), but the joke depends
on the former: seeing Καλλίστιον naked, one would think that her name
was actually Καλλίσχιον, i.e. "with attractive hips." The joke is facilitated by
the graphic similarity of χ and τ in some old scripts.   Συρηκοσίων: perhaps a reference to the view that the Syracusan comic poet Epicharmus
was responsible for the introduction of Χ into the Greek alphabet (Arist.
fr. 501 Rose ap. Pliny, *NH* 7.192; cf. Willi 2013: 139).

CXXXVIII. *Meleager* AP *12.52 (81 GP)*

The speaker wishes to become a dolphin in order to convey his beloved
safely on a sea voyage. The poem is a version of what came to be called
a προπεμπτικόν (cf. Men. Rh. pp. 395.1–399.10 Spengel), in which the
speaker wishes that someone departing on a journey might arrive safely;
in the Hellenistic period, several of these have an overtly erotic flavor (cf.
Erinna, *SH* 404, Call. fr. 400 = *AP* 13.10, Theocr. 7.52–6). The conclusion
incorporates another erotic *topos*, in which the speaker prays for physical
transformation.

1[749] οὔριος . . . ναύταις . . . δυσέρωτες: the "favorable wind for sailors" is implicitly contrasted with the misfortune it brings the speaker,
who belongs to the group of unlucky lovers he addresses.   **Νότος:** the
speaker is imagined to be somewhere to the south of Rhodes; there are
no grounds, however, for believing that the imagined geography reflects
Meleager's biography.   **ὦ δυσέρωτες:** the speaker presumes a sympathetic audience of others who share his misfortune in love. δυσέρωτες are
those who experience ἔρως obsessively and thus unhappily (cf. Eur. *Hipp.*
193 with Barrett's note.).

2[750] The verse reworks Call. *Epigr.* 41.1–2, where the speaker says that
one half of his soul (ἥμισύ μευ ψυχῆς) is intact but speculates that the other
has been snatched (ἥρπασε) by Eros or Hades. It also draws on a theme
found at Call. fr. 400 = *AP* 13.10 ἁ ναῦς, ἃ τὸ μόνον φέγγος ἐμὶν τὸ γλυκὺ τᾶς
ζόας | ἁρπάξας, ποτί τε Ζανὸς ἱκνεῦμαι λιμενοσκόπῳ. Hor. *Odes* 1.3.8 looks
both to this passage and to its Callimachean models; cf. Nisbet–Hubbard's
note.   **ἥρπασεν:** the verb is commonly used of sudden death, and
here, as in the Callimachean model (above), it suggests that the speaker
experiences the boy's departure as a form of death (cf. ψυχῆς, ζόας). The
violence it suggests also evokes the threat that winds in Greek epigrams
typically pose to sailors, and prepares for the speaker's desire to protect
his beloved.   **Ἀνδράγαθον:** the name suggests the boy's virtue; Men. Rh.

398.20–3 recommends that προπεμπτικά include praise of the traveler's character.

3–4[751–2] A surprising μακαρισμός personifying the ships and elements of the natural world responsible for Andragathus' voyage: rather than express concern about the potential threat that these pose to the boy, the speaker remarks on their good fortune in conveying him. The passage is a "tricolon crescendo" (three clauses of increasing length), with variation of the predicate (μάκαρες . . . ὄλβια . . . εὐδαίμων) and with the final word forming a ring with 1 οὔριος . . . Νότος. The adverbs τρὶς . . . τρὶς . . . | τετράκι are common in similar contexts; e.g. *Od.* 5.306 τρὶς μάκαρες Δαναοὶ καὶ τετράκις, 6.154–5, Hes. fr. 211.7 τρὶς μάκαρ Αἰακίδη καὶ τετράκις ὄλβιε Πηλεῦ, Ar. *Wealth* 851–2 καὶ τρὶς κακοδαίμων καὶ τετράκις καὶ πεντάκις | καὶ δωδεκάκις καὶ μυριάκις.   **παιδοφορῶν:** only here. The word prepares for the following couplet, in which the speaker wishes that he might be the one to convey the boy.

5–6[753–4] The usual wish for safe arrival (e.g. Sappho, fr. 5) is embedded in a prayer that the speaker might become a dolphin, perhaps playing on passages seeking assistance from sea-creatures; e.g. Erinna *SH* 404 πομπίλε ναύτῃσιν πέμπων πλόον εὔπλοον ἰχθύ | πομπεύσαις πρύμναθεν ἐμὰν ἀδεῖαν ἑταῖραν, A.R. fr. 8. The implicit idea is that as a dolphin the speaker could ensure the boy's survival in case of trouble at sea, as in the case of Arion (cf. Hdt. 1.23–4) and Phalanthus (Paus. 10.13.10), but the wish also evokes erotic contexts in which the speaker prays to be transformed in order to be close to the beloved (cf. *611*n.). Dolphins were sometimes said to be attracted to boys; cf. Arist. *Hist. anim.* 631a9–10 πρὸς παῖδας ἔρωτες καὶ ἐπιθυμίαι, Duris of Samos *FGrH* 76 F 7, Ael. *NA* 6.15, Oppian, *Hal.* 5.453–518, Pliny, *NH* 9.27, Gutzwiller 2002c.   **ἐμοῖς . . . ἐπ' ὤμοις:** reversing the more usual wish for the speaker to be converted into something that can be held *by* his beloved; cf. *612*, *carm. conv.* *PMG* 900–1. The speaker imagines himself retaining human characteristics as a dolphin.   **βαστακτός** "borne" (< βαστάζω); the word is attested elsewhere only in glosses.   **γλυκύπαιδα:** only here. Rhodes is associated with attractive boys because Andragathus will be there.

CXXXIX. *Meleager* AP *12.137 (118 GP)*

On a rooster who has interrupted the speaker's night with an ἐρώμενος. The poem is closely related to Mel. *AP* 5.172, addressed to the ὄρθρος, whose arrival has interrupted the speaker's time with a female lover.

1–2[755–6] The grand language is ironic in a complaint about the bird's arrogance.   ὀρθροβόας: i.e. a rooster, who crows in the ὄρθρος, the period just before dawn. Heraclides Lembus (fr. 5, *FHG* III.169) cites the word as one of several obscure glosses used by Alexarchus, brother of Cassander.   δυσέρωτι: see *749*n.   κακάγγελε: the rooster is a bearer of bad news in that he announces that the daybreak will soon arrive. Meleager is perhaps recalling myths in which birds are punished for bearing unhappy messages (cf. Call. fr. 260.48 = *Hecale* fr. 74.7 Hollis with Hollis on 74.18, Ant. Lib. 15.4).   τρισάλαστε "thrice accursed"; a rare synonym (elsewhere at adesp. *APl* 265.1) of the more common τρισκατάρατος.

2[756] κράζεις: the verb is a feature of the *koine* (cf. Moeris γ17).   πλευροτυπῆ κέλαδον "a cry as you beat your sides (with your wings)," a reference to roosters' habit of flapping their wings.

3[757] γαῦρος ὑπὲρ κοίτας "arrogant over his own bed" (cf. Moore-Blunt 1978). Roosters are notoriously libidinous (e.g. Arist. *GA* 749b13–15), and the speaker imagines that the bird is crowing after sex (cf. LSJ κοίτη III) at the very moment when his own lovemaking has to end. For γαῦρος, *26*n.   ὅτε . . . παιδοφιλεῖν "when I have only this little bit of night left for boy-loving."

4[758] ἐπ' ἐμαῖς . . . ὀδύναις: the rooster plays the role more usually occupied by Eros in Meleager's epigrams; cf. *743*n.   ἁδὺ γελᾶις has its roots in epic and refers to derisive or malicious amusement at another's pain (*LfgrE* γελάω 1.2a; cf. Theocr. 7.42 with Hunter's note).

5[759] ἅδε . . . χάρις "Is this a kind way to reward the one who raised you?" θρεπτήρ, first attested here, evokes the epic word θρεπτήρια, gifts given to parents to thank them for one's upbringing (*HHDem.* 168, 223, Hes. *WD* 188); cf. *457–8*.   τὸν βαθὺν ὄρθρον: i.e. the present moment, just before the break of dawn (cf. Theocr. 18.14 with Gow's note); the oath picks up 1 ὀρθροβόας. The speaker swears by it because the present moment will be the bird's last opportunity to crow.

6[760] ἔσχατα "for the last time."   γηρύσηι: second person singular future middle.   πικρά: see *152*n.

CXL. Meleager AP 5.151 (33 GP)

An appeal to mosquitoes to leave Zenophila alone. The epigram forms a pair with Mel. *AP* 5.152, addressed to a single mosquito to whom the speaker promises the arms of Heracles as a reward for summoning Zenophila. Both may implicitly play on the similarity of mosquitoes, small winged creatures who wound their victims, to Eros. Here, the speaker's attitude changes over the course of the poem. He initially beseeches the insects in language that suggests a prayer to the gods (Cairns 2016: 386–7), but at the midpoint of the poem he changes his attitude toward the insects, whom he represents as rivals with an erotic interest in Zenophila and whose arrogance he threatens to punish.

1–2[761–2] The asyndetic list of the mosquitoes' qualities evokes hymnic invocations. The language is elevated: ὀξυβόαι, elsewhere used at Aesch. *Ag.* 57 of the cry of vultures, suggests a louder sound than buzzing; the uncontracted ending of ἀναιδέες is characteristic of hexameter verse (cf. Call. *h.* 4.36), as is the collocation αἵματος ἀνδρῶν (cf. A.R. 2.59, Opp. *Hal.* 2.453); and κνώδαλα usually denotes bigger animals.   **σίφωνες:** a bold metaphor for blood-drinking insects; a σίφων is properly a tube used for drawing wine – a blood-red liquid – from a cask.   **κνώδαλα διπτέρυγα:** cf. Aesch. *Supp.* 1000 κνώδαλα πτεροῦντα; more usually the word designates terrestrial or aquatic animals. διπτέρυγα is a rare variant of δίπτερα, first here.

3–4[763–4] "Permit, I beseech you, Zenophila to rest peacefully in sleep for a brief moment, and – here! – eat the flesh of my limbs." The interjections reflect the speaker's excitement. Ζηνοφίλαν is the subject of the infinitival clause, βαιόν and ἥσυχον adverbial accusatives.   **πάρεθ':** second person plural aorist imperative of παρίημι.   **ὕπνωι | εὕδειν:** for the pleonastic dative, cf. Soph. *OT* 65 οὐχ ὕπνωι γ' εὕδοντά μ' ἐξεγείρετε.   **τἀμά:** the initial position is emphatic.   **σαρκοφαγεῖτε:** the verb, otherwise prosaic, is hyperbolic; Arist. *Hist. anim.* 556b21–2 distinguishes between insects that eat flesh (σαρκοφάγα) and those that suck fluids.

5[765] Similar comments about the futility of complaining or appealing are more often directed to Eros; cf. 741–2n.   **πρὸς τί μάτην** is a pleonastic combination of the more usual πρὸς τί and τί μάτην.   **ἄτεγκτοι** "unmalleable, unpersuadable"; cf., e.g., Aesch. fr. 348 ἄτεγκτος . . . παρηγορήμασιν.

6[766] The speaker reimagines the mosquitoes as prospective rivals (cf. 7–8n.) seeking the warmth of Zenophila's delicate skin. The line is elegantly arranged, with two words beginning in τ in the first hemistich, and two in χ in the second, with two verbal forms framing the noun phrase. χρωτὶ χλιαίνομεν- is a common pentameter end in Meleager (cf. *AP* 5.165.4, 5.172.2, 12.63.4), of human lovers.

7–8[767–8] The speaker asserts his own power, which resides in his status as jealous rival (ζηλοτύπων). Cairns (2016: 387) notes that δύναμις may denote the particular power(s) of individual gods, and argues that the speaker casts himself as divine avenger of the insects' unrestrained boldness (for τόλμης, cf. *47*n.); cf., e.g., Zeus's threat at *Il.* 1.566–7.   **ἀλλ' ἔτι νῦν** introduces a final attempt at persuasion, as the more common ἀλλ' ἔτι καὶ νῦν does at, e.g., *Il.* 9.259–60, Theocr. 22.169–70.   **προλέγω** "I warn you."   **θρέμματα** "creatures," here a term of abuse as at, e.g., Aesch. *Sept.* 181, Eur. *Andr.* 261.

WORKS CITED

Abbenes, J. G. J. 1990. "The middle imperative plural, type φεσέσθω in Greek," *Historische Sprachforschung / Historical Linguistics* 103: 236–44.

Acosta-Hughes, B. and Barbantani, S. 2007. "Inscribing Lyric," in Bing and Bruss 2007: 429–57.

Acosta-Hughes, B., Kosmetatou, E., and Baumbach, M. (eds.) 2004. *Labored in papyrus leaves: perspectives on an epigram collection attributed to Posidippus (P.Mil.Vogl.* VIII 309*)*, Cambridge, Mass.

Ambühl, A. 2002. "Zwischen Tragödie und Roman: Kallimachos' Epigramm auf den Selbstmord der Basilo (20 Pf. = 32 Gow-Page = *AP* 7.517)," in Harder, Regtuit, and Wakker 2002: 1–26.

2007. "'Tell, all ye singers, my fame': kings, queens and nobility in epigram," in Bing and Bruss 2007: 275–94.

Ameling, W. 1985. "φάγωμεν καὶ πίωμεν: griechische Parallelen zu zwei Stellen aus dem Neuen Testament," *Zeitschrift für Papyrologie und Epigraphik* 60: 35–43.

Andrade, N. 2014. "Assyrians, Syrians and the Greek language in the late Hellenistic and Roman Imperial periods," *Journal of Near Eastern Studies* 73: 299–317.

Arbanitopoulos, A. S. 1928. Γραπταὶ στῆλαι Δημητριάδος–Παγασῶν, Athens.

Argentieri, L. 1998. "Epigramma e libro," *Zeitschrift für Papyrologie und Epigraphik* 121: 1–20.

2003. *Gli epigrammi degli Antipatri*, Bari.

Arnaoutoglou, I. 2003. *Thusias heneka kai sunousias: private religious associations in Hellenistic Athens*, Athens.

Arnott, W. G. 1969. "Callimachean subtlety in Asclepiades of Samos," *Classical Review* 19: 6–8.

Asper, M. 2011. "Dimensions of power: Callimachean geopoetics and the Ptolemaic empire," in B. Acosta-Hughes, L. Lehnus, and S. Stephens, eds. *Brill's companion to Callimachus* (Leiden) 155–77.

Aston, E. 2004. "Asclepius and the legacy of Thessaly," *Classical Quarterly* 54: 18–32.

Barringer, J. 2001. *The hunt in ancient Greece*, Baltimore.

Bastianini, G. and Casanova, A. (eds.) 2002. *Il papiro di Posidippo un anno dopo*, Florence.

Belloni, L. 2008. "Il 'vecchio' Filita nel Nuovo Posidippo: la verità, le muse, il re (P.Mil.Vogl. VIII 309, col. X 16–25 = 63 A.–B.)," *Zeitschrift für Papyrologie und Epigraphik* 164: 21–7.

Berman, D. W. 2005. "The hierarchy of herdsman, goatherding, and genre in Theocritean bucolic," *Phoenix* 59: 228–45.

Bernsdorff, H. 1996. "Parataktische Gleichnisse bei Theokrit," in M. A. Harder, R. F. Regtuit, and G. C. Wakker, eds. *Theocritus* (Groningen) 71–90.

2001. *Hirten in der nicht-bukolischen Dichtung des Hellenismus*, Stuttgart.

Bing, P. 1988. *The well-read Muse: present and past in Callimachus and the Hellenistic poets*, Göttingen.

1990. "A pun on Aratus' name in verse 2 of the *Phainomena?*" *Harvard Studies in Classical Philology* 93: 281–5.

1993. "Aratus and his audiences," *Materiali e Discussioni* 31: 99–109.

1995. "Ergänzungsspiel in the epigrams of Callimachus," *Antike und Abendland* 41: 115–31 = Bing 2009: 85–105.

1998. "Between literature and monuments," in Harder, Regtuit, and Wakker 1998: 21–43 = Bing 2009: 194–216.

2002–3. "Posidippus and the admiral: Kallikrates of Samos in the Milan epigrams," *Greek, Roman, and Byzantine Studies* 43: 243–66 = Bing 2009: 234–52.

2005. "The politics and poetics of geography in the Milan Posidippus, Section One: On stones," in Gutzwiller 2005: 119–40 = Bing 2009: 253–71.

2009. *The scroll and the marble*, Ann Arbor.

Bing, P. and Bruss, J. S. (eds.) 2007. *Brill's companion to Hellenistic epigram*, Leiden.

Bleisch, P. R. 1996. "On choosing a spouse: *Aeneid* 7.378–84 and Callimachus' *Epigram* 1," *American Journal of Philology* 117: 453–72.

Blum, R. 1991. *Kallimachos: the Alexandrian library and the origins of bibliography*, trans. H. H. Wellisch, Madison.

Blumenthal, H. J. 1978. "Callimachus, Epigram 28, Numenius Fr. 20, and the meaning of κυκλικός," *Classical Quarterly* 1: 125–7.

Bolmarcich, S. 2002. "Hellenistic sepulchral epigrams on Homer," in Harder, Regtuit, and Wakker 2002: 67–83.

Bonneau, D. 1964. *La crue du Nil, divinité égyptienne à travers mille ans d'histoire (332 av.–641 ap. J.-C), d'après les auteurs grecs et latins, et les documents des époques ptolémaïque, romaine et byzantine*, Paris.

Bonsignore, C. 2013–14. "Testo e poetica di Alceo di Messene," diss. Rome.

Borthwick, E. K. 1969. "Fire imagery in two poems in the Anthology," *Classical Philology* 64: 114–15.

Bowman, L. 1998. "Nossis, Sappho and Hellenistic poetry," *Ramus* 27: 39–59.

Bremer, J. M. 1975. "The meadow of love and two passages in Euripides' 'Hippolytus,'" *Mnemosyne* 28: 268–80.

Bremmer, J. N. 2004. "Attis: a Greek god in Anatolian Pessinous and Catullan Rome," *Mnemosyne* 57: 534–73.

Briant, P. 1989. "Histoire et idéologie: les Grecs et la 'décadence perse,'" in M. M. Mactoux and E. Gery, eds. *Mélanges Pierre Léveque* II (Paris/Besançon) 33–47.

Bruss, J. S. 2005. *Hidden presences: monuments, gravesites, and corpses in Greek funerary epigram*, Leuven.

Bundy, E. L. 1972. "The 'quarrel between Kallimachos and Apollonios,' Part I: The epilogue of Kallimachos's 'Hymn to Apollo,'" *California Studies in Classical Antiquity* 5: 39–94.

1986. *Studia Pindarica*, Berkeley and Los Angeles.

Cairns, F. 1972. *Generic composition in Greek and Roman poetry*, Edinburgh.

1977. "Horace on other people's love affairs (*Odes* I 27; II 4; I 8; III 12)," *Quaderni Urbinati di Cultura Classica* 24: 121–47.

1993. "Asclepiades *AP* 5.85 = Gow–Page 2," *Grazer Beiträge* 19: 35–8.

1996a. "Asclepiades *AP* 5.85 = Gow–Page 2 again," *Papers of the Liverpool Latin Seminar* 9: 323–6.

1996b. "The 'New Posidippus' and Callimachus *AP* 7.447 = 35 (G–P) = 11 (Pf.)," in R. Faber and B. Seidensticker, eds. *Worte, Bilder, Töne: Studien zur Antike und Antikerezeption* (Würzburg) 77–88.

2016. *Hellenistic epigrams: contexts of exploration*, Cambridge.

Cameron A. 1991. "How thin was Philitas?" *Classical Quarterly* 41: 534–8.

1993. *The Greek Anthology from Meleager to Planudes*, Oxford.

1995. *Callimachus and his critics*, Princeton.

Celentano, M. S. 1995. "L'elogio della brevità tra retorica e letteratura: Callimaco ep. 11 Pf. = *A.P.* VII 447," *Quaderni Urbinati di Cultura Classica* 49: 67–79.

Chiasson, C. C. 1982. "Tragic diction in Herodotus: some possibilities," *Phoenix* 36: 156–61.

Clay, D. 2004. *Archilochos heros: the cults of poets in the Greek polis*, Washington, DC.

Clayman, D. L. 2009. *Timo of Phlius: Pyrrhonism into poetry*, Berlin.

Cluá Serena, J. A. 1990. "Euphorionis epigrammata," *Habis* 21: 31–9.

Cohen, G. M. 2006. *The Hellenistic settlements in Syria, the Red Sea basin, and North Africa*, Berkeley and Los Angeles.

Cole, S. G. 1998. "Domesticating Artemis," in S. Blundell and M. Williamson, eds. *The sacred and the feminine in ancient Greece* (London and New York) 27–43.

Copley, F. O. 1956. *Exclusus amator: a study in Latin love poetry*, Oxford.

Cribiore, R. 1996. *Writing, teachers, and education in Graeco-Roman Egypt*, Atlanta.

2001. *Gymnastics of the mind: Greek education in Hellenistic and Roman Egypt*, Princeton.

Csapo, E. 2006–7. "The cultural poetics of the Greek cockfight," *AAIA Bulletin* 4: 20–37.

Dale, A. 2010. "Lyric epigrams in Meleager's *Garland*, the *Anthologia Palatina*, and the *Anthologia Planudea*," *Greek, Roman, and Byzantine Studies* 50: 193–213.

Dasen, V. 1993. *Dwarfs in ancient Egypt and Greece*, Oxford.

Davidson, J. 1993. "Fish, sex and revolution in Athens," *Classical Quarterly* 43: 53–66.

Defreyne, L. 1993. "Erotes and Eros in the epigrams of Asclepiades," *Aevum Antiquum* 6: 199–236.

Dettori, E. 2000. *Filita grammatico: testimonianze e frammenti*, Rome.

Díaz de Cerio Díez, M. 1998. "La evolución de un género: elementos estructurales de los epigramas dedicados a animales de Ánite de Tegea," *Emerita* 66: 119–49.

Dickie, M. W. 1996. "An ethnic slur in a new epigram of Posidippus," *Papers of the Leeds International Latin Seminar* 9: 327–36.

1998. "Poets as initiates in the Mysteries: Euphorion, Philicus and Posidippus," *Antike und Abendland* 44: 49–77.

Di Marco, M. 2002. "Asclepiade 1 e 2 G.–P. (= *AP* 5, 169; 5, 85)," in L. Torraca, ed. *Scritti in onore di Italo Gallo* (Naples) 255–64.

Dover, K. J. (ed.) 1971. *Theocritus: select poems*, London.

Edson, C. 1934. "The Antigonids, Heracles, and Beroea," *Harvard Studies in Classical Philology* 45: 213–46.

1948. "Philip V and Alcaeus of Messene," *Classical Philology* 43: 116–21.

Elsner, J. 2014. "Lithic poetics: Posidippus and his stones," *Ramus* 43: 152–72.

Fabiano, M. G. 1997. "Οὐδ' ἀπὸ κρήνης πίνω: ancora poetica della *brevitas*?" *Materiali e Discussioni* 38: 153–73.

Fantuzzi, M. 2002. "La tecnica versificatoria del P.Mil.Vogl. VIII 309," in Bastianini and Casanova 2002: 79–97.

2004. "The magic of (some) allusions: Philodemus *AP* 5.107 (*GPh* 3188 ff.; 23 Sider)," *Harvard Studies in Classical Philology* 102: 213–36.

2005. "Posidippus at court: the contribution of the Ἱππικά of P. Mil. Vogl. VIII 309 to the ideology of the Ptolemaic kingship," in Gutzwiller 2005: 249–68.

2007a. "Dioscoride e la storia del teatro," in R. Pretagostini and E. Dettori, eds. *La cultura letteraria ellenistica: persistenza, innovazione, trasmissione* (Rome) 105–23.

2007b. "Epigram and the theater," in Bing and Bruss 2007: 477–95.

2015. "The aesthetics of sequentiality and its discontents," in M. Fantuzzi and C. Tsagalis, eds. *The Greek epic cycle and its ancient reception* (Cambridge) 405–29.

2016. "Novice pastoral eros and its epigrammatic critics," in Sistakou and Rengakos 2016: 281–95.

2019. "Epigrammatic variations/debate on the theme of Cybele's music," in M. Kanellou, I. Petrovic, and C. Carey, eds., *Greek epigram from the Hellenistic to the early Byzantine era* (Oxford) 213–32.

Fantuzzi, M. and Hunter, R. 2004. *Tradition and innovation in Hellenistic poetry*, Cambridge.

Fantuzzi, M. and Sens, A. 2006. "The hexameter of inscribed Hellenistic epigram," in M. A. Harder, R. F. Regtuit, and G. C. Wakker, eds. *Beyond the canon* (Leuven) 105–22.

Faraone, C. A. 1986. "Callimachus Epigram 29.5–6 (Gow–Page)," *Zeitschrift für Papyrologie und Epigraphik* 63: 53–6.

Fehling, D. 1969. *Die Wiederholungsfiguren und ihr Gebrauch bei den Griechen vor Gorgias*, Berlin.

Finglass, P. J. 2012. "Ethnic identity in Stesichorus," *Zeitschrift für Papyrologie und Epigraphik* 182: 39–44.

Fischer-Bovet, C. 2014. *Army and society in Ptolemaic Egypt*, Cambridge.

Fountoulakis, A. 2013. "Male bodies, male gazes: exploring *Erôs* in the twelfth book of the *Greek Anthology*," in E. Sanders, C. Thumiger, C. Carey, and N. J. Lowe, eds. *Eros in ancient Greece* (Oxford) 293–311.

Fraenkel, E. 1910–20. *Geschichte der griechischen Nomina agentis auf -τηρ, -τωρ, -της*, 2 vols., Straßburg.

1955. "Neues Griechisch in graffiti," *Glotta* 34: 42–7.

Fraser, P. M. 1970. "Greek-Phoenician bilingual inscriptions from Rhodes," *Annual of the British School at Athens* 65: 31–6.

1972. *Ptolemaic Alexandria*, 3 vols., Oxford.

Fuà, O. 1973. "L'idea dell'opera d'arte 'vivente' e la bucola di Mirone nell'epigramma Greco e Latino," *Rivista di Cultura Classica e Medioevale* 15: 50–5.

Gabathuler, M. 1937. "Hellenistische Epigramme auf Dichter," diss. Basel.

Galán Vioque, G. 2001. *Dioscórides: Epigramas*, Huelva.

Garland, R. 1985. *The Greek way of death*, Ithaca.

Garrison, D. 1978. *Mild frenzy: a reading of the Hellenistic love epigram*, Wiesbaden.

Giangrande, G. 1967. Review of Gow and Page 1965, *Classical Review* 17: 17–24.

1968. "Sympotic literature and epigram," in *L'épigramme grecque* (Vandoeuvres) 93–177.

Glucker, J. 1973. "Dioscorides, *AP* VII, 411, 2, and some related problems," *Eranos* 71: 84–94.

Goldhill, S. 1994. *Art and text in ancient Greek culture*, Cambridge.

　1995. *Foucault's virginity: ancient erotic fiction and the history of sexuality*, Cambridge.

Gorla, C. 1997. "La nascita dell'epitimbio per animali: Anyte di Tegea e suoi continuatori," *Acme* 50: 33–60.

Gow, A. S. F. (ed.) 1952. *Theocritus*, 2nd edn., 2 vols., Cambridge.

　1965. *Machon: the fragments*, Cambridge.

Gow, A. S. F. and Page, D. (eds.) 1965. *The Greek Anthology: Hellenistic epigrams*, Cambridge.

Granino Cecere, M. G. 1994. "Il sepolcro della catella Aeolis," *Zeitschrift für Papyrologie und Epigraphik* 100: 413–21.

Greene, E. 2000. "Playing with tradition: gender and innovation in the epigrams of Anyte," *Helios* 27: 15–32.

Gutzwiller, K. 1992. "The nautilus, the halcyon, and Selenaia: Callimachus's *Epigram* 5 Pf. = 14 G.–P.," *Classical Antiquity* 11: 194–209.

　1993. "Anyte's epigram book," *Syllecta Classica* 4: 71–89.

　1995. "Cleopatra's ring," *Greek, Roman, and Byzantine Studies* 36: 383–98.

　1998a. *Poetic garlands: Hellenistic epigrams in context*, Berkeley and Los Angeles.

　1998b. "Meleager: from Menippean to epigrammatist," in Harder, Regtuit, and Wakker 1998: 81–93.

　2002a. "Art's echo: the tradition of Hellenistic ecphrastic epigram," in Harder, Regtuit, and Wakker 1998: 85–112.

　2002b. "Posidippus on statuary," in Bastianini and Casanova 2002: 41–59.

　2002c. "Meleager as erotic dolphin: a reading of 'AP' 12.52," *Hermathena* 173–4: 91–105.

　2005. *The new Posidippus: a Hellenistic poetry book*, Oxford.

　2010. "Heroic epitaphs of the Classical age: the Aristotelian Peplos and beyond," in M. Baumbach, A. Petrovic, and I. Petrovic, *Archaic and Classical Greek epigram* (Cambridge) 219–49.

Habicht, C. 1994. "Namensgleiche Athener in verschiedenen Demen," *Zeitschrift für Papyrologie und Epigraphik* 103: 117–27.

Hall, E. 1988. *Inventing the barbarian*, Oxford.

Hammond, N. G. L. and Walbank, F. W. 1988. *A History of Macedonia, 336–167 BC*, Oxford.

Hangard, J. 1971. "Ipsae defluebant coronae," *Mnemosyne* 24: 398–400.

Harder, M. A. 2005. "Catullus 63: a 'Hellenistic poem?'" in Nauta and Harder 2005: 65–86.

　(ed.) 2012. *Callimachus: Aetia*, 2 vols., Oxford.

2019. "Miniaturization of earlier poetry in Greek epigrams," in Kanellou, Petrovic, and Carey 2019: 85–101.

Harder, M. A., Regtuit, R. F., and Wakker, G. C. (eds.) 1998. *Genre in Hellenistic poetry*, Groningen.

(eds.) 2002. *Hellenistic epigrams*, Leuven.

(eds.) 2004. *Callimachus* II, Leuven.

Hardie, A. 1997. "Philitas and the plane tree," *Zeitschrift für Papyrologie und Epigraphik* 119: 21–36.

Harris, W. V. 2009. *Dreams and experience in classical antiquity*, Cambridge, Mass.

Harrison, S. 2005. "Catullus 63: text and translation," in Nauta and Harder 2005: 2–7.

Hatzopoulos, M. 2000. "'L'histoire par les noms' in Macedonia," in S. Hornblower and E. Matthews, eds. *Greek personal names: their value as evidence* (Oxford) 99–117.

Headlam, W. 1901. "τοκέων 'a parent' and the kindred forms," *Classical Review* 15: 401–4.

Henderson, J. 1976. "The Cologne Epode and the conventions of early Greek erotic poetry," *Arethusa* 9: 159–79.

1991. *The maculate Muse*, 2nd edn., Oxford.

Henrichs, A. 1979. "Callimachus Epigram 28: a fastidious priamel," *Harvard Studies in Classical Philology* 83: 207–12.

Höschele, R. 2009a. "If I am from Syria, so what? Meleager's Cosmopoetics," in S. Ager and R. Faber, eds. *Belonging and isolation in the Hellenistic world* (Toronto) 19–32.

2009b. "Meleager and Heliodora: a love story in bits and pieces?" in Nilsson 2009: 99–134.

Horrocks, G. C. 1997. *Greek: a history of the language and its speakers*, London and New York.

Hunter, R. 1992. "Callimachus and Heraclitus," *Materiali e Discussioni* 28: 113–23.

1996. *Theocritus and the archaeology of Greek poetry*, Cambridge.

(ed.) 1999. *Theocritus: a selection*, Cambridge.

2001. "The poet unleaved: Simonides and Callimachus," in D. Boedeker and D. Sider, eds. *The new Simonides: contexts of praise and desire* (Oxford) 242–54.

2006. *The shadow of Callimachus: studies in the reception of Hellenistic poetry at Rome*, Cambridge.

2009. "Hesiod's style: towards an ancient analysis," in F. Montanari, A. Rengakos, and C. Tsagalis, eds. *Brill's companion to Hesiod* (Leiden) 253–69.

2014. *Hesiodic voices: studies in the ancient reception of Hesiod's Works and days*, Cambridge.

2019a. "Death of a child: grief beyond the literary?" in Kanellou, Petrovic, and Carey 2019: 137–53.

2019b. "Reading and citing the *Epigrams* of Callimachus," in Klooster, Harder, Regtuit, and Wakker 2019: 171–91.

Hutchinson, G. O. 2016. "Pentameters," in Sistakou and Rengakos 2016: 119–37.

Huxley, G. L. 1969. *Greek epic poetry from Eumelos to Panyassis*, Cambridge, Mass.

Iordanoglou, D. 2003. "Literary loves: interpretations of Dioscorides 1–5 and 6 G–P," diss. Uppsala.

2009. "Is this not a song of love? The Dioscorides epigram on the fire of Troy (*Anth. Pal.* 5.138)," in Nilsson 2009: 83–97.

Irwin, E. 1974. *Colour terms in Greek poetry*, Toronto.

Jacques, J.-M. 1960. "Sur un acrostiche d'Aratos (*Phén.* 738–787)," *Revue des Études Anciennes* 62: 48–61.

Jim, T. S. F. 2011. "The vocabulary of ἀπάρχεσθαι, ἀπαρχή and related terms in archaic and classical Greece," *Kernos* 24: 39–58.

Jones, K. R. 2014. "Lycophron's *Alexandra*, the Romans, and Antiochus III," *Journal of Hellenic Studies* 134: 41–55 .

Kanellou, M. 2016. "Ἑρμιόνην, ἣ εἶδος ἔχε χρυσέης Ἀφροδίτης (*Od.* 4.14): praising a female through Aphrodite – from Homer into Hellenistic epigram," in A. Efstathiou and I. Karamanou, eds. *Homeric receptions across generic and cultural contexts* (Berlin) 189–204.

Kanellou, M., Petrovic, I., and Carey, C. (eds.) 2019. *Greek epigram from the Hellenistic to the Early Byzantine era*, Oxford.

Kay, N. M. 1985. *Martial book XI: a commentary*, London.

Kellogg, D. L. 2013. *Marathon fighters and men of maple: ancient Acharnai*, Oxford.

Kenny, E. J. A. 1932. "The date of Ctesibius," *Classical Quarterly* 26: 190–2.

Kerkhecker, A. 1991. "Zum neuen hellenistischen Weihepigramm aus Pergamon," *Zeitschrift für Papyrologie und Epigraphik* 86: 27–34.

Kidd, D. (ed.) 1997. *Aratus: Phaenomena*, Cambridge.

Kidd, S. E. 2017a. "Greek dicing, *astragaloi* and the 'Euripides' throw," *Journal of Hellenic Studies* 137: 112–18.

2017b. "How to gamble in Greek: the meaning of *kubeia*,' *Journal of Hellenic Studies* 137: 119–34.

Kimmel-Clauzet, F. 2017. "La rhétorique du 'petit' dans les épigrammes funéraires des grands poètes grecs," in D. Meyer and C. Urlacher-Becht, eds. *La rhétorique du "petit" dans l'épigramme grecque et latine* (Strasbourg) 69–86.

Kleingünther, A. 1933. *"Πρῶτος εὑρετής"*: *Untersuchungen zur Geschichte einer Fragestellung*, Leipzig.

Klooster, J. 2011. *Poetry as window and mirror: positioning the poet in Hellenistic poetry*, Leiden.

Klooster, J., Harder, M. A., Regtuit, R. F., and Wakker, G. C. (eds.) 2019. *Callimachus revisited, new perspectives in Callimachean scholarship*, Leuven.

Konstantakos, I. M. 2015. "Machon's Alexandrian comedy and earlier comic tradition," *Aevum Antiquum* 89: 13–36.

Krevans, N. 2004. "Callimachus and the pedestrian Muse," in Harder, Regtuit, and Wakker 2004: 173–84.

Kuijper, D. 1972. "De Alcaeo Messenio unius carminis bis retractatore," in *Studi classici in onore di Quintino Cataudella* (Catania) 243–60.

Kurke, L. 1991. *The traffic in praise: Pindar and the poetics of social economy*, Ithaca.

1999. *Coins, bodies, games, and gold*, Princeton.

2002. "Gender, politics, and subversion in the *Chreiai* of Machon," *Proceedings of the Cambridge Philosophical Society* 48: 20–65.

Kwapisz, J. 2013. *The Greek figure poems*, Leuven.

Lambert, S. D. 1998. *The Phratries of Attica*, 2nd edn., Ann Arbor.

Lancelotti, M. G. 2002. *Attis between myth and history: king, priest and god*, Leiden.

Landolfi, L. 1984. "Silentium amoris: a proposito di Asclep., *AP*, 12,135; Call., *AP*, 12,134; Catull. 6 e 55," *Orpheus* 5: 167–81.

Lapini, W. 2004. "Posidippo, *Ep.* 110 Austin–Bastianini," *Zeitschrift für Papyrologie und Epigraphik* 149: 45–8.

Laser, S. 1987. *Sport und Spiel*, Göttingen.

Lasserre, F. 1946. *La figure d'Eros dans la poésie grecque*, Lausanne.

Lattimore, R. 1942. *Themes in Greek and Latin epitaphs*, Urbana.

Laurens, P. 1989. *L'abeille dans l'ambre. Célébration de l'épigramme de l'époque alexandrine à la fin de la Renaissance*, Paris.

Lausberg, M. 1982. *Das Einzeldistichon: Studien zum antiken Epigramm*, Munich.

Lauxtermann, M. D. 2003. *Byzantine poetry from Pisides to Geometres* I, Vienna.

Lee, M. 2015. *Body, dress, and identity in ancient Greece*, Cambridge.

Lehnus, L. 1996. "On the metrical inscription found at Pergamum (*SEG* 39.1334)," *Classical Quarterly* 46: 295–7.

Levine, D. B. 2002–3. "Poetic justice: Homer's death in the ancient biographical tradition," *Classical Journal* 98: 141–60.

Lidov, J. B. 2002. "Sappho, Herodotus, and the 'hetaira'," *Classical Philology* 97: 203–37.

Lightfoot, J. L. 2010. *Hellenistic collection: Philitas, Alexander of Aetolia, Hermesianax, Euphorion, Parthenius*, Cambridge, Mass.

Lilja, S. 1976. *Dogs in ancient Greek poetry*, Helsinki.

Livingstone, N. and Nisbet, G. 2010. *Epigram*, Cambridge.

Livrea, E. 1992. "L'epitafio callimacheo per Batto," *Hermes* 120: 291–8.

Llewelyn-Jones, L. 2003. *Aphrodite's tortoise: the veiled woman of ancient Greece*, Swansea.

Luck, G. 1956. "Trygonions Grabschrift (Philodemos, A.P. 7,222)," *Philologus* 100: 271–86.

1968. "Witz und Sentiment im griechischen Epigram," in *L'épigramme grecque* (Vandoeuvres) 387–408.

Ludwig, W. 1963. "Plato's love epigrams," *Greek, Roman, and Byzantine Studies* 4: 59–82.

1968. "Die Kunst der Variation im hellenistischen Liebesepigramm," in *L'épigramme grecque* (Vandoeuves) 299–334.

Luz, C. 2010. *Technopaignia: Formspiele in der griechischen Dichtung*, Leiden.

Luz, M. 1988. "Salam, Meleager!" *Studi Italiani di Filologia Classica* 6: 222–31.

Ma, J. 2013. *Statues and cities: honorific portraits and civic identity in the Hellenistic world*, Oxford.

McGlew, J. F. 1993. *Tyranny and political culture in ancient Greece*, Ithaca.

McKay, K. J. 1968. "A Hellenistic medley," *Mnemosyne* 21: 171–5.

McNelis, C. and Sens, A. 2016. *The Alexandra of Lycophron: a literary study*, Oxford.

Magini, D. 2000. "Asclepiade e le origini dell'epigramma erotico," *Acme* 53: 17–37.

Männlein-Robert, I. 2007. "Epigrams on art: voice and voicelessness in Hellenistic epigram," in Bing and Bruss 2007: 251–71.

Magnelli, E. 1999. *Alexandri Aetoli testimonia et fragmenta*, Florence.

2002. *Studi su Euforione*, Rome.

2006. "Il proemio della *Corona* di Filippo di Tessalonica e la sua funzione programmatica," in L. Cristante, ed. *Incontri triestini di filologia classica* IV: *2004–2005* (Trieste) 393–404.

2007. "Meter and diction: from refinement to mannerism," in Bing and Bruss 2007: 165–83.

Markle, M. M., III 1977. "The Macedonian sarissa, spear, and related armor," *American Journal of Archaeology* 81: 323–39.

Mastronarde, D. J. 1978. "Are Euripides 'Phoinissai' 1104–1140 interpolated?" *Phoenix* 32: 105–28.

Mattusch, C. 1996. *The fire of Hephaistos: large classical bronzes from North American collections*, Cambridge, Mass.

Mednikarova, I. 2003. "The accusative with the name of the deceased in Latin and Greek epitaphs," *Zeitschrift für Papyrologie und Epigraphik* 143: 117–34.

Meyer, D. 1993. "Die Einbeziehung des Lesers in den Epigrammen des Kallimachos," in M. A. Harder, R. F. Regtuit, and G. C. Wakker, eds. *Callimachus* (Groningen) 161–75.

2005. *Inszeniertes Lesevergnügen: das inschriftliche Epigramm und seine Rezeption bei Kallimachos*, Stuttgart.

Miller, S. 2006. *Ancient Greek athletics*, New Haven.

Momigliano, A. 1942. "Terra marique," *Journal of Roman Studies* 32: 53–64.

Mondin, L. 2011–12. "Riscrivere la storia: Alc. Mess. 4 G.–P. ed *Epigr. Bob.* 71," *Incontri di Filologia Classica* 11: 267–302.

Moore-Blunt, J. 1978. "Two epigrams by Meleager," *Emerita* 46: 83–9.

Murgatroyd, P. 1975. "'Militia amoris' and the Roman elegists," *Latomus* 34: 59–79.

1984. "Amatory hunting, fishing and fowling," *Latomus* 43: 362–8.

1989. "The amatory epigrams of Rhianus," *Echos du monde classique / Classical Views* 33: 301–13.

Nauta, R. R. and Harder, A. (eds.) 2005. *Catullus' poem on Attis: text and contexts*, Leiden.

Neri, C. 2003. *Erinna: testimonianze e frammenti*, Bologna.

Nervegna, S. 2017. "Aeschylus in the Hellenistic period," in R. F. Kennedy, ed. *Brill's companion to the reception of Aeschylus* (Leiden) 109–28.

Nilsson, I. (ed.) 2009. *Plotting with Eros: essays on the poetics of love and the erotics of reading*, Copenhagen.

Nilsson, M. P. 1945. "Pagan divine service in late antiquity," *The Harvard Theological Review* 38: 63–9.

Obbink, D. 2004. "Posidippus on papyri then and now," in Acosta-Hughes, Kosmetatou, and Baumbach 2004: 16–28.

2005. "New old Posidippus and old new Posidippus: from occasion to edition in the epigrams," in Gutzwiller 2005: 97–115.

Ogle, M. B. 1933. "The sleep of death," *Memoirs of the American Academy in Rome* 11: 81–117.

Page, D. L. 1963. "Some metrical rules in Meleager," in *Miscellanea di studi alessandrini in memoria di A. Rostagni* (Turin) 544–7.

Pappas, A. 2013. "The treachery of verbal images: viewing the Greek *technopaegnia*," in J. Kwapisz, D. Petrain, and M. Szymański, eds. *The Muse at play: riddles and wordplay in Greek and Latin poetry (Berlin) 199–224*.

Parker, H. N. 2004. "An epigram of Nossis (8 GP = *AP* 6.353)," *Classical Quarterly* 54: 618–20.

Parsons, P. J., Maehler, H., and Maltomini, F. (eds.) 2015. *The Vienna epigrams papyrus (G 40611)*, Berlin.

Pearce, T. E. V. 1983. "The tomb by the sea: history of a motif," *Latomus* 42: 110–15.

Peirano, I. 2013. *"Ille ego qui quondam*: on authorial (an)onymity," in A. Marmodoro and J. Hill, eds. *The author's voice in classical and late antiquity* (Oxford) 251–85.

Peirano Garrison, I. 2017. "'Newly written buds': archaic and classical pseudepigrapha in Meleager's *Garland*," in E. J. Bakker, ed. *Authorship and Greek song: authority, authenticity, and performance* (Leiden) 222–38.

Pelliccia, H. 1995. *Mind, body, and speech in Homer and Pindar*, Göttingen.

forthcoming. *Callimachus: Epigram 28*.

Petrovic, A. 2019. "Lessons in reading and ideology: on Greek epigrams in private compilations of the Hellenistic Age" in Kanellou, Petrovic, and Carey 2019: 35–50.

Pfeiffer, R. 1968. *A history of classical scholarship from the beginnings to the end of the Hellenistic age*, Oxford.

Pickard-Cambridge, A. W. 1968. *The dramatic festivals of Athens*, 2nd edn., rev. J. Gould and D. M. Lewis, Oxford.

Pollitt, J. J. 1974. *The ancient view of Greek art: criticism, history, and terminology*, New Haven and London.

1986. *Art in the Hellenistic age*, Cambridge.

Popkin, M. L. 2012. "Roosters, columns, and Athena on early Panathenaic prize amphoras: symbols of a new Athenian identity," *Hesperia* 81: 207–35.

Porter, J. 2011. "Against *leptotēs*: rethinking Hellenistic aesthetics," in A. Erskine, L. Llewellyn-Jones, and S. Winder, eds. *Creating a Hellenistic world* (Swansea) 271–312.

Prauscello, L. 2006. "Sculpted meanings, talking statues: some observations on Posidippus 142.12 A–B (= XIX G–P) ΚΑΙ ΕΝ ΠΡΟΘΥΡΟΙΣ ΘΗΚΕ ΔΙΔΑΣΚΑΛΙΗΝ," *American Journal of Philology* 127: 511–23.

Prescott, H. W. 1921. "Callimachus' epigram on the nautilus," *Classical Philology* 16: 327–37.

Pretagostini, R. 2000. "Vino, amore e . . . violenza sessuale: Hedyl. A.P. 5.199," in M. Cannatà Fera and S. Grandolini, eds. *Poesia e religione in Grecia: studi in onore di G. Aurelio Privitera* (Perugia) II.571–4.

Prioux, É. 2007. *Regards alexandrins: histoire et théorie des arts dans l'épigramme hellénistique*, Leuven.

Probert, P. 2015. *Early Greek relative clauses*, Oxford.

Puelma, M. 1996. "Ἐπίγραμμα–epigramma: Aspekte einer Wortgeschichte," *Museum Helveticum* 53: 123–39.

Race, W. H. 1982. *The classical priamel from Homer to Boethius*, Leiden.

Reed, J. D. 2000. "Arsinoe's Adonis and the poetics of Ptolemaic imperialism," *Transactions of the American Philological Association* 130: 319–51.

Rehm, R. 1994. *Marriage to death: the conflation of wedding and funeral rituals in Greek tragedy*, Princeton.

Reitzenstein, R. 1893. *Epigramm und Skolion: ein Beitrag zur Geschichte der alexandrinischen Dichtung*, Giessen.

Renberg, G. 2016. *Where dreams may come*, Leiden.

Renehan, R. 1964. "The *Collectanea Alexandrina*: selected passages," *Harvard Studies in Classical Philology* 68: 375–88.

1976. *Studies in Greek texts*, Göttingen.

Rengakos, A. 1994. *Apollonios Rhodios und die antike Homererklärung*, Munich.

Rickert, G. 1989. *EKΩN and AKΩN in early Greek thought*, Atlanta.

Ridgway, B. S. 1981. *Fifth-century styles in Greek sculpture*, Princeton.

1997. *Fourth-century styles in Greek sculpture*, Madison.

Robertson, N. 2013. "The concept of purity in Greek sacred laws," in C. Frevel and C. Nihan, eds. *Purity and the forming of religious traditions in the ancient Mediterranean world and ancient Judaism* (Leiden) 195–243.

Rosen, R. M. 2007. "The Hellenistic epigrams on Archilochus and Hipponax," in Bing and Bruss 2007: 459–76.

Rosenmeyer, P. A. 1997. "Her master's voice: Sappho's dialogue with Homer," *Materiali e Discussioni* 39: 123–49.

Rossi, L. 2001. *The epigrams ascribed to Theocritus: a method of approach*, Leuven.

Rouse, W. H. D. 1902. *Greek votive offerings: an essay in the history of Greek religion*, Cambridge.

Ruijgh, C. J. 1971. *Autour de "τε épique." Études sur la syntaxe grecque*, Amsterdam.

Sandin, P. 2000. "An erotic image in Asclepiades 5," *Mnemosyne* 53: 345–6.

Sansone, D. 1993. "Towards a new doctrine of the article in Greek: some observations on the definite article in Plato," *Classical Philology* 88: 191–205.

Sbardella, L. 2000. *Filita: testimonianze e frammenti poetici*, Rome.

Schönbeck, G. 1962. *Der locus amoenus von Homer bis Horaz*, Heidelberg.

Schur, D. 2004. "A garland of stones: Hellenistic *Lithika* as reflection on poetic transformations," in Acosta-Hughes, Kosmetatou, and Baumbach 2004: 118–22.

Scodel, R. 1980. "Hesiod redivivus," *Greek, Roman, and Byzantine Studies* 21: 301–20.

2003. "Two epigrammatic pairs: Callimachus' epitaphs, Plato's apples," *Hermes* 131: 257–68.

Sealey, R. 1994. *The justice of the Greeks*, Ann Arbor.

Selden, D. 1998. "Alibis," *Classical Antiquity* 17: 289–412.

Sens, A. (ed.) 1997. *Theocritus: Dioscuri (Idyll 22)*, Göttingen.

2002. "An ecphrastic pair: Asclepiades *AP* 12.75 and Asclepiades or Posidippus *APl* 68," *Classical Journal* 97: 249–62.

2003. "Asclepiades, Erinna, and the poetics of labor," in P. Thibodeau and H. Haskell, eds. *Being there together: essays in honor of Michael C. J. Putnam on the occasion of his seventieth birthday* (Afton, Minn.) 78–87.

2004. "Doricisms in the new and old Posidippus," in Acosta-Hughes, Kosmetatou, and Baumbach 2004: 65–83.

2005. "The art of poetry and the poetry of art: the unity and poetics of Posidippus' statue-poems," in Gutzwiller 2005: 206–25.

2006. "Epigram at the margins of pastoral," in M. Fantuzzi and T. D. Papanghelis, eds. *Brill's companion to Greek and Latin pastoral* (Leiden) 147–65.

2011. *Asclepiades of Samos: epigrams and fragments*, Oxford.

2015. "Hedylus (4 and 5 Gow–Page) and Callimachean poetics," *Mnemosyne* 68: 40–52.

2016. "Party or perish: death, wine, and closure in Hellenistic sympotic epigram," in V. Cazzato, D. Obbink, and E. E. Prodi, eds. *The cup of song: studies on poetry and the symposium* (Oxford) 230–46.

2018. "Envy and closure in the Greek Anthology," in P. Knox, H. Pelliccia, and A. Sens, eds. *They keep it all hid: Augustan poetry, its antecedents, and reception* (Berlin) 101–15.

2019. "Some aspects of closure in Callimachus' epigrams," in Klooster, Harder, Regtuit, and Wakker 2019: 205–28.

Sider, D. "Sylloge Simonidea," in Bing and Bruss 2007: 113–30.

(ed.) 2017. *Hellenistic poetry: a selection*, Ann Arbor.

Sistakou, E. 2007. "Glossing Homer: Homeric exegesis in early third-century epigram," in Bing and Bruss 2007: 391–408.

Sistakou, E. and Rengakos, A. 2016. *Dialect, diction, and style in Greek literary and inscribed epigram*, Berlin.

Skinner, M. B. 1989. "Sapphic Nossis," *Arethusa* 22: 5–18.

1991. "Nossis *thelyglossos*: the private text and the public book," in S. B. Pomeroy, ed. *Women's history and ancient history* (Chapel Hill and London) 20–47.

2001. "Ladies' day at the art institute: Theocritus, Herodas, and the gendered gaze," in A. Lardinois and L. McClure, eds. *Making silence speak: women's voices in Greek literature and society* (Princeton) 201–22.

Slings, S. R. 1973. "Callimachus, 'Epigr.' 29 Pf. = v G.–P," *Mnemosyne* 26: 284–6.

———. 1993. "Hermesianax and the Tattoo Elegy (P. Brux. inv. E 8934 and P. Sorb. inv. 2254)," *Zeitschrift für Papyrologie und Epigraphik* 98: 29–37.

Smith, M. 2004. "Elusive stones: reading Posidippus' *Lithika* through technical writing on stones," in Acosta-Hughes, Kosmetatou, and Baumbach 2004: 105–17.

Snell, B. 1958. "Die Klangfiguren im 2. Epigramm des Kallimachos," *Glotta* 37: 1–4.

Solitario, M. 2015. *Leonidas of Tarentum: between cynical polemic and poetic refinement*, Rome.

Solodow, J. B. 1986. "*Raucae, tua cura, palumbes*: study of a poetic word order," *Harvard Studies in Classical Philology* 90: 129–53.

Spanoudakis, K. 2002. *Philitas of Cos*, Leiden.

Speyer, W. 1975. "Myrons Kuh in der antiken Literatur und bei Goethe," *Arcadia* 10: 171–9.

Spyridakis, S. 1977. "Cretans and Neocretans," *Classical Journal* 72: 299–307.

Squire, M. 2010. "Making Myron's cow moo? Ecphrastic epigram and the poetics of simulation," *American Journal of Philology* 131: 589–634.

Stephens, S. 2004. "'For you, Arsinoe,'" in Acosta-Hughes, Kosmetatou, and Baumbach 2004: 161–76.

———. 2005. "Battle of the books," in Gutzwiller 2005: 229–48.

Stager, J. M. S. 2005. "'Let no one wonder at this image': a Phoenician funerary stele in Athens," *Hesperia* 74: 427–49.

Stephens, S. 2003. *Seeing double: intercultural poetics in Ptolemaic Alexandria*, Berkeley.

Stewart, A. 1990. *Greek sculpture: an exploration*, 2 vols., New Haven.

———. 1993. *Faces of power: Alexander's image and Hellenistic politics*, Berkeley.

———. 2005. "Posidippus and the truth in sculpture," in Gutzwiller 2005: 183–205.

Stewart, S. 2008. "Emending Aratus' insomnia: Callimachus *Epigr.* 27," *Mnemosyne* 61: 586–600.

Strodel, S. 2002. *Zur Überlieferung und zum Verständnis der hellenistischen Technopaegnien*, Frankfurt.

Strubbe, J. H. M. 1998. "Epigrams and consolation decrees for deceased youths," *L'Antiquité Classique* 67: 45–75.

Swinnen, W. 1970. "Herakleitos of Halikarnassos, an Alexandrian poet and diplomat?" *Ancient Society* 1: 39–52.

Taplin, O. 1993. *Comic angels and other approaches to Greek drama through vase-paintings*, Oxford.

Tarán, S. L. 1979. *The art of variation in the Hellenistic epigram*, Leiden.

1985. "ΕΙΣΙ ΤΡΙΧΕΣ: An erotic motif in the Greek Anthology," *Journal of Hellenic Studies* 105: 90–107.

Thomas, R. F. 1979. "New Comedy, Callimachus, and Roman Poetry," *Harvard Studies in Classical Philology* 83: 179–206.

1998. "Melodious tears: sepulchral epigram and generic mobility," in Harder, Regtuit, and Wakker 1998: 205–23.

Thompson, D. B. 1973. *Ptolemaic oinochoai and portraits in faience: aspects of the ruler-cult*, Oxford.

2005. "Posidippus, poet of the Ptolemies," in Gutzwiller 2005: 269–83.

Thomson, J. A. K. 1941. "ΕΙΠΕ ΤΙΣ ΗΡΑΚΛΕΙΤΕ ΤΕΟΝ ΜΟΡΟΝ," *Classical Review* 55: 28.

Tsagalis, C. 2008. *Inscribing sorrow: fourth-century Attic funerary epigrams*, Berlin.

Tueller, M. 2004. "The origins of voice and identity ambiguity in Callimachus' epigrams," in Harder, Regtuit, and Wakker 2004: 299–315.

2008. *Look who's talking: voice and identity in Hellenistic epigram*, Leuven.

2016. "Words for dying in sepulchral epigram," in Sistakou and Rengakos 2016: 215–33.

Tzochev, C. 2016. "Markets, amphora trade and wine industry: the case of Thasos," in E. M. Harris, D. M. Lewis, and M. Woolmer, eds. *The ancient Greek economy: markets, households and city-states* (Cambridge) 230–53.

van Nijf, O. 1997. *The civic world of professional associations in the Roman East*, Amsterdam.

Venit, M. S. 1998. "Women in their cups," *Classical World* 92: 117–30.

Vertsetis, A. V. 1988. "Ο ΜΕΣΣΗΝΙΟΣ ΠΟΙΗΤΗΣ ΑΛΚΑΙΟΣ ΚΑΙ ΤΑ ΠΟΛΙΤΙΚΑ ΤΟΥ ΕΠΙΓΡΑΜΜΑΤΑ," *Platon* 40: 130–40.

Wallis, W. 2016. "Ancient portraits of poets: communities, canons, receptions," diss. Durham.

Walsh, G. B. 1990. "Surprised by self: audible thought in Hellenistic poetry," *Classical Philology* 85: 1–21.

Watkins, C. 1967. "An Indo-European construction in Greek and Latin," *Harvard Studies in Classical Philology* 71: 115–19.

Webster, T. B. L. 1963. "Alexandrian epigrams and the theatre," in *Miscellanea di studi alessandrini in memoria di Augusto Rostagni* (Turin) 531–43.

West, M. L. 1967. "Epica," *Glotta* 44: 135–48.

1969. "Near Eastern material in Hellenistic and Roman literature," *Harvard Studies in Classical Philology* 73: 113–34.

1977. "Erinna," *Zeitschrift für Papyrologie und Epigraphik* 25: 95–119.

1982. *Greek metre*, Oxford.

1992. *Ancient Greek music*, Oxford.

White, S. A. 1994. "Callimachus on Plato and Cleombrotus," *Transactions of the American Philological Association* 124: 135–61.

Wickkiser, B. L. 2013. "The IAMATIKA of the Milan Posidippus," *Classical Quarterly* 63: 623–32.

Willi, A. 2013. "Epicharmus, Simonides, and the 'invention' of the Greek alphabet," *Museum Helveticum* 70: 129–40.

Wise, S. 2007. "Childbirth votives and rituals in ancient Greece," diss. Cincinnati.

Ypsilanti, M. 2003. "Notes on Anyte," *Hermes* 131: 502–7.

INDEXES

1. SUBJECTS

2. GREEK WORDS

3. PASSAGES DISCUSSED

For EU product safety concerns, contact us at Calle de José Abascal, 56–1°,
28003 Madrid, Spain or eugpsr@cambridge.org.

www.ingramcontent.com/pod-product-compliance
Ingram Content Group UK Ltd.
Pitfield, Milton Keynes, MK11 3LW, UK
UKHW020451240426
470322UK00016B/300